ORGANIZATIONAL STRESS AND PREVENTIVE MANAGEMENT

McGraw-Hill Series in Management

Fred Luthans and Keith Davis, *Consulting Editors*

ORGANIZATIONAL STRESS AND PREVENTIVE MANAGEMENT

James C. Quick, Ph.D.

College of Business Administration
University of Texas at Arlington

Jonathan D. Quick, M.D.

Family Physician

McGRAW-HILL BOOK COMPANY

New York   St. Louis   San Francisco   Auckland   Bogotá
Hamburg   Johannesburg   London   Madrid   Mexico   Montreal   New Delhi
Panama   Paris   São Paulo   Singapore   Sydney   Tokyo   Toronto

This book was set in Optima by Automated Composition Service, Inc.
The editor was John R. Meyer;
the production supervisor was Diane Renda.
The drawings were done by Danmark & Michaels, Inc.
The cover was designed by Jerry Wilke.
R. R. Donnelley & Sons Company was printer and binder.

ORGANIZATIONAL STRESS AND PREVENTIVE MANAGEMENT

2 3 4 5 6 7 8 9 0   DOCDOC   8 9 8 7 6 5 4

ISBN 0-07-051070-9

Library of Congress Cataloging in Publication Data

Quick, James C.
    Organizational stress and preventive management.

    (McGraw-Hill series in management)
    Bibliography: p.
    Includes index.
    1. Job stress.   I. Quick, Jonathan D.   II. Title.
III. Series.   [DNLM: 1. Psychology, Industrial.
2. Organization and administration.   3. Stress—
Diagnosis.   4. Stress—Prevention and control.
5. Stress, Psychological—Diagnosis.   6. Stress,
Psychological—Prevention and control.   HF 5548.85 Q6o]
HF5548.85.Q53   1984   658.3'82   83-11335
ISBN 0-07-051070-9

With love, affection, and deep devotion,
we dedicate this book to our family:

James Francis Quick
father
sales executive
wise elder

Otto Alois Faust, M.D.
grandfather
pediatrician
professor emeritus

Olva Fuller Faust Quick
mother
champion of causes
dynamo

Marcia Faust McNees
aunt
loving woman
patient soul

Tina Lee Quick
wife and sister
nurse and athlete
ebullient companion

David Michael Quick
son and nephew
athlete
student

CONTENTS

FOREWORD

One morning, as I was visiting Jim Quick in his office at Arlington, he told me about the book on organizational stress that he and his brother, a physician, were writing. The potential for this type of book sounded exciting. The combination of two professionals, one a Ph.D. and the other an M.D., both of whom were interested in stress, provided an eminent team for a definitive book on the subject. When Jim showed me the outline and explained the basic framework of the book, I was even more impressed with its possibilities. People in organizations needed a balanced book giving both medical and organizational insights into stress.

There also was a personal reason for my interest. I have cardiovascular disease, and a few years ago experienced a heart attack and cardiac arrest. My family tree showed cardiovascular disease for three generations, probably predisposing me to cardiovascular problems; but there was little doubt in my mind that stress also was a contributor to my heart attack. I was searching for a book that would help me better understand stress, including its causes, consequences, and prevention.

There is a long, difficult journey from a good book plan to a successful completion of that plan, but the authors have accomplished their task admirably. In thirteen insightful chapters they completely discuss the sources, consequences, and preventive management of stress. The contents of the book are readable, interesting, useful, and often very revealing about ourselves and our organizations. The result is an outstanding book of classic proportions about stress.

A major contribution of the book that will appeal to managers and employees alike is its focus on preventive management of stress and its undesirable consequences. Six chapters, about half the book, discuss prevention at the organizational level and the individual level. Stress is viewed not as a "bad guy" that should be abolished in every way possible. Rather it is a condition that can have either positive or negative consequences, depending on how we manage it. As the authors concisely state, "Stress is inevitable; distress is not." The goal is to help people optimize their stress level in both the organization and the external community. In this way, we take the distress out of stress so that people can perform more effectively.

While many of the chapters are outstanding, the one that I find particularly revealing and compelling in its discussion is Chapter 3, on individual consequences of stress. It explains in a concise and explicit way how a person responds psychologically and physically to stress, especially prolonged stress. The consequences (costs) of stress poorly handled are significant, and they can be life-threatening. After reading Chapter 3, the reader is sure to be convinced that: "This subject is too important to ignore. I must learn more about it, and I must reorder my priorities and environment to reduce stress."

Stressful events are not just a matter of what the organization does to us. They also may result from what we do to ourselves in organizational situations. We sometimes walk directly into stressful situations, even when we have a choice to stay away from them. For example, do we really need to force the manager into that meeting in which we are going to tell him in front of others that his plan for the sales campaign is all wrong and ours is much better? We are asking for distress in that kind of situation. If we are wiser and if we better understand the effects of stress, we might avoid direct confrontation and choose more indirect ways to present our point. However, we cannot take a preventive approach to events of this type unless we understand both organizations and ourselves. We need to function proactively to encourage organizations to serve our interests along with their own.

Regrettably, too many of us do not understand organizations, ourselves, or the effects of stress. We approach organizations in ignorance and suffer the consequences. And often the organization is equally uninformed about stress and its consequences, and so it negligently contributes to our distress. There is much room for improvement in this state of affairs. *We can do better, and we must do better.* The Quicks' book is a big step forward. It should be read by managers, employees, social workers, and others. They need it. They will benefit from it, and in turn, the world should be a better place in which to live.

I wish I could have read this book many years ago. It would have had a significant effect on my decision making.

Keith Davis
Arizona State University

PREFACE

Stress and strain are universal experiences in the life of every organization and every executive, manager, and individual employee. The individual and organizational costs of mismanaged stress for American industry are enormous. The American Heart Association estimated that the economic costs for individuals with cardiovascular disease in the United States were $35.2 billion during 1981, while American industry incurred additional costs of $11 billion because of lost output due to cardiovascular disability during the same year. Cardiovascular disease is the leading cause of death in the United States, and mismanaged stress is one of the causes of this dreaded disease. Mismanaged stress also leads to peptic ulcers, depression, alcohol abuse, smoking, exhaustion, dissatisfaction, absenteeism, dysfunctional turnover, poor quality productivity, and management-labor conflicts.

We contend, however, that stress is essential to our growth, change, development, and performance both at work and at home. Stress is a naturally occurring experience which may have beneficial or destructive consequences. The destructive consequences of stressful experiences are not inevitable; they only result from ineffective management of stress and stressful events. The thesis of this book, as it is presented in Chapter 1, is that the destructive consequences of stress may be avoided through proper application of diagnostic methods and preventive management interventions.

The book is intended for those professions concerned with individual and organizational health. These include academicians, practitioners, and students in management, psychology, public health, medicine, social work, administration, and related disciplines. We have approached the problem and promise of organizational stress by attempting to blend organizational, medical, and psychological viewpoints and methods. The resulting perspective has led to the distinguishing emphases of this book: the diagnosis of stress and the philosophy and practice of preventive management.

Stress Diagnosis

A good diagnosis is arrived at through collecting systematic knowledge of the individual and the organization. It then becomes the foundation for responsible intervention or treatment in medical, social, and organizational settings. There are a host of methods, proposed as "treatments" for stress disorders, yet few are directly linked to or based on a systematic diagnosis. Chapters 5 and 6 are unique in that they explicitly deal with the basic concepts and methods of organizational stress diagnosis. These chapters taken together serve as an introduction for students and as a resource for researchers and practitioners.

In Chapter 5 we consider several criteria for a good diagnostic procedure, examine the interdisciplinary nature of organizational stress diagnosis, and include a diagnostic model. In Chapter 6 we review in some detail various measures of organizational stress, individual distress, and factors which modify the stress response. These procedures are examined against the criteria discussed in Chapter 5. Chapter 6 also contains an Appendix which lists the sources of these procedures, their cost, and their approximate time of completion.

**The Philosophy and Practice
of Preventive Management**

The entire second half of the book deals with the prevention of distress and the enhancement of health. This emphasis is captured in the philosophy of preventive management, defined as *an organizational philosophy and set of principles which employs specific methods for promoting individual and organizational health while preventing individual and organizational distress*. Our notions of preventive management are founded on five guiding principles which are discussed in Chapter 7, along with other aspects of our basic philosophy of preventive management, such as the three stages of prevention.

The central principle of preventive management reflects our belief that stress is inevitable and potentially healthy, but that distress is *not* inevitable. Much of the distress which occurs in organizations is preventable and avoidable, as Keith Davis points out in his foreword. However, the prevention of distress and the enhancement of health entails not only an accurate diagnosis but also the proper application of various methods of preventive management at the organizational and individual levels. These methods are discussed in Chapters 8 through 11.

The methods of organizational-level preventive management, discussed in Chapters 8 and 9, are concerned with ways to change organizations and the demands they place on each of us. The methods of individual-level preventive management are discussed in Chapters 10 and 11. These chapters indicate how individuals may benefit from stress and stressful events rather than suffer from them.

Chapter 12 focuses on programs currently in use by several organizations to combat distress and improve health in the workplace. The exercise and fitness programs of Kimberly-Clark and Xerox Corporation and Tenneco's flexitime program are examples. The chapter concludes with a discussion of the cost benefit of preventive management and some guidelines for implementing a preventive management program.

We have tried not to weigh down the text with extensive pedantic or distracting referencing, but a lengthy bibliography at the end of the book combines current and historically interesting literature from the fields of medicine, psychology, organizational behavior, and management. A short list of selected readings appears at the end of most chapters. As in any applied field, a great deal of valuable information and resource material is not found in books and articles. Therefore, where appropriate, chapter appendixes provide information about national organizations and associations, special interest groups, audiovisual materials, and stress diagnostic procedures.

We are indebted to many individuals for their contributions to the development of our ideas and to our work. In particular, we would like to thank Jerry C. Wofford (University of Texas at Arlington) for essential resources and personal encouragement; Hunter P. Harris, Jr. (Baylor College of Medicine) for introducing the senior author to the excitement of studying individuals at work and for his encouragement and counsel; Robert L. Berg (University of Rochester School of Medicine) for introducing the second author to the challenge and diversity of preventive medicine and for his confidence and counsel; Joseph W. Kertesz (Duke-Watts Family Medicine Center) for teaching us about individual methods of stress management and personal stress management plans; John M. Ivancevich (University of Houston) for sharing his knowledge, research findings, and Stress Diagnostic Survey with us; Michele Bock, Marci Carden, Ruth E. Brock, Beverly Kale, and Mary Annette Partin for their careful preparation of the manuscript; Rose Derario for being herself— delightful and gregarious; and Kathi Benson for her encouragement, faith, and patience in the completion of this work.

We would also like to express our thanks for the many useful comments and suggestions provided by colleagues who reviewed this book during the course of its development, especially to Professor Terry A. Beehr (Central Michigan University), Professor Rabi Bhagat (University of Texas, Dallas), Dr. David C. Deubner, M.D. (Duke University Medical Center), Professor Thomas W. Dougherty (University of Missouri-Columbia), Professor Todd Jick (York University), Professor Janina C. Latack (The Ohio State University), Professor Fred Luthans (University of Nebraska), Professor Bronston T. Mayes (The University of Nebraska-Lincoln), Professor John Seybolt (University of Utah), and J. W. Streid (Tenneco, Inc.).

We would like to thank the following professionals: Ricky W. Griffin (Texas A&M University), Fritz Steele (Boston-based independent consultant), Danelle N. Carnes (U.S. Army Corps of Engineers), Therese M. Long (Surgikos), James E. Dalton, Jr. (Hospital Corporation of America), Colonel Francis Livers and Captain Donald W. Blanks (U.S. Air Force), Robert Dedmon (Kimberly-Clark Corporation), John Ayres (Quad Systems Inc.), Johannes Steenkamp (Texas College of Osteopathic Medicine), Debbie Nelson, Coleen Shannon, Patt Gray (University of Texas at Arlington), Leonard Moss (New York psychoanalyst), the late Hans Selye (International Institute of Stress), Belinda Novik (Duke-Watts Family Medicine Center), James A. Richardson (Arlington cardiologist), Thomas R. Collingwood (Institute for Aerobics Research), Jim Post (Xerox Corporation), James Manuso (The Equitable Life Assurance Society of America), C. Ewin Cooley (Metro Counseling Associates, Inc.), David Hughes (Internal Medicine Associates), and Carlton Allen, Kenneth Gates, Kent I. Groff, K. C. Ptomey, and Lelia Power (the Presbyterian Church-USA).

Several graduate students of the University of Texas at Arlington (Bryan Clark, Steve Fedorko, David Geller, Jerie Jaecques, J. D. Mosley, Phyllis Newman, and Danny Williams) contributed to the refinement of a number of notions expressed in this book through their efforts at case diagnosis and their critical, probing, questioning attitudes during the spring of 1982. We thank Marshall Klayman for being a "live case" in that spring seminar.

Very special thanks go to Suzanne Warner from the senior author. As my graduate assistant, she has been absolutely outstanding. Without her very able assistance, writing the book would have been work rather than the pleasure it has been. The second author is particularly indebted to his bride and loving wife, Tina, for shepherding him through the writing of the book and through their wedding, and for showing him the excitement of a strong marriage and the importance of a healthy balance between work and play.

Inevitably a book such as this provides only a framework and starting place for individuals interested in reducing distress and promoting well-being in themselves, their colleagues, and/or their subordinates. Countless managers, patients, and other individuals have shared accounts of their experiences with us so that we might better understand their stresses and strains. For this we are most grateful. Their experiences of stress and strain have enriched the detail of the book, as we illustrate in points with their case reports. The authors look forward to hearing from readers about their experiences with stress and strain, and about the application of preventive management concepts.

James C. Quick
Jonathan D. Quick

CHAPTER 1

STRESS IN ORGANIZATIONS

Can your company afford to pay $500,000 to replace its chief executive officer? Can your university afford the $50,000 needed to replace the president? Is your hospital willing to pay $60,000 to replace the administrator?

These are among the bottom-line costs that an organization accrues when a distressed employee walks out the door or dies of a heart attack. Death is the extreme individual consequence of poor stress management; high levels of turnover and absenteeism are among the organizational consequences of mismanaged stress. But stress is not necessarily destructive or bad: it may provide the eleventh-hour energy needed to save an ailing company or resolve a difficult labor dispute. Channeled properly, stress is zestful and stimulating and produces growth. Our popular wisdom about stress has some very healthy messages, but it also contains a number of ideas that are not confirmed by serious investigators of stress. For example, the "executive heart attack" is reserved not for the executive but rather for the middle-level manager who has not made it to the top (Moss, 1981). And it is not people who have ways of expressing their anger who will have heart disease, but those who repress it and turn it on themselves (Gentry, et. al., 1982).

The thesis of this book is that stress is essential to our growth, change, development, and performance both at work and at home. Stress is a naturally occurring experience which may have beneficial *or* destructive consequences. The destructive consequences of stressful experiences are not inevitable. They result solely from the improper management of and reaction to stressful events. The contention of this book is that the destructive consequences of stress may be avoided through the proper application of diagnostic methods and preventive management interventions.

Stress is an important managerial, medical, and public health issue. Even though stress has been a human concern for centuries, in the last few years increased attention has been devoted to considering stress in professional training programs in management, medicine, social work, health administration, public health, occupational medicine, industrial and public administration, organizational psychology, clinical psychology, and business administration. Because the adverse effects of stress are disguised in a host of human illnesses and behavior patterns, the real costs of mismanaged stress are frequently hidden in an organization. As our awareness of the diverse effects of stress has expanded, increasing concern by interdisciplinary researchers, therapists, practitioners in organizations, and theorists has brought to bear a variety of tools for examining and dealing with stress. From this work have come many new and fundamental concepts of stress.

WHAT IS STRESS?

For many people, stress has negative connotations, and it is an experience to be avoided. These individuals associate stress with incidents which create discomfort, tension, and anxiety. For example, stress occurs when you:

- Are fired the Friday before Christmas.
- Receive a 1 percent pay raise with no bonus.
- Go in for your performance review after the worst year in your career.
- Fail your first M.B.A. course after returning to graduate school.
- Have your husband announce that, since your career is so important, he's leaving with the kids.

Such situations are stressful and also have components of tension and/or anxiety which the person would experience in the situation. However, stress is not simply an unpleasant event or experience. The above situations reveal only the unpleasant face of stress. But stress also has a second face.

Situations which create great excitement, stimulation, and arousal can be stressful for the individual. This is the positive face of stress which reveals joy and excitement. And so, stress also occurs when you:

- Receive a $10,000 bonus at Christmas.
- Get a social engagement with a handsome bachelor or a gorgeous bachelorette.
- Become a full professor at age 35.
- Land the biggest sales order in company history.
- Get *the* job you wanted right out of college.

Therefore, it is immaterial whether the agent or situation one faces is pleasant or unpleasant; all that counts in determining the degree of stress that an individual experiences is the intensity of the demand for readjustment or adaptation.

Stress has its origins in the demands of organizational and personal life. *Any demand, either of a physical or psychological nature, encountered in the course of living is known as a stressor.* The stress response occurs as a result of the individual's interaction and reaction to the stressor.

The *stress response* is the generalized, patterned, unconscious mobilization of the body's natural energy resources when confronted with a stressor.

This mobilization occurs through the combined action of the sympathetic nervous system and the endocrine system, often manifested in elevated heart rate, blood pressure, and respiration. A model for understanding stress is presented in Figure 1.1. This figure identifies the major sources of demands which require a response on the part of the individual. These demands may originate within the organization, such as job deadlines, or they may be of an extraorganizational nature, such as social obligations with one's wife, husband, or children. These extraorganizational demands also include such self-imposed factors as need for achievement and elements of the superego component of the personality.

Each of us has a host of resources for managing these demands. These include our knowledge about the demand and its requirements, our skills and abilities in the behaviors required in response to the demand, as well as our biological and psychological life history. Our social support system is also important as a source of information as well as emotional comfort in dealing with various demands. These resources provide each individual with the necessary tools to manage the demands of life.

Every individual exhibits several responses to the demands that are faced. The *behavioral response* to the demand is the set of specific observable actions taken in response to the demand. For example, if your boss enters your office and demands that your report be on his desk next

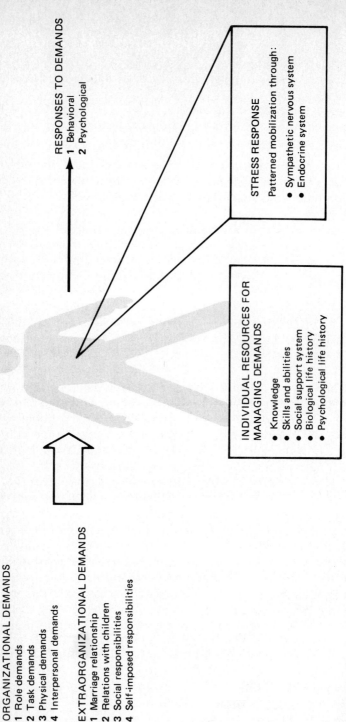

ORGANIZATIONAL DEMANDS

1 Role demands
2 Task demands
3 Physical demands
4 Interpersonal demands

EXTRAORGANIZATIONAL DEMANDS

1 Marriage relationship
2 Relations with children
3 Social responsibilities
4 Self-imposed responsibilities

RESPONSES TO DEMANDS

1 Behavioral
2 Psychological

STRESS RESPONSE

Patterned mobilization through:

● Sympathetic nervous system
● Endocrine system

INDIVIDUAL RESOURCES FOR MANAGING DEMANDS

● Knowledge
● Skills and abilities
● Social support system
● Biological life history
● Psychological life history

FIGURE 1.1
What is stress?

Monday, your behavioral response might be to work all weekend to complete the report on time. An alternative behavioral response would be to leave work at the end of the day and not return until next Tuesday, either claiming to be ill or actually becoming ill over the deadline.

In addition to the behavioral response, the individual will have a *psychological response* which takes the form of cognitive and emotional reactions. For example, in the above situation one psychological response might be an enthusiastic, positive feeling because you think the boss has finally realized how important your work really is. An alternative psychological response would be anger and hostility because you realize that the boss's demand will interfere with a planned family outing.

Regardless of the behavioral and psychological responses, the individual experiences the *stress response* when confronted with a demand. This is an innate, psychophysiological response over which an individual has little control. This instinctual response leads to the generation of stress-induced energy which plays a key role in meeting demands and dealing with emergencies. As Figure 1.1 indicates, this response and its stress-induced energy will play an instrumental role in shaping the individual's behavioral and psychological responses. Stress is often accompanied by varying degrees of strain.

Individual strain is related to individual stress but is not the same. Individual strain has its analogue in engineering, where strain is the degree of deformation or distortion that occurs in a block of material subjected to stress. It is, therefore, a form of deviation from a standard.

Individual strain is the degree of physiological, psychological, and/or behavioral deviation from an individual's normal functioning resulting from a stressful event or series of events.

Strain is exhibited in the various behavioral, psychological, and medical disorders which we commonly see, such as insomnia, depression, and cardiovascular disease.

The same demands will cause different degrees of stress and strain for different individuals. What is negatively stressful for one individual will be positively stressful for another. Therefore, the study of stress and strain entails examining the individual's psychological, emotional, and physiological evolution and life history. Each of us has great complexity and depth in our experience. Psychoanalytic practice and theory is one vehicle for approaching this complexity and depth within the individual spirit. Without delving into the depths it is often impossible to understand an individual's stress and strain in response to the demands of life.

Because each individual is unique, it is impossible to draw universal generalizations about the causes of stress or the prevention of strain. It may be possible to suggest guidelines for groups or personality types, but even these should be treated with circumspection. A careful and in-depth diagnosis of an individual or an organization is essential to effective stress management. Only through a psychodynamic understanding of the individual and the individual's ecological fit in the world can we understand stress and help prevent strain.

The Stress Response

The nature of the human response to stressful events was first studied in the mid-1920s by Hans Selye, known to many as the "father of stress." As a young medical student, Selye became curious about the general syndrome of "being sick." He noticed that patients suffering from a variety of illnesses demonstrated many similar physiological responses.

Through subsequent work on both animals and humans, Selye identified a rather predictable sequence of responses which he termed the "general adaptation syndrome (GAS)." There are three stages to the GAS: the alarm reaction, the stage of resistance, and the stage of exhaustion. The alarm reaction is the immediate and fairly predictable psychophysiological (mind-body) response to any type of stress. It is the stage of the GAS which is of primary concern here. This stage of the GAS has been called the "emergency reaction" (Cannon, 1932), the "ergotropic reaction" (Hess, 1957), or simply the "fight-or-flight" response.

The response is rooted in human evolutionary development and was essential for survival in an environment of primarily physical stressors (lions, opposing warriors, or the pursuit of game). Such a response is still functional in saving pedestrians from speeding cars and miners from collapsing mine shafts. In addition, this response, if channeled wisely, can improve performance in both physical and nonphysical work environments.

Many of the components of this response are familiar: increased heart rate, rapid breathing, increased blood pressure, the feeling of pounding in the chest (resulting from the fast heart rate and higher blood pressure), perspiration, increased alertness, and, often, a feeling of jitteriness or nervousness. This alarm reaction is mediated by the sympathetic nervous system and the endocrine system. In conjunction with the activation of these systems, several "stress hormones" are released which may contribute to longer term effects of stress.

The second stage of the GAS is the stage of resistance in which the immediate response to stress has enabled the individual to adapt to the stressor. But when the alarm reaction is elicited too intensely and too frequently over an extended period without an effective outlet, the third stage of the GAS, the stage of exhaustion, is reached. As Selye (1973) points out, "One would think that once adaptation has occurred and ample energy is available, resistance should go on indefinitely. But just as any inanimate machine gradually wears out, so does the human machine sooner or later become the victim of constant wear and tear."

It is at the stage of exhaustion that many of the negative, destructive consequences of stress become manifest. These may include behavioral changes such as increased cigarette smoking and accident proneness, psychological effects such as depression or marital discord, and medical consequences including the onset or worsening of heart disease and diabetes. These are manifestations of individual strain.

Optimum Stress: The Yerkes-Dodson Law

That stress has both beneficial and destructive effects upon the individual was first suggested by Yerkes and Dodson (1908), who discovered that performance improved with increasing amounts of stress up to an optimum point. Beyond that point, additional amounts of stress resulted in a reduction in performance level. This relationship is depicted in Figure 1.2 and suggests that too little stress may be just as bad as too much stress. In other words, there is an optimum level of stress which

FIGURE 1.2
The Yerkes-Dodson law. [*Based on Robert M. Yerkes and John D. Dodson, "The Relation of Strength of Stimulus to Rapidity of Habit-Formation,"* Journal of Comparative Neurology and Psychology, *vol. 18, 1908, pp. 459–482.*]

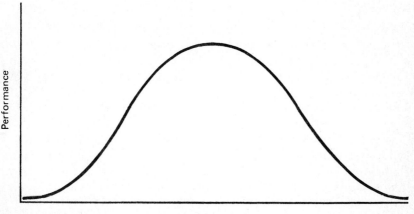

will elicit the best performance. This optimum stress level will vary among individuals and among organizations.

Selye makes a similar point in describing the differences between racehorses and turtles. Some individuals will perform well when they are experiencing many demands and high levels of stress. These individuals are the racehorses who have a high optimum stress level. Other individuals will perform best when they experience fewer demands and less stress. They are the turtles who have a relatively low optimum stress level. Each individual's and each organization's optimum level of stress is healthy and appropriate for them.

For stress to have its most beneficial effects, individuals and organizations must be working and living at *their* optimum stress level. If they attempt to operate above or below that level, they will experience the distress of overload or underload, both of which will result in a reduction in performance effectiveness.

The two major outcomes of the stress response, alluded to previously, are eustress and distress.

Eustress is the healthy, positive, constructive outcome of the stress response. It includes the individual and organizational well-being associated with growth, flexibility, adaptability, and high performance levels.

Distress is the unhealthy, negative, destructive outcome of the stress response. It includes such adverse individual and organizational consequences as cardiovascular disease and high absenteeism rates associated with illness, decay, and death.

Stress Is Not . . .

There are numerous notions about stress, some of which are unfounded. In attempting to clarify some of these misperceptions, Selye (1974) cautions people to be aware of several things which stress *is not*. Following Selye's approach, it will be helpful to address some of these common misperceptions.

Stress is not simply anxiety. The psychoanalysts who have studied anxiety have found it to be a signal that something is out of balance in the individual's psychological sphere. Anxiety is often one of many reactions to stressful events. Anxiety originates in fear, apprehension, and/or dread. Stress may originate in apprehension and thus have an anxiety component. Or, it may originate in positive anticipation and be devoid of an anxiety component.

Stress is not simply nervous tension. Even individuals who are unconscious have been observed to exhibit the stress response. As in the case of anxiety, nervous tension *may* result from a stressful situation. Whether or not it does depends in part upon whether the individual stores the stress-induced energy *or* releases it through various behavioral and psychological channels.

Stress is not necessarily bad or damaging. Daily activities—a round of golf or a passionate embrace—can cause considerable stress without producing measurable damage. Eustress is not damaging, but distress *may* be damaging. The outcome of a stressful event depends on how the individual manages it. For example, individuals who stress themselves in the process of creative, exhaustive work may actually benefit from their self-imposed demands.

Stress is not an event or a circumstance, but a response to it. The actual event or circumstance which demands a response and produces stress is the *stressor*. Stress is the patterned, unconscious response to this stressor. This distinction will become important in later discussions of diagnosis (Chapters 5 and 6) and preventive management (Chapters 7 through 12). Too often the term "stress" is used ambiguously to mean "stressor," "distress," "the stress response," or the consequences of stressful events.

Stress is not always overstimulation or overexcitement. Stress may result from the experience of too many demands which lead to overstimulation. It also may result from too few demands, such as might result from repetitive, boring work. This form of stress leads to understimulation which may in turn lead to depression.

Stress should not necessarily be avoided. As long as an individual is alive, demands are placed upon him or her and, thereby, the individual is stressed. What can be avoided, or at least modified, are the negative consequences of stress. Stress is inevitable; distress is not. It is the maximization of the beneficial aspects of stress and the minimization of the harmful effects of stress at which much of this discussion is aimed.

WHY STUDY ORGANIZATIONAL STRESS?

Students of management pursuing their chosen course of study, the busy manager concerned with keeping daily operations going smoothly, and the executive who is occupied with major corporate decisions may all justifiably ask, "Why should I worry about organizational stress?" We all know that life in organizations can be stressful and that the stresses can sometimes wear on people. But what is organizational stress and why should we study it?

> *Organizational stress* is the general, patterned, unconscious mobilization of the individual's energy when confronted with any organizational or work demand.

Organizational stress originates in organizational demands and is experienced by the individual. It should not be confused with the stress which an organization experiences. That is, when an entire organization is subject to a demand, like adjusting to a new competitor in its task environment or government deregulation, it will respond in a general, patterned way to mobilize its resources to meet the demands. This parallels the individual's response to a stressful situation, but occurs at the organization level. Organizational stress occurs at the individual level and is caused by organizational demands placed upon the individual.

There are at least two compelling and related reasons for studying organizational stress. First, mismanaged organizational stress can produce individual strain and distress which is detrimental for an organization's human resources. The damage done to the organization's human resources due to strain and distress then has negative economic implications, such as low productivity or poor quality workmanship. Second, when organizational stress is expertly managed, it can lead to improved performance, worker satisfaction, and productivity.

The human and economic costs of distress are rather substantial at the national level. The American Heart Association has estimated the total costs of cardiovascular diseases alone to be in excess of $46 billion annually. Alcohol abuse has been estimated to cost the nation $40 billion annually. Ivancevich and Matteson (1980) estimate that the total cost of distress may be approximately 10 percent of the United States gross national product—or even greater. It may be hard to link stress with short-term, bottom-line cost figures in a given organization. However, there is increasing evidence that distress does have adverse consequences, and we know these consequences cost money.

Therefore, mismanaged stress can lead to varied costly, dysfunctional consequences for the organization. Macy and Mirvis (1976) have delineated the economic costs accrued by organizations for various dysfunctional behaviors. Absenteeism and turnover are among these dysfunctional behaviors. On the other hand, the effective management of organizational stress can lead to improved organizational functioning and reduced costs.

As Yerkes and Dodson (1908) have pointed out, an optimum level of stress leads to higher levels of performance. Therefore, the proper management of stress involves working to arrive at this optimum stress level for individuals and organizations. Effective stress management will result in eustress and the various benefits in performance, satisfaction, and functioning.

Managers may find an understanding of organizational stress important to their practices as supervisors. The managerial function entails communicating work-related expectations, creating job responsibilities and tasks, conducting performance evaluations, and influencing the behavior of any number of subordinates and other organizational members. Stress inevitably plays an integral role in each of these aspects of a manager's work life. For example, the effective manager will want to reduce stress at performance evaluation times while increasing stress to appropriate work levels to increase motivation and performance. In addition, an understanding of organizational stress and its prevention can enhance the manager's own coping ability.

If an understanding of stress can help managers deal with organizational stress more effectively, it should enable their subordinates to function better also. These individuals typically have less decision-making latitude than their managers. This lack of authority has been found to be very stressful when coupled with heavy job demands (Karasek, 1979). Therefore, supervisors and managers who experience heavy job demands without much decision-making latitude may benefit from understanding other mechanisms for coping with organizational stress.

Finally, from a societal perspective, the American industrial system has always been concerned with profitability and productivity. Productivity has become emphasized as a theme and focus for government as well as industry because of recent declines in productivity. As noted earlier, too much or too little stress both result in a reduction in individual and also organizational performance. Finding optimum stress levels for individuals and organizations would be expected to lead to higher levels of performance and productivity.

THE PREVENTIVE MANAGEMENT MODEL
FOR ORGANIZATIONAL STRESS

The study of organizational stress involves an understanding of the sources of stress within the organization, a view of the positive as well as negative consequences of these stressors, a framework for diagnosing organizational stress, and some appreciation for the methods of change which may be used to deal with these stressors and/or the individual's response to them. The central framework for dealing with these issues and developing them in the book is presented in Figure 1.3, which also shows the chapter in which each topic is discussed in detail.

Organizational stressors which generate demands for the employee can be classified into four primary categories: task demands, role demands, physical demands, and interpersonal demands. Task demands include the deadline and the decision-making responsibilities which the individual has at work. Role demands include the expectations that others have of the individual's behavior as well as the confusion often associated with work requirements. Physical demands include the extremes of temperature and the design of one's working environment.

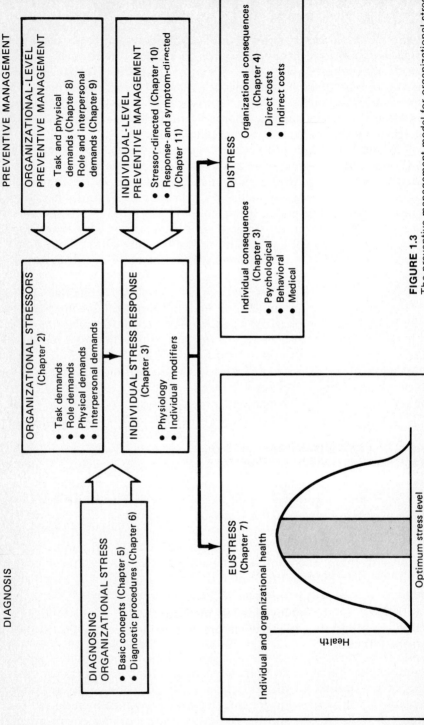

FIGURE 1.3
The preventive management model for organizational stress.

Interpersonal demands include dealing with social status incongruence and dealing with abrasive personalities at work.

All these stressors have one general effect upon the employee: to varying degrees they all elicit the stress response. This natural psycho-physiological alarm reaction is functional in preparing the individual to deal with the demands of a stressful, emergency situation. The physiological changes associated with this response are universal, although the degree and intensity of the changes will vary from individual to individual. What is not universal is the individual's action following elicitation of the stress response.

Eustress and Distress

The two alternative outcomes from the stress response are identified in Figure 1.3. *Eustress* is the adaptive, constructive, healthy response to a stressful situation. This healthy response leads to effective employee performance and normal organizational functioning. However, not everyone responds to stress in a healthy manner. When someone does not, the resulting maladaptive, detrimental, dysfunctional response leads to *distress*, with its associated individual and organizational consequences. The adverse individual and organizational consequences of distress are not inevitable. It is possible for stress in organizations to be regularly channeled into eustressful outcomes, instead of the undesirable distressful outcomes. However, for this to occur, individuals and organizations must take responsible action to bring about the positive benefits of eustress.

Two essential aspects of this responsible action are the accurate diagnosis of stress and the use of prevention methods which enhance eustress and minimize distress. These diagnostic and preventive elements are incorporated in Figure 1.3. Diagnosing organizational stress involves careful observation and assessment of both individuals and organizations. The two prevention blocks in the figure capture the two levels of prevention involved in preventive management.

Preventive Management: Taking the Strain Out of Stress

Preventive management is an organizational philosophy and set of principles which employs specific methods for promoting individual and organizational health while preventing individual and organizational distress.

Preventive management is concerned with how organizations and individuals adapt, respond to change, and grow. Organizations may respond to the variety of internal and external changes that they encounter in one of three ways (Basil and Cook, 1974). One model for organizational response is the reactive one. In this model the organization reacts to crises. It is the traditional, "firefighting," crisis-oriented model of organizational change. A second model is the adaptive one, in which the organization reacts to external events in an adaptive, non-crisis mode. This is a transitional model in which the organization keeps abreast of changes. In this model, the organization is able to effectively respond to changing circumstances, but does little to shape or alter these events. The third model is the proactive one. It is a responsive change model in which the organization anticipates and averts most crises that might befall it. It does not react to events; it shapes events.

It is the proactive model which captures the essential philosophy of preventive management. Preventive management is oriented to dealing with stress in organizations in a proactive manner, not a reactive manner. Preventive management is carried out in three stages. First, it is aimed at reducing or eliminating the unreasonable and unnecessary demands of organizational life. This involves altering or eliminating the stressors to which organizations subject individuals at work. Second, preventive management is concerned with helping individuals and organizations manage the reasonable and necessary demands of work life. This involves helping people optimize their stress level. Third, when there are failures in these two efforts, preventive management helps individuals deal with the resulting behavioral, psychological, and medical distress. This may include medical and/or psychological treatment.

Preventive management is a philosophy of managing stress in organizations for constructive, healthy, productive results. It is based upon the notion that individuals and organizations can and should assume responsibility for their actions as well as the notion that our physiological functioning can and does influence psychological processes. Therefore, taking the strain out of stress involves the realization that stress is a natural experience, one that can be constructively channeled for individual or collective benefit, and one whose dysfunctional outcomes can be minimized.

The core of the preventive management philosophy is this orientation to managing individual and organizational stress. The philosophy is founded on the principles of preventive management discussed in Chapter 7. The specific techniques for enhancing individual and organizational health, which are also an important part of preventive management, encompass the two levels of prevention activities identified in Figure 1.3. Organizational-level preventive management involves the organizationwide preventive actions taken by a responsible manager. These actions are discussed in detail in Chapters 8 and 9. Individual-level preventive management focuses on the individual employee and is concerned with individual actions an employee may engage in for the purpose of improved health and performance. These actions are discussed in detail in Chapters 10 and 11. In Chapter 12, both levels of prevention are exemplified by programs currently used in various organizations.

SUMMARY

This chapter has defined stress and strain in organizations and discussed the reasons for managers, individuals, researchers, and change agents to be concerned about such stress and strain. *Organizational stress* was defined as the general mobilization and patterned response of the individual to any organizational demand. It may cause varying degrees of *individual strain*, but is always characterized by the patterned set of physiological changes identified in Figure 1.1. A key premise of this chapter has been the notion that stress is not necessarily bad or dysfunctional. It may have either healthy *(eustressful)* or unhealthy *(distressful)* consequences. The set of consequences which individuals and organizations experience depends largely upon their own coping mechanisms and the responsible, preventive actions of the organization's management.

The preventive management model of organizational stress presented in the chapter incorporates the sources of organizational stress, the individual's alarm reaction to these demands, as well as the outcomes of *eustress* and *distress*. This model incorporates the philosophy of *preventive management* in the form of organizational-level and individual-level methods which may be employed to implement this philosophy of responsible organizational management. These prevention techniques are the tools of preventive management which enable individuals and organizations to achieve the beneficial, eustressful consequences of stress. These techniques are employed based upon the results of an *organizational stress diagnosis,* which is a key aspect of the preventive management model.

CHAPTER 2

SOURCES OF ORGANIZATIONAL STRESS

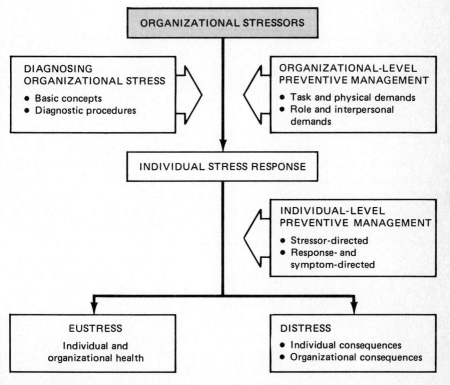

This chapter will examine the major origins or sources of stress within an organization. While stress is an individualized experience, there are a variety of demands which serve as stressors for groups of individuals. Therefore, there will be stressors discussed in this chapter which may have little or no impact upon *you*, yet they may be major stressors for someone else. Conversely, the stressors examined here may not focus on a specific part of *your* work environment which is particularly stressful. In addition to organizational stressors, extraorganizational stressors (for example, marital discord) and transitional factors (for example, preparing for retirement) can be of equal or greater importance to an understanding of an individual's stress and strain. As found in working with cardiovascular patients, it is essential to look at an individual's entire life experience (that is, work plus nonwork) and psychodynamics if one is to understand the individual's stress and strain. Therefore, the extraorganizational stressors and transitional factors will be discussed briefly at the end of this chapter and then throughout the book only as they relate to and/or tie in with stress in organizations.

Four major categories of organizational stressors are identified and discussed in this chapter. These are presented in Table 2.1. The first of these is a set of task demands. Any job is composed of a specific set of tasks and activities which are assigned to the employee who "occupies" the job. The task demands discussed in this chapter are included in the table. Task demands as sources of stress are distinguished from other stressors by their task-oriented origin (Beehr and Newman, 1978). Occupations, which are the groupings of similar jobs, as well as careers, which are the sequencings of different jobs, will therefore be considered here as task factors. All of the task stressors are based upon the nature of the work itself.

The second set of stressors is composed of role demands associated with the process of making and assuming an organizational role (Kahn et al., 1964). A role is typically defined in terms of the expectations others in the work environment attribute to it. It is the dysfunctional aspects of this role-making and role-taking process which cause an individual stress. The third major source is composed of the elements in one's physical setting or environment (Gunderson, 1978; Steele, 1973). Discomforts caused by too little free space in the physical environment exemplify this category of stressor. Finally, there are a set of interpersonal demands that occur as people work together and interact on a regular basis (Blau, 1964). All four sets of demands require a behavioral response on the part of the individual, and therefore they generate stress.

What we do not deal with separately as stressors are global organizational factors such as centralization or formalization. These factors do influence the work stress individuals experience, but their effects have been found to occur through the more specific factors which have

TABLE 2.1
SOURCES OF STRESS IN ORGANIZATIONS

Task demands	Role demands
• Occupational category	• Role conflict:
• Managerial jobs	intrasender
• Career progress	intersender
• Routine jobs	person-role
• Boundary-spanning activities	interrole
• Performance appraisal	overload
• Work overload	• Role ambiguity
• Job insecurity	
	Interpersonal demands
Physical demands	• Status incongruence
• Temperature	• Social density
• Illumination and other rays	• Abrasive personalities
• Sound waves and vibrations	• Leadership style
• Office design	• Group pressures

been identified here. Specifically, Moorhead (1982) has found in studies of managers in high-technology manufacturing organizations and in studies of hospital residents that the organizational factors do not have an *independent* effect upon work stress. Rather, they affect the individual *through* the demands which will be discussed. For example, he found that the absence of rules and procedures created role ambiguity for the managers, which in turn increased their stress. Therefore, global organizational stressors will be discussed only as they affect the four categories of stressors presented in this chapter.

TASK DEMANDS

According to Drucker (1954), organizations are goal-directed entities which have an existence of their own beyond that of the individuals who compose them. An organization's basic structural building block is the job, which is typically defined in terms of various tasks and activities. There are several task characteristics of these structural units which generate stress for individuals.

Occupational Category

The occupational category that a job falls into has been found to be an important determinant of the amount as well as the type of stress an individual experiences (French, Caplan, and Harrison, 1982; Smith, Colligan, and Hurrell, 1977). In a study of 22,000 individuals in 130 occupations who either died, were admitted to a hospital, or admitted to a mental health center owing to stress-related disease, the National Institute for Occupational Safety and Health (NIOSH) was able to distinguish high- and low-stress occupations. Office managers, administrators, first-line supervisors, and secretaries were in occupations with the most stress-related disorders, while personnel employees, craftsmen, and university professors were in occupations with the lowest incidence of stress-related disorders.

In a study of the Goddard Space Center, French, Caplan, and Harrison (1982) found that the administrators were subject to different sources of stress than were the engineers and scientists. For example, the administrators reported more stress because of too much work than did the engineers or scientists. On the other hand, the engineers and scientists reported more stress due to the challenges and demands of the tasks than did the administrators. Therefore, there are differences not only in the total *amount* of stress that various occupations cause but also in the *nature* and *source* of the stresses across occupations.

In a study of over 2,000 individuals in 23 blue- and white-collar occupations, Caplan et al. (1980) detailed a variety of occupational differences in terms of stress physiology (for example, differences in blood pressure, heart rate, and cholesterol), personality factors (for example, Type A/B patterns and defense mechanisms), and psychological factors (for example, dissatisfaction and anxiety). They were particularly interested in job stress and individual strain, either of a physiological, psychological, or behavioral nature. Their conclusions suggest that some occupations, such as supervisor, are more stressful than others, such as research scientist.

Occupational differences in stress are exemplified in the case of one university colleague who initially started a career as a young entrepreneur. His laborious and time-consuming work as a small businessman was tremendously demanding, stressing not only himself but his family. His stressful occupational activities manifested themselves in several health disorders and the recommendation of his physician that he change jobs. Following a change into the low-stress occupation of university professor, his self-reported stress is lower, his personal comfort is greater, and his health disorders are currently quiescent.

While there is variance across occupations regarding the level of stress caused by the jobs in a given occupation, there are inevitable individual differences with regard to how much stress an occupation may cause. For example, an individual who had an abundance of energy and a low sleep requirement (less than four hours per night) might find the occupational activities of an entrepreneur to be very gratifying and stimulating while not detracting unduly from family time. Therefore, another individual in the same position as our colleague might find entrepreneurial work most rewarding and quite positively stressing.

Managerial Jobs

One occupation included in the NIOSH studies was that of manager. Managerial jobs were listed twice among the twelve most stressful occupations. This may be caused by a variety of factors, such as time deadlines and performance evaluation activities (Cooper and Marshall, 1978). However, managerial work is not easily nor concisely defined. Mintzberg (1973), in an effort to more systematically study and define the nature of managerial work, has found that a major component of a manager's work involves a variety of decision-making activities. Therefore, one stress-related factor appears to be the latitude the manager has in the decision-making process (Karasek, 1979). Specifically, the increasing demands of managerial work will not be experienced as especially stressful so long as there is increased decision latitude for the manager accompanying the increased demands. This is illustrated in Figure 2.1, which depicts active, passive, high-strain, and low-strain jobs. Without this latitude, the high demand levels and pressures of managerial responsibility can become unbearable.

Therefore, managerial jobs will be particularly stressful if they are demanding in time requirements and decision-making activities yet the incumbent has little freedom of action and must continually clear decisions with the immediate boss or with other superiors. The manager in a very demanding job who has the associated freedom of action is more likely to experience the job as very exciting and active. For example, one young corporate officer in the health care industry spends from sixty to eighty hours a week on his job, which is consistent with the

FIGURE 2.1
A job strain model. [Source: *Robert A. Karasek, Jr., "Job Demands, Job Decision Latitude, and Mental Strain: Implications for Job Redesign,"* Administrative Science Quarterly, *vol. 24, June 1979, p. 288. Used by permission of* The Administrative Science Quarterly. *Copyright © 1979 Cornell University. All rights reserved.*]

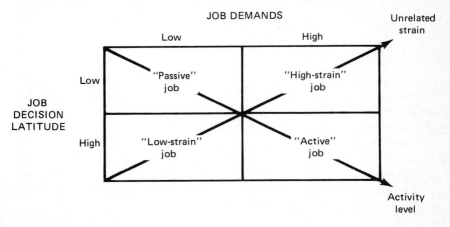

time commitments outlined in a 1982 *Wall Street Journal* article, but does not experience his job as unduly stressful. This is because he has an appropriate amount of decision power and authority to accompany his demands. He experiences his job as an "active" one because it both demands much of him and provides him ample opportunity to exercise his talents and discretion.

In addition to the decision-making activities of managerial jobs, there is another characteristic which may make them very stressful, and that is the responsibility for people which characterizes managerial work. Research suggests that responsibility for budgets or material property, such as incorporated in the strict property accountability system utilized by the United States Air Force, is not as stressful for managers as is the accountability for the work of other people (Cooper and Payne, 1978). This is painfully illustrated in the untimely death in August 1981 of Alvin Feldman, president of Continental Airlines, at a time when it seemed imminent that Texas International would take over his airline (Anderson, 1981). One of his closest associates noted: "He was also alone with the responsibility, and he took it too far. . . . He felt he was responsible for letting us down." Such responsibility for other people can be a stressful burden to carry.

First-line supervisors find themselves in a particularly stressful managerial position. One of the reasons, especially for new supervisors, is the uncertainty that goes with the new role as well as the need to learn new skills and develop new abilities. A second reason for the especially stressful nature of the position is the low decision latitude that frequently accompanies such lower-level managerial positions. A third reason for the stress of these positions is the boundary-spanning activities (discussed in detail on page 24) that the supervisor must engage in between management and labor. Because of the frequently conflicted relationship between these two groups, the supervisor is often caught as the person-in-the-middle. For these reasons, first-line supervisory positions are especially stressful.

Career Progress

One's occupation is normally characterized by the technical or professional activities in which he or she engages, but that does not constitute a career unless one pursues the occupation over an extended period of time. Occupying a job or position in an organization does not constitute a career either. One's career refers to the vocational activities which one pursues over time. It often requires involvement in several jobs and, possibly, occupations over the course of time (Hall, 1976).

The process of changing jobs in pursuing one's career can be stressful in and of itself. This is especially true if the job change also involves a relocation, which then involves family readjustments as well as a host of minor changes for the individual. These many minor hassles may contribute to the individual's overall experience of stress and strain (R. Lazarus, 1981). This change may be either positive, as in the case of a promotion or captured opportunity, or negative, as in the case of a demotion or a dead-end assignment. In either case, the change will be stressful.

The lack of change in jobs may be equally stressful. Any job requires a period for mastery, which may vary from several days to a few years. Once the individual has mastered his job through knowledge acquisition and skill development, substantial additional time in the job may be stressful due to a lack of challenge. Thus, the lack of stimulation and growth opportunities can be distressing. It may be possible, through work-redesign activities of various kinds (for example, see Hackman, 1977), to alter a job so as to revitalize its potential for challenging the individual.

Lack of career maturity may be another major stressor for the individual. Career maturity refers to the individual's readiness to effectively cope with the developmental tasks associated with one's stage of career development (Hall, 1976). The individual who possesses career maturity exhibits behavior appropriate for his stage of life development and copes with the issues of that stage as well or better than other people of that stage. Therefore, each life stage presents new demands and stresses to which the individual must adjust. The inability to make that adjustment creates genuine distress for the individual.

Routine Jobs

While managerial jobs and career development may be demanding and stressful for the reasons just discussed, blue-collar jobs can be just as stressful for different reasons. Jobs which demand too much of the incumbent in terms of demonstration of skills or utilization of knowledge and experience are just as stressful as those which underutilize the person's abilities, talents, and skills. Repetitive work is one example of a job situation which does not provide the employee with adequate physiological and/or psychological arousal (T. Cox, 1980). The problem with repetitive work is not in temporary exposure to it but rather in the prolonged exposure to such a job situation. The result is stress attributable to low levels of both self-reported and physiological arousal, which leads to boredom, shifts in attention, and associated physiological problems.

Mass production technology frequently leads to the design of jobs which are stressful because they are *understimulating* (Levi, 1981; Thompson, 1967). Jobs that support this technological process are dominantly characterized by robotic activities. In an intensive study conducted in the auto industry, Walker and Guest (1952) identify the characteristics of these assembly line jobs which make them stressful.

They are (1) a mechanically controlled work pace, (2) repetitiveness, (3) minimum skill demands of the worker, (4) predetermination of tools and techniques, (5) a high degree of task specialization, and (6) a requirement for only surface mental attention. One aspect of their field study involved intensive interviews with many of the assembly line workers, during which it was revealed that many of the workers interviewed aspired to better jobs which would provide greater opportunities for interpersonal contact (arousal) and help overcome the boredom associated with their current jobs.

Whenever employees' talents are underutilized as a result of occupying jobs such as these, then a number of dysfunctional behaviors, such as absenteeism, may be manifested. These behaviors have various individual and organizational costs, which will be discussed in detail in Chapters 3 and 4. However, the key point to note here is the very stressful nature of routine work.

A sometime characteristic of routine work is the piece-rate method of payment for work accomplishment. Taylor (1911) originally proposed this method to increase the employee's task motivation. Subsequent research supports his contention (Levi, 1981). What occurs under the piece-rate system of compensation is an increased experience of physical discomfort and fatigue as well as increased adrenaline excretion into the bloodstream. These changes suggest that there may be a physiological basis for the increased motivation of individuals working under incentive compensation systems. While this *may* be positively stressful, there is also the possibility that such incentive systems may contribute to the distress associated with routine work. Whether such pay systems are distressful or not may depend upon factors like the proportion of pay which is incentive pay, the minimum standard levels to be achieved before incentives are earned, and the magnitude of the incentive for each piece produced.

Boundary-Spanning Activities

Some jobs require individuals to work with people in other departments or organizations, thus crossing an organizational boundary in the process. Because these boundaries are designed to protect the organization, boundary-spanning activities are often stressful for the individuals who engage in such work (French and Caplan, 1972; Miles, 1980). Jobs that involve boundary-spanning activities include sales, procurement, public information, and the like. Employees who occupy these boundary-spanning jobs engage in various tasks concerned with managing the "face" of the organization (how it presents itself publicly), processing various kinds of environmental information, and managing relations with organizations in the environment (Miles, 1980).

Boundary-spanning activities are inherently stressful for individuals. A number of key factors which contribute to the high stress associated with boundary-spanning activities include:

1 Having required and nonroutine activities
2 Maintaining frequent and long-term relations with individuals in other organizations
3 Relating to dynamic, complex environments
4 Dealing with very diverse organizations
5 Lacking screening mechanisms, like secretaries
6 Being evaluated with very exact, precise performance standards

An example of how such activities may generate stress was seen in a computer services organization. Rather than using a customer service unit as a single point of contact for the organization's customers (i.e., explicitly identifying a boundary-spanning job for the organization), the customers regularly contacted members of both the computer operations and systems and programming departments. As a result of this procedure, the employees were cast into boundary-spanning activities which they reported to be very stressful. That is, they were cast into positions characterized by a number of the factors identified above as being very stressful, such as being unprotected from customers in the client organizations.

While most boundary-spanning activities occur *between organizations,* as in the example above, there are also boundary-spanning activities which occur *between departments* within one organization. The same factors which contribute to the stress of boundary-spanning activities between organizations also apply to the internal boundary-spanning activities within one organization. For example, there is an internal boundary between the medical and surgical staffs and the administrative personnel in most hospitals. In a university another internal boundary exists between the research and teaching faculty and the administrative personnel. Still another example would be the internal boundary between the engineering and production departments within a manufacturing company. Therefore, while boundary-spanning activities may be more prevalent at the organization's external boundary, they are also carried out between various departments within an organization. Exchanges and transactions across these boundaries will cause stress for individuals involved in such activities.

Performance Appraisal

In addition to the above-mentioned sources of job stress, the activity of appraising an employee's job performance is not infrequently stressful for supervisor and employee alike. As one new supervisor described it,

"You get a lump in your throat and your hands get sweaty" just before appraisal interviews. The reactions of employees are not altogether different.

The appraisal interview, when conducted in a thorough manner, will review both the positive and negative aspects of an employee's job performance (Meyer, Kay, and French, 1965). While employees may respond well to positive feedback, the General Electric investigators found that they rarely responded constructively to criticisms about their work. Over 50 percent of their responses were defensive. The employees in the General Electric study typically shifted the responsibility for their shortcomings to others, denied the shortcoming outright, or presented one of a variety of excuses for the shortcoming. These defensive behaviors resulted in the employees not fully hearing the negative feedback and may well be viewed as a way of coping with the stress attached to receiving it.

So, it is not the positive performance feedback during the appraisal interview which generates stress for the employee. Rather, it is the negative performance feedback and criticism which causes the stress, as evidenced by the assortment of observed defensive behaviors. The anticipation of this defensiveness on the part of the employee may be a contributing factor in the evaluator's (supervisor's) own experience of stress.

Another stressor for the supervisor is present in unionized organizations, as well as in other organizations which have formalized grievance procedures. This concerns the appeal of the supervisor's appraisal if the employee deems it sufficiently unfair. This possibility creates some anxiety for supervisors, who know that if they do not do a good job of appraising an employee or if they have a particularly difficult or rebellious employee, they will have to answer a grievance action. An extreme example of what supervisors have to contend with at appraisal time occurred in south Texas in a data processing organization. One disgruntled computer operator stood up following his appraisal interview and stuck a screwdriver in his supervisor's chest, seriously injuring, but not killing, the man.

Work Overload

Work overload is a stressor which may be manifested in one of two ways. The first is quantitative overload resulting from the employee being assigned too many tasks or insufficient time to accomplish the assigned tasks. As reported in the *Wall Street Journal*, this form of work overload occurred noticeably during the inflationary period of the late 1970s and early 1980s for many blue-collar workers. As organizations trimmed their payrolls, they would assign some operating employees the equivalent of

1.5 or 2.0 jobs. This resulted in more frequent accidents in some cases, as well as in union grievances regarding the practice.

The second form of work overload is qualitative in nature. This occurs when an employee does not feel that he possesses the required skills, knowledge, abilities, or competencies to do the job. This form of over-load is frequently experienced by the new first-line nursing supervisors who have been promoted on the basis of excellent clinical practice but who have no knowledge or skill training in such supervisory practices as performance appraisal or delegation. They simply do not have the skills and knowledge to manage because their clinical training excluded management training.

Job Insecurity

Another stressor exacerbated by the economic difficulties of the late 1970s and early 1980s is job insecurity. The uncertainty about the effects of budgetary cutbacks and organizational downsizing efforts will create stress for many employees. Jick (1984) has formulated a topology for examining the degree of stress caused by a budgetary cutback. Argyris (1952) previously identified additional aspects of budgets which cause pressure and stress for employees. In the case of budget cuts, one's vulnerability will be determined in a large degree by the new goals of the organization and one's marginal knowledge, ability, skill, and resources to meet these organizational requirements vis-à-vis another employee.

One's vulnerability to termination is not the only factor which will influence the experience of stress and strain due to job insecurity. Even if one is vulnerable to termination, the insecurity caused by this will be moderated by the number of alternatives for employment one has available. While such alternatives are generally less available in difficult economic times, their presence will reduce the stress of job insecurity and vulnerability to termination. The greatest degree of stress and strain is caused by the prospect of termination coupled with few or no prospects of alternative employment.

ROLE DEMANDS

A second major category of stressors at work is associated with the organizational role that an individual assumes. While task demands are concerned with specific work activities that must be accomplished, role factors are related to the behavior others expect of us as we fulfill our organizational roles. Therefore, roles are typically defined in terms of the behavioral expectations that various individuals and groups of individuals communicate to an individual at work. One's role set is therefore composed of all the various individuals, called role senders,

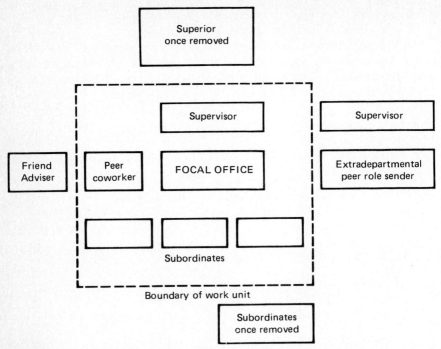

FIGURE 2.2
Composition of a hypothetical role set. [Source: *Robert L. Kahn, Donald M. Wolfe, Robert P. Quinn, J. Diedrick Snoek, and Robert A. Rosenthal,* Organizational Stress: Studies in Role Conflict and Ambiguity, *John Wiley & Sons, Inc., New York, 1964, p. 41.*]

who have expectations of that person. A typical organizational role set might look like that shown in Figure 2.2. In this illustration, the role senders include the superiors and superior once removed, the various peers and friends, the subordinates as well as the subordinate once removed. All these individuals together with the individual in the focal office compose the role set. Each role sender places unique demands on the focal person. For example, the supervisor will establish certain deadlines and assign various projects to the focal person. The subordinates will be concerned with certain performance review procedures to be used. They will also expect a consistency in managerial style on the part of the focal person. The various behaviors that these different role senders expect of the focal person are not always consistent or compatible.

There are two broad dysfunctions in role-making and role-taking activities in organizations, as identified by Kahn and his associates (1964) during their extensive examination of organizational role stress. These are role conflict and role ambiguity. These problems may be caused in a number of ways, which we will discuss separately. Both role dysfunctions cause stress and strain for the individual who is subject to them.

Role Conflict

Role conflict occurs for an individual when a person in his work environment communicates a certain expectation about how he should behave and this expectation makes it difficult or impossible to fulfill another behavioral expectation, or set of expectations. Therefore, stress is caused by the inability or difficulty in meeting the various expectations of his behavior (Van Sell, Brief, and Schuler, 1981).

Intrasender role conflict occurs when a single person in the work environment communicates conflicting or incompatible expectations. This form of role conflict typically occurs in one's relationship with the supervisor or boss, though it is not limited to that relationship. An example of how this form of conflict might exist occurred in a sales manager's job. The marketing vice president expects the sales manager to increase sales by 10 percent per year for the next five years. At the same time, the vice president expects the sales manager to keep advertising and entertainment expenses at approximately their current level so that the marketing unit can show improved profitability. The sales manager experiences these two expectations as conflicting since he thinks that he needs to spend money to increase sales.

Intersender role conflict occurs when two or more role senders communicate conflicting or incompatible expectations. This may occur in relationships with two or more supervisors, two or more colleagues, a superior and a subordinate, a superior and a client or customer, or any combination of these. This is a very common situation in matrix forms of organization where an individual will have a functional manager as well as a project manager. It is not uncommon for the two managers to disagree somewhat in their expectations, leaving the individuals caught in the middle. An illustration of how such a circumstance may be harmless occurred during an interview in a large insurance company. The manager being interviewed said that he had his boss narrowed down to one of two people, both of whom he liked. Since they did not give him conflicting assignments, he said he had no problem with the management.

Person-role conflict is a third form of role conflict which occurs when there is a perceived incompatibility between an individual's values or beliefs and the expectations held by various role senders. This form of conflict puts an individual in rather direct opposition to the behaviors that others expect. Examples of this form of role conflict arose for various military personnel during the Vietnamese war. In some cases, Air Force bomber pilots found that they could not carry out certain bombardment missions because such missions violated specific moral or ethical beliefs which they held. Thus, the fulfillment of their combat roles would have violated their personal value schemes.

Interrole conflict occurs when the requirements of one role are incompatible with requirements of a second role occupied by the incumbent. This form of conflict might arise, for example, when a director of nursing in a hospital is expected by the hospital administration in the "manager" role to place primary emphasis on administrative duties. Nursing colleagues, on the other hand, may expect the director to place primary emphasis on direct-care activities as part of the professional "nurse" role.

Role overload is the final form of role conflict and is analogous to work overload. The difference is that work overload is based upon actual tasks and activities, while role overload is based upon the behaviors which are expected of the individual. This form of role conflict would occur when too many behaviors are expected of an individual in a period of time or when the behavior expected is too complicated or difficult for the individual to execute.

While all these forms of role conflict are notably different, they all can contribute to increased stress levels for those who encounter them. However, this is not the only dysfunction that occurs in the role-making and role-taking process. Role ambiguity is a second major role dysfunction encountered in organizations.

Role Ambiguity

Role ambiguity results whenever there is inadequate information about what role behavior is expected, unclear or confusing information about expected role behaviors, unclear or confusing information about what behaviors will enable the incumbent to fulfill the role expectations, or uncertainty about the consequences of certain role behaviors (Van Sell, Brief, and Schuler, 1981).

In the first case, the ambiguity arises because the role senders, especially the key ones such as the supervisor, simply *do not communicate adequate information* to the role incumbent about what is expected. As a result, the incumbent does not understand his role in terms of specific behaviors. An example of this occurred for a young graduate student who worked in the merchandise distribution department of a major retailer. Told by the supervisor on the first day to "do what that guy does," the student was then left to do the job with no further information.

In the second case, the ambiguity arises because the role sender(s) communicate *information that is unclear or confusing*. This is prone to occur in work environments where technical terms or jargon unfamiliar to the role incumbent are prevalent. For example, administrative or nonprofessional staff employees in health care or hospital settings might initially experience role ambiguity because of the use of large amounts of medical and surgical terminology.

In the third case, ambiguity is attributable to *uncertainty about what behaviors* will enable the incumbent to fulfill the role expectations, which are clear in and of themselves. For example, a personnel manager for a major airline is given responsibility for improving several personnel practices for the maintenance, data processing, and finance personnel at a given location. The assignment is to reduce the intraorganizational conflicts at that location, improve the performance appraisal processes, and reduce the number of union grievances. While these role expectations are relatively clear, it is not at all clear immediately what behaviors and activities will enable the manager to fulfill these expectations.

Finally, ambiguity for the role incumbent may arise if *the consequences of a specific role expectation are unclear.* For example, a sales representative may be required to establish a sales goal for the territory as a result of a new corporate MBO program. This task of estimating and stating such a goal may not be difficult at all. However, ambiguity intrudes into the situation because what is not clear is the result of meeting the goal (a bonus?); exceeding the goal (a bigger bonus? or no bonus because the goal was too low?); or failing to meet the goal (no consequence because it was a difficult goal? or a commission penalty for failure to meet the goal?).

Again, as in the case of role conflict, these various forms of role ambiguity generate stress for the role incumbent. For the vast majority of office employees and professionals, these role dysfunctions, and the job factors previously discussed, are the major sources of stress. However, they are not the only sources of organizational stress. Other sources of stress are found in an employee's physical and interpersonal environment.

PHYSICAL DEMANDS

Many of the stressors which have been considered so far have either a psychological or interpersonal origin, and that may be in part due to our sociological and cultural evolution as a species. In many ways humans have removed themselves one step from the vagaries of their physical environment by the creation of physical settings which function to protect their shelter and security needs (Steele, 1973). However, this natural, cultural, and developmental evolution has not placed them in a position of immunity from physical sources of stress. Rather, the physical settings they create simply buffer them to some degree, lessening the stressful impact of the physical environment.

Selye (1976b) was among the most attentive to the issues of physical stressors. According to him, there are a host of physical agents which cause the individual stress. These include temperature variations; burns; sound and ultrasound (like sonic booms); ionizing, light, and ultra-violet rays; vibrations; airblasts; compression and decompression; gravity, magnetism, electricity, and electroshock; as well as osmotic pressure. While many offices are buffered against these stressors, a manager may well encounter various of these stressors in times of travel and during office modification and/or work at construction sites.

In a series of research studies of United States Navy surface vessels in the Atlantic and Pacific, Gunderson and his associates (see Gunderson, 1978) found various divisions of the ship to be unfavorable and hazardous work environments. These divisions included the boilers, machinery, and deck divisions. The key environmental concerns of the research team were temperature, ventilation, cleanliness, odor, size, number of people, lighting, color, privacy, noise, and safety. They found that poor physical settings, based upon these various environmental conditions, not only generated more stress for the crew members working in them but also resulted in a number of adverse individual and organizational outcomes. A number of these environmental areas of concern have applicability to other working areas in industry as well.

Temperature

People will vary in terms of both their physiological and psychological responses to various temperature levels. While some peoples are more adapted to hotter climates (black and Arabian peoples), others have made an adjustment to much colder climates (Nordic and Eskimo peoples). Still, temperature extremes at either end of the continuum will cause a stress reaction. Individuals need both physical setting pro-tections as well as garment and other sorts of safeguards as temperatures move into the freezing region (32°F) or over 100°F. With the energy crisis of the 1970s, the issue of temperature as a stressor impacted even office workers in the Sun Belt during the summer months.

Illumination and Other Rays

Lighting and illumination levels were the concern of the original Haw-thorne investigators back in the 1920s. They did discover that workers tended to produce less work under moonlight intensity. However, be-yond that they did not uncover the systematic relationship between illumination level and productivity that they had anticipated. It was not until later that they would understand that it was because of unaccounted for variables, such as the individual attention the workers received, that this was so.

Most physical and office work environments require 20 to 40 foot-candles of light (Ivancevich and Matteson, 1980). However, this may need to be increased markedly for especially fine or detailed work tasks. Extremes in lighting cause stress which is manifested in a variety of ways, such as headaches and nervous tension.

Rays outside of the visible spectrum also have the potential for generating stress, though their effects are much more subliminal and therefore further from the individual's awareness. X-rays, infrared, and ultraviolet rays are now used in a host of settings, such as dental offices, inspection stations, military operations of various sorts, and welding activities, such as in shipbuilding. Precautions are increasing so as to protect workers from the harmful effects of overexposure to these physical stressors.

Sound Waves and Vibrations

Exposure to excessive noise (roughly 80 decibels) on a recurring, prolonged basis can cause stress (Ivancevich and Matteson, 1980). Anyone who has been exposed to a noisy, second-generation computer printer or to an airplane such as the Air Force's C-130 or a naval aircraft carrier flight deck is well aware of the stress that can be caused by excessive noise levels. In extreme cases, temporary and permanent hearing losses may result from overexposure without proper protection, such as the ear protectors issued to Air Force personnel who are exposed to such noise.

This kind of overexposure occurred for a young warehouseman who wanted to startle the secretarial staff in the second-story offices in one of the warehouses. He rigged up a huge firecracker on a long clothesline pole, lit it, held it up by the outside of the office window, and awaited the loud explosion. The secretaries were quite startled, to say the least, when the firecracker exploded, but the poor warehouseman suffered a temporary two-day hearing loss. Because he was standing in the narrow alley between two warehouses, the noise had been amplified at his level. The incident would not have been at all amusing had the hearing loss been permanent.

Closely associated with sound waves is vibration, which, according to Selye (1976b), is a very powerful stressor. Vibrations typically occur as a result of some rotary or impacting motion, or a combination of the two. Choppers, ramming machines, pneumatic and riveting hammers, aircraft propellers, and the like generate vibrations. Therefore, construction sites and aerospace activity centers are common locations where such stress would occur. A central element of the stress response is elevated catecholamine levels, which have been noted in response to vibration (Selye, 1976b). In addition, there are various alterations that occur in psychological and neurological functioning as a result of exposure to this stressor.

Office Design

According to Steele (1973), physical settings fulfill one or more of six basic functions, which are to (1) provide shelter and security, (2) facilitate social contact, (3) provide symbolic identification, (4) enhance task instrumentality, (5) heighten pleasure, and (6) stimulate growth. If physical settings are not designed to fulfill the function for which the space is intended, then those attempting to use the space will experience stress. Thus, if office settings do not serve their first function effectively, then they expose the inhabitants to some of the environmental vagaries already discussed. But even if they are well designed for meeting this function, they may cause stress because other functions are not fulfilled by the design of the work environment.

For example, physical settings should facilitate certain kinds of social contact associated with the work. When a large office of a state department of human resources was temporarily relocated to an unused supermarket, all of the social workers were spread out in long rows and aisles with no partitions between them. An entering social welfare client was struck by the overwhelming nature of this sprawl (see Figure 2.3). This was a very stressful environment in which to discuss such private matters as child abuse.

An example of how too much physical dispersion may cause stress occurred in a military computer installation which had units located in four different buildings. The computer operations were all in one main building, but there were programmers spread out through three other buildings. This physical dispersion caused some disruptions in communications, contributed to distrust among the groups, and heightened the stress and tension between them.

Therefore, physical settings and office space can cause stress for employees in a variety of ways when their basic functions are not adequately fulfilled. They do not have the direct, immediate impact of extremes in temperature and sound waves, but their importance is no less a potential source of stress.

INTERPERSONAL DEMANDS

Interpersonal stressors at work are concerned with the demands placed upon us in the normal course of social, personal, and working relationships in the organization. As individuals, we have various distinctive personality and behavioral characteristics which are a source of stimulation for some people (positively stressful) and a source of aggravation

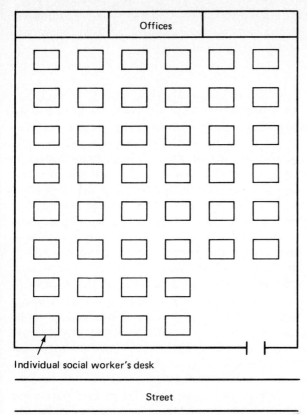

Individual social worker's desk

Street

FIGURE 2.3
A temporary office of a department of human resources.

and irritation for others (negatively stressful). Individuals with clear-cut, powerful personalities may be more stressful for us to deal with than bland, withdrawn individuals, although the reverse could also be the case. As Selye (1974) points out, learning to live with other people is one of the most stressful aspects of life. There are various individual characteristics which we possess as well as various aspects of informal group behavior within organizations that make this so.

The interpersonal stressors should not be confused with individual characteristics which are moderators of the stress response. These individual modifiers of the stress response will be discussed in detail in the next chapter where the individual consequences of stress are examined. The interpersonal stressors come from the demands and pressures of social system relations at work. The demands of these social relationships are in part related to the role stressors previously discussed but are different from them in that they are not based upon expected behaviors.

There are five specific interpersonal stressors which will be examined here. They are status incongruence, social density, abrasive personalities, leadership style, and group pressures.

Status Incongruence

Each individual occupies a unique social status within a group in an organization. This social status is based upon many factors, such as educational and family background, technical competence, professional accomplishment, membership in associations and clubs, income level, as well as formal position and responsibilities. Individuals of higher social status within an organization receive prerogatives and privileges not enjoyed by individuals of lower social status. Individuals of lower social status also defer more frequently to those in higher status positions. Stress is caused for the individual who does not perceive himself in a social status commensurate with the various social attributes which normally are used to determine such status.

For example, one manager in the aerospace industry reported a strong sense of frustration and stress over not being in a higher social status at work. Based upon his various professional accomplishments, technical competence, and positions of responsibility in professional associations, he perceived a clear incongruence between his actual status at work and what it should be. He saw a distinction between his formal job position and this social status. In other words, he thought he should be entitled to more influence than he in fact perceived having. Therefore, his stress was caused by the incongruence of having a lower social status than he was entitled to have.

Status incongruence may also occur if an individual is in a higher status position than that to which the individual feels entitled. This form of status incongruence will cause less frustration and more insecurity. The insecurity is caused by not having all of the social attributes the individual views as necessary for the higher level status position. This was exemplified in the case of a nursing administrator who had to regularly deal with the hospital's board of directors. She did not feel secure in relating to the various board members on an equal level although she was accorded that position by the board members.

Social Density

Social density, either too much or too little, may also be a source of interpersonal stress. Each individual has varying needs for interpersonal space and distance. When this distance is violated and people are too close, they experience stress. The effects of crowding have been studied in a variety of settings by V. C. Cox and his associates. Their findings suggest that crowding leads to significant psychological stress which in turn contributes to increases in *both* contagious and noncontagious illnesses (V. C. Cox et al., 1982). On the other hand, when there is not an adequate proximity for social contact, that also is perceived as stressful. As in the case of all the stressors, there will be individual differences in terms of the amount and intensity of stress caused by a particular social density.

In contrast, a study of 96 professionals in the headquarters of a petroleum-related company by Szilagyi and Holland (1980) refuted the commonly held notion that increasing social density increases stress for individuals. The changes in social density occurred in the context of an office relocation. The employees reported a greater sense of closeness and social density as a result of the change. They also reported greater work satisfaction, more friendship opportunities, and lower levels of stress, suggesting that a balance in social density is desirable.

Increasing social density may be overdone. Evans (1969) found that where social density was too high, individuals did not have an adequate amount of space to work in. In addition, he found that their performance suffered and their work satisfaction declined. Physiologically, individuals working in these crowded conditions also had increases in their blood pressure. This suggests that both too great or too little a social density will cause stress for individuals at work.

Abrasive Personalities

Another interpersonal stress to which an individual may be subject is an abrasive personality (H. Levinson, 1978). Such individuals may not intend to create stress and strain for others at work, but they do. Abrasive personalities cause stress for others by ignoring the interpersonal aspects of human intercourse, the feelings and sensibilities of fellow employees, and the depth and richness of their own emotional lives. Abrasive personalities are often achievement-oriented, hard-driving, and intelligent. Thus, they may function very well at the conceptual level but not do nearly as well at the emotional level.

There are several other ways in which abrasive personalities cause stress and strain for others at work. First, their condescending and critical style places others in a constantly subordinate position in which they are also viewed as "unimportant." Second, their need for perfection in each task they undertake often causes others to feel inadequate or "outdone." Third, their attention to self leaves little energy for thoughtful and sensitive attention to the needs of other individuals at work. Fourth, they prefer to do all work themselves, leaving others out of their projects and activities. This provides a fertile ground for feelings of uselessness and inadequacy in others. Finally, their competitive nature fosters a conflicted and divisively competitive work environment as opposed to a cooperative and mutually achievement-oriented environment.

H. Levinson (1978) provides some useful illustrative examples of the adverse effects of abrasive personalities at work. Abrasive individuals can be difficult enough to deal with as colleagues and coworkers, but in positions of management and leadership they may scatter stress and strain throughout an organization. However, it is not only abrasiveness within a leader which may cause stress and strain for subordinates but also leadership style.

Leadership Style

Managers and supervisors are in a unique position to cause stress for their subordinates, either wittingly or unwittingly. The interpersonal leadership style, as opposed to the technical aspects of supervision, adopted by a manager has long been seen as a potential source of tension for subordinates (Lewin, Lippitt, and White, 1939). For example, authoritarian behavior on the part of a leader tends to cause pressure and tension for subordinates because of the high number of influence attempts undertaken by the leader. This is unrelated to the task functions of the leader. The underlying tension among subordinates under authoritarian leadership tends to be expressed in one of two ways. One way is for the subordinates to become very outwardly calm and passive, repressing much of the tension and hostility which they experience. This repressed (as opposed to expressed) anger may be converted into elevated blood pressure over extended periods of time. The second way is for the tension to be expressed in spontaneous outbursts of conflict and aggression in the workplace. While this may be healthier for the expression of anger and tension, the conflicts will generate some stress for others around them to cope with.

These effects of authoritarian supervision were illustrated in a contemporary American industrial setting among a group of seven supervisors who worked for an autocratic section chief. When asked what their boss expected during an intensive group interview, a one-legged supervisor responded by saying that he had ordered pontoons for his crutches. Another supervisor, in describing his perceptions of the work environment, related his recurring night dreams of hurricanes, tornadoes, and ocean storms which constantly raged over him (his boss?) and around him (his tense, fellow supervisors?), though he was never seriously hurt by the storms. Virtually no overt signs of conflict and tension were exhibited in the workplace. Rather, a deceptive calm existed which could be seen through during in-depth interviews with the supervisors. The emotionally turbulent, stressful work environment was apparently attributable to the interpersonal behavior of the section chief, since supervisors working for another section chief in the same environment did not have similar descriptions of the work environment.

This is one way in which the interpersonal style of the leader may be a source of stress for subordinates at work. These patterns may also be self-defeating and destructive for the work group as a whole. However, all of the stress generated by these characteristics is not destructive. Some of it is positive and stimulating, as in the case of the extrovert who stresses an individual into greater growth and development.

Group Pressures

Many groups in an organization place pressures on their individual members which are a source of stress and tension. These groups are often part of an informal organization which evolves within any formal organization (Roethlisberger and Dickson, 1939). The informal organization has as its fundamental building block the informal group, which overlaps in varying degrees with work groups in the organization. These informal groups have a dual impact upon the individual in that they may be either a cause of stress because of various pressures and group sanctions or a refuge and source of strength because of the social support they provide the individual. The latter is the case in cohesive groups that enable individuals to meet certain emotional needs, such as interpersonal and physical safety. It is those situations in which these groups pressure their members and cause stress that are of concern here.

As a group matures through its developmental stages, it establishes a variety of behavioral norms which function as standards of conduct for members of the group. These behavioral norms are frequently unwritten and operate through a process of consensual understanding. A violation of these informal codes of behavior typically results in group sanctions to realign the individual's behavior with the norms. The silencing treatment given a West Point cadet is an example of such sanctioning behavior on the part of a group. The purpose of such group sanctioning behavior is to establish control over individual group members. As such, it causes stress and tension for the individual involved.

The stress caused by group pressures and behavioral norms results in part from the frustration of an individual's natural drives and urges (Freud, 1961). When an individual is required to work or function in a group context, he must curb his aggressive urges. This frustration of natural drives and urges that must occur as part of being able to get along with other people in the world (or a group) is inevitably distressful for the individual because it inhibits the release of natural energies that arise within the individual.

It was the later psychoanalysts such as Laing (1971; with Esterson, 1964) and especially Sullivan (1953), who were concerned with how these interpersonal, group pressures caused various psychological and behavioral disorders for the individual. Their theory and therapy were both predicated on the notion that interpersonal exchanges within all sorts of groups place pressures, stresses, and strain on the individual members. Therefore, they considered it to be inevitable that group membership would cause stress for the individual, primarily from a psychological point of view.

An example of how an individual's membership within a group may cause stress was illustrated by a service manager in a manufacturing organization. As a young man, he described going to work in a shop that manufactured wheel hubs for cars. Most workers turned out about 50 hubs per week. He thought he might be able to turn out 100, so he tried. He actually turned out 125 with a great effort. However, several of his coworkers "counseled" him at the end of the week about not "over-exerting" himself. The subtle message and clear pressure caused him stress, tension, and anxiety, but he fully understood the message. This is just one example of how groups can cause stress for their members.

EXTRAORGANIZATIONAL STRESSORS

It is difficult to understand an individual's stress and strain without examining the whole experience, at work as well as away from work. Stressful life events of a personal nature also have an effect upon an individual's performance effectiveness and adjustment at work (Bhagat, 1983). Therefore, we cannot totally ignore the extraorganizational stressors to which an individual is subject in studying organizational stress. For example, individuals working in heavily populated urban areas, such as Houston or New York, may experience significant extraorganizational stress from the process of commuting to and from work.

While some individuals can compartmentalize the different aspects of their lives well, other individuals have difficulty in doing so. For individuals who can compartmentalize well, extraorganizational stressors will have less impact upon their stress at work than for those who cannot. Regardless of how well one can separate the different aspects of one's life, one's marriage and family relationships are important extraorganizational stressors (Hall and Hall, 1980; Handy, 1978). There is a clear potential for role stress in this area due to the conflicts inherent in assuming work roles and family roles, such as husband, son, father or mother, wife, and daughter. As with the case of any stressor, these family relationships may contribute to improved work performance and adjustment or they may detract because of the distress they cause (Bhagat, 1983).

The distinction between the demands of personal and work life is a conceptual and somewhat artificial one. While our major focus will be on organizational stressors, the role of extraorganizational stressors cannot be ignored in diagnosing and preventing distress for individuals and organizations.

TRANSITIONAL FACTORS

Individuals and organizations go through stages of growth and evolution over the course of time. The periods of transition from one life stage to the next stage give rise to stress and strain within either the individual or the organization (D. J. Levinson, 1978; Kimberly, Miles, and Associates, 1980). These passages and transitions will contribute to the overall stress one experiences at a given point in time and will have an effect upon behavior and performance. These transition periods may become crises, although not necessarily. If they take on the character of crises, then they will contribute to distress for the individual or organization in transition.

One particularly important transition period is that from active work life to retirement (Hall, 1976). How this transition is managed has important implications for individuals as well as for the organizations from which they retire. Retirement is a very stressful transition for a majority of individuals, but it need not be distressful. How individuals and their organizations manage this transitional factor will influence not only the individual's stress with regard to the experience, but also the stress of others in the individual's work environment. For these reasons, retirement and other transitions are of some concern in the study and management of organizational stress.

SUMMARY

This chapter has focused on four major categories of organizational stressors: task demands, role demands, physical demands, and inter-personal demands. Which set or sets of demands create the most stress for you will undoubtedly differ from the demands which create the most stress for another person. However, there are some conclusions that may be drawn from the chapter. First, role demands will be very dominant and pervasive sources of stress for most individuals working in large or small organizations. It is inevitable that conflicts and con-fusion at work will cause employees stress. Second, the amount of stress attributable to task and interpersonal demands will vary markedly by job and individual. These two sets of demands will probably vary the most in their importance as stressors. Third, while such physical de-mands as extreme temperature and office designs are sources of organizational stress, man's mastery of his physical environment over the past century has contributed to reducing the amount of stress directly attributable to his physical setting.

Finally, in developing a stress profile for an individual, it is important to consider a number of unique life demands which are beyond those originating in an organization. Of particular importance may be such *extraorganizational stressors* as the general business climate (which may affect job security), family considerations (which may create interrole conflicts with one's work role), commuting and travel activities (which can increase one's sense of being hassled), and social change. In addition, there may be *transitional factors*, such as adult life transitions, passages, and crises, such as impending retirement, which contribute to an individual's stress. Therefore, a number of sources of stressors, including the organizational ones discussed in this chapter, must be considered in accurately determining an individual's stress profile.

FURTHER READINGS

Beehr, T. A., and J. E. Newman: "Job Stress, Employee Health, and Organizational Effectiveness: A Facet Analysis, Model, and Literature Review," *Personnel Psychology*, vol. 31, 1978, pp. 665–699.

Bhagat, R. S.: "Effects of Stressful Life Events upon Individual Performance Effectiveness and Work Adjustment Processes within Organizational Settings: A Research Model," *Academy of Management Review*, vol. 8, 1983.

Cooper, C. L., and R. Payne: *Stress at Work*, John Wiley & Sons, Chichester, England, 1978.

Cooper, C. L., and R. Payne: *Current Concerns in Occupational Stress*, John Wiley & Sons, Chichester, England, 1980.

Kahn, R. L., D. M. Wolfe, R. P. Quinn, J. D. Snoek, and R. A. Rosenthal: *Organizational Stress: Studies in Role Conflict and Ambiguity*, John Wiley & Sons, New York, 1964.

McLean, A. A.: *Work Stress*, Addison-Wesley, Reading, Mass., 1979.

Moss, L.: *Management Stress*, Addison-Wesley, Reading, Mass., 1981.

CHAPTER 3

INDIVIDUAL CONSEQUENCES OF STRESS

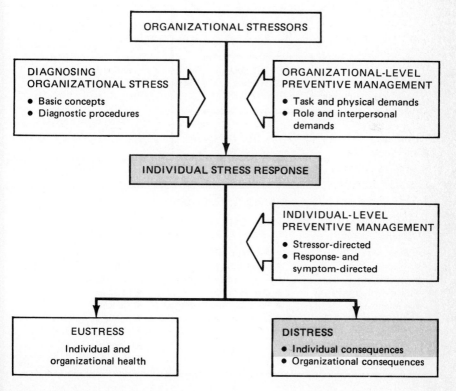

The organizational stressors described in Chapter 2 are rather diverse, yet they lead to a common result: when perceived by the individual as a stressor, each of these factors leads to a stereotypic psychophysiological reaction known as the stress response. Each individual exhibits the same *basic response*, although the immediate and long-term *consequences* of the stress response vary greatly among individuals. These consequences may be behavioral, psychological, or medical. When determining the ultimate individual costs of organizational stress, these various consequences must be considered collectively.

This chapter contains a review of the physiology of the stress response; a description of the major behavioral, psychological, and medical con-

FIGURE 3.1
Organizational stressors and individual distress.

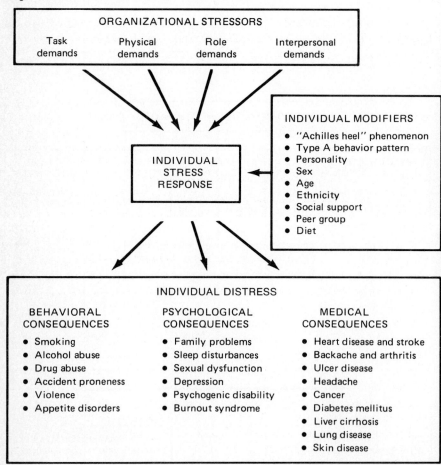

sequences of mismanaging the response; and, finally, a discussion of individual factors which modify and shape those consequences. Figure 3.1 illustrates the pivotal role which the individual stress response plays in the organizational stressor–individual distress connection. As depicted in the figure, any one of a number of organizational stressors may lead to an even greater variety of distressful consequences. Our focus in this chapter is on these consequences and the individual differences which modify their occurrence.

PHYSIOLOGY OF THE STRESS RESPONSE

When confronted with news reports and journal articles describing the spectrum of conditions which have been associated with stress and stressful events, it is reasonable to ask, "How can this be?" "How can accidents, heart attacks, and diabetes *all* be associated with something such as stress?" Inevitably, the answer will be found in the biological and psychological linkages which govern inner human workings. Through the work of Hans Selye, Walter B. Cannon, other medical scientists, and students of psychosomatic medicine, many of these linkages are now known.

As indicated in Chapter 1, the stress response consists of a generalized pattern of psychophysiological (mind-body) reactions. The response is generalized in that its pattern is not determined by the individual stressor, nor the individual being stressed, and there is a generalized mobilization of the individual as a result of the response.

Much of the pattern is familiar. Imagine, for example, that you have just taken over Chrysler Corporation, which is having financial difficulty. You have a host of ideas on how to save the company, but you know you will have to fire thousands of the over 125,000 employees. You are confident that you will save the company, but inevitably many individuals will be hurt and terminated in the process. You know that many will be upset. Not everyone will agree with your recommended solutions and course out of the current problems. In fact, some may be irate about certain of your ideas.

While you're looking over your notes, one of your officers is calling for order and beginning to introduce you. In about 30 seconds you'll be standing in front of these employees with only your notes. If you pause and observe your own body, you will notice a sense of pounding in your chest—your heart is beating about 120 times a minute, rather than its usual 60 times, and each beat is more powerful as it raises your blood pressure. Your breathing is deeper, yet somewhat tighter. Your stomach is a bit queasy; you are aware of a feeling of gnawing in the pit of your stomach. Despite the air conditioning, your brow and palms are sweating, moistening your scribbled notes.

As you step to the center, you realize that your mouth is dry, cottony. You take a sip of water and raise the glass with a slightly tremulous hand. You clear your throat and begin to speak, focusing all your attention on the audience and the comments you are about to make. Your muscles are tense as you rock forward on your feet.

What you are experiencing is the normal response to an emergency or stressful situation. This response is sometimes called the fight-or-flight response. At this point, the flight option probably feels very attractive. Through biological mechanisms which developed in our primitive past, your body is preparing for a physical response to a challenging situation.

The stress response consists of a well-organized series of events involving the sympathetic nervous system and the endocrine (hormone) system. The anatomy of the stress response is summarized in Figure 3.2. Our basic understanding of the role of the sympathetic nervous system and, in particular, the role of adrenaline comes from the work of the physician-researcher Walter B. Cannon and his colleagues at Harvard University. Much of the information regarding the role of the endocrine system is provided by Selye's research.

The combined effects of the sympathetic and endocrine responses to stress are to redirect blood flow to the muscles and brain and away from the skin, intestines, and other "vegetative" organs; to mobilize glucose (blood sugar) and fatty acids from storage sites and pour them into the blood stream to provide readily available fuel for the body; to increase alertness; and to reduce less emergent activities such as digestion. These responses are logical and highly adaptive preparation for physical challenges such as wild animals or warring neighbors. As we will see below, however, these responses may be highly maladaptive for responding to nonphysical stressors.

The Sympathetic Nervous System

The human nervous system has two major divisions: the somatic nervous system, which controls the skeletal muscles, and the autonomic nervous system, which controls the visceral organs. It is now recognized that the actions of the autonomic nervous system are not entirely involuntary, as was once thought. Nevertheless, basic life functions such as heartbeat, blood pressure, digestion, and breathing are maintained by the autonomic nervous system without our conscious effort.

The autonomic nervous system is further divided into the sympathetic nervous system, which is responsible for activating functions such as the stress response, and the parasympathetic nervous system, which stimulates vegetative or reparative activities.

Figure 3.3 summarizes the organization of the sympathetic nervous system and describes its major actions. Sympathetic activity is caused by

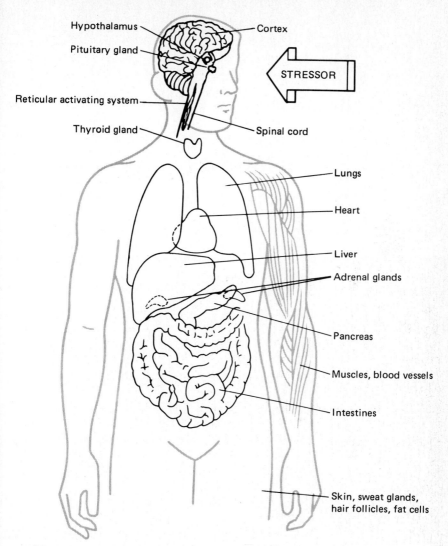

Hypothalamus —
Cortex
Pituitary gland —
STRESSOR
Reticular activating system —
Thyroid gland —
Spinal cord
Lungs
Heart
Liver
Adrenal glands
Pancreas
Muscles, blood vessels
Intestines
Skin, sweat glands,
hair follicles, fat cells

FIGURE 3.2
Anatomy of the stress response.

the release of catecholamines, primarily adrenaline and noradrenaline, into the bloodstream. Catecholamine release has a direct, activating effect on the central nervous system and, in particular, the reticular activating system (RAS) or reticular formation. This structure has a deep, central location in the brain, and in terms of evolution it is one of the oldest parts of the brain. Stimulation of the RAS leads to the awake, alert state which usually occurs in stressful situations.

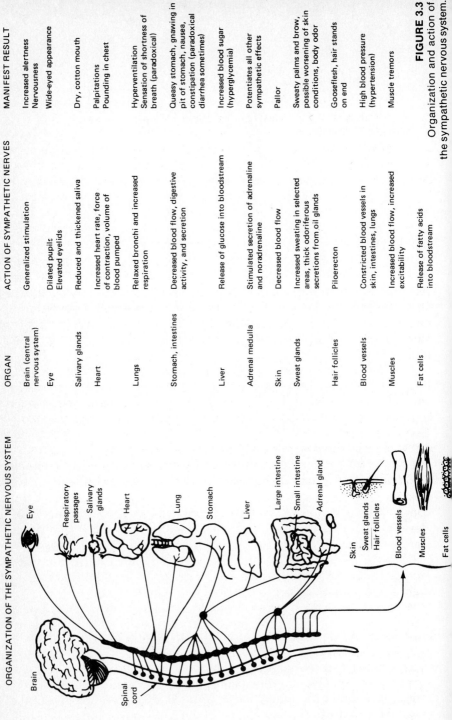

ORGANIZATION OF THE SYMPATHETIC NERVOUS SYSTEM	ORGAN	ACTION OF SYMPATHETIC NERVES	MANIFEST RESULT
Brain	Brain (central nervous system)	Generalized stimulation	Increased alertness Nervousness
Eye	Eye	Dilated pupil Elevated eyelids	Wide-eyed appearance
Respiratory passages Salivary glands	Salivary glands	Reduced and thickened saliva	Dry, cotton mouth
Heart	Heart	Increased heart rate, force of contraction, volume of blood pumped	Palpitations Pounding in chest
Lung	Lungs	Relaxed bronchi and increased respiration	Hyperventilation Sensation of shortness of breath (paradoxical)
Stomach	Stomach, intestines	Decreased blood flow, digestive activity, and secretion	Queasy stomach, gnawing in pit of stomach, nausea, constipation (paradoxical diarrhea sometimes)
Liver	Liver	Release of glucose into bloodstream	Increased blood sugar (hyperglycemia)
Large intestine Small intestine Adrenal gland	Adrenal medulla	Stimulated secretion of adrenaline and noradrenaline	Potentiates all other sympathetic effects
Skin	Skin	Decreased blood flow	Pallor
Sweat glands Hair follicles	Sweat glands	Increased sweating in selected areas, thick odoriferous secretions from oil glands	Sweaty palms and brow, possible worsening of skin conditions, body odor
	Hair follicles	Piloerecton	Gooseflesh, hair stands on end
Blood vessels	Blood vessels	Constricted blood vessels in skin, intestines, lungs	Pallor
Muscles	Muscles	Increased blood flow, increased excitability	High blood pressure (hypertension) Muscle tremors
Fat cells	Fat cells	Release of fatty acids into bloodstream	

Spinal cord

FIGURE 3.3
Organization and action of the sympathetic nervous system.

The Endocrine System

The second major system which is involved in the stress response is the endocrine or hormone system. Hormones are, in essence, chemical messengers released by specific organs to travel in the bloodstream to stimulate special responses by the target organs. The most important stress hormones are ACTH, cortisol (a form of cortisone), glucagon, adrenaline, and noradrenaline. Adrenaline and noradrenaline serve both as transmitters for the sympathetic nervous system and as hormones in their own right. Thyroid hormone, growth hormone, and aldosterone are also stimulated by stress, but their primary role is to serve other functions.

Within seconds after an individual has been presented with a condition or event which is perceived as stressful, a message is transmitted from the cortex to the hypothalamus and finally to the pituitary gland, a pea-sized organ located behind the eyes. The pituitary releases ACTH (adrenocorticotrophic hormone), which travels in the bloodstream to the adrenal cortex. There ACTH stimulates the conversion of cholesterol to steroid hormones and the release of cortisol and similar steroids in the hormone group known as glucocorticoids. Figure 3.2 illustrates this sequence.

Cortisol acts on a variety of organs, with its major effect being to increase the supply of glucose and fatty acids in the bloodstream. It stimulates the liver to produce and release glucose, it stimulates fat cells to release fat, and it causes tissues such as skin to consume less glucose. Cortisol also has several other effects on the body, some of which can be quite harmful at times. It causes the breakdown of protein for use as energy, inhibits immunity and inflammatory responses, shrinks lymphoid tissue (like the glands in the neck which swell with infection), and weakens bones. Moderate levels of cortisol can strengthen muscle contraction, but prolonged or excessively high levels can weaken muscles. Cortisol in large doses, such as those used to treat certain inflammatory diseases, can also cause psychosis or other mental changes.

Glucagon, like insulin, is released from the pancreas. It stimulates increased blood glucose and release of fatty acids. In addition, it causes a slight increase in the rate and strength of the heartbeat.

When ACTH acts on the adrenal cortex, it also causes the release of aldosterone and related hormones known as mineralcorticoids. Mineralcorticoids help to regulate blood pressure by causing the kidney to retain salt and, thereby, to increase blood pressure. Although ACTH is not the primary stimulant for aldosterone release, persistently high levels of ACTH can lead to increased blood pressure.

Thus the sympathetic nervous system and the endocrine system work together to mobilize the body's various resources. With regard to the immediate behavioral and psychological consequences of stress, the heightened alertness and the sense of apprehension which result from increased adrenaline are the predominant effects. At the same time, it is the cardiovascular and metabolic effects of stress which lead to many of the adverse medical consequences.

INDIVIDUAL DISTRESS

When the stress response is elicited too intensely or too frequently and the individual is unable to find a suitable outlet, the result is individual *distress*. The manifestation of this distress varies with the individual and may include behavioral, psychological, and medical consequences. The impact of distress on mental and physical well-being can be substantial; the extreme result might be sudden death from, for example, suicide or a stress-induced cardiac arrhythmia.

Behavioral Consequences

The behavioral changes which can accompany rising levels of stress include increased cigarette smoking, greater alcohol and drug abuse, accident proneness, and appetite changes. Each of these behavioral changes can, in turn, have an important health impact.

Smoking　Cigarette smoking and the use of other tobacco products constitutes the single most devastating preventable cause of death in the United States today. It contributes substantially to hundreds of thousands of deaths each year from heart attacks and strokes; tens of thousands of deaths from lung, bladder, and other cancers; and immeasurable suffering and disability from chronic bronchitis and emphysema, angina pectoris, nonfatal strokes, and other tobacco-induced diseases.

Cigarette consumption may serve as pleasure smoking, social smoking, or stress smoking. There are occupational differences in the frequency of smoking which may represent in part social influences in the work environment. But stress is also an important factor. In a survey of 12,000 professional men in fourteen occupational categories, Russek (1965) found 46 percent of men in high-stress occupations to be smokers versus 32 percent in low-stress occupations. Both stress and cigarette consumption were related to the incidence of heart disease. Similarly, in a study of U.S. Navy petty officers, Conway and colleagues (1981) found a significant correlation between occupational stress and cigarette consumption. Not only have studies confirmed the relationship between smoking and stress, but they have shown that the tendency to increase smoking under stress appears to be proportional to the number of stressors within a given period of time (Lindenthal et al., 1972; Hillier, 1981).

Alcohol abuse   Alcohol consumption is one of the most widely recognized and probably the most common serious stress reaction. As such, it constitutes a major personal and societal hazard. About 10 million Americans and up to 10 percent of the work force are alcoholics. Alcohol consumption is a major factor in one-half of this country's motor vehicle fatalities and homicides, one-third of the reported suicides, the majority of the nation's 30,000 annual deaths from liver cirrhosis, and a substantial number of serious birth defects (Trice and Roman, 1981). The problem of alcohol abuse is also costly in economic terms. Former HEW Secretary Califano, in the third special report to Congress on "Alcohol and Health" (Noble, 1978), estimated that the cost of alcohol-related problems in 1975 was $43 billion, including about $20 billion in lost production.

Alcohol abuse varies widely from occupation to occupation. For the assembly line worker or night guard, stressed by the boredom of his job, alcohol addiction may become a part of his daily work routine. Drinking may begin before the workday even starts, with routine drinking leading to increased accident rates and decreased productivity. For the white-collar alcohol abuser, alcohol consumption may not begin until the "three-martini lunch." When drinking continues throughout the rest of the day, its most destructive impact may be on the executive's home life.

Several studies have suggested that occupation may be the most influential factor in determining drinking habits and consequent alcohol-related problems (Plant, 1979a; Ojesjo, 1980). Various reasons have been given for the strong relationship between occupation and alcohol use, including differences in social pressures and social controls which allow or encourage drinking within some group, recruitment and selection trends which attract alcoholism-prone individuals to certain careers, and variations in occupational stress (Cosper, 1979; Plant, 1979b).

Whatever other occupational factors influence drinking behavior, organizational stress must be considered a major contributor and the individual consequences of alcohol abuse should be seen in part as stress-related illness.

Drug abuse   Alcoholism has been the most visible form of drug abuse, but other forms are now gaining increased attention. Recent reports regarding the widespread use of marijuana, cocaine, and other recreational drugs by armed services personnel underline the vulnerability of individuals in repetitive or monotonous jobs.

Drug abuse can take several forms, including the use of illegal "recreational drugs" such as cocaine and the misuse of prescription drugs. Although physicians concerned with occupational health have noted this to be a problem of increasing significance, the extent of the problem and costs are unknown. Nevertheless, the potential impact of drug abuse on absenteeism, productivity, and accidents makes this an important area for management concern.

Accident proneness   A much subtler but potentially as important effect of organizational stress is to predispose the individual to both industrial and nonindustrial accidents. "A person under stress is an accident about to happen" (Warshaw, 1979, p. 193).

The role of stress in industrial accidents has long been noted anecdotally, but the classic studies of the accident process were conducted in the mid-1960s by two Cleveland psychiatrists who reviewed about 300 cases of industrial accidents leading to disability (Hirschfeld and Behan, 1963; 1966). Not only was stress found to contribute significantly to the occurrence of an accident, but it was also found to slow the recovery process and prolong disability.

More recent studies have shown that work-related stressful events may immediately precede automobile and domestic accidents as well as industrial accidents (Whitlock et al., 1977). In addition, automobile drivers who experienced recent social stress, including job stress, have been found to be five times more likely to cause a fatal accident as drivers without such stress (Brenner and Selzer, 1969).

Violence   Perhaps the most extreme, but fortunately less common, manifestation of stress is violence on the part of the stressed individual. Occasional news stories record the more publicly visible episodes of violence: the overworked, unassertive secretary who, asked once too often to do too much in too short a time, sends the boss to an emergency room for stitches with a well-directed throw of an ashtray; the disgruntled graduate student who wounds the professor with a shot from a small service revolver; or the distraught assembly line supervisor who returns at night after being fired to "torch" the former employer's factory. Less visible, but probably more common, forms of violence precipitated by stressful events are spouse abuse and child abuse.

In examining the dynamics of violence, Newman (1979) suggests that violence grows out of frustration. The frustration of natural urges and drives then leads to aggression, which may even be displaced from the original source of frustration. This is illustrated by the husband who comes home and beats his wife because his boss was very critical of his work at the office. It is important to note that not all aggression is violent or destructive. Fromm (1973) indicates that aggression may be either benign or malignant. It is malignant aggression which is at the root of human destructiveness and violence.

Appetite disorders   Individuals may respond to stress with either markedly increased appetite or markedly decreased appetite. Loss of appetite is a common symptom of depression in older people. Extreme weight loss may also be seen in younger women with a psychological condition known as anorexia nervosa. People under stress frequently respond to stress by overeating or by consuming high-fat diets such as those commonly found at fast-food chains. The resulting obesity is associated with higher rates of heart disease, greater difficulty with backaches and arthritis, and more difficulty with respiratory problems.

Psychological Consequences

Closely related to the behavioral consequences of distress are the psychological effects. Among the problems to consider are family problems, sleep disturbances, sexual dysfunction, depression, conversion reactions, and the "burnout" syndrome.

Family problems   Marital discord and family conflict result from a variety of sources. The home and work stress combination may have been a particularly significant factor in the last several decades. Steiner (1972) uses a highly enlightening case illustration in asking individuals to examine the home and work balance and the potentially destructive effects of professional success. Burke and his associates (1979) examined the view of women married to men who exhibited unbalanced professional striving and competitive overdrive. The wives of men with such unbalanced striving and competitive overdrive reported greater levels of depression, less satisfaction, fewer friends and less contact with those friends, and more feelings of tension, anxiety, isolation, worthlessness, and guilt.

A marriage may serve as a source of support to sustain one spouse through stress at work, or it may serve as a further source of stress and frustration. The determining factor is the marriage pattern established by the two partners. For the traditional working husband, this means that the wife is supportive and derives her sense of security from him. This is sometimes termed the "hidden contract," by which the wife agrees to be the "support team" so that the husband can pursue his professional aspirations.

Studying the marriages of twenty-three successful midcareer executives training at the Sloan Programme at the London Business School, Handy (1978) found four principal marital patterns, as defined by the attitudes and values of each spouse. Certain patterns were associated with low-stress, supportive relationships, while others were associated with resentment and discontent. Thus, the impact of organizational stress on a marital relationship is in part determined by the structure of the relationship.

The relationship of organizational stress to family life will also be influenced by the particular life stage. Take, for example, the young executive in a traditional family setting. He must devote a great deal of energy and time to building his career, while at the same time his wife, housebound with small children, is in need of increasing time and attention. The executive frequently responds by creating distance between his wife and the organization. That this response is in fact dysfunctional is now recognized by some companies. These companies try to integrate the wife and family into the husband's work so that they might better understand his situation and provide him with emotional and instrumental support.

The kind of support base at home in the traditional marriage is not always available in the dual-career marriage. Unless the two partners consciously work at the support functions for each other, this form of marriage is especially vulnerable to the shattering effects of outside stressors, such as those from work. A dual-career marriage is less at risk if there are others—for example, extended-family members—who play key roles in the support functions.

Family businesses provide a unique setting for interactions between family pressures and work pressures. When stressful situations develop, they may be intensified in this setting as the distinction between family business fades and both suffer (Barnes and Hershon, 1976; H. Levinson, 1971). Such a situation was reported by a nationally prominent lawyer whose wife was also his legal secretary. In assessing the end of his twenty-eight-year marriage, he attributed the decay of the relationship largely to the home-work combination.

Sleep disturbances   Inability to fall asleep the night before a stressful event, such as a key briefing of the company's senior officers or a difficult performance-review session, is a common, if not universal, experience. However, occupational stress can lead to chronic and sometimes debilitating sleep disturbances.

Insomnia, the inability to fall asleep or to stay asleep, is an extremely common problem. Each year up to 30 percent of the general population seek help for sleep disturbances (Mendelson et al., 1977). Worries over promotion, conflict at work, or project deadlines frequently cause difficulty in falling asleep. Shift work, with its inevitable disruption of usual sleep patterns, is another work-related cause of insomnia. Excessive use or evening use of caffeinated liquids, such as coffee, tea, cola drinks, chocolate drinks, and many noncola drinks, can exacerbate the problem. Excess nicotine consumption from stress-induced cigarette smoking can also lead to difficulty falling asleep.

Sleep disturbances may be aggravated by the common home remedy for insomnia: alcohol. The depressant effect of beer, wine, or liquor often helps a person to fall asleep, but alcohol disrupts sleep cycles and leads to a rebound increase in adrenaline in the middle of the night. This may awaken the person, making it difficult to get back to sleep. The person is left fatigued in the morning, which sets up a self-replicating cycle of stress-alcohol-awakening-fatigue-stress.

An example of this is seen in the case of Steve W., a 42-year-old director of sales whose increasing concern with the poor performance of his salesmen led to his having three to five shots of bourbon each evening. He would quickly fall asleep around midnight, but by 3 a.m. he was wide awake again, alert, and often unable to return to sleep. He was eventually hospitalized for stress-induced palpitations, and by the third night in the hospital he was sleeping soundly through the night—without alcohol.

Because sleep deprivation has a negative impact on mood and performance, it can exacerbate the work situations which caused the sleep disturbance to begin with. Thus it is important to recognize insomnia as a possible consequence of stress at work and to confront the problem as soon as it is recognized.

Sexual dysfunction   Another potential consequence of mismanaged stress is inability to function sexually and to enjoy sexual relations. Several studies have shown that stress can reduce sex hormones in both men and women. This reduction, in turn, leads to a reduced interest in sexual relations. In men, reduction in testosterone, the principal male hormone, also leads to a slowing of sperm production. In women, progesterone is reduced along with other female hormones, resulting not only in reduced sexual interest but at times in disruption of menses and temporary infertility.

Thus, stress reduces interest in lovemaking not only because stress-related problems are distracting, but also because of the impact of stress on an individual's hormone physiology. Deterioration in sexual relations is undoubtedly one of the factors contributing to marital difficulties among executives and other individuals experiencing significant stress at work. Since satisfying sexual relations are an important part of one's mental health and well-being, preventing or resolving sexual dysfunction is a necessary element of stress management.

Depression   Depression is the most common significant psychological condition seen by the family physician and by many psychiatrists and psychologists. It is often accompanied by extreme anxiety. It may be mild and self-limited, or it may be severe enough to lead to suicide. Stressful events such as business failure, termination, and interestingly enough, promotion have led some employees and managers into varying depths of depression and even suicide (Paykel, 1976). Although family and personal events such as death of a spouse or illness in the family show the strongest relationship to the onset of depression, work-related events are also important.

The experience of a young company president is a case in point. He rose through the ranks of his company very quickly and by his early forties was president of a strong, but small, growth company which was listed on the over-the-counter exchange. His personal worth was about $8 million, largely based on company-owned stock. His company got overextended, wrote orders it could not fill, and within a one-year period had its stock trading frozen. The board of directors relieved the president, who subsequently went into a deep depression of several years' duration. His is a dramatic example of how work stresses may induce depression.

Psychogenic disability   Psychological trauma or conflict is sometimes converted and expressed as a somatic or physical symptom. This process is termed a *conversion reaction*. While the disability or discomfort associated with a conversion reaction is very real to the patient, no objective basis for the complaint can be found. Sudden speech difficulty and/or laryngitis for a manager just prior to a major presentation is an example of such a reaction. Frequently the symptoms are of brief duration and are resolved without intervention. At times, however, conversion symptoms can be quite disabling and require skilled psychiatric care.

The burnout syndrome   *Burnout* is a relatively new term which has rapidly gained acceptance and popularity in both the lay and professional stress literature. It refers to a pattern of exhaustion one experiences when subject to unavoidable pressures at the same time that there do not appear to be available sources of satisfaction (Moss, 1981). The symptoms of this syndrome are outlined in Table 3.1.

Burnout tends to occur in individuals and professions characterized by a high degree of personal investment in work and high performance expectations. Often these individuals have a strong emotional commitment to work, as is true with executives (H. Levinson, 1981). Much of their self-image and sense of worth may be derived from their occupation. This limits the amount of investment in recreational and sometimes family activities. When difficulties arise at work or there are limited rewards for increasing labor, burnout-prone individuals begin to invest even more time at work and further neglect outside supports.

Increasing recognition of the burnout syndrome probably reflects the

TABLE 3.1
SYMPTOMS OF THE BURNOUT SYNDROME

1 Early stages

   a Work performance
- Decline in efficiency
- Dampened initiative
- Diminished interest in work
- Progressively lessened ability to maintain work performance in times of stress

   b Physical condition
- Exhaustion, fatigue, run-down physical condition
- Headaches
- Gastrointestinal disturbances
- Weight loss
- Sleeplessness
- Shortness of breath

   c Behavioral symptoms
- Changing or dampened moods
- Quickness to anger and increasing irritability
- Diminished frustration tolerance
- Suspiciousness
- Feelings of helplessness
- Increased levels of risk taking

2 Later stages

   a Attempts at self-medication (tranquilizers, alcohol)

   b Increased rigidity (thinking becomes closed, attitudes become inflexible, negativistic, or cynical)

   c Questioning of abilities of self, coworkers, and organization

   d Increase in time spent working, with dramatic decline in productivity

Source: Adapted from *Management Stress* by Leonard Moss, M.D., copyright © 1981, by permission of Addison-Wesley Publishing Co., Reading, Mass. All rights reserved.

effect of popularization of the term rather than a significant increase in the number of individuals who fit the syndrome. Nevertheless, special attention is now being paid to the burnout phenomenon, especially in health-related professions. Several techniques have been recommended for coping with the "stressfulness of striving" which leads to burnout, such as delegation of workload to subordinates (Moss, 1981).

Medical Consequences

While the behavioral and psychological effects of organizational stress are in themselves immense, they may in turn have a potentially more devastating and irreversible effect on an individual's medical health and physiological well-being. A combined set of empirical research studies and skilled clinical observations have confirmed the association between a wide range of stressors and serious physical disease. Heart attacks, strokes, peptic ulcers, asthma, cancer, diabetes, hypertension, headache, back pain, and arthritis are among the many diseases and symptoms which have been found to be caused or worsened by stressful events. Early studies of strictly job-related stress concentrated primarily on heart disease and peptic ulcer disease, but there is growing evidence that the same relationship exists between organizational stress and disease that exists between other life stressors and disease.

Table 3.2 lists the major causes of death in the United States. Several well-known scientific commentators have referred to many of these conditions—including heart disease, hypertension, peptic ulcer disease, certain cancers, and numerous other illnesses—as "diseases of adaptation" or "diseases of civilization." Organizational stress, as well as other sources of stress, has cumulative effects which contribute to the development of such illnesses. Although genetics, biological development, and many other factors influence the appearance and course of these diseases, and although stress cannot be said to be the sole cause of any of these diseases, the following pages should highlight the important role which stress plays in hastening the appearance of disease and in worsening the impact of disease.

TABLE 3.2
MORTALITY FOR LEADING CAUSES OF DEATH
United States, 1978

Rank	Cause of death	Number of deaths (1,000)	Deaths per 100,000 population	Percent of all deaths
1	Heart disease	729	334	37.8
2	Cancer	397	182	20.6
3	Strokes	176	80	9.1
4	Accidents	106	48	5.5
5	Pneumonia and influenza	58	27	3.0
6	Diabetes mellitus	34	15	1.8
7	Liver cirrhosis	30	14	1.6
8	Arteriosclerosis	29	13	1.5
9	Suicide	27	12	1.4
10	Diseases of infancy	22	10	1.1
11	Homicide	20	9	1.1
12	Emphysema	16	7	0.9
All causes		1,928	883.4	100.0

Source: U.S. Bureau of Census, 1980, Table 116.

Heart disease and stroke   For the past several decades the leading cause of death in the United States has been disease of the heart, primarily myocardial infarction or heart attack. Heart disease is a multifactorial illness, meaning that there are numerous conditions which influence the likelihood that a person will develop a heart condition or die from a heart attack. The most important factors are family history of heart disease, smoking, hypertension, blood lipids (cholesterol and triglycerides), Type A personality, and diabetes. Lack of exercise and poor diet may also be contributing factors. Except for family history, all of these risk factors are related or potentially related to stress.

We noted earlier that increased consumption of cigarettes and other tobacco products frequently occurs under stress. When these increases are sustained, the process of arteriosclerosis is accelerated and heart attacks are more likely. Recurrent or persistent organizational stress can also increase an individual's blood pressure and, thereby, the risk of heart attack or stroke.

Another means by which organizational stress may contribute to coronary artery disease is through its impact on blood lipids, including cholesterol and triglycerides. Recent studies have demonstrated that the relationship between blood lipids and cardiac risk is much more complex than originally thought. Nevertheless, cholesterol levels are still predictors of cardiac risk, and these levels appear to be related to stress. In one of the earliest studies of this relationship, Friedman and his associates (1958) studied tax accountants and found that, as the deadline for filing federal income tax returns approached, their cholesterol levels increased.

Aside from having a long-term impact on risk factors such as smoking and hypertension, stress can have the immediate effect of precipitating a heart attack in a coronary-prone individual. For example, Russek and Zohman (1958) found that among 100 young adults who had suffered heart attacks, 91 percent experienced prolonged emotional strain associated with job responsibilities prior to the coronary. This rate of similar occupational stress appeared in only 20 percent of the controls, those who did not suffer heart attacks. The precipitating occupational stress need not be a negative one. For example, Jenkins, Rosenman, and Friedman (1966) found that men who had recently been promoted experienced more heart attacks than a control group matched for age and occupation who had not been promoted.

The effect of even positively stressful events was illustrated in the case of a recently retired 89-year-old pediatrician and child psychoanalyst who was to be honored at his ninetieth birthday by the pediatrics department he had once chaired. The night before the big event, while anxiously rehearsing his reflections of sixty-five years of practice, he developed severe left-sided chest pain and was hospitalized for an acute heart attack. He had no previous manifestations of heart disease and quickly recovered from this attack. Unfortunately, the carefully rehearsed recollections were never presented.

In profiling individuals who self-report or are referred by their family physician to a heart clinic, we discover one or two dominant patterns. Either there are several, related major sources of stress in the individual's organizational environment or there is significant stress at home, frequently in the marital relationship. Not all the individuals have heart disease, though some may be in the early stages of developing it. The organizational stress may therefore be either a long-term contributing factor or the short-term precipitating event which brings on chest pain and suffering.

The impact of organizational stress on heart disease has been studied much more extensively than its impact on strokes. The risk factors which lead to stroke are quite similar to those for heart attacks and include smoking, hypertension, poor diet, and diabetes. To the extent that organizational stress influences these risk factors, it can also be expected to influence death and disability from strokes.

Backache, arthritis, and related conditions   Backache is one of the most common causes of lost time at work and one of the most frequent conditions seen by the family physician. Although many acute backaches can be attributed to various strains and sprains suffered from over-exertion, chronic backaches frequently have no association with trauma or any other identifiable pathology. Those who treat patients with chronic backaches attribute much of the problem to muscle spasms induced by stress and to the lack of strength and flexibility which results from a sendentary occupational and recreational life.

Stress-induced muscle spasms can also lead to chronic neck pain, jaw pain, and other musculoskeletal complaints. In addition, although stress does not appear to cause rheumatoid arthritis or osteoarthritis, stressful conditions can worsen these conditions.

Peptic ulcer disease and other stomach and intestinal conditions   Ulceration of the stomach and duodenum (first part of the small intestine) represents the classic psychosomatic illness. This description is due in part to the early work of Wolff, a neurologist from Cornell University and a pioneer in psychosomatic medicine (Wolf and Wolff, 1943). For many years Wolff studied the gastric functioning of a patient named Tom, who had a gastric fistula (an artificial opening between the stomach and the outside). Wolff noted that during times of prolonged emotional conflict, the stomach lining became engorged with blood and finally its surface developed minute, bleeding erosions.

The same process can occur as a result of chronic stress at work or at home. Certain individuals appear to be prone to stomach ulcers in that they respond to stress with a higher production of stomach acid. When stressed sufficiently, such individuals can readily develop ulcer symptoms.

In addition to ulcers, other digestive diseases can result from chronic stress. Ulcerative colitis, a condition of the large intestine characterized by bleeding ulcerations, may be induced in part by stressful circumstances (Selye, 1976a). Irritable bowel syndrome, a condition characterized by painful spasms of the large intestine, is another common stomach malady in which stress plays an important role.

Headache The tension headache is one of the universal symptoms of stress. It appears to be caused by spasm of the facial and scalp muscles. Such headaches can sometimes become chronic and quite difficult to treat. Migraine headaches, by contrast, seem to be caused by spasm of the blood vessels which supply the brain. Although migraine headaches can sometimes be caused by stress, they can also result from several other factors. Headache is one of the features of a syndrome described by Sewil (1969) as "Wall Street sickness." Investors plagued by this sickness develop headache, stomach trouble, and fatigue.

Cancer Frequently cancer is pictured at one extreme of a disease continuum which lists "psychological-induced illness" at the opposite end. Such a formulation implies that stress can have little to do with development of cancer. However, a more careful consideration of the problem reveals that stress may have a rather profound impact on the appearance of cancer in an individual, especially with the general reduction in immunity associated with prolonged stress.

The leading cause of cancer deaths is lung cancer, a rapidly fatal form of cancer for which early detection has proven difficult and current treatments rather unsatisfactory. It has been estimated that three-quarters of lung cancer cases are attributable to cigarette smoking. Thus, to the extent that organizational stress increases tobacco consumption, it also increases lung cancer. In addition, cigarette smoking contributes to the development of bladder cancer, stomach cancer, and cancer of the mouth, throat, and larynx.

As early as the second century a physician by the name of Galen concluded that women with "melancholic dispositions" were more inclined to develop breast cancer. This idea is supported by recent studies which indicate that the appearance of cancer is often preceded by a significant increase in potentially stressful life events as well as by chronic stress. This is further supported by research showing that widowed persons have the highest cancer mortality rate and divorced persons have the next highest level (LeShan, 1966).

Diabetes mellitus   The origin of diabetes mellitus, or "sugar diabetes," is still being studied, but it is apparent that the adult form of diabetes is closely related to diet and obesity, which may be symptoms of distress. While it is unlikely that stress can cause diabetes in a nonsusceptible individual, in someone predisposed to diabetes, stress-induced obesity and stress-related stimulation of blood sugar increases may tip the balance.

Diabetes is defined as the existence of abnormally high glucose in the bloodstream. As you will recall from the opening section of this chapter, one of the predominant effects of the stress response and, indeed, of all stress hormones is to increase the availability of blood glucose for fast energy. Therefore, it should not be surprising that stress induced by a high intensity of life changes is associated with the appearance of diabetes or disturbance of blood glucose control (Grant, 1974).

Liver cirrhosis   Cirrhosis of the liver, largely due to excessive alcohol consumption, remains a leading cause of death and disability despite widespread occupational and community efforts to help the alcoholic worker and citizen. Excessive alcohol consumption also contributes to the incidence of heart disease and diabetes.

Lung disease   The occurrence of pneumonia, influenza, and in particular, emphysema is also strongly influenced by cigarette smoking, which is in turn influenced by stress levels. In addition to this indirect effect, stress appears to have a direct effect, at least with regard to asthma.

Asthma is another of the "classic" psychosomatic illnesses in that the impact of psychosocial events on asthma attacks has been frequently studied. It is clear that stress is an important precipitating factor for individuals prone to having asthma attacks. Stress can also be a factor in the development of tuberculosis (Holmes et al., 1957).

Skin disease   Perhaps the most visible medical consequences of stress are the skin diseases which appear to be precipitated or worsened by stressful events. Although the common skin disorders rarely pose a serious threat to one's health, their unsightliness can be a major source of anguish. Eczema, neurodermatitis, hives, and acne are all skin conditions which are generally felt to be associated with stress. For example, laboratory studies of eczema—a condition characterized by itching, redness, swelling, and, eventually, scaling and fluid discharge—have demonstrated that in eczema-prone individuals emotional arousal leads to specific changes in the skin cells. Similarly, it can be shown that individuals prone to develop hives often do so under stressful conditions.

INDIVIDUAL MODIFIERS OF THE RESPONSE TO STRESS

From Figure 3.1 it is apparent that the wide range of organizational stressors can each contribute to one or more of a large number of behavioral, psychological, or medical consequences. But how is it that shift work, for example, may lead to alcoholism in one individual and hypertension in another? Why do some individuals develop recurrent ulcers, while other individuals never develop ulcers? The answer lies in the individual modifiers of the body's response to stress. There are important and significant individual differences which account for these diverse results.

Selye (1976a) identifies two categories of such modifiers, internal conditioning factors and external conditioning factors. Internal conditioning factors include such things as family patterns of stress response, past experiences, age, sex, and personality. As Selye (1976a, p. 123) notes, "Heredity and past experiences have some trace, some 'tissue memories,' which influence the way we react to things." In addition to the internal factors, there are external conditioning factors such as diet, climate, drugs, and social setting.

Social scientists and medical researchers have not sorted out all the complex relationships which determine the relative importance of the various internal and external conditioning factors. Indeed, the importance of many of these factors has been recognized only recently. Nevertheless, several modifiers of the individual stress response are well-recognized and warrant discussion.

In thinking about the dynamics of the stress response, it is important to distinguish modifiers of the stress response from coping mechanisms and other intervention techniques. Individual modifiers are preexisting conditions or characteristics which influence the way in which a person will respond to various stressors. Fortunately, some of these individual modifiers can themselves be modified by the individual. Coping mechanisms and related intervention techniques will be considered in Chapters 10 and 11.

The Achilles Heel Phenomenon

Part of the explanation for different patterns of distress lies in individual response specificity. The "Achilles heel" or "organ inferiority" hypothesis was developed in part through the work of Harold Wolff, the psychosomatic medicine pioneer, in the 1950s. He and others since suggest that there is an individual response stereotype whereby each individual reacts to stress with a particular preferred pattern of psychophysiological responses. On the basis of his work, Wolff (1953, p. 35) concludes:

> An individual may have been a potential "nose reactor" or "color reactor" all his life without ever actually having called upon a particular protective pattern for sustained periods because he did not need to. A given protective pattern may remain inconspicuous during long periods of relative security, and then with stress, becomes evident as a disorder involving the gut, the heart and vascular system, the vasorespiratory system, the skin or general metabolism.

Medical research supports this hypothesis. Studies have shown that individuals with stomach ulcers tend to respond to stress with gastric secretion (Wolff, 1953), that individuals with diabetes respond to stress with greater changes in blood glucose than do normal individuals (Hinkle and Wolf, 1952), and that individuals with cardiovascular disease show greater variability in heart rate and respiration than do other people (Masuda et al., 1972). The influence of family medical history was clearly demonstrated in a study of hypertensive and nonhypertensive people. Rise in blood pressure in response to three different stressors (a frustration task, intravenous injection of normal saline, and a cold stimulus test) was greater not only in hypertensive patients but also in normal subjects with a family history of hypertension (Shapiro, 1961.)

After learning of the importance of family history as an internal conditioning factor, some people fearfully conclude that, for example, "If my father died of a heart attack at age 48, so will I." In most cases, however, family history represents only a *predisposing* influence—possibly a necessary, but by itself not a sufficient, condition for the development of an illness. Family history does not make family illness inevitable! It is this fact that motivates the discussion of preventive management undertaken in the second half of the book.

Type A Behavior Pattern

It was in the late 1950s that two experienced cardiologists, Friedman and Rosenman, began to recognize a pattern in the behavior of the coronary patients they were treating. In the years since then, the Type A behavior pattern has been more clearly defined and its relation to coronary artery disease has been extensively studied. After twenty years of research, Type A behavior remains one of the best predictors of the likelihood of developing coronary disease.

Competitive overdrive, devotion to work, and time urgency are the predominant features of the pattern. Friedman and Rosenman (1974, p. 84) define the Type A individual as an "action-emotion complex" in which the individual is "*aggressively* involved in a *chronic, incessant* struggle to achieve more and more in less and less time, and if required to do so, against the opposing efforts of other things or other persons." Type A behavior results in socially acceptable conflict. It is also a response to a challenge in the environment. In the absence of a challenging situation, Type A behavior patterns may not be manifested. As Friedman and Rosenman point out, "For Type A Behavior Pattern to explode into being, the *environmental challenge must always serve as the fuse for this explosion.*" Thus, it is the interaction of specific personality characteristics and an environmental challenge—usually a stressor of some sort— that results in the Type A pattern.

The complement to the Type A pattern is the Type B pattern, characterized by a less harried, less competitive existence. Type B individuals are equally intelligent and may be just as ambitious as those who are Type A, but they approach their life in a more measured way.

Early research showed a striking relationship between the Type A behavior pattern and the occurrence of heart attacks and coronary deaths. More recent studies have begun to clarify the mechanisms by which these personality traits lead to heart disease. For example, in a study of 236 managers sampled from twelve Canadian firms, Howard and colleagues (1976) found that Type A managers had higher blood pressure and cholesterol levels, were more frequent smokers, and had less interest in exercise. Other studies have found that Type A individuals have a higher resting pulse and catecholamine excretion rate during waking hours. Therefore, these individuals incorporate previously discussed risk factors in their daily living.

Even when blood pressure, smoking, cholesterol and other known risk factors are taken into consideration, Type A individuals have 1½ to 2 times the risk of heart attack in comparison with Type B individuals. The most convincing evidence comes from the Western Collaborative Group Study (WCGS), a long-term study of 3,524 men in the San Francisco Bay area. At the end of 8½ years of study, the men judged at the outset to be Type A had twice the rate of primary coronary heart disease and an even higher rate of recurrent coronary events than had Type B individuals. These differences remained even after statistical adjustment for all other risk factors, and the relative risk was even greater for younger men.

Whatever other observations are made in future research, it is apparent that the Type A behavior pattern constitutes an important cardiac risk factor and that the appearance of the pattern is provoked by stress in the individual's environment.

Personality

The coronary-prone behavior pattern has provided the strongest link between individual differences, stress, and disease patterns. However, other individual traits have also been found to mediate the relationship between organizational stressors and individual responses.

Locus of control   One of the more clearly defined and widely studied personality concepts is that of locus of control. This refers to the extent to which individuals *perceive* that they have control over any given situation. *Internally oriented* individuals believe that their decisions and their actions will influence what happens to them.

Externally oriented individuals, in contrast, tend to believe that rewards or positive reinforcements are beyond their control and not contingent upon their actions; they are believers in luck or fate.

When the two types of individuals face a potentially stressful situation, their responses appear to be different. Internals, perceiving themselves to have greater control, tend to be less threatened by stressful situations and conditions and, therefore, experience fewer adverse reactions. They may, however, experience more anxiety in situations in which they, in fact, perceive that they have little or no control.

The impact of locus of control on stressful occupational events is illustrated by C. R. Anderson's study (1977) of 102 owner-managers of small businesses in a small Pennsylvania community which was extensively damaged by a flood. Following the flood, the internally oriented managers responded in a more task-oriented way and demonstrated less stress. The externals responded with anger, greater anxiety, and hostility.

Although the concept of perceived personal control does not indicate why one individual responds to stress with a headache and another with increased smoking, it does provide insight into why the same events will appear stressful to some individuals and not to others.

Self-esteem   The most extreme demonstration of the relationship of self-esteem to individual responses to stressful situations is provided by Bettelheim's studies (1958) of individual behavior in concentration and forced-labor camps. In trying to discover why some of those who escaped death at the hands of their captors were able to maintain a degree of physical and mental health, while others succumbed to mental and physical deterioration, Bettelheim concluded that a key factor was regaining the self-esteem initially shaken by the shock of the camps.

Self-esteem also appears to be an important factor in the workplace. Research at the University of Michigan (Mueller, 1965) demonstrated that individuals reporting low self-esteem were also more likely to perceive greater job overload. The importance of self-esteem as a buffer against adverse stress reactions is demonstrated by several studies of occupational groups which indicate that coronary heart disease risk factors rise as self-esteem declines (J. S. House, 1972; Kasl and Cobb, 1970).

Other personality traits   In addition to perceived personal control and self-esteem, there are numerous other personality factors which have been associated with individual responses to organizational stress. Among these traits are tolerance for ambiguity (Ivancevich and Matteson, 1980), anxiety (Chan, 1977), and introversion/extroversion, flexibility/rigidity, and dogmatism (Brief et al., 1981). Common to all these traits is the assertion that the presence or absence of the trait increases or decreases the likelihood that a particular event or condition will be perceived as a stressor.

Sex

Over the past two decades an increasing amount of attention has been paid to the impact of sex differences on relationships in the workplace. Interest has been focused primarily on the changing role of women. But it is important to recognize that, on the basis of stress-related illness, being male is much riskier than being female. Death rates at all ages are higher for men than for women, and the overall life expectancy for men is almost eight years less than for women. Part of the difference in death rates may be genetically and hormonally based, but much of it is attributable to the greater prevalence among men of smoking, alcohol consumption, and Type A behavior patterns, as well as homicide and suicide. However, there are indications that some of these risk factors may be on the rise among women and that this may be related to women's expanding work roles.

For example, B. Jacobson (1981) reports that female managers smoke more than women in other occupational groups and more than their male counterparts. Cooper and Melhuish (1980) found that female executives take significantly more tranquilizers, antidepressants, and sleeping pills than male executives. Finally, Cooper and Davidson (1982) indicate that the proportion of women alcoholics more than doubled between the early 1960s and the late 1970s. While there are few data directly tying these adverse personal health effects to the organizational stress of working women, there are several sources of stress at work which are unique to women. These include role stress, occupational stereotypes, and conflict related to sexuality.

Role stress   Role conflict, to include role overload, presents particular difficulties for working women. The basic conflict is between the traditional role of the woman as mother, homemaker, and wife and the contemporary role of the woman as a professional. In an attitude study of over 2,000 executives, Bowman, Worthy, and Greyser (1965) found that the home-job conflict was the most frequently cited obstacle to women's success in management. Terborg (1977) identified a variety of studies documenting the pressures exerted by vocational counselors and family members to discourage women from pursuing occupations other than those traditionally assigned to women, for example, school teacher.

Even in families and social settings where the home and work roles are viewed as compatible, the demands of both roles may create role overload. Housekeeping activities, child care, and work demands coupled with a husband's low involvement in home management may be particularly difficult. A similar problem does not exist for men, who spend about half as much time on housework and shopping as women (Brief, Schuler, and Van Sell, 1981). The overload problem appears worse for women in upper management (Ritzer, 1977).

Not surprisingly, role stress appears to have important organizational and individual consequences. Bhagat and Chassie (1981), for example, found that role stress was a strong predictor of organizational commitment in working women, second only to satisfaction with promotional opportunities. There is also some evidence to suggest that working women with several children are more likely to suffer from stress-related heart disease than are single working women or housewives with children (Brief, Schuler, and Van Sell, 1981).

Occupational stereotypes   Many occupations are dominated by one or the other sex, although this is changing somewhat. For example, nurses and secretaries are traditionally stereotyped as women, while truck drivers and business executives are traditionally stereotyped as men. The existence of these occupational stereotypes can provide at least two types of stress. The first is the stress of adhering to the stereotype and taking an undesirable and unsatisfying job. For example, a given secretarial job may be boring, low-paying, and dead-end work in which a capable woman may feel quite underutilized. But her own acceptance of occupational stereotypes or her employer's adherence to such stereotypes may prevent her from transferring to a potentially more satisfying "man's job."

The second type of stress would be experienced by a woman who accepted a traditionally male job as a manager. Successful managers are generally described in masculine terms (Schein, 1975) by both men and women and, when surveyed, both men and women prefer having a man as their boss (Gallup Opinion Index, 1978). Thus, the female manager will feel pressure to meet the male stereotype standards.

Sexuality issues   As Brief, Schuler, and Van Sell (1981) point out in their discussion of sexuality and work stress, western culture has built an image of "woman as temptress," enticing men to intoxication, to folly, and in modern times, to buy a car, a farm tool, or virtually anything else advertised to men. In addition, throughout adolescence and young adulthood, interactions between men and women generally revolve around sexuality. As a result of our cultural images and early life experiences, proximity to women, particularly in pairs or small groups, is sometimes avoided by men in order not to create "the wrong idea." This inhibition may influence planning for overnight business trips, office arrangements, dinner meetings, and other business activities. It may also limit the involvement of women in the "informal organization," the importance of which is considered below in the section on ethnicity.

In contrast to the phenomenon of avoidance based on sexuality is the phenomenon of sexual harassment. Unwanted, repeated, and coercive sexual advances are reported by 70 to 90 percent of working women (Lindsey, 1977; Mackinnon, 1979). Although sexual harassment of employees by their supervisors has been officially considered a civil rights violation since 1980 and although several states are moving to make sexual harassment a criminal violation, it remains a common problem and, too often, efforts to end such harassment jeopardize a woman's job or lead to frustrating or time-consuming bureaucratic or legal action.

These unique sources of stress for women in organizations have given rise to a variety of books aimed at assisting the professional working woman, including works by Adams and Lenz (1979), Barnett and Baruch (1978), Kinzer (1979), Newton (1979), and Stewart (1978).

Age

The impact of stress on the individual may be influenced by the person's age in at least two ways. First, age may in part determine whether a given situation or condition is perceived as a stressor by an individual. Second, the individual's biological age may determine how the stress response is manifested.

The concept of career stages was introduced in Chapter 2. Although "career maturity" need not progress exactly in age, individuals at the same stage tend to be in roughly the same age range. The objectives are different at each stage and, therefore, the types of events and conditions which are perceived as stressful will be different.

As the body ages, the overt manifestations of stress may change. For example, a young executive in a highly stressful situation, such as the presentation of a deficit financial report to the board of directors, may respond with an imperceptible rise in pulse and blood pressure, while an older executive with many years of high cholesterol and cigarette smoking behind him may experience severe chest pain or even a heart attack. Conversely, some ailments become less likely with age. For example, "slipped disks" and the resulting back pain are less likely to occur among older workers.

Ethnicity

Racial and other minority group differences have a complex and constantly changing impact on relationships in the workplace. With regard to organization stress, minority group members can have two important effects. First, there are certain stressors unique to particular minority groups. Second, there are several cultural and social factors which magnify the impact of the stressors described in Chapter 2 on minority group members. Although they do not deal specifically with organizational stress and ethnicity, Ford's *Readings in Minority-Group Relations* (1976) and the work of Burack, Staszak, and Pati (1972) are the basis for much of the following discussion and provide more detailed consideration of many of the relevant issues.

Blatant racial prejudice is the most obvious source of stress for ethnic individuals. The impact of racist attitudes and behavior at work can be magnified by a sense of inferiority, inadequacy, or low self-esteem which minority group members may bring from their social setting. This is especially true when a black is hired into a "white man's job," that is, a supervisory or management-level job in a predominantly white organization with no previous examples of successful black supervisors or managers.

Minority groups represent subcultures which often establish their own norms and values. These are not always understood by the majority group. For example, Triandis and his colleagues (1974) note that ghetto social relations are sometimes characterized by an outlook which they describe as *ecosystem distrust*. Ecosystem distrust "subsumes such phenomena as lower interpersonal trust, rejection of institutions in one's environment, suspicion of authority figures, and . . . weaker perceived connections between behavior and outcomes" (Triandis et al., 1974, p. 688). Lack of awareness of these phenomena can easily lead to the false assumption by management that an unresponsive worker is lazy or dumb, rather than to the more likely explanation that the worker does not yet trust the supervisor and the organization. Due to such cultural differences, Triandis and his associates (1974) suggest crosscultural training of *both* minority and majority group members.

At the managerial level, blacks and other minorities are often disadvantaged by lack of familiarity with the business world. This deficit begins building in childhood. Just as white suburbanite children do not grow up with the customs and physical skills necessary to succeed in daily life "on the street," ghetto blacks do not grow up in an environment which allows them to assimilate the terminology, analytic problem-solving skills, and behavior patterns necessary for the daily challenges of management (Nason, 1976, p. 304).

Performance evaluations are a major source of stress for many individuals, but for minority group members the stress of these evaluations is sometimes exacerbated by the confusion which results from basing evaluations on nonwork behaviors. For example, in a study of a training program for forty-eight black supervisors, Beatty (1973) found that employers tended to evaluate performance not on task-oriented behaviors related to the training program but on other behaviors demonstrated at work. The confusion and anguish generated by inconsistency or unexplainable subjectivity in performance appraisals is vividly described in E. W. Jones's autobiographical review of life as a rising black manager (1973).

Jones also describes the difficulties which black managers have because of lack of access to the "informal organization," or network of informal personal contacts at work. Unfortunately, racial prejudice or simply a nonjudgmental personal discomfort with blacks often excludes them from these informal networks and relationships. As a result, the social support needed to deal with common demands, such as boundary-spanning activities and work overload, as well as the guidance needed to recognize and resolve role conflicts or ambiguity are lacking. As Jones points out, lack of acceptance tends to amplify other shortcomings or difficulties.

Minority group managers and supervisors may also suffer from lack of support from the formal organization. A frequent criticism of affirmative action efforts is that management develops effective procedures for locating and recruiting minority supervisors but then fails to recognize their unique ongoing training and support needs. This leads to stress and strain for the minority manager, who is already under pressure in a new position because of the inevitable visibility of a minority group member. This high visibility simply magnifies the common demands of managerial jobs.

Social Support

It is striking that more recently, as traditional societal structures such as the extended family and the township are being attenuated and individual mobility is increased, social and medical scientists have become interested in a phenomenon they term *social support*. J. House

(1981) points out that social support may come in one of four forms, either emotional, instrumental, informational, or appraisal. Each individual derives these forms of social support from a variety of social relationships at work, at home, and in the community. For example, while one's spouse may be the key source of emotional support, it is the supervisor who provides much informational and appraisal support at work.

Social support appears to be beneficial primarily through its buffering effect (J. House, 1981). The individual's *existing* support system at work and at home may then be viewed as a wealth of resources that the individual may draw upon in managing various stressful situations. Informational or instrumental resources help the individual meet the demands causing the stress, thereby reducing the level and intensity of the stress.

Thus the concept of social support further contributes to understanding individual variations in the response to organizational stressors. Unlike some of the other factors which influence individual stress responses, *additional* social support may be engendered by management and, to the extent that this is possible, it can serve as an important preventive intervention. This possibility will be pursued further in Chapter 9.

Peer Group

Why do some people smoke more cigarettes when they are under stress, other people drink more alcohol, and still other people increase their lunch-hour athletic activities? Part of the answer may lie in the occupational peer group. It was noted above that certain occupations are prone to alcohol abuse. Similarly, there are differences in cigarette and drug consumption among various occupations.

The hypothesis, then, is that individuals are more likely to turn to alcohol under stress if they are in an occupational group with a higher baseline level of alcohol use. Unfortunately, there is little evidence to support or refute this hypothesis. Future studies of organizational stress may shed more light on this possibility. In the meantime, however, the behavior patterns of the occupational peer group should be one area in which to look for possible explanations of individual responses to stress.

Diet

In medicine, as in many other fields, conjecture precedes fact, and all too often the distinction between the two is quickly lost. Nowhere is this truer than in the area of nutrition and health. Despite the plethora of articles and books on nutrition and stress, there are a small number of points at which diet and stress interact. With or without outside stress, most dietary extremes are associated with adverse health effects. Extreme weight reduction, as sometimes seen among young women (anorexia nervosa), can be associated with specific nutritional deficiencies and, commonly, with temporary hormonal abnormalities. Overeating and the resulting obesity are, of course, associated with cardiac and respiratory ills. Moderation is clearly the healthiest route. But diet and stress can interact in some rather striking ways.

An individual predisposed to hypertension may be able to maintain a normal blood pressure even under stress, but when high stress is combined with excess consumption of table salt, abnormally high blood pressure can result. Similarly, an individual predisposed to peptic ulcers may be free of symptoms until the stress of a report deadline combines with the ulcer-inducing effects of caffeinated drinks (coffee, tea, and many carbonated beverages), smoking, and alcohol to develop a typical ulcer or severe gastritis.

This phenomenon is illustrated by the case of Mr. A., a 58-year-old businessman with occasional chest pain from mild heart disease, but no previous stomach trouble. As the rush of Christmas orders accelerated and he became tense, he treated the resulting headaches with up to eight aspirin each day. After attending several Christmas parties one weekend, at which he drank moderate amounts of Scotch, he developed some stomach discomfort and vomited up a small amount of fresh blood and clots. He was hospitalized for two weeks and treated for an acute bleeding ulcer, attributed by his doctors to the combination of stress, aspirin, and alcohol. During the hospitalization he developed persistent chest pain, which was finally relieved when the anemia caused by his bleeding was treated with blood transfusions. Fortunately, he did not suffer a heart attack, and his ulcer healed. He did miss the rest of the Christmas business activity, however.

Other examples where the impact of stress on illness may be modified by dietary factors include diabetes (stress plus overeating or high consumption of sweets), the common cold (some high-risk individuals may benefit from vitamin C), and certain heartbeat irregularities (arrythmias caused by caffeinated drinks).

SUMMARY

The consequences of individual distress appear to result from frequent or intense arousal of the stress response and, in particular, from the mental arousal which is induced by stress. The stress response represents an inherent biological pattern of sympathetic nervous system and endocrine reactions. Familiar symptoms of the stress response are pounding in the chest, palpitations, shortness of breath, gnawing feeling in the stomach, sweaty palms and brow, muscle tension, and nervousness. In addition, the blood pressure, heart rate, blood glucose, fatty acids in the blood, and stress hormones, such as cortisol, glucagon, and adrenaline, are elevated.

In response to this state of arousal, individuals may experience behavioral, psychological, or medical effects. Some of the more significant behavioral changes include increased cigarette smoking, alcohol abuse, and accident proneness. Psychological effects, which may be profound, include family trouble, sleep disturbance, depression, and possibly suicide. Medical conditions which may be influenced by stress are heart disease, stroke, backache, stomach ulcer, cancer, and diabetes.

An apparent paradox is the observation that a wide variety of stressors can lead to a rather stereotyped psychophysiological stress response, which in turn can be manifested by the range of behavioral, psychological, and medical effects just mentioned. The explanation for this paradox can be found, in part, in the individual modifiers of the stress response. Among these modifiers are the Achilles heel phenomenon, coronary-prone behavior patterns, personality differences, sex, age, ethnicity, social support, peer group, and diet.

The individual consequences of organizational stress can in themselves be devastating. In addition, however, the organization may suffer significant adverse consequences as a result of stress. To a large extent these organizational consequences follow from the individual consequences. Accident proneness increases medical claims, alcoholism increases absenteeism, exacerbation of medical conditions increases sick time, and so on. These and other organizational consequences of stress are the subject of the following chapter.

FURTHER READINGS

Benson, Herbert: *The Relaxation Response*, Avon Books, New York, 1975.

Girdano, D. A., and G. S. Everly: *Controlling Stress and Tension: A Holistic Approach*, Prentice-Hall, Inc., Englewood Cliffs, N.J., 1979.

Mazzaferri, Ernest (ed.): *Endocrinology: A Review of Clinical Endocrinology*, 2d ed., Medical Examination Publishing Company, Inc., New Hyde Park, N.Y., 1980.

Morse, Donald R., and M. Lawrence Furst: *Stress for Success: A Holistic Approach to Stress and its Management*, Van Nostrand Reinhold Company, New York, 1979.

Selkurt, E. E. (ed.): *Basic Physiology for the Health Sciences*, Little, Brown and Company, Boston, 1975.

Selye, H.: *Stress in Health and Disease*, Butterworths, Boston, 1976.

Selye, H.: *The Stress of Life*, 2d ed., McGraw-Hill, Inc., New York, 1976.

CHAPTER 4

ORGANIZATIONAL CONSEQUENCES OF STRESS

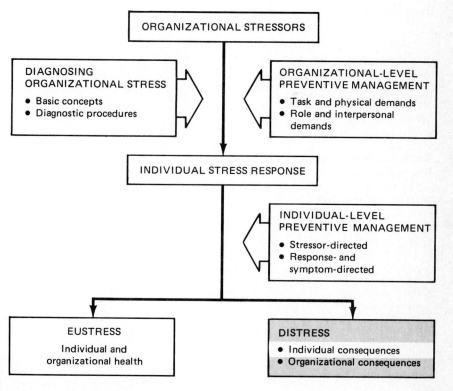

Organizations and individuals benefit from the experience of an optimum level of stress, but both pay a price for the mismanagement of stress. Chapter 3 examined the individual consequences of stress and the individual costs associated with mismanaged stress. This chapter will look first at the nature of the relationship between the organization and the individual and the meaning of organizational health. Then the direct and indirect consequences associated with the management and mismanagement of organizational stress will be examined. The consequences of mismanaged stress are summarized in Table 4.1.

The organizational costs of distress at work can be quite substantial. For example, the American Heart Association (1980) has developed a relatively simple procedure for roughly calculating the direct hiring and training costs associated with replacing just those employees who suffer heart attacks. This procedure, which is outlined in Figure 4.1, may be applied to any type of organization. For example, if the procedure were applied to Tenneco, Inc., a large, diversified corporation encompassing shipbuilding, life and health insurance, auto parts manufacturing, real estate, oil and gas, and other business activities, the results would indicate that its "cost of doing business" with 106,000 employees in 1981 would be $882,450. Applying item 7 in Figure 4.1 to Tenneco shows that this company can anticipate eventually losing 53,000 employees to heart

TABLE 4.1
ORGANIZATIONAL CONSEQUENCES OF MISMANAGED STRESS

Direct costs	Indirect costs
Participation and membership	**Loss of vitality**
• Absenteeism	• Low morale
• Tardiness	• Low motivation
• Strikes and work stoppages	• Dissatisfaction
• Turnover	
	Communication breakdowns
Performance on the job	• Decline in frequency of
• Quality of productivity	contact
• Quantity of productivity	• Distortions of messages
• Grievances	
• Accidents	**Faulty decision making**
• Unscheduled machine	
downtime and repair	**Quality of work relations**
• Material and supply	• Distrust
overutilization	• Disrespect
• Inventory shrinkages	• Animosity
Compensation awards	**Opportunity costs**

You may wish to use the following to determine the amount cardiovascular diseases could eventually cost your company, business, or industry.

1. Number of employees.   _____

2. Men in age range 45–65. (¼ of line 1)   _____

3. Estimated heart deaths per year — six of 1000.
   (.006 × line 2)   _____

4. Estimated premature retirement due to heart problems
   per year — three of 1000. (.003 × line 2)   _____

5. Company's annual personnel losses due to heart disorders.
   (sum of lines 3 and 4)   _____

6. Annual replacement cost. (line 5 × $3,700, the average cost
   of hiring and training replacements for experienced employees)   _____

7. Number of employees who will eventually die of heart
   diseases if present rates are allowed to continue.
   (½ of line 1)   _____

FIGURE 4.1
The cost of doing business. [Source: *American Heart Association, 1980.*]

diseases alone if present rates are allowed to continue. This is just *one* of the direct costs of mismanaged stress. These costs will of course be more substantial for companies with an older work force and less for companies with a comparatively younger work force, such as Xerox Corporation and Hospital Corporation of America. While most organizations at this time are not systematically accumulating the kinds of cost data on their human resources that will be discussed in this chapter, organizations like AT&T and Johnson & Johnson are beginning to do so.

THE ORGANIZATIONAL-INDIVIDUAL RELATIONSHIP

The individual costs of distress translate in various ways into organizational costs. Therefore, it is important to have a more complete understanding about how individuals and organizations interrelate. Fundamentally, this relationship is founded upon the notion of social exchange. That is, each party in the exchange makes certain demands on the other, and each party in the exchange has specific resources and assets which they are willing to commit to the exchange relationship. Each party benefits from the exchange, and each is dependent upon the other for meeting certain needs. The nature of this social exchange relationship is depicted in Figure 4.2. This figure shows the demands each party places on the relationship as well as the contributions or resources that each party has available for the relationship.

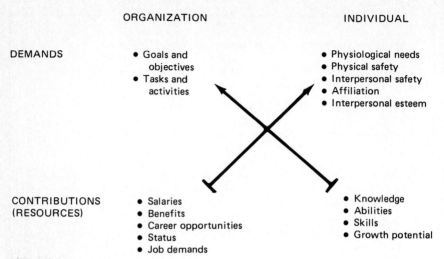

FIGURE 4.2
The basis for individual-organizational exchange. [*Based on Lyman W. Porter, Edward E. Lawler, III, and J. Richard Hackman*, Behavior in Organizations, *McGraw-Hill, New York, 1975, p. 109.*]

Organizational Contributions to the Exchange

Every organization has specified tasks and activities to accomplish in the pursuit of its goals and objectives. These tasks and activities, as well as goals and objectives, form the core of demands which the organization places upon the individual. Whether offering products, as in the case of General Motors Corporation, or delivering services, as in the case of American Telephone & Telegraph, the survival of the organization hinges upon its capacity to achieve its goals effectively and efficiently.

In exchange for having its goals and objectives achieved, the organization is prepared to contribute various resources. In particular, the organization is prepared to pay various levels of salary and benefits for particular tasks and jobs, to provide career advancement opportunities for individuals contributing importantly to organizational goal attainment, and to give social status for affiliation with the organization. Every organization will allocate these resources differentially to its various members in exchange for their contributions to the relationship.

Individual Contributions to the Exchange

To earn these organizational resources and meet the organization's goals, the individual has various resources to contribute to the exchange relationship. Most employees are selected on the basis of a variety of skills, abilities, and knowledge that they can contribute to the organization. In addition to these resources for task accomplishment, individuals have varying degrees of growth potential. That is, they have the capability of expanding their knowledge or skill base so as to contribute more effectively to the organization.

However, individuals will be willing to contribute these resources only if their own demands in the exchange relationship are met. These demands take the form of human needs. While the classical management theorists assumed that basic human motivational needs were economic, the later behaviorists and human relationists assumed that humans were primarily social beings. Of course, both groups were in part right, but the approaches of Maslow (1943) and Alderfer (1972) are more accurate portrayals of the diversity of human needs. Meeting the diversity of human existence, relatedness, and growth needs is a central aspect of human health and a key aspect of the exchange relationship with the organization. While the medical profession has known for decades that various debilitating illnesses result from psychological and physiological deprivation, it has only been comparatively recently that McGregor (1957) and others have identified the emotional illness that results from failure to meet relatedness and growth needs at work.

Need deprivation at any level will be a contributing stressor leading to employee distress with the attendant individual consequences discussed in the last chapter. These individual consequences of stress will in varying degrees lead to the individual's difficulty or inability to use the resources at his disposal for organizational goal attainment. Thus, the individual experience of stress has organizational consequences. Excessively high levels of stress lead to exhaustion and burnout, while too little stress leads to debilitation and boredom. Both are undesirable from an organizational point of view. An optimum level of stress on the individual at work will stimulate him or her to grow and develop within the organization, thus contributing to the exchange relationship.

Each organization and individual should seek a good match as well as a dynamic equilibrium in this exchange. A good match will contribute to both individual and organizational health. Individual health is one of several prerequisites for organizational health. And, organizational health will contribute to individual health through need gratification, as well as through opportunities for growth and development.

ORGANIZATIONAL HEALTH

Organizational health is a concept central to an understanding of the management of stress. Beer (1980, p. 41) talks about organizational health as "the capacity of an organization to engage in ongoing self-examination aimed at identifying incongruities between social systems components and developing plans for needed change." This process-oriented definition implies that healthy organizations will not necessarily stay that way. They must engage in a systematic process of adaption and change to maintain their relative degree of healthy functioning and well-being. This is accomplished through a process of examining the internal functioning of the organization as well as its relationship with its task environment.

There are several characteristics which distinguish healthy organizations from unhealthy ones. These characteristics relate to the effectiveness of the organization. Mott (1972) has identified three such characteristics: adaptiveness, flexibility, and productivity. These are consistent with the dominant characteristics identified by Steers (1975). The *adaptiveness* characteristic refers to the ability of an organization to change and to resist becoming rigid in its functioning and operating procedures, especially vis-à-vis its task environment (i.e., the part of the organization's environment related to its goal attainment efforts). Related to this characteristic is that of *flexibility*. Flexibility differs from adaptiveness in terms of response time. Adaptiveness is concerned with long-term adjustment while flexibility is concerned with adjusting to internal and external emergencies. The *productivity* characteristic is concerned with the amount of product *or* service provided by the organization.

Healthy organizations will be self-renewing and self-examining in an effort to maintain their adaptiveness, flexibility, and productivity. They will make planned changes in key internal dimensions in order to achieve (1) integration and congruity among these dimensions as well as (2) consistency and congruity with their task environments. These key internal dimensions of the organization in which planned changes may be made are identified in Figure 4.3 and include *people, structure, technology,* and *task*.

The first aspect of organizational health refers to the *internal adjustment* activities aimed at having the people, structure, technology and task of the organization work in harmony. A misfit between two or more of these dimensions will cause internal health problems for the organization. Such a problem would be illustrated in the case of a manager placed in a job for which the individual was not fully qualified. In this example, the organization may *change the manager* through a training and development effort. Or, the organization may *change the job*, reassigning those job functions for which the manager is not qualified to another job. In either case, the organization achieves an improved person-job fit with the associated improvement in health.

The second aspect of organizational health refers to the organization's adjustment to the demands of the task environment. Important agents in

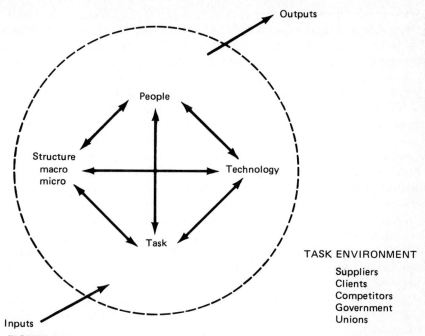

FIGURE 4.3
A framework for viewing organizational health. [*Based on Harold Levitt, "Applied Organizational Change in Industry: Structural, Technological and Humanistic Approaches," in J. G. March (ed.),* Handbook of Organizations, *Rand McNally, Chicago, 1965, p. 1145.*]

the task environment are identified in Figure 4.3. This *external adjustment* dimension is essential primarily because of the organization's dependence upon these environmental agents in achieving its objectives. Good external adjustment is essential to organizational health and vitality and is best achieved through the mutual, reciprocal exchange of knowledge, products, and other resources between the organization and the agents in its task environment (Alderfer, 1976).

An example of the problems that occur when there is poor external adjustment to the task environment is the experience of a small, family-owned printing company in the late 1970s. After nearly seventy-five years of successful operations, the firm bordered on bankruptcy for a year's period. This circumstance arose because the firm had developed too large a debt structure for the fragmented, turbulent market that it operated in. Had it been more sensitive to its task environment and therefore more conservative in its debt structure, it would not have risked bankruptcy and near dissolution. In this case, the lack of health was attributable to poor adjustment to the task environment.

The maintenance of organizational health requires an active process of planned change and adjustment to avoid a crisis like the one illustrated above. There must be constant efforts to achieve integration and wholeness within the four internal dimensions of the organization as well as with the task environment. This ongoing process of adjustment to internal and external demands requires both resources and commitment from the organization's management as well as a long-range perspective. Short-run cost effectiveness should not be achieved at the expense of long-term health and growth. For example, failure to invest sufficient capital and resources for retooling and updating organizational technology on a regular basis can lead to even greater costs at a later date. This is illustrated in the American automobile and steel industries, both of which face major capital investment programs in the 1980s.

If the organization does not maintain a relative state of health, it risks its long-run effectiveness and survival. Healthy organizations are not only better equipped to survive and grow; they are also in a better position to contribute to individual health and well-being. The inconsistencies and flaws in an organization's health will lead to the various direct and indirect costs to be discussed later in this chapter. The thrust of preventive management is to minimize these various costs while encouraging the maximum degree of organizational health.

DIRECT COSTS OF DISTRESS

When the organizational costs of mismanaged stress are examined, it is seen that there are two general categories of costs. There are the *direct costs* associated with the loss of an individual through absenteeism or turnover or with the poor performance of that individual while in the workplace (Macy and Mirvis, 1976). There are also direct costs associated with paying distressed employees compensation awards. The second category of organizational costs is the *indirect costs*—for example, broken or disrupted communication channels due to individual stresses or lowered self-esteem, and reduced production attributable to declining morale triggered by a poor performer or a lost employee. The direct costs of distress will be discussed first.

It should be pointed out here that the diseases of adaptation discussed in Chapter 3 have an organizational cost correlate. For example, the American Heart Association has found that cardiovascular diseases— high blood pressure, hardening of the arteries, heart attack, stroke, rheumatic heart disease, congenital heart defects, and congestive heart failure—cost the United States a total of $46.2 billion in 1981. Approximately 25 percent of this total amount was attributable to lost production: the nation lost about 52 million worker-days of production during that year. Medical care, loss of managerial skills, and retraining account for most of the remaining costs. Not all the diseases of adaptation are directly attributable to mismanaged stress. Similarly, not all the organizational costs of detrimental behaviors are *directly* attributable to mismanaged stress.

One of the real difficulties in tracing cause-and-effect relationships in the stress area is the pervasive nature of stress. Virtually all the experiences and demands of work and life stimulate the stress response. The mismanagement of this response causes distress, but distress may be manifested in a host of ways. There is not *one* individual or *one* organizational manifestation of distress. To isolate the precursors and the consequences as well as their causal relationships is an extremely complex task. However, this is an important area of investigation if organizations and individuals are to succeed in the preventive management of stress. Some preliminary efforts are underway in this regard.

One of the most comprehensive efforts to identify the direct economic costs of various employee attitudes and behaviors was undertaken at the Institute for Social Research by Mirvis, Macy, Lawler, and others (Mirvis and Macy, 1982). These investigators developed a detailed guide to behavioral costing which traces the variety of direct costs associated with a specific employee behavior, such as absenteeism. They developed costing procedures for behaviors related to participation and membership (for example, turnover) and to performance on the job (for example, poor-quality work). In addition to the direct economic costs associated with specific employee behaviors, organizations are now being held compensatorily responsible by some courts for on-the-job distress encountered by employees. Each of these three general categories of costs will be examined separately.

Participation and Membership

There are numerous reasons why an individual may not be available to work in the organization. If an employee is not participating in work at the appointed time or if an employee elects to leave the organization altogether, then the organization pays a price for unperformed work. *Absenteeism* and *tardiness* are two behaviors associated with non-participation. As short-term coping strategies for the individual, these behaviors may benefit the organization in the form of improved morale and quality of work. In the aggregate, they cost the organization in terms of both lowered morale for other workers and money for the overstaffing needed to cover the absent worker's station.

For example, an automobile assembly plant located near a major university runs approximately 10 percent absenteeism on the Friday and Monday shifts. The plant's response to the absenteeism is to hire a pool of local university students to serve as "fillers" for the absent workers. This response therefore inflates the personnel payroll. While studying a similar automobile production plant in the rural south, Mirvis and Lawler (1977) calculated the cost of each absence for the plant. This cost was $55.36 per absence. Using the same method, they determined that the absence of a bank branch manager in the midwest cost $218.15. Therefore, each occurrence of nonparticipation has a direct cost for the organization.

Strikes and *work stoppages* are other forms of nonparticipation which are in varying degrees costly to the organization. There are not only the direct costs associated with loss of production and/or replacement of personnel, as occurred in the Air Traffic Controllers' attempted strike, but also the indirect costs of lost opportunities and/or disruption of relations with suppliers, clients, and others in the task environment. These indirect costs will be discussed in more detail later in the chapter.

Just how costly a work stoppage may be is shown by an incident in a southern automobile assembly plant. One disgruntled employee, who was not getting adequate attention, effectively "pulled the power plug" on the entire assembly line. He idled 3,000 or so workers at once and prevented a resumption of normal activities for several hours. By applying the pertinent costing rules from the Mirvis procedures, it became evident that in addition to lost production, this incident cost the assembly plant several thousands of dollars in wages, salaries, and fringe benefits.

Turnover is the final cost in this category. Turnover has functional as well as dysfunctional consequences for the organization (Dalton, Tudor, and Krackhardt, 1982). Turnover may have functional consequences by enabling the organization to maintain a state of relative health by improving the quality of its human resources. Thus, if overpriced employees or unproductive employees leave and make room for new, vital personnel, then turnover is healthy. Or, if individuals leave because of a change in organizational tasks and goals, then such turnover can be good. While very high rates of turnover or unstable rates of turnover are costly for the organization, it is important to note that the functional aspects of turnover have often been overlooked (Dalton, Krackhardt, and Porter, 1981).

The actual costs of turnover vary with several factors; however, they frequently range around five times the employee's monthly salary. In empirically determining the economic costs of turnover, Mirvis and Macy (1982) determined that the cost of replacing one toll operator for a northeastern telephone company was approximately $1,900, while the cost of replacing a top manager for a midwestern manufacturing company was $30,000. Even these costs may be outweighed by the benefits of terminating a nonproductive employee who is absorbing

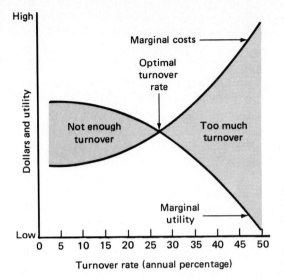

FIGURE 4.4
The economics of turnover management. [Source: *Allen C. Bluedorn, "Managing Turnover Strategically,"* Business Horizons, *vol. 25, no. 2, March/April 1982, p. 8.*]

organizational resources while giving nothing substantive to the organization in return.

The organization's objective should be to achieve an optimum level of turnover, which is determined by considering both the functional and dysfunctional aspects of turnover within a group of employees. Bluedorn (1982) has attempted to do this in economic terms by considering both marginal utility and marginal costs, as opposed to considering economic costs alone. Figure 4.4 shows a hypothetical example in which the optimum turnover rate is about 25 percent. The determination of a specific optimum turnover rate for a company, or for one of its employee groups, is based upon both functional and dysfunctional aspects of turnover. The key point to note here is that an optimum turnover rate may be determined for an organization so as to realize maximum economic benefit.

Performance on the Job

Stress not only influences the various degrees of participation, or lack of it, by an individual in the work organization; it also affects behavior at work. For example, while one individual may choose to be absent because of distress, another individual may well show distress in poor-quality performance. Or, distress might manifest itself in aggressive conflicts at work. Therefore, job performance is a second major realm in which there are direct consequences of organizational stress. Amount of productivity, quality of production, grievances, accidents, unscheduled machine downtime and repair, material and supply overutilization, and inventory shrinkages are all aspects of job performance (Mirvis and Macy, 1982).

Performance decrements attributable to excessive levels of stress were identified by Yerkes and Dodson at the turn of the century. When stress becomes distress because the degree has passed the optimum level for the individual, then either the *quality* or the *quantity* of the employee's work suffers, or both. This may occur routinely in repetitive work situations in which the employee starts losing concentration after approximately thirty minutes. When the employee's attention starts drifting because of the repetitiveness of the work, then quality and quantity of performance can both suffer. Fatigue due to work overload or role overload can also contribute to poor quality and/or quantity of work.

Executive burnout is a form of distress at work which results in individuals losing enthusiasm and vitality for their work; it is often accompanied by declining job performance. Burnout is a form of emotional and psychological fatigue, akin to depression, which appears to result from work and/or role overload. This condition appears to influence both the quality and quantity of work that an individual will produce. People who work directly with employee problems are particularly prone to experience this form of distress, as discussed in Chapter 3.

Grievances and *accidents* are also behaviors that take away from an employee's performance on the job. Informal complaints or suggestions that get acted on by managers or supervisors and thus never reach the formal grievance action stage are not included here. Such informal action may well be very beneficial to improved organizational health and cost the organization little beyond supervisory and employee time to resolve the issue. What is relevant here are formal actions such as those which resulted from work overload during the economic difficulties of 1980 and 1981 (see Chapter 2). Some organizations responded to the tight economy of this period by seeking cost savings through reductions in their labor force. In cases where commensurate reductions in work activities did not accompany the labor reductions, some workers experienced a work overload. This in turn led to grievance actions and accidents.

The Wall Street Journal's coverage of this practice suggested the presence of two consequences. One consequence was that unions and employees were filing more grievances about the practice of job loading. This consequence has only organizational cost implications. The other consequence of job loading was increased incidence of employee accidents. Accidents have both individual and organizational cost implications. The individual cost implications were discussed in Chapter 3.

The organizational costs associated with these forms of employee behavior are identified by Mirvis and Macy (1974) in their behavioral costing procedures, the applicable sections of which are identified in Figure 4.5. (The entire set of procedures includes some ten pages of thirty or more costing rules.) To these direct costs for the organization,

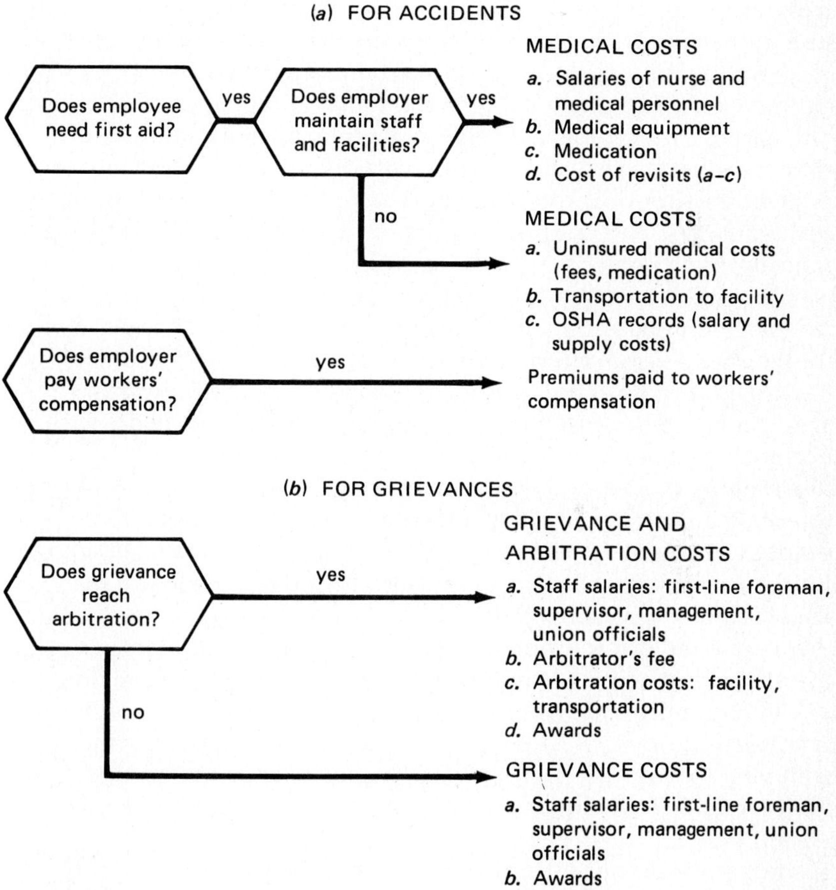
(a) FOR ACCIDENTS
Does employee need first aid?
yes
Does employer maintain staff and facilities?
yes
MEDICAL COSTS
a. Salaries of nurse and medical personnel
b. Medical equipment
c. Medication
d. Cost of revisits (a–c)
no
MEDICAL COSTS
a. Uninsured medical costs (fees, medication)
b. Transportation to facility
c. OSHA records (salary and supply costs)
Does employer pay workers' compensation?
yes
Premiums paid to workers' compensation
(b) FOR GRIEVANCES
Does grievance reach arbitration?
yes
GRIEVANCE AND ARBITRATION COSTS
a. Staff salaries: first-line foreman, supervisor, management, union officials
b. Arbitrator's fee
c. Arbitration costs: facility, transportation
d. Awards
no
GRIEVANCE COSTS
a. Staff salaries: first-line foreman, supervisor, management, union officials
b. Awards

FIGURE 4.5
Direct costs of distress. [*Use of these behavioral costing guidelines is reported in B. A. Macy and P. H. Mirvis, "Organizational Change Efforts: Methodologies for Assessing Organizational Effectiveness and Program Costs versus Benefits,"* Evaluation Review, *vol. 6, no. 3, 1982, pp. 301–372, and B. A. Macy and P. H. Mirvis, "A Methodology for Assessment of Quality of Work Life and Organizational Effectiveness in Behavioral-Economic Terms,"* Administrative Science Quarterly, *vol. 21, 1976, pp. 212–226.*]

it may be necessary to add the costs associated with nonparticipation if the employee involved in the accident or grievance is absent from the work station. Still additional costs are incurred if such an employee is permanently disabled or leaves the organization.

Mirvis and Macy (1982) also delineate the direct costs associated with *unscheduled machine downtime and repair, material and supply overutilization,* and *inventory shrinkages.* Not all incidents of these employee behaviors will be attributable to employee distress, but some will. Fatigue, poor judgment, anger, inattention, and other outcomes of distress at work will be factors contributing to occurrence of these dysfunctional behaviors. In addition to the direct costs of performance decrements attributable to the above-mentioned behaviors, poor job performance may be attributable to the sublimation of negative feelings on the part of the employee. Feelings of anger, hostility, and anxiety are normal responses to stressful situations at work such as conflict with one's boss or other superior, role ambiguity about expected work perform-ances, work overload, and other related experiences. However, many organizations do not legitimize the formal verbalization or expression of these normal feelings. While the repression of these feelings may lead to some of the psychosomatic disorders discussed in Chapter 3, the employee has some alternative ways of expressing these feelings behaviorally. For example, one of the ways in which individuals find expression for these hostilities is through subversive behaviors such as intentional machine malfunctions or poor-quality work.

Illustrations of these circumstances may be seen in the American automobile industry during the past several years. Ford Motor Company attempted to counteract this trend through a mass media campaign by pointing out that "quality is job 1." This effort was occasioned by cases in which employees sabotaged individual car quality by slipping bottles in the assembled door, dropping bolts in the engine cylinders just prior to assembly, or placing notes like "I'll be gone by the time you find this one!" in an empty soda can in a fender housing. There are numerous "humorous" stories of such subversive activities, all of which are detrimental to product quality. Employees use these means to express negative feelings which have found no more effective channels for release.

Some of these poor performance behaviors are consciously or unconsciously designed to get the individual attention at work, for there is interpersonal stress associated with being ignored at work. In surveying 4,500 workers in six occupational groups, the Academy of Family Physicians recently found that employees change jobs to seek greater self-fulfillment and because they experience a lack of appreciation in their present organizational circumstances. Therefore, employees will seek dysfunctional ways of gaining attention if they cannot get adequate attention in a functional manner.

Compensation Awards

The third category of direct organizational costs associated with mis-managed stress takes the form of court-ordered compensation awards to distressed employees. The awards take the form of disability com-pensation and are based primarily upon adverse psychological or emotional reactions to stressful events at work. A difficulty that courts and companies, as well as employees, encounter in some instances is locating or identifying the true locus of the stress that causes the dis-order. Thus, an unhappy and tense family environment may be the real source of an individual's anxiety, not tension and conflict at work.

The amount of compensation that an organization is held accountable for varies with a number of considerations. For example, Burroughs Corporation had to pay one of their secretaries $7,000 for hysteria resulting from her boss's constant criticism of her restroom trips. The secretary is filing an appeal for a larger award. In another case, the Los Alamos Scientific Laboratory had to pay an employee working with ra-dioactive materials $75,000 for anxiety that resulted from one bout with cancer.

Organizations must follow both state and federal court rulings to determine what the trends will be for such direct costs. For employees who become permanently disabled, an organization may be looking at long-term financial commitments to that employee, or large lump-sum severance payments. There is at least one precedent in the case of the Los Alamos Scientific Laboratory employee.

In summary, the direct costs of mismanaged stress fall into one of three categories: participation and membership, on-the-job performance, and compensation awards. The actual measurement of the first two categories has been the subject of recent investigations in several diverse industries. Organizations have been aware of these costs for a long time, even though they have not always placed economic figures on them. Com-pensation awards for distress at work are only recently emerging as an organizational cost.

INDIRECT COSTS OF DISTRESS

In addition to the various direct economic costs of mismanaged stress, there are a number of indirect costs which the organization may suffer in various forms and which may be contributing factors to previously discussed direct costs. While research by Mirvis, Macy, Lawler, and others on the quality of work life has made some notable progress in developing behavioral-costing guidelines for many of the direct costs and the courts will help determine compensation costs, the same sorts of guidelines, procedures, and precedents are not available for the indirect costing. The absence of such indirect costing procedures does not make the indirect costs any less important for organizational managers and investigators. The absence of such procedures does suggest that it may be very difficult to trace such costs so as to develop accurate estimates of what they are.

Loss of Vitality

Selye (1974) argues that all individuals have both superficial and deep adaptive energy. The superficial adaptive energy is what enables individuals to cope with immediate emergency or stress situations. Individuals who are constantly experiencing too high a level of stress for their particular abilities and energy resources will not have sufficient recuperative time to replenish the superficial adaptive energy supply that gets consumed on a daily basis. Employees who are so expended on a regular basis in this way may end up accruing some direct performance costs for the organization in the form of lowered work quality. Even in the absence of such direct costs, there may be indirect costs associated with the inability to effectively cope with changes and adjustments at work. Long-term work overload would reasonably create such a condition with its associated problems. Therefore, individuals who are chronically distressed lose their responsiveness and resiliency because they do not have the necessary superficial adaptive energy to cope with stress. Employees who are expended in this way are not able to contribute constructively and consistently to organizational health and functioning.

This loss of vitality may well manifest itself in varying degrees of *low morale, low motivation,* and *dissatisfaction* in the work force. These indirect costs have been shown to contribute to some of the direct costs previously discussed, such as the connection shown between low morale and high turnover or dissatisfaction and low productivity. However, these manifestations of loss of vitality have implications other than their contribution to the direct costs. They are also evidence of poor quality work life, which has humanitarian implications over and above the economic considerations discussed. The work environment need not be a dissatisfying place. On the contrary, there are long-term benefits available to organizations which are concerned with humanitarian and morale considerations, such as the goodwill which leads individuals to seek employment with the organization.

Communication Breakdowns

Distress at work also has adverse effects upon communication patterns of employees. Kahn and his associates (1964) found that as role conflicts and role ambiguity intensified, there was a decline in the frequency of communication between the individual and others in the working environment. The *decline in communication frequency* was much more notable in the case of role conflict, where the individual experiencing the conflict attempts to reduce it by withdrawing from conflicted relationships. This reduction in the frequency of communication interactions may lead to disruption and to misunderstanding in the accomplishment of especially interdependent tasks and activities.

Especially at the managerial level, much of the work in an organization gets accomplished through verbal and written instructions, directions, information sharing, and clarification of objectives and activities. An example of how miscommunication can disrupt work activities occurred at a large photochemical company one summer. When told to go paint the windows in one building, the crew never asked clarification and simply painted the windowpanes in the entire building, rather than the frames as had been intended!

In addition to the reduced frequency of communication that may occur due to stress, there is a clear potential for *distortions* to occur in communication linkages. One of the associated events of a stressful situation is the arousal of defense mechanisms. While the psychological defense mechanisms which individuals have in protecting ego integrity have some functional value, they may also distort both the messages that one sends and the interpretation of messages that one receives. Either is dysfunctional for effective working relationships.

Faulty Decision Making

Effective managerial decision making requires information about the decision situation and goal judgmental processes upon the part of the decision maker (MacCrimmon and Taylor, 1976). The communication breakdowns discussed above not only are an organizational cost of distress but also may contribute to faulty decision-making processes in the organization. That is, as communication flows and patterns are disrupted, information will either be lost or not transmitted within the organization. The lack of this lost or untransmitted information can have a detrimental effect upon any decisions to which it is relevant. Therefore, distress at work may lead to faulty managerial decision making due to lost or incomplete information about the decision.

A second way distress at work can lead to faulty decision making is by impairing the judgment of the manager. When a manager is distressed, his or her physiological and psychological processes will be adversely affected. Specifically, a manager who is bored because of too little stress may be inattentive and lack alertness in making a decision, while a manager who is overloaded with demands may not carefully weigh and evaluate the decision alternatives and the information relevant to these alternatives. Both poor judgment and lost information due to communication breakdowns can contribute to costly bad decisions for the organization.

Quality of Work Relations

The communication problems that result from distress are one aspect of the overall quality of working relationships in an organization. In addition to the reduced communications noted by Kahn and his associates, they found a marked increase in *distrust*, *disrespect*, and *animosity* occurring under conditions of stress. That is, individuals who are experiencing role distress tend to have markedly less trust in, less respect for, and less liking for those with whom they are working.

A deterioration in the quality of work relations in the organization can have at least two dysfunctional side effects. First, distrust and dislike will both contribute to destructive conflict and animosity in the relationship. The more energy that is consumed in this manner, the less constructive energy is available for people to use in work performance. This form of conflict is different from constructive conflict, which when managed in a confrontational manner, can lead to change and growth.

Second, poor working relationships have the effect of reducing employee satisfaction and, in turn, an employee's attendance behavior (Steers and Rhodes, 1978). Thus, the reduced quality of relationships within the organization will contribute to the direct costs of absenteeism and to reduced organizational health in the long term.

Opportunity Costs

As was seen earlier, healthy organizations will respond and adapt to their task environments so as to minimize the impact of threats while working to take advantage of opportunities. Distressed employees and organizations are at a disadvantage in this regard because they do not have energy available for such a positive response. The distressed individual is utilizing available energy for coping—or survival. Under such extended conditions, the longer time perspective needed for examining future opportunities may be lost.

SUMMARY

Organizations and individuals engage in exchange relations for mutual benefit, health, and growth. The health of one member in the exchange also affects the health of the other member. Organizational health is an ideal state of flexibility, adaptability, and productivity toward which an organization may work, though it is never fully achieved. Optimum levels of stress within an organization enhance this process and contribute to organizational health, while excessive levels lead to various sorts of dysfunctions and organizational costs discussed in this chapter.

The direct costs of distress are those related to nonparticipation and nonmembership, nonperformance, and court-ordered compensation awards. Of the three categories of direct costs, more is currently known about nonparticipation and nonmembership and about nonperformance than about compensation awards. Additional information about compensation award costs awaits the establishment of court precedents and case law development in the states as well as in the federal sector.

The indirect costs of distress are much less easily quantified but may be no less destructive for organizational health. Some of these indirect costs, such as poor quality in work relations, may be connected to the more measurable direct costs, such as absenteeism and tardiness. Both sets of costs are detrimental and should be managed in a proactive, preventive manner so that an optimum level of stress is established for organizational health. But the preventive management of organizational stress must be based upon an accurate and information-based understanding of the stresses operating in a *particular* organization. This understanding may be arrived at through the diagnostic process discussed in the next chapter.

FURTHER READINGS

Beer, M.: *Organization Change and Development: A Systems View*, Goodyear Publishing Company, Santa Monica, Calif., 1980.

Blau, P. M.: *Exchange and Power in Social Life*, John Wiley & Sons, New York, 1964.

Kahn, R. L., D. M. Wolfe, R. P. Quinn, J. D. Snoek, and R. A. Rosenthal: *Organizational Stress: Studies in Role Conflict and Ambiguity*, John Wiley, New York, 1964.

Seashore, S. E., E. E. Lawler, P. H. Mirvis, and C. Cammann: *Observing and Measuring Organizational Change: A Guide to Field Practice*, Wiley Interscience, New York, 1982.

Steers, R. M.: *Organizational Effectiveness: A Behavioral View*, Goodyear Publishing Company, Santa Monica, Calif., 1977.

CHAPTER 5

BASIC CONCEPTS FOR DIAGNOSING ORGANIZATIONAL STRESS

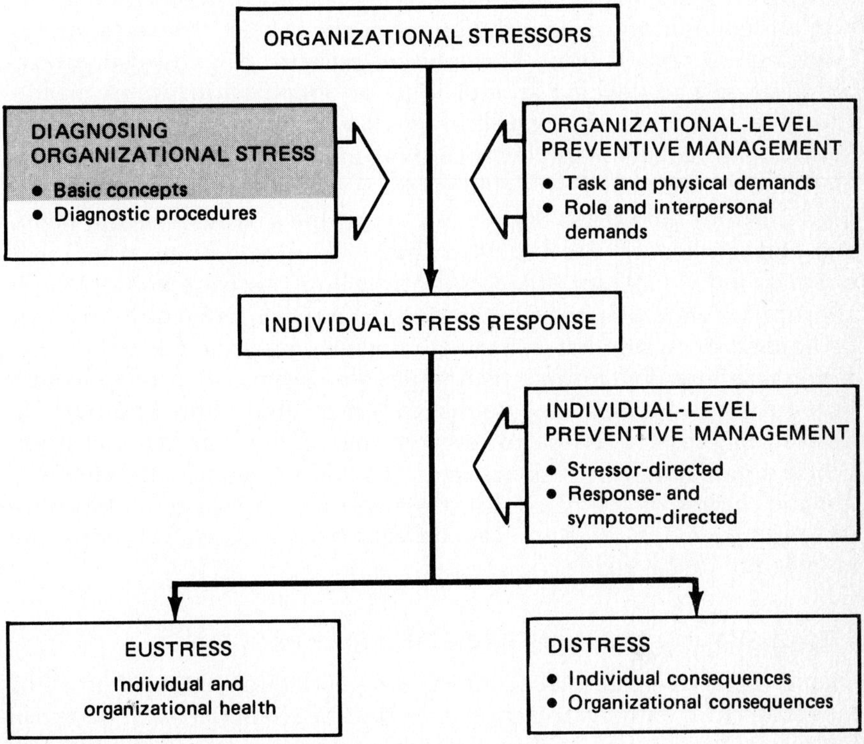
ORGANIZATIONAL STRESSORS
DIAGNOSING ORGANIZATIONAL STRESS
• Basic concepts
• Diagnostic procedures
ORGANIZATIONAL-LEVEL PREVENTIVE MANAGEMENT
• Task and physical demands
• Role and interpersonal demands
INDIVIDUAL STRESS RESPONSE
INDIVIDUAL-LEVEL PREVENTIVE MANAGEMENT
• Stressor-directed
• Response- and symptom-directed
EUSTRESS
Individual and organizational health
DISTRESS
• Individual consequences
• Organizational consequences

The purpose of this chapter is to examine several relevant aspects of the process of organizational stress diagnosis. The word "diagnosis" comes from *dia*, "through"; *gnosis*, "knowledge of". In this case, organizational stress diagnosis is concerned with knowledge of the causes and consequences of the stress that specific organizations and individuals encounter. The role of diagnosis in organizational stress and preventive management was suggested in Chapter 1 (see Figure 1.3). One of the aims of preventive management is to enhance individual and organizational health. However, to undertake activities toward that end without proper diagnosis would be ill-advised under most circumstances. The diagnostic process is not a one-time activity. Rather, it is an ongoing component of effective preventive management. The relevant aspects of the diagnostic process covered in this chapter are the philosophy of stress diagnosis, the different types of diagnostic procedures available, the criteria for evaluating diagnostic procedures, and the characteristics of the diagnostician. Specific procedures and instruments will be reviewed in Chapter 6.

There are actually several purposes for conducting stress diagnostic activities. One purpose is to determine the cause of a current dysfunction, such as cardiovascular disease or high turnover rates. The focus here is on determining the major stressors that the individual or the organization are encountering, with the intent of altering the stresses upon the individual or organization. A second purpose for diagnosing organizational stress is to develop an individual or organizational stress profile. The stress profile would then allow the diagnostician to determine if the individual or organization is functioning at an optimum level or if they might be at risk for stress-related organizational or individual distress. A third purpose for a stress diagnosis is to provide a basis for recommending and evaluating preventive managerial interventions which will enhance individual and organizational health. There are no universally appropriate ways of managing stress, but there are techniques that may be applied once one has a thorough knowledge of the current organizational setting. Once these techniques are applied, their effectiveness in reducing stress must be systematically evaluated. A final purpose for a stress diagnosis is related to research regarding organizational stress. While organizational stress has been studied for years, additional systematic studies of the causes of stress and evaluations of methods for preventing distress at work can be very beneficial to furthering our knowledge in this field.

STRESS DIAGNOSIS: AN INTERDISCIPLINARY PROCESS

Diagnostic activities are appropriate for a variety of settings, including medical, social, and organizational. According to Laing (1971), diagnosis in social settings involves identifying the underlying causes of individual behavior and interpersonal dynamics within the setting. Laing indicates that the causes for behaviors and interactions may not be what the individuals in the setting say they are. Diagnosis does not assume that there is a problem, although most diagnostic activities are undertaken on the basis of some symptom or anticipated problem.

As discussed earlier, the rationale for careful diagnostic procedures when dealing with organizational stress is to provide a responsible basis for preventive management activities, to include treatment actions. The organizational stress diagnostician needs an understanding of individual and organizational functioning since both the organizational unit of analysis and the individual unit of analysis are important in the diagnostic process.

It is very important in stress diagnosis to identify the underlying causes of the stress rather than the manifestations of that stress. It is altogether too easy to deal with visible *symptoms* in stress and not properly diagnose the underlying *causes* of a problem, or the *preconditions* which lead to the occurrence of the symptom. Therefore, the objective of good stress diagnostic activities in organizations should be aimed at determining the underlying causes of distress.

Interdisciplinary Nature

In dealing with a multifaceted problem such as organizational stress, it is valuable to incorporate the perspectives of several disciplines in developing an accurate diagnosis. Three key disciplines relevant to stress diagnosis are organizational science, psychology, and medicine. Most organizations, especially large ones like IBM and Mobil Oil Corporation, have individuals who specialize in each of these three areas. While they may be employed in personnel management, organizational development, or medical departments, these specialists are often available somewhere within the organization. What is important in stress diagnosis . is the integration of the diverse professional expertise of these various groups. Each discipline's relevance to the diagnostic process will be examined separately.

The first key discipline is *organizational science*. The discipline of organizational science takes the organization as its primary unit of analysis, although the individual and the group are of importance also. Organizational science starts with an understanding of organization design, job design, and technology, and of their impact on individuals and groups at work. People who study organizational behavior have learned over the years that it is not possible to understand an individual's behavior in organizations on the basis of psychological principles alone. An understanding of administrative and organizational principles is also needed before one can fully explain and predict organizational behavior. Without an open-system framework of organization, as presented in Chapter 4, and a mastery of the fundamental concepts of organizational science, it is not possible to identify or recognize stress-related dysfunctions. While individuals who are trained in organizational science have special skills and knowledge in this area, many managers and executives also have intuitive and/or explicit knowledge in this discipline.

The second key discipline is *psychology*, including the related medical discipline of *psychiatry*. While organizational science takes the organization as its primary unit of analysis, psychology and psychiatry take the individual as their primary unit of analysis. This discipline is important in diagnosing stress due to the role of emotions, ideas, and cognitive processes in influencing or altering individual physiological processes. If the diagnostician does not have an adequate understanding of depth psychology, then it may not be possible to go beyond the medical symptoms to possible underlying psychological causes. Certainly not all distress comes from underlying psychological issues, but psychological processes play an instrumental role in diagnosing organizational stress.

The third key discipline is *medicine*, which is concerned traditionally with the biological and physiological functioning of the individual. An adequate understanding of physiological processes is important to identifying when an individual is encountering distress. Medicine is of primary importance because it is within the human body that the symptoms of distress are most commonly revealed. An individual's psychological distress very frequently will lead at some point to one or another physiological disorder. Therefore, it is important to recognize the symptoms of strain within the physiology of the individual.

These three key disciplines are essential underpinnings to the stress diagnostic process in organizations. In addition, as McLean has pointed out, there are several related disciplines, such as industrial sociology and occupational medicine, that play a role in understanding stress. These disciplines make contributions to the diagnostic process through their own unique perspectives and blend of experiences, thus rounding out the core of knowledge and skills contained in the pure disciplines. Therefore, they should be incorporated in the diagnostic process. Again, it should be pointed out that most organizations have professionals employed, either on a full-time or on a consulting basis, in each of these disciplines.

Basic Philosophy

There are several fundamental notions about organizational stress which shape the underlying diagnostic philosophy of this chapter. One notion is that stress is not necessarily bad. That is, it may be either functional or dysfunctional depending upon its intensity, source, and the individual's psychophysiological response to it. Therefore, the identification of certain forms of stress in organizations will require no preventive or remedial managerial response.

A second notion is that distress may manifest itself in any one of a host of individual or organizational problems. If you subscribe to the "Achilles heel" phenomenon discussed in Chapter 3, this means that the particular manifestation of distress in individuals or in organizations will occur at their weakest point. For example, one individual may suffer ulcers as a result of distress while another individual may manifest cardiovascular disease. At the organizational level, one organization may experience high levels of turnover in response to distress while another organization may experience a crippling labor strike. As a result, the diagnostician who attends only to the presenting disorders is not always able to identify underlying causes or may miss symptoms and causes by having too narrow a diagnostic focus. The key point here is that there are substantial and significant differences across individuals and organizations. It is the *differences*, not the similarities, which are of particular importance to the skilled diagnostician.

The third notion is that effective stress diagnosis, at both the individual and organizational levels, is never complete. While an individual or an organization may not be encountering notable distress at one point in time, this does not mean that they will never experience distress. Thus, the ongoing diagnostic activities ensure the maintenance of optimum individual and organizational health.

The Process of Organizational Stress Diagnosis

The overall process for organizational stress diagnosis is presented in Figure 5.1. This model presents assessments of health and functioning at both the organizational and individual levels. On the basis of diagnostic assessments, the diagnostician must (1) propose individual and organizational prevention activities to be used to preclude distress as well as (2) list the points of dysfunction at the organizational and individual levels. The points of dysfunction are identified by the problems and/or inconsistencies in the individual's or organization's functioning. To identify these dysfunctions requires both skill and sensitivity on the part of the diagnostician. As H. Levinson (1972, p. 7) puts it, "Any fool can tell that a river flows. Only he who understands its cross-currents, its eddies, the variations in the speed, the hidden rocks, its action in drought and flood, is the master of its functioning." So it is with individuals and organizations. Until the diagnostician has fully familiarized himself with the subject of the diagnosis, it is not possible to delineate the points of dysfunction.

Individual and organizational prevention activities should be tailored

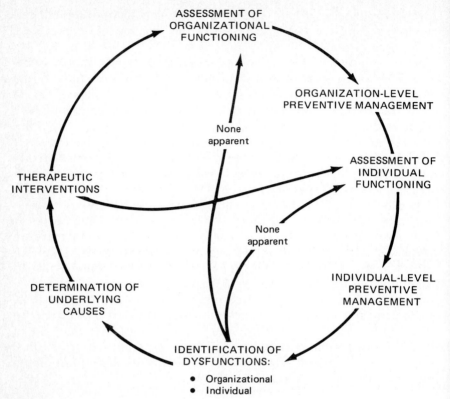

FIGURE 5.1
The process of organizational stress diagnosis.

to the specific individual or organization on the basis of the diagnostic findings, taking into consideration the individual differences previously discussed. It is possible that the diagnosis will reveal no notable, current dysfunctions. Even if no distress is revealed, it is still necessary to continue the organizational and individual assessment activities at periodic intervals. Failure to do so invites the potential problem of dealing with a distressing crisis in a full-blown form. Periodic assessments, say on an annual basis, provide a more fertile ground for effective implementation of preventive management.

Therapeutic interventions are also a part of preventive management and are identified in Figure 5.1. Any therapeutic interventions must be based upon a determination of the underlying causes of stress, not the surface symptoms. The therapeutic activities must also be tailored to the specific individual and organization. The purpose of the therapeutic interventions is to prevent further deterioration in functioning or to rectify problems which were not precluded by other preventive activities introduced on the basis of the diagnostician's assessment activities. For example, health maintenance programs, such as exercise and fitness activities, will not prevent all cardiovascular disease. It may be necessary in individual cases to intervene therapeutically with surgery and/or drugs.

TYPES OF DIAGNOSTIC PROCEDURES

In conducting the diagnostic assessments of individual and organizational functioning, there are a wide variety of procedures that may be used. In this chapter, the general procedures or methods of making diagnostic assessments will be considered. In Chapter 6, specific instruments will be examined. Because of the nature of stress, and the dual levels of assessment, it is appropriate for the diagnostician to draw upon more than one type of diagnostic procedure in conducting a thorough assessment at either the organizational or individual level.

Interviews

Interviews may be used to diagnose either organizational or individual stress, depending upon the structure and focus of the interview. The loosely structured interview gives the interviewee an opportunity to depict in more detail both perceptions and feelings about stressful events. As such, the loosely structured interview may be used without constraining the subject too narrowly in terms of what he or she reports. The difficulty with this procedure is in its user and not in its nature. That is, the success of using interviews hinges upon the skills and characteristics of the interviewer as much as upon the structure and design of the interview protocol. While the protocol should have some structure, it is important that it be sufficiently open-ended to allow for unsolicited inputs from the interviewee.

Athos and Gabarro (1978) discuss the use of a reflective technique with its attendant reflective responses as a way of enhancing interpersonal communication. This technique is based upon the listening skills of the interviewer, whose purpose is to understand the interviewee's experience in detail and depth. That is a key advantage of this reflective technique. However, the effective use of this technique requires skill and sensitivity. Some characteristics of the interviewer will inhibit an effective process while others will enhance that process. For example, in conservative settings such as many oil companies and military units, an interviewer decked out in jeans and a tee shirt may well erect some barriers to effective communication which would not be present in another setting such as a loading dock. The importance of these reactive effects have been discussed by Laing (1971), who points out that a situation immediately changes as soon as a diagnostician enters it.

A key advantage of the interview is the detail and depth of perspective which it can afford the diagnostician. This depth and detail are not as feasible when using other procedures. The interview combines a procedure for self-report data collection with some observation on the part of the interviewer. The limitation of the interview is its time-consuming nature and the potential difficulties in summarizing a number of interview results. There is much room for both faulty interpretation and unconscious bias being introduced in the analysis of interview data. Feeding back the results of interviews to management also becomes more complicated and cumbersome, if the open-ended interview procedure is employed.

Questionnaires

Structured questionnaires are an alternative method for conducting diagnostic activities. The bipolar adjectives used in a semantic differential may be used to describe potential stressors at work in terms of various feeling states. For example, an employee might be asked to describe "the job" in terms of: frustrating versus not frustrating, stressful versus not stressful, tense versus relaxed, and pressured versus not pressured. In this way, adjective sets could be developed which would describe a stressor. The use of numbered scales, such as those used by Likert, would allow the diagnostician to determine the degree of stress caused by a large number of stressors. That is, the Likert procedure would allow for an assessment of the degree of stress caused, while the semantic differential would allow for an adjective picture of the stressor.

Questionnaires are suitable for either individual or organizational use. In addition, they enable the diagnostician to develop data from large groups of people much more easily than would be possible through interviews. Because of the quantifiable responses that result from most social science questionnaires, this type of diagnostic procedure allows for more measurable intersubject comparisons. Even with semistructured interview protocols, it is often difficult to do more than make qualitative comparisons regarding the data.

Questionnaires can be very useful in developing perceptual data and some feeling-state data. However, it is more difficult for the diagnostician to develop a sense of these feeling states through questionnaires. The most that can be hoped for when using this procedure is a rough approximation of those feeling states. What is lost in detail in using questionnaires may be made up in the volume of data that can more effectively be collected.

Questionnaire results are often more easily communicated to management. Such results do not require as much interpretation as needed when reviewing interview data, although there is some need for explanation and clarification. While questionnaire results may look more objective because of their quantitative nature, one must keep in mind the still subjective nature of the individuals completing the instrument. Some of the individual biases that distort interview results will still operate, but will be compensated for when larger samples are included for questionnaire surveys.

Observational Techniques

There are two categories of observational techniques which lend themselves to use in stress diagnosis. The first of these is *behavioral* observation, and the second of these is *medical* observation. Both must be employed by a trained observer who is skilled at selecting and evaluating those aspects of the field to observe. Either category of observation may be of a quantitative or qualitative nature (Van Maanen, 1979). Qualitative and quantitative observation are both important and may be used to complement and supplement each other. Neither is necessarily better or more valuable than the other.

Behavioral observations can be useful in individual stress diagnosis. They are difficult to use alone without alternative types of diagnostic procedures but can be very helpful as supplemental sources of data. Their use requires familiarity on the part of the diagnostician with the particular individual. That is, there are culturally acceptable patterns of behavior which specific individuals exhibit in varying degrees. Behavior that varies substantially from such norms should be more closely monitored to determine its origin. Stress is only one of a number of possible causes for such deviant behavior. Within the culturally accepted norms, there are individual variations which may be considered normal. Therefore, it is important to understand a specific individual's normal patterns of behavior prior to ascertaining their degree of deviance. When deviant behavior is observed, it may be attributable to stress-related causes and thus used as supplemental diagnostic data.

Behavioral observations may also be made at the organizational level in diagnosing stress. Observations at this level are frequently, but not always, collected in the form of institutional records or archival data. The relevant behavioral observations are those associated with organizational health, as discussed in Chapter 4. These behaviors, which will be detailed in Chapter 6, include (1) absenteeism and tardiness rates, (2) turnover rates, and (3) strikes and other forms of work stoppages. Some occurrences of these behaviors should be anticipated in any organization. Judgment is required in the diagnostic process to determine what are "normal" or "healthy" occurrences of these behaviors and what rates suggest organizational distress.

Medical observations are the second category of observational data. These consist of a set of possible observations made by a clinician or by a laboratory technician using urine or blood analyses. These observations are used in individual stress diagnosis and may supplement organizational stress diagnosis. There are several key medical observations that may be made. These will be detailed in Chapter 6 but include, among others, (1) heart rate as measured by pulse, (2) blood pressure as measured using a sphygmomanometer, and (3) HDL and LDL cholesterol levels as measured in blood analyses. There are normal ranges for all of these observations. Observations outside of the normal ranges would suggest that the individual may well be experiencing distress.

Both categories of observational data should really be used in conjunction with other types of diagnostic procedures. They are limited primarily to the diagnosis of individual stress, which is not the case with interviews and questionnaires as types of diagnostic procedures. Interviews and questionnaires should therefore be used as primary methods, supplemented at the individual level by medical observation and at the organizational level by selected behavioral observations.

CRITERIA FOR A DIAGNOSTIC PROCEDURE

There are several criteria that should be considered in determining the relative merit or value of any stress diagnostic procedure. A good diagnostic instrument or method should meet certain minimum standards or selected criteria. It may be improved by also having some additional characteristics which, if absent, do not necessarily make it a poor instrument or method. There are three necessary and three additional criteria for a good diagnostic procedure. These are listed in Table 5.1.

Necessary Criteria

Validity is probably the most important characteristic of a good diagnostic instrument, and it is probably the most difficult criterion to meet. Validity is concerned with whether the methods and procedures that are used to measure organization stress are in fact measuring what they are designed to measure. While there are psychometrically different procedures that may be used in evaluating the various forms of validity, each comes down to a point of judgmental evaluation by some investigator. Of the various forms of validity, several are relevant to our

TABLE 5.1
CRITERIA FOR A DIAGNOSTIC PROCEDURE

Necessary criteria	Additional criteria
• Validity	• Comprehensiveness
• Reliability	• Depth
• Feasibility	• Instrumentation

purposes. *Construct validity* is concerned with the extent to which the diagnostic procedure measures the theoretical construct "stress." What makes addressing construct validity very difficult in the context of stress is the current theoretical difficulties in definition. There is not *one* unified, agreed upon construct called "stress," which then leaves the construct validity issue problematic.

Of more current relevance is the issue of *discriminant validity*. This form of validity is concerned with the distinction of organizational stress from such related constructs as anxiety, job tension, frustration, anger, hostility, joy, and other such phenomena. A good diagnostic procedure should then be able to separate organizational stress symptoms from some of these other experiences. While it may be reasonable to see some relationship or occurrence of one or more of the related experiences when diagnosing stress, they are not the same; and a good procedure or instrument should be able to separate the difference.

A final form of validity that is of concern here is *concurrent* and/or *predictive validity*. That is, if the procedure used yields a stress diagnosis, then one would expect to also observe various of the consequences of stress either concurrently or at some point in the future. These consequences would most commonly take the form of the various individual and organizational dysfunctions previously discussed in Chapters 3 and 4. If the diagnostic procedure cannot predict these consequences of the stress, then it will have little value in preventive or remedial intervention.

Reliability is the second central criterion for a good diagnostic procedure. Here the concern is with the accuracy of the diagnostic measures. This is sometimes determined by taking measures at two time points (test-retest reliability) and examining their degree of relationship. However, in the case of organizational stress, it would be expected that the stress levels would vary over time. Because of this, it would be difficult to establish test-retest reliability unless the individual's or organization's circumstances have not changed at all over time. Therefore, of more concern here are the issues of interrater reliability and internal consistency.

Reliability is particularly important as a criterion for a diagnostic procedure because it limits the validity criterion. That is, regardless of how valid the diagnosis is, its usefulness will be limited by the reliability of the diagnosis. That is why the *interrater reliability* and the *internal consistency* of the diagnostic procedure should be good. The first of these suggests that the procedure should yield the same result regardless of the diagnostician who uses it. Or, different diagnosticians should get the same result when using a particular interview or questionnaire procedure. In addition to getting the same results from different diagnosticians, a procedure should be internally consistent. That is, the questions related to a particular source of stress should elicit a common response from the same individual.

An unreliable procedure, in either regard, can yield one of two errors. Either the diagnosis will identify stress where none really exists or it will *not* identify stress where it does exist. The latter error is potentially harmful, while the former may simply lead to wasted time and energy in preventive or remedial treatment. Failing to diagnose stress which is actually operating has the potential for allowing serious disease to evolve beyond the point of preventive action, leaving remedial or therapeutic action as the only alternatives. For these reasons, the reliability of the diagnostic procedure is particularly important.

Feasibility is the third key criterion for a diagnostic procedure. It must not be too complex either for the diagnostician to use or, in the case of questionnaires, for the operating-level employee with minimal formal education to use. Unless it is a feasible procedure for a variety of organizational settings, then it will not yield the needed results even if it meets the validity and reliability criteria. The procedure must be valid and reliable, but it must also be sufficiently simple and economical to use.

Additional Criteria

In addition to these three key criteria for selecting a diagnostic procedure, there are three other criteria that one may want to consider. The *comprehensiveness* of the procedure may be very relevant when there are few apparent indications or symptoms. Because distress may be manifested in such a variety of ways, it is important to ask whether the diagnostic procedure considers all the possible symptoms and causes. Greater comprehensiveness in the diagnostic process can be achieved by using multiple types of procedures as previously discussed. The limiting consideration here is whether the use of multiple procedures will become so complex as to violate the simplicity criterion. Sequential use of multiple procedures as indicated may yield the necessary comprehensiveness without encumbering the procedure with too much complexity.

Related to the comprehensiveness criterion but distinct from it is the criterion of *depth*. While comprehensiveness is concerned with how well the procedure will identify all forms of stress, the depth criterion is concerned with how well the procedure will detail the relative importance or magnitude of any particular stressor. For example, a questionnaire procedure may identify one's marriage relationship as a source of stress without providing detailed information on the nature of that stress. In this case, an interview procedure would afford the opportunity for exploring the nature of the stress in more detail. Or, open-ended questionnaires rather than structured questionnaires would provide a similar opportunity.

Another criterion to consider is the degree of *instrumentation* in the procedure. That is, to what degree is the procedure quantitative versus qualitative? If it is a very quantified procedure, then it allows for greater cross-subject (either individual or organization) comparison. This is of some concern when considering concurrent and predictive validity. The alternative to a highly quantified procedure is a highly qualitative one, which may leave more discretion and judgment in the hands of the diagnostician but provide for richer detail in the diagnosis. The more instrumented the procedure, the more readily useful it may be for managers. However, highly instrumented procedures are not necessarily better than qualitative procedures and even have disadvantages, such as lack of contextual detail, which handicap the diagnosis (Payne, 1978).

Any diagnostic procedure should be evaluated using the key criteria as well as the additional criteria. In Chapter 6, selected procedures, methods, or instruments will be examined in light of the criteria established here. These same criteria should be considered in evaluating any procedure for use in organizational stress diagnosis.

THE DIAGNOSTICIAN

While the procedure is important to the diagnostic process, the characteristics of the diagnostician are also an integral part of the process if a formal diagnosis of organizational stress is to be undertaken. It is debatable who the diagnostician should be. There are two considerations here. One consideration is the organizational affiliation of the individual. That is, is the individual an academician with a primary commitment to the university? An internal consultant whose primary commitment is to the organization? Or a professional consultant who must earn a living? The nature of the diagnostician's primary affiliation will color the person's perceptions in degree and should be considered as one aspect of selecting a diagnostician.

As a rule, the cost of the diagnosis will be less when internal diagnosticians and resources are used. The quality of such internal diagnosis is not necessarily less than the quality of a diagnosis completed by an external professional. Considerations such as the internal diagnostician's independence and freedom from political reprisals will influence the quality of the diagnostic findings. The professional consultant may be similarly subject to pressures internal to the organization, depending upon how the initial relationship is structured. And hiring a professional consultant will not necessarily yield a higher-quality diagnosis.

A second consideration is the professional grounding of the diagnostician. This grounding will shape this individual's world view and interpretation of the observations and information uncovered during the diagnostic process. Each professional will have limitations. The primary disciplines which have been discussed as being involved in the diagnostic process are organizational science, psychology and psychiatry, and medicine. Each of the disciplines has its own norms and values as well as preferred orientations. It is important that the diagnostic process not be prejudiced by any set of predispositions in this regard.

This professional diversity entails an interdisciplinary dialogue. No professional can entirely overcome the perspectives of a particular profession, but he or she can be open to interdisciplinary efforts. This open dialogue involves individuals from other professions in the diagnostic process and/or makes use of referrals to the appropriate professional group. Without this sort of willing exchange, the diagnostic process will be prejudiced in an examination of such a multifaceted issue as stress.

One critical requirement of a diagnostician, regardless of affiliation or profession, is confidentiality. Without confidentiality, individuals and organizations will not talk freely about their stresses and strains. It is inevitable that the diagnostic process will leave individuals and/or groups vulnerable and exposed with regard to their inner selves. Therefore, it is critical that the diagnostician and the organization be sensitive to this point so that individuals will not be hurt while in this vulnerable position.

SUMMARY

This chapter has examined the process of diagnosing organizational stress. There are various purposes for engaging in formal stress diagnostic procedures, which include (1) determining the cause(s) of various individual and organizational dysfunctions, (2) developing stress profiles for individuals and groups at risk, (3) recommending and evaluating preventive managerial interventions, and (4) providing a basis for research regarding organizational stress. The diagnosis should be an interdisciplinary one which considers organizational science, psychology, and medicine in the process. The actual diagnosis may be conducted by means of interviews, questionnaires, or behavioral and medical observations. Whatever procedure is chosen for the diagnosis, it should be valid, reliable, and feasible. Actual instruments and procedures for diagnosis will be reviewed in Chapter 6. In addition to the methods and procedures, the characteristics of the diagnostician should be considered when using a formal procedure. The process of organizational stress diagnosis is an integral aspect of the philosophy of preventive management.

FURTHER READINGS

Campbell, D. T., and J. C. Stanley: *Experimental and Quasi-Experimental Designs for Research*, Rand McNally, Chicago, 1973.

Dunham, R. B., and F. J. Smith: *Organizational Surveys: An Internal Assessment of Organizational Health*, Scott, Foresman and Company, Glenview, Ill., 1979.

Feinstein, A. R.: *Clinical Judgment*, Williams & Wilkins, Baltimore, 1967.

Feinstein, A. R.: *Clinical Biostatistics*, C. V. Mosby, St. Louis, 1977.

Nunnally, J. C.: *Psychometric Theory*, McGraw-Hill, New York, 1967.

CHAPTER 6

SURVEY OF STRESS
DIAGNOSTIC PROCEDURES

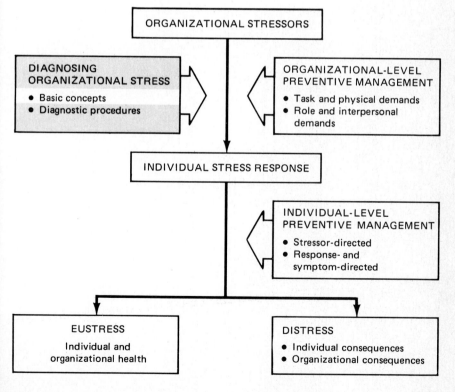

There are a wide variety of questionnaires, interview procedures, and other measurement devices which may be used in the stress diagnostic process. These various instruments are found in both professional and popular stress literature. They are intended to measure the sources, consequences, or potential cures for individual and organizational stress. Most of these measurement devices are ad hoc inventions of individual authors, designed as much to stimulate and challenge the subject of the measurement as to provide an objective or verifiable measure of stress. Nevertheless, for the investigator or student of organizational stress as well as for the manager interested in the health and performance of his organization, there are several assessment devices which warrant consideration.

TABLE 6.1
SELECTED STRESS-RELATED
DIAGNOSTIC INSTRUMENTS

Organizational stressors

- Objective organizational measures of stress
- Stress Diagnostic Survey
- Michigan Stress Assessment
- Quality of Employment Survey
- Adams' Stress Evaluation
- Stressors Checklist
- Organizational Diagnosis
- The Management Audit
- Life Events Scale
- The Hassles and Uplifts Scales
- Other measures related to organizational stress

Individual distress

- Physiological measures
- Behavioral measures
- Cornell Medical Index
- Daily Log of Stress-Related Symptoms
- SCL-90-R
- Maslach Burnout Inventory
- State-Trait Anxiety Inventory
- Alcoholic Stages Index
- Other measures related to individual distress

Individual modifiers of the stress response

- Type A behavior pattern
- Social support
- Workaholic Questionnaire
- Coping Mechanisms Assessment
- Locus of Control
- Other measures

Available stress diagnostic procedures fall into at least three basic categories, depending upon their primary focus: (1) measures of organizational stressors, (2) measures of individual distress, and (3) measures of individual modifiers of the stress response. This chapter will discuss selected instruments in each of these three areas and consider the advantages and disadvantages of individualized or customized measurement devices. Table 6.1 lists the major stress-related diagnostic procedures which will be reviewed.

MEASURES OF ORGANIZATIONAL STRESSORS

When a specific organizational stress causes a major disruption, the source of the stress is usually apparent. In most instances, however, the impact of stressors is less obvious. There is a need, therefore, to systematically diagnose the sources and impact of organizational stress. There are objective measures which can be used, but these tend to be rather nonspecific in identifying organizational stressors. Questionnaires and interviews provide more specific information about the sources of stress. Some of the objective measures of stress and selected stress questionnaires and interview formats are reviewed in the following pages.

While it is possible to examine work-related stress and non-work-related stress separately, it is not really possible to fully understand overall stress level or experience without considering the two in combination. Therefore, this section also includes a consideration of relevant instruments which incorporate both aspects of an individual's life. It would be a mistake to ignore either work-related or non-work-related factors in diagnosing an individual's stress level.

Objective Organizational Measures of Stress

The objective measures which are available to evaluate organizational stress are to a large extent the measures used to assess organizational health and effectiveness. Such measures include the following:

- Tardiness rate
- Absenteeism rate
- Grievances filed
- Rate and severity of work-related accidents
- Interdepartmental employee transfer rate
- Employee turnover rate
- Performance of specific cost/profit centers in standard terms (time per unit of service, unit produced per time period, percent utilization of raw materials, etc.)

- Sales volume and revenue, change in volume and revenue
- Return on equity

These and similar measures are appealing because they are objective and quantifiable. Unfortunately, they are rather nonspecific with regard to organizational stress. Each of the measures can be influenced by many factors other than stress. Even when a high absentee rate is attributable to organizational stress, knowing the absentee rate does not in itself indicate the source of the stress.

Objective measures can be useful in several specific instances. Comparison of tardiness, absenteeism, or turnover rates among subgroups within the organization may serve to identify high-risk groups worthy of further scrutiny. After these groups are identified, more specific stress questionnaires or interviews can be used to determine the reasons for poor performance. Comparing performance measures over time may help to alert management to potential difficulties. A fall in productivity or a rise in tardiness, absenteeism, or turnover may be an indicator of growing stress levels. What is important to note in this regard is the extent and degree of *change* that occurs.

When preventive management procedures or other stress reduction activities are undertaken, the impact of the interventions can be followed by some of the objective measures. If such measures are used to assess the impact of management interventions, it is important to carefully select those measures which are intended to be affected by the intervention.

While the objective organizational measures of stress may indicate the existence of organizational stress, they will not give much data or detail about the specific source of the stress. However, they provide an independent means for comparing groups within the organization and for assessing the impact of management interventions.

Stress Diagnostic Survey

One of the most comprehensive questionnaire-type measures of organizational stress is the Stress Diagnostic Survey (SDS) developed by Ivancevich and Matteson at the University of Houston. The questionnaire is designed to help individual employees identify specific areas of high stress at work. In addition to the work version of the SDS, there is a nonwork version which profiles individuals' personal stressors. It has also been used to profile worker subgroups and as a research tool to assess the impact of specific management interventions on individual perceptions of stress.

The work version of the SDS consists of eighty brief statements of conditions, each of which the respondent is supposed to rate on a 7-point

TABLE 6.2
SAMPLE ITEMS FROM THE STRESS DIAGNOSTIC SURVEY

My job duties and work objectives are unclear to me.
I work on unnecessary tasks or projects.
I have to take work home in the evenings or on weekends to stay caught up.
I lack the proper opportunities to advance in this organization.
I am held accountable for the development of other employees.
People do not understand the mission and goals of the organization.
I am not able to control the activities in my work area.
My supervisor does not go to bat for me with the bosses.
I am not a part of a close-knit work group.
My work group does not support my personal goals.

Source: J. M. Ivancevich and M. T. Matteson, *Stress and Work*, Scott, Foresman, Glenview, Ill., 1980, pp. 118 and 140. Copyright © 1980 Scott, Foresman and Company. Used with permission.

scale according to whether the condition is never, sometimes, or always a source of stress. Several sample statements are shown in Table 6.2. The responses to these questions are totaled in such a way as to yield separate scores for fifteen categories of work stressors. These scores are then plotted to yield a stress profile. The scales in the work version of the SDS were determined by factor analysis with data from over 2,000 business executives, hospital nursing personnel, graduate management and engineering students, and medical technologists. The coefficient alphas for the fifteen categories were 0.58 to 0.87 for the organizational measures and 0.64 to 0.95 for the job stressors, indicating a good degree of internal consistency.

Two sample work stress profiles are shown in Figures 6.1 and 6.2. The stress profile in Figure 6.1 is that of a 43-year-old female administrative secretary. In addition, she is a heart patient. Her primary source of work stress is lack of career progress. The underutilization of her abilities and the lack of rewards for her performance are also stressful and consistent with her primary work stress. The stress profile in Figure 6.2 is that of a 56-year-old male head-of-staff in a church. He also is a heart patient. His primary sources of work stress are found in the overload of work he undertakes, which then causes him some notable stress from a sense of time pressure. Both profiles illustrate how the work version of the SDS can be used in diagnosing sources of stress.

The nonwork version of the SDS is not as well-developed psychometrically. It still may be a useful global guide to stress points in the individual's nonwork life. It assesses stress levels in nine different areas: marital and personal relationships, children, extended family, neighborhood, criminal and legal matters, educational activities, financial matters, vacations, and health matters. An 11-point scaling procedure is used.

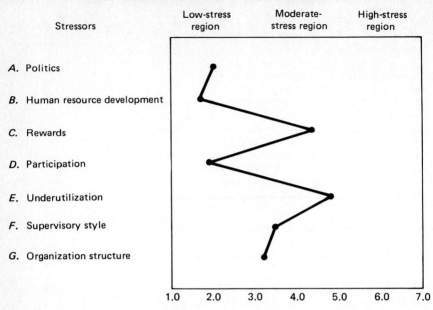

HER VIEW OF ORGANIZATIONAL STRESSORS

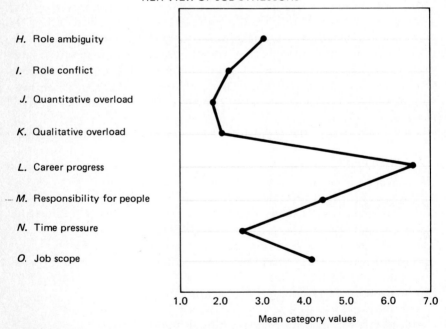

HER VIEW OF JOB STRESSORS

Mean category values

FIGURE 6.1
Work stress profile for a 43-year-old female administrative secretary and heart patient. [Source: *J. C. Quick, J. D. Quick, and J. A. Richardson*, Stress Diagnostic Survey Results, *University of Texas at Arlington, Arlington, Texas, 1982. Used with permission from J. M. Ivancevich and M. T. Matteson.*]

HIS VIEW OF ORGANIZATIONAL STRESSORS

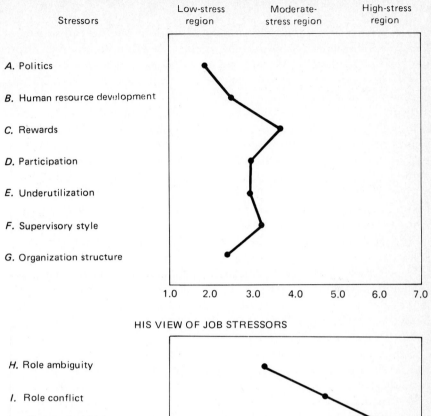

| Stressors | Low-stress region | Moderate-stress region | High-stress region |

A. Politics

B. Human resource development

C. Rewards

D. Participation

E. Underutilization

F. Supervisory style

G. Organization structure

1.0　2.0　3.0　4.0　5.0　6.0　7.0

HIS VIEW OF JOB STRESSORS

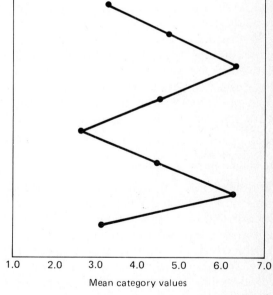

H. Role ambiguity

I. Role conflict

J. Quantitative overload

K. Qualitative overload

L. Career progress

M. Responsibility for people

N. Time pressure

O. Job scope

1.0　2.0　3.0　4.0　5.0　6.0　7.0

Mean category values

FIGURE 6.2
Work stress profile for a 56-year-old male head of staff in church and heart patient.
[Source: *J. C. Quick, J. D. Quick, and J. A. Richardson*, Stress Diagnostic Survey
Results, *University of Texas at Arlington, Arlington, Texas, 1982. Used with
permission from J. M. Ivancevich and M. T. Matteson.*]

While this version of the SDS may lead to determining the source of stress, it will not always indicate its nature. For example, the procedure can be used to identify marital stress for a male or female, but the specific nature or cause of the stress in that relationship is not identified without supplemental interviewing.

With regard to the work version of the SDS, Ivancevich and Matteson point out that "while there are no norms for this form, the ideal situation would be for all fifteen of the categories to be in the low-stress region below 2.0." They hasten to add that few people are likely to have achieved such a low-stress state. The mean scores for the studies listed above ranged from 2.0 to 4.0 in most cases. Scores of 6.0 and above are taken by the originators to be indicators of areas in which specific stress reduction activities should be undertaken.

The SDS has proven to be a fairly reliable test instrument and its relative brevity makes it easy to administer. The construct validity of the SDS is based upon factor analysis. Testing among health care and managerial personnel, technicians, and graduate business students over a period of years has yielded sufficient data to conduct a series of factor-analytic refinements of the scales in the SDS. In addition, the SDS has face validity regarding both items and scales.

Aside from its simplicity, the major advantage of the work version of the SDS is that it identifies *specific areas* of high stress, rather than simply providing a global measure of the *amount* of stress. To the extent that the SDS provides a true representation of what is occurring for individuals at work, it can serve as a useful tool in identifying priority areas for preventive interventions. In considering the applicability of the SDS to various settings, it should be recognized that it is suited more for use with managerial employees in large organizations than for use in small businesses and professional organizations.

Michigan Stress Assessment

Another approach to measuring organizational stress is found in the work of French and Kahn (1962). The work arose out of an interest in identifying the factors in the industrial environment which play a role in coronary artery disease. Self-report questionnaires were used to provide a subjective index of environmental stress. The principal variables were role ambiguity, work load, role conflict, responsibility for persons, responsibility for things, participation, and relations with work group. Respondents rated each item on the questionnaire with a 5-point scale according to whether the item constituted a "very little" or "very great" amount of stress.

In addition to the self-report questionnaires, French and Kahn also included a tally sheet for obtaining objective work-load data. The tally sheet was filled out by another individual, for example, the respondent's secretary. The tally sheet covered such items as phone calls, office visits, meetings, and other daily activities.

The construct validity for each of the scales in the questionnaire was determined by factor analysis and judged to be acceptable. Studies by the originators using the questionnaire report reliabilities of roughly 0.70 to 0.85.

Like the SDS, external validation of these scales has been limited, but they have been used extensively by Caplan (1971), Sales (1969) and other behavioral scientists. The most important difference between the Michigan measure and the SDS is in the subcategories of organizational stress which are identified by the scales. The SDS provides a slightly more detailed breakdown of stress areas, but the Michigan measures have been more widely used.

Quality of Employment Survey

Researchers from the National Institute of Occupational Safety and Health (NIOSH) and the Institute for Social Research at the University of Michigan have developed and tested a series of questions which they have used to assess job-related stress in personal interviews (Quinn and Shepard, 1974; Margolis et al., 1974). Separate scores are obtained for six individual indexes of job stress, and an overall job-stress score is obtained from these indexes. The six indexes are role ambiguity, underutilization, overload, resource inadequacy, insecurity, and nonparticipation.

Role ambiguity is a measure of the extent to which work objectives or the expectations of the worker are unclear. *Underutilization* questions assess whether individual capabilities are untapped because there is too little to do or the work tasks are too easy. The *overload* index is just the reverse, a measure of the extent to which there is too much work or work tasks that are too difficult. *Resource inadequacy* questions determine whether there are adequate resources and information to do the job. *Insecurity* refers to job uncertainty. Will there be continued employment? Finally, the *nonparticipation* index considers whether there is a lack of "say" in the organization's decisions, particularly those decisions that affect one's job.

Compared to the SDS, the stress-related portion of the Quality of Employment Survey is somewhat less convenient to use because it is in an interview format. In addition, the individual stress indexes are less specific than the fifteen categories found in the SDS. Nevertheless, the Quality of Employment Survey does provide a reliable overall measure of organization stress as perceived by the individual.

Adams's Stress Evaluation

In his questionnaire measure, Adams makes an important distinction between chronic stress and episodic stress as well as between work-related and non-work-related stress. These two distinctions taken in combination result in four types of stress, as indicated in Figure 6.3. Adams uses thirty items paralleling the Holmes and Rahe (1967) procedures to assess episodic, work-related stress (Type I). He uses forty items in a similar format to assess episodic non-work-related stress (Type II). He uses twenty-five items responded to on a 5-point Likert scale to assess chronic, work-related stress (Type III). Finally, he uses sixteen items and a similar 5-point Likert scale to assess chronic, non-work-related stress (Type IV). This evaluation has the advantage of building upon the importance of both frequency and intensity of stressor in determining its overall impact upon an individual.

There are no reliability or validity data reported by Adams regarding any of the four types of stress included in the evaluation. However, on the basis of data from 570 managers, administrators, and educators, Adams has developed scores for each of the four categories which relate to percentile rankings in increments of 10. He has also examined the relationship between work-related stress, both episodic and chronic, and various stress-related disorders, such as hypertension, mentioned in Chapter 3. He has found that as the stress evaluation scores increase, there is a significant increase in the number of health-related disorders (Adams, 1978).

Stressors Checklist

Yet another questionnaire measure of organizational stress is McLean's (1979) Stressors Checklist. The checklist consists of twelve items representing common situations or problems which the respondent rates on a 5-point scale as to whether they are never, seldom, sometimes, usually, or always a concern or obstacle to doing one's job.

The results of the questionnaire provide scores for four stress-related areas: conflict and uncertainty, job pressure, job scope, and rapport with management. The scores in each area can range between 3 and 15; the author suggests that scores of 9 or above indicate that "the area may be presenting a problem for you warranting attention." The total score can range from 12 to 60, and a score of 36 or more is felt to suggest a "more than desirable" amount of stress in the work environment.

The checklist is easily administered and includes several areas of general relevance. Lack of published data on the reliability and validity of the list makes any objective interpretation difficult. Therefore, it should be considered a tool for raising employee awareness of stress, rather than a diagnostic instrument for identifying areas requiring intervention.

SOURCE OF STRESS

	Work-related	Non-work-related
Episodic	Type I (e.g., reorganization)	Type II (e.g., marital crisis)
Chronic	Type III (e.g., too much work)	Type IV (e.g., concern over economy)

DURATION OF STRESS

FIGURE 6.3
Adams's stress evaluation. [Source: *John D. Adams*, Understanding and Managing Stress: A Workbook in Changing Life Styles, *University Associates, San Diego, Calif., 1980, p. 15. Used with permission.*]

Organizational Diagnosis

There are many objective measures of organizational effectiveness, such as profit margins and productivity indexes, and there are several stress questionnaires such as those listed above. But methods for conducting a comprehensive assessment of organizational effectiveness are limited. In his 1972 publication, *Organizational Diagnosis*, Harry Levinson and his coauthors provide a systematic approach to the study and assessment of organizational performance. Drawing on psychoanalytic theory, sociology, and systems theory, they describe an orderly diagnostic method aimed at understanding the operation of an organization and ascertaining areas of dysfunction. The data obtained through the diagnostic process serves as the basis for intervention and organizational change efforts. *Organizational Diagnosis* is aimed primarily at individuals involved in organizational consultation and executives interested in assessing their own managerial efforts.

The four major areas in the diagnostic process and their subheadings are:

1 Genetic data
  a Identifying information (organization name, location, etc.)
  b Historical data (reason for the study, organization problems, circumstances of the study, etc.)
2 Description and analysis of current organization as a whole
  a Structural data (table of organization, personnel, etc.)
  b Process data (communication systems, previous reports, etc.)
3 Interpretive data
  a Current organizational functioning (organizational knowledge, emotional atmosphere, organizational action)

   b Attitudes and relationships (attachments, relations to things and ideas, authority)
4 Analysis and conclusions
   a Organizational integrative patterns (appraisal of the organization in terms of assets and impairments, relationship of the organization with the environment)
   b Summary and recommendations (present status, prognostic conclusions, recommendations)

Organizational Diagnosis uses a wide range of case studies and published accounts to illustrate the approach to gathering and using the information listed in each of these sections.

   In addition, the book includes a detailed Organization and Job Attitude Inventory. Although "stress diagnosis" is not specifically identified as an area of investigation, numerous stress-related items are included in the questionnaire. Rather than providing a quantitative measure of organizational well-being and organizational stress, *Organizational Diagnosis* provides a method for assessing these items in the context of a comprehensive study of the organization.

The Management Audit

Cooper and Marshall (1978) have proposed a general framework within which to diagnose the stress of managerial work. They have not developed nor proposed quantitative nor qualitative instrumentation to accompany their audit. Theirs is a useful conceptual framework from which some may work. They suggest that there are seven relevant aspects of a manager and/or his work which contribute to stress and strain. (The seventh aspect is Type A behavior pattern, which they have treated as a moderator of the stress-strain relationship, just as this book has. The Type A behavior pattern is not relevant to this section of the chapter.)

   The six sources of managerial stress which Cooper and Marshall propose that we examine are (1) the job of management, (2) interpersonal relations at work, (3) role in the organization, (4) organizational structure and climate, (5) career prospects, (6) home and work interface. While they do not propose specific measurement devices for conducting a diagnosis, this conceptual framework does lend itself to the design of interview protocols which investigate each of these six sources of stress.

   The audit has primarily two limitations. First, no specific measurement device is proposed by the authors; therefore, the diagnostician is left even more on his own than in the case of Levinson's organizational-diagnosis approach. Second, this diagnostic approach is limited to managerial work and as such has very limited applicability in other occupational areas.

Life Events Scale

Probably the most widely used research instrument for studying the long-term effects of stress is the Life Events Scale (LES) also known as the Social Readjustment Rating Scale (SRRS), the Schedule of Recent Experiences (SRE), the Social Readjustment Rating Questionnaire (SRRQ), or the Schedule of Recent Life Events (SRLE). The earliest version of the scale was developed at the University of Washington in the late 1950s (Hawkins et al., 1957). For several years the relative degrees of life change inherent in the various life events were not taken into consideration, but in 1964 scaling studies were carried out to establish a method for weighing the different life changes (Holmes and Rahe, 1967). The numbers in parentheses after each of the scale items in Table 6.3 represent the number of life change units (LCU) for each item. These units were established by assigning an arbitrary value to marriage and then asking individuals to rate the other forty-two items in comparison to marriage.

The LES has been tested in a wide variety of settings and has been shown to have a high degree of reliability and validity. LCU ratings of the different life events have been found to follow the same basic pattern among individuals of different ages and among white Americans, black Americans, Mexican Americans, Danes, Swedes, and the Japanese (Rahe, 1972; Coleman, 1973).

Much of the recent research relating life stresses to illness has used the LES as the primary measure of stress. Early research with the scale demonstrated that 80 percent of people with scores over 300 and 53 percent of the people with scores between 150 and 300 suffered a significant health impairment during the period following the stressful events. People with scores under 150 had a low incidence of major health problems. Significant medical problems whose onset has been associated with significant increases in LES scores include sudden death, myocardial infarction, acute respiratory illnesses, and a variety of musculoskeletal problems (Rahe, 1972).

Although the LES is the most widely tested and perhaps the most extensively used stress scale, its application to the assessment of organizational stress is limited by the fact that only seven of the forty-three items are work-related. In the work area, as in other areas of the LES, a wide range of events which may be significant stressors to many individuals are omitted. The LES may be a useful tool to assess the general level of stress among a group of individuals and to predict the likelihood

TABLE 6.3

LIFE EVENTS SCALE

Below is a list of events that you may have experienced during the past year. In the left-hand column, please check off those events that did occur. In the right-hand column, please rate how stressful you perceived each event to have been, on a scale of 1 to 5. (Scale values: 1—not at all stressful; 2—slightly stressful; 3—moderately stressful; 4—somewhat stressful; 5—extremely stressful)

Personal

___	Personal injury or illness (53)	___
___	Outstanding personal achievement (28)	___
___	Revision of personal habits (24)	___
___	Change in recreation (19)	___
___	Change in church activities (19)	___
___	Change in sleeping habits (15)	___
___	Change in eating habits (15)	___
___	Vacation (13)	___
___	Christmas (12)	___

Family

___	Death of a spouse (100)	___
___	Divorce (73)	___
___	Marital separation (65)	___
___	Death of a close family member (63)	___
___	Marriage (50)	___
___	Marital reconciliation (45)	___
___	Change in health of a family member (44)	___
___	Pregnancy (40)	___
___	Gain of a new family member (39)	___
___	Change in number of arguments with spouse (35)	___
___	Son or daughter leaving home (29)	___
___	Trouble with in-laws (29)	___
___	Wife begins or stops work (26)	___
___	Change in number of family get-togethers (15)	___

Financial

___	Change in financial state (38)	___
___	Mortgage over $10,000 (31)	___
___	Foreclosure of mortgage or loan (30)	___
___	Mortgage or loan of less than $10,000 (17)	___

Social

___	Jail term (63)	___
___	Sexual difficulties (39)	___
___	Death of a close friend (37)	___
___	Begin or end school (26)	___
___	Change in living conditions (25)	___
___	Change in schools (20)	___
___	Change in residence (20)	___
___	Change in social activities (18)	___
___	Minor violations of the law (11)	___

Work

___	Fired at work (47)	___
___	Retirement (45)	___
___	Business readjustments (39)	___
___	Change to a different line of work (36)	___
___	Change in responsibilities at work (29)	___
___	Trouble with boss (23)	___
___	Changes in work hours or conditions (20)	___

Source: Adapted from T. H. Holmes and R. H. Rahe, "The Social Adjustment Rating Scale," Journal of Psychosomatic Research, vol. 11, 1967, pp. 213–218. Copyright © 1967, Pergamon Press. Ltd.

of future illness. It does not, however, provide specific diagnostic information to guide organizational or individual interventions.

The Hassles and Uplifts Scales

Kanner et al. (1981) report an alternative method for measuring stressful life events. As in the case of the standard life events methodology, their concern is with the prediction of psychological symptoms. Both scales developed by Kanner et al. (1981) identify work and nonwork sources of stress in an interspersed fashion. The Hassles Scale contains 117 items identified as possible irritants for an individual which may range from minor annoyances to fairly major pressures, problems, or difficulties. The Uplifts Scale contains 136 items identified as sources of good feelings, peace, satisfaction, or joy. Each scale contains the option for adding hassles or uplifts experienced by the individual which were not covered in the scale. The items in the Hassles Scale are rated on a 3-point severity scale and those in the Uplifts Scale are rated on a 3-point frequency scale.

In a ten-month study, Kanner et al. (1981) found the Hassles Scale to predict concurrent and subsequent psychological symptoms such as anxiety, depression, and psychoticism better than the LES. They also found the Uplifts Scale to be positively related to symptoms for women but not for men. The test-retest reliabilities were 0.79 for frequency and 0.60 for intensity of the Uplifts Scale. As in the case of the LES, the Hassles Scale and Uplifts Scale may be useful tools to assess the general level of stress, but they provide little diagnostic information to guide preventive interventions.

Other Measures Related to Organizational Stress

In addition to the diagnostic procedures already mentioned, there are numerous other questionnaires, structured interview formats, and measures of organizational stress reported by various authors, such as Albrecht (1979). The Job-Related Tension Scale (Kahn et al, 1964) and the Work Environment Scale (Billings and Moos, 1982) are specific additions which one may want to consider. Since some of these are ad hoc instruments without supporting data, they might best be used simply as thought-provokers, to stimulate workers to reflect on their own stress levels, and as qualitative assessments of stress.

Job satisfaction surveys can be a useful adjunct measure in analyzing organizational stress and its impact. Such measures include the Job Description Index (Smith, Kendall, and Hulin, 1969), the Context Survey (McLean, 1979), the Minnesota Satisfaction Questionnaire (Weiss et al., 1967), and other scales reviewed by Dunham and Smith (1979).

MEASURES OF INDIVIDUAL DISTRESS

Individual distress, like organizational stressors, can be measured with objective or subjective techniques. The discussion of individual consequences in Chapter 3 provides a good indication of the range of behavioral, psychological, and medical factors which might be evaluated in the measurement of individual distress. This chapter will focus on some of the standardized measures of individual distress. Unfortunately, these measures do not have the specificity and comprehensiveness that individual psychological testing or a complete medical examination offer. They are, however, more feasible measures in the context of most organizations.

Physiological Measures

There are literally dozens of physiological parameters which have been used in the study of stress. These range from obvious and easily obtained measures such as heart rate to obscure and poorly understood parameters such as newly discovered hormones and hormonelike substances. Table 6.4 lists some of the frequently used physiological measures. These measures raise several issues for the executive, manager, or organization consultant which are different from the issues faced with questionnaire or interview material.

First, there is the question of interpretation of physiological data. Under standard conditions the parameters in Table 6.4 can be reliably measured, but assessing their validity as stress measures is more difficult. The validity of medical tests is determined both by the *sensitivity* and *specificity* of the test. Sensitivity and specificity are complementary measures which together indicate how well a test identifies people with a given condition (sensitivity) and separates them from people without the condition (specificity).

As tests of organizational stress, physiological measures have potential problems with both specificity and sensitivity. For example, specificity of blood or urinary measures of catecholamines is limited by the fact that there are many factors other than stress which influence catecholamine assays. These factors include severe illness, use of one or more of a wide variety of prescription and nonprescription drugs, and ingestion of tea, coffee, or one of several other drinks or foods. Similarly, heart rate can be influenced by a wide range of factors in addition to stress. Other measures may be limited by their lack of sensitivity. Cholesterol levels, for example, tend to change slowly and, if used as an objective measure of stress, might remain relatively constant despite the occurrence of some highly stressful events.

A second factor to consider in the use of physiological measures is feasibility—both in terms of cost and convenience. Pulse and blood

TABLE 6.4
PHYSIOLOGICAL PARAMETERS USED IN STRESS ASSESSMENT

Physical measures

- Pulse
- Blood pressure
- Body weight
- Respiratory rate

Measures with specialized electronic equipment

- Muscle tension (facial muscles, neck muscles, and others)
- Galvanic skin response (GSR) (sweating or cutaneous conduction)
- Blood flow (measured by plethysmography)
- Electrocardiogram
- Electroencephalogram (brain waves)

Hormone levels*

- Catecholamines (adrenaline, noradrenaline, and metabolites)
- Cortisol, related hormones and metabolites
- ACTH
- Glucagon
- Other hormones (thyroid, angiotensin, growth hormone, renin, etc.)

Glucose, lipids, and related metabolites

- Glucose
- Cholesterol
- Triglycerides
- Lipoproteins
- Free fatty acids

*May be measured in blood or urine, depending on the hormone and assay involved.

pressure are easily determined. Company nurses can teach others to take pulses and blood pressures in a matter of minutes, and a minimum of equipment is required. Measurement of muscle tension or GSR is also quite easy to teach nonmedical personnel, but both require special, sometimes costly equipment. Serum hormonal measures not only require someone skilled at blood drawing (and the employee's consent to be stuck with a needle!), but can also be quite costly to process. Urinary measures of catecholamines, for example, will cost $30 to $40 per sample in commercial laboratories, and blood samples are usually more expensive.

The third issue of importance in evaluating physiological measures of stress is applicability. How will the results be used? For instance, demonstrating that cholesterol levels increase in accountants near tax time does not help to determine what it is about tax time that is stressful or what can be done about it. Similarly, demonstrating that urinary catecholamines rise during public speaking does not provide much information about the reasons for the rise or the impact of public speaking on the individual who is speaking.

Some physiological measures, however, do have direct application to stress management. Blood pressure control, for example, is a valid objective of stress management as well as a measure of stress. Equipment used to assess muscle tension can also be used in biofeedback techniques discussed in Chapter 10.

In summary, the major advantage of physiological measures is their objectivity. Disadvantages include the lack of sensitivity and specificity of many of the measures, the inconvenience of some measures, and the high individual cost which is sometimes involved. Physiological measures can be useful when objective measures are needed for preintervention and postintervention assessments to evaluate a stress reduction program or when objective measures are desired for comparing different occupational groups or corporate divisions. Finally, some physiological parameters represent therapeutic targets in themselves. Blood pressure and muscle tension are two such measures. Further information on the measures listed in Table 6.4 can be found in Selye (1976b) and Bridges (1974).

Behavioral Measures

The behavioral and psychological consequences of individual distress which were discussed in Chapter 3 suggest several possible measures of individual stress. Such measures might include the number of cigarettes smoked (possibly divided between on-the-job and at-home smoking), self-report of alcohol consumption and other drug use, recent weight change, sleeping pattern, and number and severity of accidents, both work-related and non-work-related. Some specific measures which have been used in general studies of health status include:

- Number of days per year lost from work
- Number of days per year of illness-related restricted activity
- Number of days per year of bed-bound disability

Although there are no standard values for absenteeism and disability, the National Center for Health Statistics (1978) provides some useful comparative disability information, presented by occupational category.

Cornell Medical Index

The Cornell Medical Index (CMI) is one of the oldest and most widely used standard questionnaires for medical symptoms. It was developed in the 1940s to provide a rapid, reliable means of obtaining a patient's medical history without expending the physician's time. It consists of 195 "yes" and "no" questions which take ten to thirty minutes to answer as a self-administered questionnaire. It can also be administered by an interviewer. There are four types of items (symptomatology, past history, family history, and behavior) which fall into the eighteen categories listed in Table 6.5.

The questionnaire was validated by comparison of hospital case records with the CMI responses (Brodman et al., 1951). There was 95 percent agreement between the case-records and the questionnaire. Furthermore, physicians were able to correctly infer the specific medical condition from the CMI answers in 87 percent of cases. As a general screening tool, however, the CMI has been found to be most predictive of impaired emotional health and general physical health. For example, affirmative response to thirty or more items and, in particular, to the "psychiatric subsections" (M-R) is highly correlated with emotional disturbances of various sorts.

The CMI is easy to administer, and it is readily scored. Specific symptom areas felt to be related to particular occupational risks can be scored and reported separately. There are no "standard values" for the

TABLE 6.5
CORNELL MEDICAL INDEX SECTIONS

Sections	Number of questions
A. Eyes and ears	9
B. Respiratory system	18
C. Cardiovascular system	13
D. Digestive system	23
E. Musculoskeletal system	8
F. Skin	7
G. Nervous system	18
H. Genito-urinary system	11
I. Fatigability	7
J. Illness frequency	9
K. Miscellaneous disease	15
L. Habits	6
M. Inadequacy	12
N. Depression	6
O. Anxiety	9
P. Sensibility	6
Q. Anger	9
R. Tension	9

Source: Adapted from Keve Brodman, A. J. Erdmann, Irving Lorge, and Harold G. Wolff, "The Cornell Medical Index," *Journal of the American Medical Association*, vol. 140, no. 6, 1949, p. 531. Copyright 1949, American Medical Association.

total affirmative scores on the CMI, but there are comparative data regarding total scores for specific subgroups (Abramson, 1966).

Self-report questionnaires should always be viewed with caution when trying to assess the incidence of specific medical conditions. However, the CMI is a reliable and comprehensive measure of assessing *perceived* impairment and for this reason may be a useful tool in assessing the impact of job stress. An alternative to the CMI is the General Health Questionnaire (GHQ), which is often used as a psychiatric screening instrument. It is a thirty-item, self-administered questionnaire whose results have been significantly correlated with independent clinical assessments (Goldberg, Richels, Downing, and Hesbacher, 1976). The results of the GHQ have also been found highly correlated with symptoms of anxiety and depression.

Daily Log of Stress-Related Symptoms

One of the most detailed and individualized instruments for assessing individual distress is the Daily Log of Stress-Related Symptoms (Manuso, 1980). The log is intended as a self-assessment tool for use in a comprehensive stress management workshop. It is designed to help participants identify symptoms which have causes other than stress, to discover their own unique patterns of stress response, and to establish goals for stress management.

A sample daily log is shown in Figure 6.4. Using the symptom checklist (Table 6.6), participants record the development of any symptoms by putting a dot on the log over the time of day at which the symptom began. The symptom is rated by its intensity (vertical axis of the log) and by the extent to which it interferes with ongoing activities (number in parentheses next to each dot). Interference with ongoing activities is rated from 1, no interference, to 100, total incapacity. The log also has space to record number of hours at work, percent of time interacting with others, use of medications, daily accomplishments, avoidance strategies, use of alcoholic beverages, use of relaxation and other stress-control techniques, and cigarette consumption. The daily log can be scored to establish one's relative stress level.

The log's degree of detail limits its use as a screening or group assessment instrument. However, it is the amount of detail and individual-ization inherent in the daily log which makes it a valuable tool in intensive stress management workshops.

FIGURE 6.4
Sample daily log. [Source: J. Manuso, Manage Your Stress, *Preworkshop Packet, CRM Multimedia Module*, McGraw-Hill Book Company, New York, 1980.]

DAILY LOG *William Shakespeare* Date *April 1, 1590*

If a workday, indicate (1) how many hours spent in relation to your job _9½_ ; and (2) estimate of % of on-the-job time spent interacting with others (meeting, supervising, consulting, etc.) _25%_.

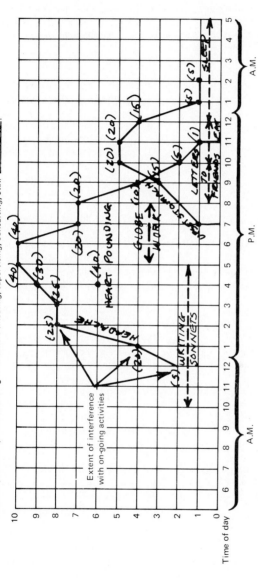

Extent of interference with on-going activities

Time of day

(40) (40)
(30)
(25) (25)
(40)
HEART POUNDING
(20)
(20) (20)
GLOBE (10)
WORK (15)
(5) (5)
JOB STRESS
(5)
(6)
LETTERS (1)
TO FRIENDS CUT
(5) (5)
SLEEP
HEADACHE
(5) WRITING SONNETS

A.M. 6 7 8 9 10 11 12 1 2 3 4 5 6 7 8 9 10 11 12 1 2 3 4 5 P.M. A.M.

Medications taken: Name	# &/or mg.	Time	Accomplishments of the day	Wanted to do but did not do	Avoidance strategies used & # times used	Alcoholic beverages: Name & number	No. times tense, slow relax & O.R. exercise performed	Times of day relaxation & O.R. exercise done	Cig's smoked
Valium	5 mg	9am	COMPLETED 2 SONNETS	INTERVIEW 2 ACTORS	DAYDREAM	WINE	4	8:30 A.M.	17
"	"	5PM	THEATRE SEATING	CLEAN HOUSE	NO PRODUCTIVE PURPOSE	3 GOBLETS		7:30 P.M.	
DONNATAL	1 TAB.	9PM	2 LETTERS						

TABLE 6.6
SYMPTOM CHECKLIST FOR USE WITH THE DAILY LOG

Instructions: Here are 58 symptoms or problems that people sometimes have. Please read each one carefully and decide how much the symptom bothered or distressed you during the past week and enter where appropriate on your Daily Log.

1 Headaches
2 Nervousness or shakiness inside
3 Being unable to get rid of bad thoughts or ideas
4 Faintness or dizziness
5 Loss of sexual interest or pleasure
6 Feeling critical of others
7 Bad dreams
8 Difficulty in speaking when you are excited
9 Trouble remembering things
10 Worried about sloppiness or carelessness
11 Feeling easily annoyed or irritated
12 Pains in the heart or chest
13 Itching
14 Feeling low in energy or slowed down
15 Thoughts of ending your life
16 Sweating
17 Trembling
18 Feeling confused
19 Poor appetite
20 Crying easily
21 Feeling shy or uneasy with the opposite sex
22 A feeling of being trapped or caught
23 Suddenly scared for no reason
24 Temper outbursts you could not control
25 Constipation
26 Blaming yourself for things
27 Pains in the lower part of your back
28 Feeling blocked or stymied in getting things done
29 Feeling lonely
30 Feeling blue
31 Worrying or stewing about things

32 Feeling no interest in things
33 Feeling fearful
34 Your feelings being easily hurt
35 Having to ask others what you should do
36 Feeling others do not understand you or are unsympathetic
37 Feeling that people are unfriendly or dislike you
38 Having to do things very slowly in order to be sure you were doing them right
39 Heart pounding or racing
40 Nausea or upset stomach
41 Feeling inferior to others
42 Soreness of your muscles
43 Loose bowel movements
44 Difficulty in falling asleep or staying asleep
45 Having to check and double-check what you do
46 Difficulty making decisions
47 Wanting to be alone
48 Trouble getting your breath
49 Hot or cold spells
50 Having to avoid certain things, places or activities because they frighten you
51 Your mind going blank
52 Numbness or tingling in parts of your body
53 A lump in your throat
54 Feeling hopeless about the future
55 Trouble concentrating
56 Weakness in parts of your body
57 Feeling tense or keyed up
58 Heavy feeling in your arms or legs

Source: J. Manuso, "Manage Your Stress," CRM Multimedia Module, McGraw-Hill Films, Del Mar, CA, 1980.

SCL-90-R

Derogatis (1981) has developed a ninety-item, multidimensional self-report symptom inventory which measures symptomatic psychological distress. The SCL-90-R results in three global measures of distress as well as nine primary symptom dimensions. These primary symptom dimensions are (1) somatization, (2) obsessive-compulsive, (3) interpersonal sensitivity, (4) depression, (5) anxiety, (6) hostility, (7) phobic anxiety, (8) paranoid ideation, and (9) psychoticism. Each item is rated on a 5-point scale as to the degree of distress which it causes. The internal consistency of the nine symptom dimensions ranges from 0.77 to 0.90 and the test-retest reliability of the dimensions ranges from 0.78 to 0.90. Derogatis has established some normative data for psychiatric outpatients, psychiatric inpatients, and nonpatient populations.

The SCL-90-R has been used as an evaluation tool in examining the effects of meditation and other relaxation techniques for the purpose of stress reduction. It has also been used with cancer patients to establish clinical levels of psychological symptoms.

Maslach Burnout Inventory

Maslach has developed a twenty-two-item measure of burnout which assesses three aspects of the burnout experience (Maslach and Jackson, 1981b). These three aspects of burnout are incorporated in the three subscales found in the overall measure. These subscales are emotional exhaustion, depersonalization, and lack of personal accomplishment. While burnout is a stress-related experience most commonly found in human-service professions, anyone under stress, including business executives, may be subject to it (H. Levinson, 1981). The Maslach measure of this syndrome normally takes less than thirty minutes to complete and is easily scored using the scoring key. It has been administered to a variety of occupational groups, including police officers, nurses, agency administrators, teachers, counselors, social workers, probation officers, mental health workers, physicians, psychologists, and psychiatrists (Maslach and Jackson, 1981a; 1981b).

With a sample of over 1,000 respondents from these various occupations, the internal consistency of the three subscales in the inventory was found to be very acceptable. Cronbach's coefficient alpha ranged from 0.71 for the lack-of-personal-accomplishment subscale to 0.90 for the emotional-exhaustion subscale. The reliability of the subscales was also examined in a limited sample ($n = 53$) by using a test-retest interval of two to four weeks. These results were not quite as encouraging, although all retest correlations were above 0.50 and significant at the 0.001 level. Preliminary convergent validity tests also suggest that the subscales are related to independent behavioral ratings of burnout, certain job characteristics (e.g., high client volume) expected to contribute to burnout, as well as other outcomes expected to be related to burnout, such as the impairment of various interpersonal relationships (Maslach and Jackson, 1981a). They have also discriminated burnout from job dissatisfaction in preliminary validation research.

State-Trait Anxiety Inventory

As pointed out in Chapter 1, stress and anxiety are not the same. Stress is often accompanied by the experience of tension and anxiety, although not always. However, it may be useful and/or appropriate to develop measures of anxiety in conducting a stress diagnosis individually or organizationally. Spielberger, Gorsuch, and Lushere (1970) have developed a self-administered questionnaire for this purpose. It was developed for normal individuals, although it has also been used in clinical settings and with emotionally disturbed individuals. It may be completed in less than ten minutes by normal individuals, although it may take up to twenty minutes for emotionally disturbed individuals to complete the instrument.

The instrument will assess both state (i.e., transitional) and trait (i.e., stable individual proneness for anxiety) anxiety. The reliability and validity data available on the state-trait anxiety scale suggest that it is a psychometrically sound measure. In addition, norms are established for some groups, such as students.

Alcoholic Stages Index

One of the most common manifestations of increasing stress is alcohol abuse and, eventually, alcoholism. The "wino" in the park is readily recognized as an alcoholic, but the early stages of alcoholism are sometimes difficult to recognize in the white-collar executive or the blue-collar factory worker. Several different questionnaires have been developed to help individuals to identify themselves as alcoholics or alcohol abusers.

One such questionnaire is reported by Mulford (1977) and is called The Alcoholic Stages Index. The index consists of twenty-seven items which compose four subscales. These subscales are (1) trouble due to drinking, (2) personal-effects drinking, (3) preoccupied drinking, and (4) uncontrolled drinking. The questionnaire may be best used as a device to provoke the respondents into recognizing their own alcohol abuse, although in the right setting it may be helpful in identifying individuals to whom the organization should recommend alcohol counseling.

Other Measures Related to Individual Distress

In addition to the above-mentioned diagnostic and assessment instruments, there are a myriad of psychological test batteries and published questionnaires covering a wide range of topics, including anxiety, depression, sleeping habits, sexual satisfaction or dysfunction, specific psychiatric conditions, and symptoms of specific diseases. In general, such techniques should be used under special circumstances and with the guidance of a physician, psychologist, or other professional familiar with the use and interpretation of the tests. These often provide an indication that an individual consequence of stress is impending or already operating. What is important is the rather early identification of the symptom before severe damage occurs. Sensitivity to employee privacy and confidentiality becomes increasingly important with some of the more personal, potentially threatening areas of inquiry. This factor must be considered in any significant stress diagnostic effort based on individual responses to questionnaires or interviews.

MEASURES OF INDIVIDUAL MODIFIERS OF THE STRESS RESPONSE

As pointed out in Chapter 3, there are several factors which act to determine the manner in which the generalized stress response will be manifested in a particular individual. In the case of the Achilles heel phenomenon, there are no good measures or indicators of the individual's differential responsiveness, or Achilles heel weakness. In the case of other characteristics, such as the Type A behavior pattern, there are measures available. This section will review a small number of the better known or more directly applicable measurement techniques. Possible uses for these devices in the diagnosis of organizational stress are considered in the final section of this chapter.

Type A Behavior Pattern

The original research on the Type A behavior pattern is based on assessment of Type A behavior using a *structured interview* (SI) developed by Rosenman, Friedman, and their colleagues (1964). Audiovisual recordings of the interviews are rated by judges who, despite the apparent subjectivity of the assessment, have an interrater reliability of 0.64 to 0.84. In an attempt to reduce the subjectivity and avoid the cost of the SI, self-report questionnaires have been developed for making the Type A/B classification. The Jenkins Activity Survey (JAS), developed by Jenkins in conjunction with Rosenman and Friedman (Jenkins, Rosenman and Friedman, 1967), has been the subject of the greatest amount of research and the most careful validation. A review of the studies using the fifty-four-item JAS indicates that it is a strong predictor of coronary artery disease, but not as strong as the SI (Chesney and Rosenman, 1980). Sample items from the JAS* are as follows:

- Frequently hurries speaker to the point
- Tends to get irritated easily
- Frequently brings work home at night
- Gives much more effort than the average worker

Attempts to develop alternative, usually briefer, Type A scales include the ten-item Framingham Type A Scale (FTAS) (Haynes et al., 1978), a Type A scale developed by Vickers and Sales for use by the University of Michigan's Institute for Social Research in occupational stress research (Caplan et al., 1975), and the twelve-item Behavior Activity Profile (Ivancevich and Matteson, 1980). Caution should be used in selecting these briefer questionnaires, since there is little predictive data to confirm their ability to reliably identify individuals at risk for coronary artery disease (Chesney and Rosenman, 1980).

Currently, only the SI rated by trained judges, the JAS, and to a lesser extent the FTAS should be considered reliable measures of Type A behavior patterns. Data derived from the use of other scales should be considered tentative in the absence of further cross-validation studies.

Social Support

Another indicator of an individual's vulnerability is found in examining or profiling his social support network. House has conducted several studies in this area using a brief questionnaire as the primary measure of social support. The three central questions asked (House and Wells, 1978) were:

1 How much can each of the following people be relied on when *things get tough at work*? (immediate supervisor or boss; other people at work; spouse; friends and relatives)

2 How much is each of the following people *willing to listen to* your *work-related problems*? (immediate supervisor or boss; other people at work; spouse; friends and relatives)

3 How much is each of the following people *helpful to you in getting your job done*? (immediate supervisor; other people at work)

For each potential support person mentioned, respondents were asked to indicate whether the individual was a source of support by answering, "not at all, a little, somewhat, or very much." In addition, respondents were asked about their supervisors' competence, concern, and tendency to give praise.

This questionnaire and minor modifications of it have been used in several large studies of organizational stress and social support. It has clear face validity and is easy to administer. A copy of the questionnaire appears in the monograph *Work Stress and Social Support* (House, 1981, p. 71).

Workaholic Questionnaire

The *workaholic* is described by one management consultant as, "the 'successful' executive or manager who works sixty to seventy hours a week, rises high in the organization, and makes a handsome salary while his marriage falls apart, his health declines, he smokes and drinks too heavily, and lives only for his work. . . ." (Albrecht, 1979, p. 217).

The idea that overinvestment in work is a form of addiction with attendant negative health consequences is gaining increasing acceptance. McLean has proposed a questionnaire (Table 6.7) designed to help individuals to recognize whether or not they are becoming workaholics. Although McLean provides an "answer key," the point at which investment in work becomes overinvestment is not known. Thus, as with several of the other stress-related questionnaires, the Workaholic Questionnaire should be considered a qualitative self-assessment tool, rather than a definitive assessment instrument.

Coping Mechanisms Assessment

McLean (1976) has also developed a coping checklist designed to provide individuals with a very rough and admittedly superficial assessment of the way in which they are coping with their job. The checklist consists of twenty statements to which the respondent expresses varying degrees of agreement or disagreement on a 5-point scale. The questionnaire is totalled according to five subcategories which assess the extent to which the individual accepts his or her own strengths and weaknesses; the degree to which the person has developed interests outside the workplace to balance the investment in work; the individual's ability to respond to stress with a variety of actions, depending on the nature of the situation, rather than to also respond with, for example, anger or depression; the person's flexibility in accepting or at least tolerating other people's values; and finally, the individual's assessment of how

TABLE 6.7
WORKAHOLIC QUESTIONNAIRE

1 Do you seem to communicate better with your secretary (co-workers) than with your spouse (or best friend)?
2 Are you always punctual for appointments?
3 Are you better able to relax on Saturdays than on Sunday afternoons?
4 Are you more comfortable when you are productive than idle?
5 Do you carefully organize your hobbies?
6 Are you usually much annoyed when your spouse (or friend) keeps you waiting?
7 When you play golf is it mainly with business associates? (or: are most recreational activities with work associates?)
8 Does your spouse (or friend) think of you as an easygoing person?
9 If you play tennis do you occasionally see (or want to see) your boss's face on the ball before a smash?
10 Do you tend to substitute your work for interpersonal contacts; that is, is work sometimes a way of avoiding close relationships?
11 Even under pressure, do you usually take the extra time to make sure you have all the facts before making a decision?
12 Do you usually plan every step of the itinerary of a trip in advance and tend to become uncomfortable if plans go awry?
13 Do you enjoy small talk at a reception or cocktail party?
14 Are most of your friends in the same line of work?
15 Do you take work to bed with you when you are home sick?
16 Is most of your reading work related?
17 Do you work late more frequently than your peers?
18 Do you talk "shop" over cocktails on social occasions?
19 Do you wake up in the night worrying about business problems?
20 Do your dreams tend to center on work-related conflicts?
21 Do you play as hard as you work?
22 Do you tend to become restless on vacation?
23 If you are a homemaker, do you tend to prepare most of the food for the week on Sunday?

(1) Yes	(2) Yes	(3) Yes	(4) Yes	(5) Yes	(6) Yes	(7) Yes
(8) No	(9) Yes	(10) Yes	(11) Yes	(12) Yes	(13) No	(14) Yes
(15) Yes	(16) Yes	(17) Yes	(18) Yes	(19) Yes	(20) Yes	(21) Yes
(22) Yes	(23) Yes					

active and productive he or she is at work as well as at home and in the community.

The coping checklist is strictly a self-assessment tool. McLean provides some guidelines for evaluating one's score on the checklist, but there are no "norms" or standard values. Thus, it is useful primarily for stimulating employees' own thinking about stress management. As such, it may be useful in stress management workshops and other organized interventions aimed at helping employees to understand and strengthen their own coping mechansisms.

A related scale which measures personal coping resources is the Uplifts Scale, a 136-item scale which measures sources of peace, satisfaction, or joy (Kanner et al., 1981). It too may be useful as a tool in organization stress management programs.

Locus of Control

Locus of control is a personality characteristic which may modify an individual's experience of stress as well as response to it. This characteristic is concerned with the degree to which individuals perceive that they have control over events occurring in their lives. An individual with an *external* locus of control perceives that circumstances, bad or good luck, other people, or events are responsible for what occurs in life. An individual with an *internal* locus of control perceives that individuals are the masters of their own destinies and responsible for their own fortunes or misfortunes.

Rotter (1966, and reprinted in Rotter, Chance, and Phares, 1972) has developed a twenty-nine-item, forced-choice measure of the tendency toward an internal or external locus of control. The twenty-nine-item scale includes six filler items intended to disguise the aim of the test and twenty-three items used to determine an individual's locus of control. His measure has demonstrated internal consistency, test-retest reliability, as well as discriminant validity.

Other Measures

Several other individual characteristics may influence the response to stress. For some of these characteristics there are readily available and easily administered assessment scales. Among these characteristics are personal rigidity (Wesley, 1953), tolerance for ambiguity (Lyons, 1971), self-esteem (for example, Kasl and Cobb, 1970; House, 1972), and need for achievement (McClelland, 1961). The Minnesota Multiphasic Personality Inventory (MMPI) is the broadest, most widely used, and best-validated assessment of psychological parameters. It has been used in a variety of stress-related studies, but its breadth limits its routine use in the stress diagnostic process.

SUMMARY

There has been too little practical application of many of the stress assessment measures to provide definitive recommendations regarding the selection of specific diagnostic instruments. It is possible, however, to offer a logical approach to using these instruments based on the purpose of the inquiry.

Chapter 5 mentioned several purposes which might be served by efforts to diagnose organizational stress. One purpose which stress assessment can serve is to determine the cause of current organizational or individual dysfunction. For this purpose a fairly specific and sensitive approach is needed. The Stress Diagnostic Survey would provide some useful insights into specific areas which are troubling employees. In addition, the more individualized approach described in Levinson's *Organizational Diagnosis* could be fruitful. Less specific measures such as productivity rates or global stress ratings would serve only to confirm the existence of a problem and would probably not contribute substantively to determining the cause of the problem.

Stress diagnostic procedures can also be used to develop an individual or organizational stress profile. This can be useful in assessing whether an individual or an organization is operating at an optimal level and whether there is potential risk for stress-induced dysfunction. For this purpose, any of the general organizational stress measures discussed above, and the Cornell Medical Index at the individual level, may prove useful. For individuals interested in their own risk factors, assessment of the Type A/B behavior pattern, coping mechanisms, social supports, and such things as alcohol consumption (Alcoholic Stages Index) can be beneficial.

Objective measures such as productivity, absenteeism rates, turnover, and possibly some of the individual physiological and behavioral measures may be most useful in assessing the impact of preventive interventions. Although these measures are not specific to stress effects, the impact of an intervention can be inferred from changes in these measures not explained by other changes in the organization.

With regard to organization stress research, any of the diagnostic instruments discussed in this chapter may be of interest, depending on the research question. The field of organization stress research has roots which go back for many decades, but the last few years have seen a rapid expansion of interest in the area. Efforts to validate existing measures and to develop new, reliable measures in specific areas of need will be important in the development of this field.

In considering the use of any of the measures described in this chapter, executives, managers, and organizational consultants should bear in mind that experience in organizational stress diagnosis with these techniques is limited in some cases. Many of these instruments which have been developed by medical, organizational, and psychological professionals should be used or applied with caution. Some of the scales are restricted to use by qualified professionals while others have fewer restrictions on their use. Therefore, the interpretation and extrapolation of the findings from these stress instruments should be tempered by these comments. Nevertheless, the techniques described here can serve a useful purpose in stimulating management and individual employees to systematically reflect upon their own stress and their own positive and negative responses to stress.

FURTHER READINGS

Buros, O.: *Eighth Mental Measurements Yearbook*, 2 vol., Gryphon Press, Highland Park, N.J., 1978.

Dunham, R. B., and F. J. Smith: *Organizational Surveys: An Internal Assessment of Organizational Health*, Scott, Foresman and Company, Glenview, Ill., 1979.

Ivancevich, J. M., and Matteson, M. T.: *Stress and Work: A Managerial Perspective*, Scott, Foresman and Company, Glenview, Ill., 1980.

Selye, H.: *Stress in Health and Disease*, Butterworths, Boston, 1976.

APPENDIX: Sources of Diagnostic Instruments

ORGANIZATIONAL STRESSORS

1 *Stress Diagnostic Survey* (work and nonwork versions)
   Source: Dr. John M. Ivancevich and Dr. Michael T. Matteson, College of Business Administration, University of Houston, Houston, Tex. 77004
   Cost: None applicable at this time
   Approximate completion time: Forty minutes for both

2 *Quality of Employment Survey*
   Source: Dr. Robert D. Caplan, Survey Research Center, Institute for Social Research, The University of Michigan, Ann Arbor, Mich.
   Cost: None applicable at this time
   Approximate completion time: Thirty minutes each

3 *Adams' Stress Evaluation*
   Source: University Associates, Inc., 8517 Production Avenue, P.O. Box 26240, San Diego, Calif. 92126
   Cost: $45.00 for a complete package with workbook
   Approximate completion time: Thirty minutes

4 *Stressors Checklist*
   Source: Dr. Alan McLean, *Work Stress*, Addison-Wesley Publishing Company, Reading, Mass.
   Cost: $6.95 per book
   Approximate completion time: Ten minutes

5 *Organizational Diagnosis*
   Source: Dr. Harry Levinson, *Organizational Diagnosis*, Harvard University Press, Cambridge, Mass.
   Cost: $10.00 per book
   Approximate completion time: Varies from hours to days

6 *The Management Audit*
Source: Dr. Cary L. Cooper and Dr. Judi Marshall, "An Audit of Managerial (Di)Stress," *Journal of Enterprise Management*, vol. 1 (1978), pp. 185–196.
Cost: None
Approximate completion time: Varies by individual and organization

7 *Life Events Scale*
Source: T. H. Holmes and R. H. Rahe, "The Social Readjustment Rating Scale," *Journal of Psychosomatic Research*, vol. 11, 1967, pp. 213–218.
Cost: None
Approximate completion time: Fifteen minutes

8 *The Hassles and Uplifts Scales*
Source: A. D. Kanner, J. C. Koyne, C. Schaefer, and R. S. Lazarus, "Comparison of Two Modes of Stress Measurement: Daily Hassles and Uplifts versus Major Life Events," *Journal of Behavioral Medicine*, vol. 4, 1982, pp. 25–36.
Cost: None
Approximate completion time: Fifteen minutes each

INDIVIDUAL DISTRESS MEASURES

1 *Cornell Medical Index*
Source: Cornell University Medical College, 1300 York Avenue, Box 88, New York, N.Y. 10021
Cost: $4.00 per fifty questionnaires, $1.50 per fifty diagnostic sheets
Approximate completion time: Thirty minutes

2 *General Health Questionnaire*
Source: Institute of Psychiatry, DeCrespigny Park, Denmark Hill, London, S.E.5, *ENGLAND*
Cost: £3.50 per manual, 2p per long form, 4p per short form
Approximate completion time: Ten minutes for long form, five minutes for short form

3 *Daily Log of Stress-Related Symptoms (in Managing Your Stress)*
Source: CRM McGraw-Hill, 110 15th Street, Del Mar, Calif. 92014
Cost: $6.95 per workbook
Approximate completiom time: Twenty minutes each time

4 *SCL-90-R*
Source: Leonard R. Derogatis, Ph.D., 1228 Wine Spring Lane, Baltimore, Md. 21204
Cost: $25.00 per hundred questionnaires, $10.00 per manual, $15.00 per hundred score profiles
Approximate completion time: Thirty minutes

5 *Maslach Burnout Inventory*
  Source: Consulting Psychologists Press, 577 College Avenue, Palo Alto, Calif.
       94306
  Cost: $4.25 for twenty-five booklets, $4.00 for twenty-five demographic data
       sheets, $1.25 for a scoring key, $5.50 for a manual, $7.00 for a specimen set
  Approximate completion time: Twenty to thirty minutes

6 *State-Trait Anxiety Inventory*
  Source: Consulting Psychologists Press, 577 College Avenue, Palo Alto, Calif.
       94306
  Cost: $2.25 for twenty-five (quantity discounts available), $.75 for the scoring
       key, $6.00 for the manual
  Approximate completion time: Ten minutes

7 *Alcoholics Stages Index*
  Source: Harold A. Mulford, "Stages in the Alcoholic Process," *Journal of
       Studies in Alcohol*, vol. 38, no. 3, 1977, p. 565
  Cost: None
  Approximate completion time: Ten minutes

INDIVIDUAL MODIFIERS OF DISTRESS

1 *Jenkins Activity Survey (Type A Behavior)*
  Source: Psychological Corporation, 575 3rd Avenue, New York, N.Y. 10017
  Cost: $13.75 for twenty-five questionnaires, $4.00 for the manual, $4.50 for a
       specimen set
  Approximate completion time: Fifteen minutes

2 *Workaholic Questionnaire* and *Coping Mechanisms Assessment*
  Source: Dr. Alan McLean, *Work Stress*, Addison-Wesley Publishing Company,
       Reading, Mass.
  Cost: $6.95 per book
  Approximate completion time: Fifteen minutes each

3 *Locus of Control*
  Source: Julian B. Rotter, "Generalized Expectancies for Internal Versus
       External Control of Reinforcement," *Psychological Monographs*, vol.
       80, no. 1 (Whole No. 609), 1966
  Cost: None
  Approximate completion time: Fifteen minutes

CHAPTER 7

PREVENTIVE MANAGEMENT: PRINCIPLES AND METHODS

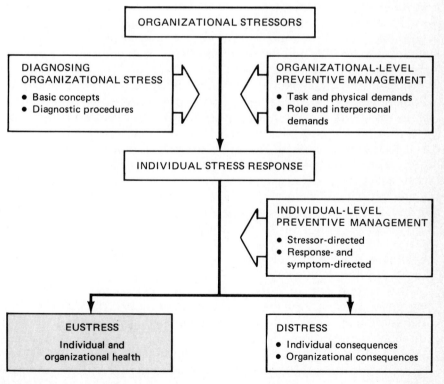

Chapters 1 through 6 discussed sources of stress in organizations, the stress response, individual and organizational consequences of stress, and methods of diagnosing stress and measuring the stress response. Chapters 7 through 13 will consider specific methods and implementation strategies for minimizing distress and promoting health and well-being in both the individual and the organization. This chapter will introduce the principles and methods of preventive management which serve as the basis for Chapters 8 through 12.

PREVENTIVE MANAGEMENT DEFINED

In Chapter 1 preventive management was defined in the following way:

> *Preventive management* is an organizational philosophy and set of principles which employs specific methods for promoting individual and organizational health while preventing individual and organizational distress.

Thus preventive management consists of a set of basic notions about how an organization should operate and what sort of an attitude management should take toward the demands of organizational life. These notions are ones that may be implemented by managers and executives in any organization. The actual implementation strategy and specific techniques should be suited to a particular organization, but the basic thrust is the same for all organizations.

The specific implementation strategy must consider both organizational-level and individual-level methods of preventive management. Organizational-level methods aim at altering the task, role, physical, and interpersonal stressors described in Chapter 2. Individual-level methods aim at altering the individual's ability to manage various demands and the individual's response to these demands. Preventive management follows a proactive model of organizational change, as was noted in Chapter 1. Under this model, an organization anticipates and averts most crises by shaping events rather than reacting to them.

The above definition of preventive management captures its two major aims. The first aim is to promote individual and organizational health. Achieving this objective requires efforts directed toward increasing productivity, adaptiveness, and flexibility.

The second aim of preventive management is to minimize and, wherever possible, avert individual and organizational distress. The three stages of prevention involving organizational or individual interventions directed at the stressor, the stress response, or the resulting symptoms of stress, will be described later in this chapter.

Before defining the stages of prevention and outlining specific prevention methods, it will be useful to consider some of the basic principles which guide our thinking about preventive management. These guiding principles form the central elements of our philosophy of preventive management and the basis of preventive action taken by management.

GUIDING PRINCIPLES

The notion of preventive management is, in part, a convenient conceptual framework for organizing and describing existing organizational and individual stress management methods. However, it also reflects the authors' philosophy about the way in which an organization should operate. This philosophy is based on five fundamental principles which motivate and guide the practice of preventive management. These principles are offered as guidelines for managers and executives interested in designing and implementing their own preventive management programs as well as for investigators interested in developing and evaluating stress management techniques. In considering this section the reader should bear in mind that these are indeed *principles*; they are not directives for implementation, nor are they necessarily verifiable facts.

Principle 1: Individual and Organizational Health Are Interdependent

The major conclusions which can be drawn from Chapters 2 through 4 are that organizational stressors can create substantial ill-health among employees and that distressed employees can create considerable organizational dysfunction. This seemingly obvious but too often overlooked interdependency is the essence of principle 1.

In addition to its financial assets, an organization has human assets which can be liquidated as surely as its capital assets can be. The well-being or ill health of human assets does not have an immediate effect upon organizational health. It takes time—sometimes as much as a year or two years or even five years—for the benefits of human resource development to have an effect upon the health of the organization. It may take an equivalent time period for the detrimental effects of the liquidation of human assets to be felt in the declining health of the organization.

Organizations cannot achieve a high level of productivity, adaptability, and flexibility without vital, healthy individuals. By the same token, individuals will have a great deal of difficulty maintaining their psychological and physical health in unproductive, rigid, unchanging organizations. This interdependency is expressed more formally in the concept of the *person-organization fit*. As Harrison and his associates (1978) have pointed out, this fit occurs in two ways. First, there is the degree to which *individual resources meet organizational goals and requirements*. Individual health and vitality contribute to organizational health. Second, there is the degree to which *organizational resources meet individual needs*. Thus organizational health and vitality contribute in turn to individual health. The individual-organizational fit represents an exchange relationship, both aspects of which are important.

Principle 2: Management Has a Responsibility for Individual and Organizational Health

The responsibility for the active pursuit of the development of an organization lies with management. It must take the initiative to pursue the entrepreneurial role; it must continually look for ways to improve the functioning of the organization (Mintzberg, 1973). Apathetic or passive leadership on the part of management is an irresponsible posture which will lead to organizational decay and decline.

But the corollary to the interdependency described in principle 1 is that management also has a responsibility for individual health and well-being. Although this interest can be based partly on altruism, it is rooted in enlightened self-interest: individuals who are highly distressed are not as effective as those who are not. Management's responsibilities include diagnosing organizational stress, selecting appropriate organizational-level and individual-level methods of preventive management, and implementing programs tailored to the particular needs of the organization.

Although management has the leading role in pursuing individual and organizational well-being, it does not have exclusive responsibility for either individual or organizational health. Managers and employees acting as individuals and employees acting in groups also have a responsibility for the organization and the individuals within it. This too is a corollary of the person-organization interdependency contained in principle 1. An individual who accepts employment with an organization has a responsibility to contribute to his own work environment and to participate in efforts to combat organizational distress.

A detailed consideration of the role of organized labor in organizational stress management is outside the focus of this chapter. Many of the key issues in this area have been addressed by Shostak (1980) in *Blue-Collar Stress*.

While management has a responsibility for individual health, it is important to recognize that the ultimate responsibility for one's health lies with the individual. Each person must take responsibility for his or her own life, health, and well-being. To surrender that responsibility is both immature and hazardous. Principle 2 does not in any way attempt to relieve individuals of responsibility for their own health and well-being.

Principle 3: Individual and Organizational Distress Are Not Inevitable

Task, role, physical, and interpersonal demands are an inescapable part of participating in any organization. Unfortunately, too many of these demands and too much of the resulting distress are accepted as "the price of success," "part of the industrial revolution," or "a necessary evil of work." These cruel myths are used to rationalize inaction and neglect by management and employees alike. In fact, many stressors can be reduced or eliminated, the impact of other stressors can be softened, and the resulting distress can be greatly reduced. While the stress and demands of work life are inevitable, distress resulting from stress and demands is *not* inevitable.

From the assertion that management has a responsibility for individual and organizational health (principle 2), it follows that management has a responsibility to identify and assault preventable sources of organizational and individual distress. The organizational- and individual-level weapons for this assault are the subject of Chapters 8 through 12. Distress is averted through preventive managerial action using these methods.

Principle 3 is based on the use of a proactive model of organizational change. It is difficult to avert distress when its consequences are already being experienced at the individual or organizational level. Therefore, it is necessary to anticipate and influence those demands which are the source of stressful events as well as to employ methods for shielding the individual or organization from their harmful effects. Management will be able to prevent distress through the use of such a proactive posture.

Principle 4: Each Individual and Organization Reacts Uniquely to Stress

There are considerable individual differences in the demands that are perceived as stressful, in the response to these demands, in the recognition and toleration of distress, and in response to stress management interventions. These differences have important implications for diagnosing organizational stress and for designing effective preventive management programs.

For example, routine, monotonous work may be quite distressing for one person, but reassuring and secure for another; social isolation at the job may be quite upsetting for one person, but a virtual employment requirement for another. An effective preventive management program must address itself to the stressors which are relevant to the individuals concerned. This observation highlights the importance of the diagnostic process described in Chapters 5 and 6.

There are also variations in the response to stress, as we noted in Chapter 3. For example, some individuals might respond to a surprise short deadline with increased cigarette consumption, others with a headache, and still others with nothing but quiet, efficient productivity. Signs of distress may also be perceived differently by different organizations. For instance, a company dependent upon large numbers of unskilled laborers who require minimal training may have little interest in reducing a stress-related high turnover rate. In contrast, a firm which uses internally-trained technicians might be alarmed by stressors which cause even a modest increase in turnover.

Finally, the feasibility, acceptability, and effectiveness of preventive management interventions will vary among organizations and individuals. A small firm often cannot afford on-site counselors, fitness trainers, or special health facilities. An effective system for identifying and referring individuals having particular difficulties might suffice. At the individual level, techniques which are attractive to one individual may be entirely unacceptable to another individual.

Thus it is important to recognize from the outset that the discussion of preventive management methods in Chapters 8 through 12 is not meant to provide a "cook book" for organizational stress management. Distress prevention methods will be presented, and guidelines for designing stress management programs will be considered. Nevertheless, the uniqueness of individuals and organizations requires that interventions be chosen and implemented in light of the particular characteristics and needs of the individual or organization being served.

Principle 5: Organizations Are Ever-Changing, Dynamic Entities

Organizations, like individuals, are open systems which have a life cycle of growth, maturation, and death as well as varying degrees of health and vitality (Alderfer, 1976; Kimberly, Miles, and Associates, 1980). They are at any given point in time a blend of health, vitality, and decay. They will face different developmental issues at various stages in their growth, just as individuals face different developmental issues at various stages of their lives. The nature of the stressors faced by an organization as well as the nature of the demands generated within it will change over the course of its life cycle. The strategies and techniques which are effective in managing stress at one stage may be ineffective at a later stage.

Essentially, preventive management is concerned with enhancing organizational health, vitality, and functioning while minimizing the amount of decay and illness within the organization. This can only be accomplished by attending to the ever-changing, dynamic nature of the organization. It requires the active involvement and participation of all organizational members in the process of organizational growth and change.

Application of the Principles

These five principles constitute the central elements of the preventive management philosophy. Their application requires a knowledge of the three stages of prevention as well as the methods of individual- and organizational-level preventive management. Using these principles and methods, management may formulate a specific preventive management plan for the organization. We will turn next to a discussion of the stages of prevention and then an overview of the methods of preventive management.

STAGES OF PREVENTION

Chronic diseases do not arise suddenly; instead, they develop gradually through a progression of disease stages, a "natural life history." The natural history of most diseases is one of evolution from a stage of susceptibility, to a stage of early disease, to a stage of advanced or disabling disease. At the stage of susceptibility, the individual is healthy, but is exposed to certain risk factors or disease precursors. For example, individuals who choose a sedentary life or who choose to smoke cigarettes are at the stage of susceptibility for coronary artery disease as well as several other diseases. When these and other risk factors lead to the development of arteriosclerotic plaques or "hardening of the arteries" to the heart, the individual is at the stage of early disease or "preclinical" disease. In other words, the person's body has responded to the disease precursors, but there are few, if any, symptoms. As the disease advances further, it becomes symptomatic or clinical disease. Angina pectoris ("heart pains") and heart attacks are advanced manifestations of coronary artery disease.

One of the fundamental concepts of public health and preventive medicine is that there is an opportunity for preventive intervention at each stage in the life history of a disease. These interventions are aimed at slowing, stopping, or—unfortunately, in too many instances—reversing the progression of disease. *Primary prevention* is directed at the stage of susceptibility and aims to eliminate or reduce the impact of risk factors; *secondary prevention* aims at detecting and treating early disease; *tertiary prevention* is directed at symptomatic or advanced disease and aims to alleviate discomfort and restore effective functioning (Morris, 1955).

The impact of organizational stress also proceeds through several stages and, therefore, there are several possible points for preventive management intervention. Figure 7.1 presents the essential elements of the organizational stress model described in Chapter 1 and indicates the stages of preventive management. *Primary prevention* is aimed at

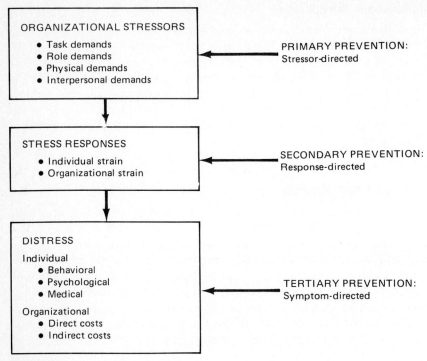

FIGURE 7.1
The stages of preventive management.

modifying the organizational stressors which eventually lead to distress. *Secondary prevention* aims at identifying and reversing—or at least arresting—individual and organizational strain. *Tertiary prevention* is directed at the symptoms of organizational stressors; it attempts to minimize the amount of individual and organizational distress which results when organizational stressors and resulting stress responses have not been adequately controlled.

For example, multiple-reporting relationships (stressor) might lead to chronic anxiety (stress response) and in turn to absenteeism (organizational consequence of distress). Primary prevention would attempt to simplify the reporting relationships. Secondary prevention might address the problem by providing a program of relaxation training to help alleviate signs of tension among affected subordinates. Tertiary prevention might include an employee counseling program designed to help employees cope with conflicting expectations.

What is preventable really is dependent upon the nature of the demand(s), the characteristics of the individual, and the resources available in the situation. The appropriate stage of prevention for precluding or arresting distress is, therefore, often situationally determined. Sometimes it is not possible to change a demand or reduce one's vulnerability to the demand, which then indicates that tertiary prevention is most appropriate. Thus, what is realistically preventable at each stage may be as much a function of circumstances as rational choice. There are available at each stage of prevention individual-level and organizational-level interventions.

At the organizational level, primary prevention is aimed at controlling the number of stressors and their intensity. At the individual level, primary prevention is intended to help individuals control the frequency and intensity of the stressors to which they are subjected. The goal is not to eliminate stressors, but to optimize the frequency and intensity of stressors. When the stress response is elicited too frequently or too strongly at work, organizational and individual strain and disease become inevitable. This leads to the exhaustion stage of Selye's general adaptation syndrome (see Chapter 1). When the stress response is not elicited frequently enough, lethargy as well as lack of growth and adaptation occur. Either extreme is to be avoided and an optimum level is to be sought. This optimum level varies substantially among individuals and different groups of individuals. This point is an underlying theme in many of Selye's writings on stress.

Secondary prevention is directed at controlling the stress response itself and includes efforts to optimize the intensity of each stress response an individual experiences. While low-intensity stress responses may provide insufficient impetus for adaptability and growth, high-intensity reponses may lead to sudden death or other serious individual consequences. Because of individual differences, the optimum intensity for one individual may not be optimum for another. The importance of optimizing both the frequency and the intensity of the stress response is reflected in the expanded Yerkes-Dodson curve shown in Figure 7.2.

Tertiary prevention is concerned with minimizing the organizational costs and the individual discomfort, disability, and death resulting from frank manifestations of too much stress. At the organizational level this usually takes the form of crisis intervention, while at the individual level it often consists of traditional medical and psychiatric care.

Folkman, Schaefer, and Lazarus (1979), Folkman and Lazarus (1980), and Herold and Conlon (1982) have discussed coping strategies for alleviating distress which parallel the notions of primary and secondary prevention presented here. Coping is a cognitive and behavioral process of mastering, tolerating, or reducing internal and external demands (Folkman and Lazarus, 1980). The problem-focused function of coping is

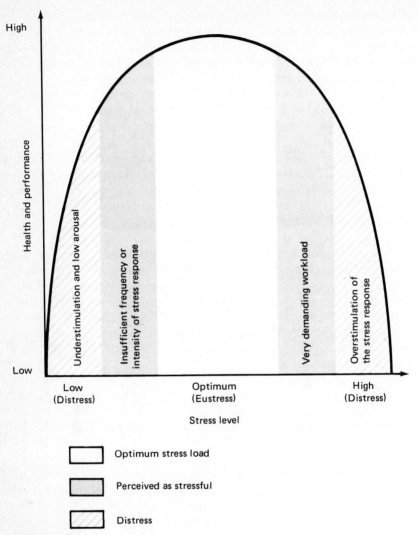

FIGURE 7.2
An expanded Yerkes-Dodson curve.

concerned with managing or altering the source of stress in the person-environment relationship and parallels preliminary prevention. The emotion-focused function of coping is concerned with regulating stressful emotions and parallels secondary prevention. The coping scheme of Folkman and Lazarus does not incorporate a notion which parallels tertiary prevention.

PREVENTIVE MANAGEMENT METHODS

The three stages of prevention provide a useful means to understand the process of preventive management. However, the specific methods are described more readily as organizational-level preventive management and individual-level preventive management. The distinction between these two levels of intervention will serve to organize the following four chapters. Figure 7.3 identifies these two levels of preventive action and identifies the methods at each level which will be discussed in the following chapters. It is not our intention to provide a cursory review of all possible interventions. Instead, we will selectively review in detail those methods which are feasible for implementation in a variety of

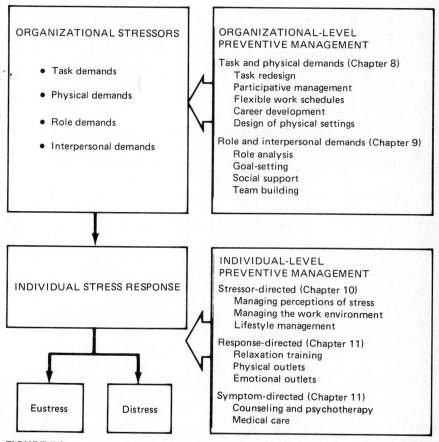

FIGURE 7.3
Organizational-level and individual-level preventive management.

organizations and which, in most instances, have some empirical evidence to support their effectiveness in prevention.

Organizational-Level Preventive Management

Organizational-level preventive management is aimed primarily at the task, role, physical, and interpersonal demands discussed in Chapter 2. Many of the organizational-level methods are aimed at changing the organization's structure and practices by altering the nature of these different demands. This means that organizational-level methods of preventive management are used to eliminate unnecessary demands while sharpening the focus of necessary demands and helping employees better manage these necessary demands in healthy ways. Nine organizational-level methods of preventive management are discussed in Chapters 8 and 9.

As shown in Figure 7.3, five prevention methods are examined in Chapter 8. Of these five methods three are concerned with the task demands of work: task redesign, flexible work schedules, and career development. Each of these methods is concerned with the design, structure, and sequence of an individual's work. Task redesign is explicitly concerned with the core characteristics of an individual's job and the processes whereby person-job fit may be improved. Flexible work scheduling is concerned with a specific dimension of one's job and affords the individual increased discretion in managing both professional and personal demands. Career development focuses on the sequence of jobs an individual might hold over time as well as the knowledge and skills required to grow in these different jobs.

Also discussed in Chapter 8 are participative management and the design of physical settings. Participative management is concerned with the task and interpersonal demands of work. Its thrust is to increase job-decision latitude, improve organizational decision making, and increase the individual's investment in as well as adjustment to organizational life. The design of physical settings is concerned with the physical and task demands of work. Through this method of prevention, an individual's physical work environment is designed to facilitate task accomplishment as well as to stimulate pleasure and growth on the job.

Chapter 9 examines four methods of organizational-level preventive management. Two of these methods, the role analysis technique and goal-setting programs, focus on the demands of the individual's work role. The role analysis technique is designed to clarify, focus, and minimize the conflicts present in the role demands of work. Goal-setting programs, on the other hand, are concerned with task demands as well as role demands. The emphasis in goal-setting programs is on explicitly identifying the manager's task-related role demands of his employees through a participative process.

Social support and team building are also explored in Chapter 9. These related methods of preventive management focus not on changing or restructuring the different demands at work but rather on providing groups of employees with support and resources in managing the necessary yet stressful demands of work. These methods complement the other techniques of organizational-level preventive management aimed at changing the organizational stressors listed in Figure 7.3.

The emphasis in organizational-level preventive management is at the primary stage of prevention, as depicted in Figure 7.1. While the secondary and tertiary stages of prevention are not ignored at the organizational level, a greater number of individual-level methods of preventive management are available for these stages of prevention. It is to this individual level that we now turn.

Individual-Level Preventive Management

Individual-level preventive management provides an alternative and, in many cases, more effective means for dealing with organizational stress. As shown in Figure 7.3, the major individual-level methods of preventive management fall under the three stages of prevention.

Chapter 10 describes some of the primary or stressor-directed techniques which are essential to a personal stress management plan. Managing personal response patterns includes changing Type A behavior patterns, talking constructively to oneself, and uninhibiting emotional expression. Management of the personal work environment includes managing time, learning how to obligate and "deobligate," and planning work activities systematically. Achieving a healthful balance between work, home, and other activities, using leisure time effectively for relaxation, and finding satisfying artistic outlets are all part of lifestyle management.

Although stressor-directed techniques may form the basis for a comprehensive individual stress management plan, it is important to recognize that these techniques have not been as widely accepted nor as systematically studied as the secondary and tertiary individual-level preventive techniques described in Chapter 11. Secondary or response-directed techniques include relaxation training and physical exercise. Tertiary or symptom-directed techniques include counseling, psychotherapy, and medical care.

The types of relaxation training described in Chapter 11 are the relaxation response, progressive relaxation, clinically standardized meditation, transcendental meditation, Zen and other eastern meditative systems, hypnosis, autogenic training, biofeedback, momentary relaxation, and traditional forms of relaxation. Physical exercise can be beneficial in any of several ways, depending in part on whether it is aerobic exercise, recreational sports, flexibility and relaxation exercises, or muscle strength and endurance building.

The tertiary prevention measures considered in Chapter 11 include symptom-directed programs such as those for alcoholics, individual counseling, behavioral therapy, group therapy, and career counseling as well as standard medical care using medications, physical therapy, and surgery.

Chapter 11 concludes with a brief discussion of the process for creating a personal stress management plan. The actual plan will vary considerably among individuals, but the process for developing such a plan can be fairly standard.

Implementing Preventive Management

Implementing the principles of preventive management and applying the organization-level and individual-level methods of preventive management takes an organizationally specific strategy. Chapter 12 contains a description of what Xerox Corporation, Kimberly-Clark Corporation, Southern Connecticut Gas Company, and several other firms are actually doing to combat the effects of distress. The chapter also contains a model for implementing and evaluating preventive management, along with several key questions to consider in the implementation process.

SUMMARY

This chapter contains a discussion of the principles and methods of preventive management. The principles constitute the central element in the philosophy of preventive management. These guiding principles are:

1 Individual and organizational health are interdependent.
2 Management has a responsibility for individual and organizational health.
3 Individual and organizational distress are not inevitable.
4 Each individual and organization reacts uniquely to stress.
5 Organizations are ever-changing, dynamic entities.

These principles underlie the concept of preventive management which was first defined in Chapter 1. The two aims of preventive management are (1) to promote individual and organizational health and (2) to minimize individual and organizational distress, as manifested in a variety of asymptomatic and symptomatic diseases.

The principles of preventive management and the organizationally specific strategy for implementing these principles guide both the selection and the use of specific preventive management methods. These methods were briefly discussed in the last section of the chapter and are listed in Figure 7.3. They will be considered in detail in the following five chapters which deal first with organizational-level preventive management, second with individual-level preventive management, and finally with sample industrial programs using a selection of these methods.

CHAPTER 8

ORGANIZATIONAL METHODS FOR MODIFYING WORK DEMANDS

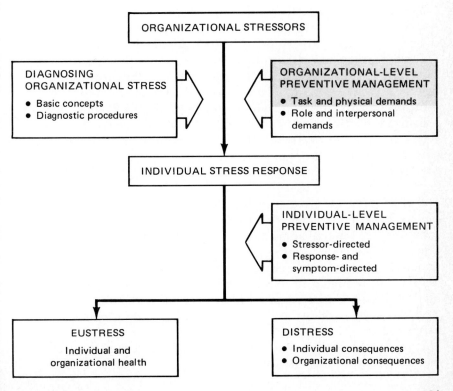

ORGANIZATIONAL STRESSORS

DIAGNOSING ORGANIZATIONAL STRESS

- Basic concepts
- Diagnostic procedures

ORGANIZATIONAL-LEVEL PREVENTIVE MANAGEMENT

- Task and physical demands
- Role and interpersonal demands

INDIVIDUAL STRESS RESPONSE

INDIVIDUAL-LEVEL PREVENTIVE MANAGEMENT

- Stressor-directed
- Response- and symptom-directed

EUSTRESS

Individual and organizational health

DISTRESS

- Individual consequences
- Organizational consequences

This is the first of two chapters dealing with the use of preventive management techniques at the organizational level. The aim of these organizational strategies is to modify and shape the organization, altering the demands it places upon the individual. The intention is *not* to minimize the stress individuals experience at work, but rather to optimize it in accordance with the expanded Yerkes-Dodson curve discussed in Chapter 7 (see Figure 7.2). To achieve this objective, organization-level preventive management attempts to buffer the effects of organizational stressors upon individuals by increasing stress where too little exists and reducing stress where it may become overwhelming. This should be done through an organizationally specific implementation strategy which incorporates individual-level and organizational-level methods of preventive management discussed in this chapter and in Chapter 9.

This chapter presents five prevention methods aimed specifically at one or another category of demands to which the individual is subject at work. These methods, summarized in Table 8.1, are primarily concerned with modifying the formal organization in order to alter the demands that it places upon individuals. It is these organizational demands which are the sources of organizational stress.

Principle 2 of prevention management is: *Management has a responsibility for individual and organizational health.* Organization-level preventive management is concerned with the implementation of this principle in specific organizational settings. The methods of preventive management discussed in this chapter are designed to maintain organizational health by preventing the occurrence of structural conditions, such as insufficient job autonomy, which may lead to various individual and organizational disorders. These methods have the major focus at the primary stage of prevention, since they are directed at organizational stressors. However, they function at the secondary stage of prevention to the extent to which they are directed at how groups respond to organizational demands.

It is important to note at the outset of our discussion of prevention methods that each is aimed at improving organization health through some form of internal adjustment. The process of making an organizational change and internal adjustment will in and of itself create uncertainty and stress for some individuals. There is the risk of increasing rather than reducing stress within the organization if the prevention method is poorly implemented or mismanaged. The risk of problems with any of the following methods will be greatly reduced through careful planning and active collaboration with the groups and individuals affected by the change. Therefore, thoughtful and cautious use of the methods of preventive management is recommended.

TABLE 8.1
ORGANIZATIONAL-LEVEL METHODS OF PREVENTIVE MANAGEMENT
Task and Physical Demands

Task redesign
This method is aimed at changing the task demands which jobs place upon individuals holding them. This is accomplished by restructuring one or more core job dimensions. The result of task redesign efforts is to improve person-job fit and to increase the job occupant's level of motivation, thus reducing distress on the job. (Griffin, 1982)
Participative management
This method increases the amount of discretion and autonomy that individuals have at work by decentralizing decision making and increasing participation in decision-making processes as much as possible. The individual is able to exert greater control at work and to channel stress-induced energy, while minimizing the frustration of working under authoritarian management. The result of practicing participative management is to reduce conflict and tension while increasing productivity. (Likert, 1961)
Flexible work schedules
This method enhances the individual's control and discretion in the work environment. It makes possible greater flexibility for integrating and managing organizational and personal demands. The increased discretion over one's work time leads to a reduction in unresolved strain. (Ronan, 1981)
Career development
Based upon structuring career paths, this method encourages eustressful individual growth and development. This is accomplished through a process of self-assessment as well as an analysis of opportunities within the organization. This is done through individual initiative as well as in conjunction with counselors in the organization. The result is reduced individual frustration and distress. (Hall, 1976)
Design of physical settings
This method minimizes the distressful effects of the physical work environment, for example noise and excessive heat. The use of pleasant or growth-oriented settings (e.g., fitness center) promotes eustress. If the work environment is properly designed, it will also facilitate task accomplishment. The elicitation of eustress will also be important if the functions of the physical setting are pleasure or growth, such as found in a fitness center. (Steele, 1973)

TASK REDESIGN

In any organization there are many points at which stress-reducing interventions can be made. Because of the direct and immediate impact which job content has upon the individual, the job is one of the critical intervention points. *Task redesign* is the most advanced technique for analyzing and improving job structure. The thrust of task redesign is to enhance employee motivation by altering specific task dimensions to achieve a better "fit" between individual needs and the structure of the job (Hackman, 1977). It is an approach which can be applied to managerial as well as nonmanagerial work.

Too often managerial jobs are characterized by heavy responsibilities without commensurate authority and autonomy. The stress of managerial jobs which results from high demands and low decision latitude has already been noted (Figure 2.1; Karasek, 1979). Job redesign addresses this dilemma by allowing for an increase in the autonomy dimension of a job. By increasing job autonomy along with increasing task demands, the amount of unresolved strain, which is often manifested in dissatisfaction, depression, and sick days, does not necessarily increase for the individual.

At the other extreme, the boredom of routine jobs is both psychologically and physiologically stressful. Task redesign addresses this problem by focusing on the motivating potential score associated with a given job.

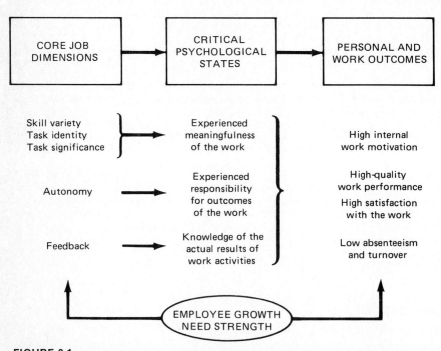

FIGURE 8.1
A model for task redesign. [Source: *J. R. Hackman, "Work Design," in J. Richard Hackman and J. Lloyd Suttle (eds.),* Improving Life at Work, *Goodyear Publishing, Santa Monica, Calif., 1977, p. 129. Copyright © 1977, Scott, Foresman and Company. Used by permission.*]

This *motivating potential score* (MPS) is a measure of a particular job's potential for motivating the individual to work. It is only when a job achieves a minimum, yet unspecified, motivating potential score that it can create the optimum amount of stress specified in the Yerkes-Dodson law.

The way in which the individual interacts with a job is depicted in Hackman's task redesign model shown in Figure 8.1. In the model, five core job dimensions are postulated to impact three key psychological states within the individual. For individuals with high growth needs, the interaction of the core job dimensions with the critical psychological states will result in the personal and work outcomes listed in the figure. The motivating potential score of any particular job is determined through an additive and multiplicative combination of the five core job dimensions. The range of this score is from 1 (a job characterized by virtually none of the core dimensions) to 343 (a job in which these dimensions are very high). Hackman (1977) suggests that the average motivating potential score is about 125.

This relationship between the structure of a job, as measured by Hackman's motivating potential score, and the amount of stress the employee will experience is shown in Figure 8.2. As the figure shows, stress increases linearly with the scope of a job. Both ends of the task-scope continuum result in distress caused by too little or too much motivating potential. The figure also shows how employee satisfaction will increase as eustress is achieved and decline again at the upper end of the task-scope continuum.

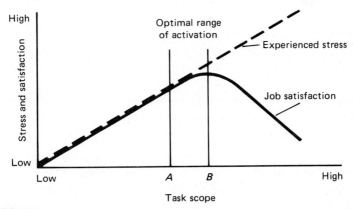

FIGURE 8.2
Task scope, activation, and experienced stress. [Source: *J. C. Quick and R. W. Griffin,
"Situational Determinants of Goal Setting Behavior and Evaluation: Task Variability,"
paper presented at the annual meeting of the Southwest Division of the Academy of
Management, San Antonio, 1980.*]

Implementing Task Redesign

Hackman and Oldham (1980) and Griffin (1982) suggest that we first decide whether to change individual jobs or to create self-managing groups out of existing work teams. There is not always a choice, since one or the other alternative is sometimes not feasible. In cases where choice exists, the selection of the appropriate strategy should be based on preliminary diagnostic data. Griffin (1982) also suggests two key questions for those considering task redesign: (1) Is there a need for task redesign? (2) Is task redesign feasible? The first question in particular should be addressed through the organizational diagnostic activities undertaken by management. Hackman (1977) also suggests a diagnostic approach to task redesign which may be usefully modified for our purposes here.

Diagnose the work setting   Problems in the work setting suggested by such symptoms as absenteeism and/or poor quality performance are not necessarily attributable to poorly designed jobs. Symptoms may result from alternative sources, such as authoritarian supervision or interpersonal conflicts with peers. The diagnostic procedure should lead to a determination of the underlying ills *or* precursors for future symptoms. If the diagnosis suggests that task design is the root problem, then we should follow with the task redesign procedure. If not, then an alternative method of preventive management would be suggested.

One aspect of the diagnostic procedure in this case should be the examination of the motivating potential score (MPS) for the group of jobs being examined. Hackman and Oldham (1974) have developed some normative data regarding the MPS for various categories of jobs. The MPS is derived in each case using Hackman's (1977) additive and multiplicative equation which combines the scores for each core job dimension. Comparing the MPS of the target job to normative scores for similar jobs will provide a basis for determining whether or not there are problems with the design of the target job.

Are specific core dimensions the problem?   If the design of the job is the real problem, then it is necessary to examine the scores for each core job dimension, which are defined by Hackman as follows:

Skill variety. The degree to which a job requires a variety of different activities that involve the use of a number of different skills and talents.

Task identity. The degree to which the job requires completion of a whole and identifiable piece of work—that is, doing a job from beginning to end with a visible outcome.

Task significance. The degree to which the job has a substantial impact on the lives or work of other people, whether in the immediate organization or in the external environment.

Autonomy. The degree to which the job provides substantial freedom, independence, and discretion to the individual in scheduling the work and determining the procedures to be used in carrying it out.

Feedback. The degree to which carrying out the work activities required by the job results in the individual obtaining direct and clear information about the effectiveness of his performance.

Each core dimension is examined to determine if it alone is the problem. For example, we have seen cases where a very low score on *feedback* alone resulted in a low MPS for a job. Other dimensions of the core job were well-designed in these cases. We also know of a case where the *autonomy* dimension of a job was identified as the major stressor for incumbents. It is important to note that individual perceptions of the core job dimensions will be shaped in some degree by such social influences as supervisor and coworker behaviors and communications. It is important to separate out such social and perceptual influences from the structural aspects of the job under examination.

Once the problems with one or more of the five core job dimensions have been identified, Hackman (1977) suggests that one of five principles for task redesign may be employed to alter the job. These principles are:

1 *Form natural work units.* This involves organizing people whose work is interrelated into work groups or teams.

2 *Combine tasks.* This is done by despecializing a job and allowing individuals to do several different activities.

3 *Establish client relationships.* This enables the worker to interact directly with people who use or are affected by the work.

4 *Use vertical loading.* This allows the worker more responsibility and discretion over the work and decisions affecting the work.

5 *Open feedback channels.* This involves increasing the ways in which feedback from the work process itself may be made available to the worker.

The effects of these five change principles on the core job dimensions are shown in Figure 8.3.

What unique problems and opportunities are present?   Each work setting is unique: it has specific problems that will resist task redesign efforts as well as opportunities that will enhance the efforts. Among the problems are insecurity, anxiety, and resistance on the part of those affected by the redesign effort. For example, during one change effort we undertook, the computer operations manager was so insecure about the changes in his job that he was temporarily paranoid, believing that we as change agents were out to get him. This was due to his emotional insecurity. Once the change was finalized, his emotional disturbances and upset dissipated.

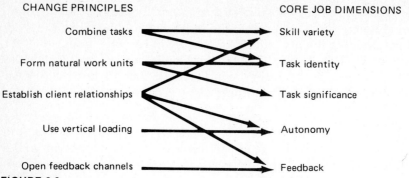

FIGURE 8.3
Principles for redesigning jobs. [Source: *J. R. Hackman, "Work Design," in J. R. Hackman and J. L. Suttle (eds.),* Improving Life at Work, *Goodyear Publishing, Santa Monica, Calif., 1977, p. 136. Copyright © 1977, Scott, Foresman and Company. Used by permission.*]

Similar problems will be present in varying degrees for all change efforts in organizations, but they will be more pronounced in some cases, as in the example above, and less pronounced in others. Unless the individuals affected are prepared for and open to the redesign efforts, there will be substantial difficulty in carrying out the changes, no matter how beneficial they may be from a managerial or engineering perspective. Other unique problems may lie in the fixed, unchangeable aspects of the task's physical setting or in the technology used in the job. For example, there are limits to increasing the autonomy an individual may have in an assembly line job.

There will also be opportunities in any given job setting which may be of advantage in carrying out redesign efforts. For example, if the life expectancy of the equipment has been reached and it is time to make capital investments for new technology, the redesign efforts can be actively integrated with the technology decisions. Unfortunately, such freedom and opportunity are not always possible.

Evaluation of the redesign activities   There needs to be a systematic evaluation and follow-up to determine the effectiveness, or lack of effectiveness of any redesign actions. A procedure similar to the one used in diagnosis should be followed in order to compare the results of the evaluation with the diagnostic base data established before the change. Without such comparability, the evaluation loses its usefulness. Where action is based upon such symptoms as excessive absenteeism or poor quality performance, the evaluator should look for the elimination of such symptoms.

In a well-designed field experiment, Orpen (1979) used Hackman's theory to increase the MPS of 36 randomly assigned clerical employees. He did not alter the MPS or task scope of an additional 36 clerical employees. His evaluation focused on changes in individual motivation, satisfaction, and performance. Data collected six months after the task redesign effort had been completed indicated a significant improvement in both motivation and satisfaction, which would be consistent with the relationships suggested in Figure 8.2. Orpen did not find a similar increase in performance among these clerical employees.

Job Enrichment

Job enrichment has been viewed as a practical approach to improving employee motivation and is the historical predecessor to Hackman's task redesign work. Motivational factors are designed into a job to make it more challenging and stimulating. According to Herzberg's theory, a job has specific *motivational factors* (for example, recognition, responsibility, and the opportunity for achievement) which serve to stimulate employee motivation. In addition, each job has specific *hygienic factors* (for example, lighting levels, company regulations, and employee benefit programs) which, if poorly conceived or implemented, can cause significant dissatisfaction.

As a job redesign strategy, job enrichment *may* be useful in the prevention of organizational distress in two ways. First, it can increase functional stress in the workplace by building mildly stressful motivational factors into specific jobs. This provides for the constructive stress associated with movement up the Yerkes-Dodson curve to the optimum region. These additional motivational factors should provide *regular, mildly intense* stress for the job's incumbent, rather than severe, irregular stress.

Second, attention to the hygienic factors in the workplace can alleviate some of the distress associated with physically or psychologically poor working conditions. We will discuss the relevant physical hygienic factors when we talk about the analysis of physical settings later in the chapter. Other hygienic factors, such as company benefit programs, tuition reimbursement, or sabbatical leaves, may cause distress by their absence.

The bulk of the job enrichment research and practice has been flawed, leaving this technique open to criticism. In contrast, experience with and research on task redesign are more extensive and more convincing. Proponents of task redesign have developed more psychometrically sound and advanced diagnostic tools. In addition, normative data on motivating potential scores are available for a variety of jobs. Thus, theoretically, empirically, and practically, task redesign is a more acceptable technique than job enrichment.

PARTICIPATIVE MANAGEMENT

Participative management is a strategy for managing the resources and people in an organization. It incorporates the ideas and thoughts of individuals as well as groups into the decision-making processes of the organization. Much of this managerial decision-making strategy is founded on the early research of Lewin, Lippitt, and White (1939). In their original work, they identified three distinct styles of leadership: authoritarian, democratic, and laissez faire. The distressful effects of authoritarian leadership were discussed in Chapter 2. The adverse consequences of the laissez faire style of leadership are found in the confusion, turmoil, and anarchy that result in the workplace under this leadership style. Participative management is the style of the democratic leader.

Lewin, Lippit, and White (1939) found that participative leaders had less tension, destructive conflict, and rigidity in their work groups. Subsequently, Likert (1961) found that work groups managed in a participative fashion were ones in which the manager focused on the human aspects of the work environment and on teamwork. Subordinates in such an environment had considerably more freedom. The work groups under participative managers tended to be more productive than those working under authoritarian leadership. In addition to improved productivity, Tannenbaum and Massarik (1950) identified five other benefits of participative management, which are (1) a reduction in turnover, absenteeism, and tardiness; (2) a reduction in grievances and an improvement in management-labor relations; (3) a greater readiness to accept change; (4) a greater ease in managing subordinates; and (5) an improvement in the quality of managerial decisions. Several of these benefits directly address various organizational consequences of stress discussed in Chapter 4.

Karasek's (1979) work seems to complement these findings. It suggests that demanding jobs must allow incumbents commensurate decision latitude and autonomy, unless management wants unresolved strains in the workplace. Restricting an individual's opportunities for participation and autonomy increases depression, exhaustion, illness rates, and pill consumption. Increasing participation and autonomy leads to greater freedom of action, still within defined limits, which enables an individual to more naturally channel and release stress-induced energy.

Decentralization

The process of decentralizing organizational decision making has a rather direct effect upon the degree of job autonomy throughout an organizational hierarchy. It is a process that increases the decision latitude of individual managers in that hierarchy. The Japanese have taken the American notions of participative management, including decentralization of decision making, and implemented them through the mechanism of quality circles (Ouchi, 1981). Quality circles allow organizational problems to be solved at the lowest practical organizational level by having a peer group identify problem areas as well as potential solutions to the problem. The Department of Defense has undertaken a quality-circle program in the last few years. The results of the program have been mixed, with some quality circles working very well and others being disbanded by higher-level managers. Karasek's (1979) research suggests that the process of decentralization should reduce the amount of unresolved strain which individuals experience at work.

The benefits of decentralization in terms of reduced distress and strain are illustrated in the experience of an officer of a hospital equipment corporation. Over a ten-year period, this officer had worked for two different corporations. One company was very centralized; the other used a very decentralized decision-making approach. During his years in the centralized corporation, he had insomnia, depression, and nightmares about going to jail and about running afoul of corporate policies and procedures. His family reported that he was increasingly difficult to live with. After a year of this distress, he left the centralized corporation and subsequently joined the decentralized corporation. Following the move to the new corporation, his insomnia and depression cleared. His nightmares about legal and procedural problems became less frequent and then stopped. His family reported that he was much easier to be around and he was more the man they used to know.

While this executive's experiences may be more extreme than the average individual subject to centralized decision making, it illustrates how centralized decision making and lack of decision latitude can create distress and unresolved strain, with the attendant psychological and physiological consequences, for individuals subject to such a management strategy.

Implementing Participative Management

Participative management is not appropriate in all circumstances; even under a participative approach, the boss is still the boss. What is important in the implementation of participative management is an understanding of the circumstances and conditions in which it is appropriate. When this approach to management is responsibly executed, it is effective in achieving the sorts of benefits outlined at the beginning of this section. There are two sets of conditions for effective participative management: one is psychological in nature and the other is organizational in nature (Tannenbaum and Massarik, 1950).

Psychological conditions   If participative management is to be effective, the individual participants must meet certain psychological preconditions. These include the ability to become psychologically involved in participative decision making, the interest in participating in decision making, the ability to express oneself and one's thoughts about decisions under consideration, and the perception that participation has personal relevance to one's own future. Unless individuals meet these preconditions, participative management will not be highly effective. Even if they do meet these preconditions, the effectiveness of participation will be hampered unless certain organizational conditions are met.

Organizational conditions   The organizational conditions for effective participation are availability of time for individuals to participate in a decision (e.g., crisis decisions in military combat or in hospital emergency room settings should not be made participatively); existence of benefits which outweigh the costs of time and effort in participative decision making; relative stability of working relationships between managers and subordinates; absence of decision-making situations in which the participants have a conflict of interest; shared goals and values; presence of channels whereby individuals may effectively contribute to decisions; and sufficient training and education about participation.

If the psychological and organizational conditions for participative decision making are met, an organization should achieve the benefits identified by Tannenbaum and Massarik (1950). As a strategy of preventive management, participation allows individuals to contribute their resources to improved organizational functioning and health. It also enables individuals to improve the degree of personal fit with the organization, which in turn provides a vested interest in organizational performance.

Program Buck Stop

Even military organizations have come to realize that there are substantial benefits to be realized through participative management and decentralized decision making. The Air Force's Strategic Air Command (SAC) has implemented a program called Buck Stop, which illustrates the practice of participative management. This program is designed to have all operational and staff decisions made at the lowest practical level within the command. It is implemented by the SAC commander through his wing commanders. While there is no formalized training associated with the implementation process, there is a formal monitoring procedure established through the command's inspector general. Each team of inspectors is instructed to query junior noncommissioned officers during unit inspection tours regarding their understanding and use of Buck Stop.

Experience with Buck Stop, although limited, suggests that commanders and senior supervisors are less burdened with decisions that can be made at a lower level. This frees the commanders to spend more time managing the combat wings and subordinate organizations by focusing more attention on managerial planning and action.

FLEXIBLE WORK SCHEDULES

One of the ways in which participation has been implemented in organizations is through the use of flexible work schedules. These allow individuals discretion in determining their own working hours—within limited organizational constraints. Job enrichment and task redesign are both concerned with the content and structure of each job. They deal with work schedules tangentially through the autonomy and responsibility job dimensions. For preventive stress management, work scheduling is an important dimension of job design. Flexible work schedules have been a part of organizational life at least since the Hawthorne studies in the 1920s and 1930s (Roethlisberger and Dickson, 1939). During one of these series of studies the researchers experimented with allowing the women to follow alternative work schedules that might better suit them.

There has been an increase in the prevalence of such programs in the past ten years, with the general model being one of choosing a standard work schedule within certain limits. For example, an individual may choose a starting time between 7 and 9 a.m., and leave work eight hours later. The intention is to increase the individual's degree of self-control in the work environment as well as in structuring his or her overall life. It is important to keep in mind that this aspect of job design cannot be taken independent of other design considerations.

Task Interdependence

Where the work is accomplished very independently and task identity is high, there is more potential for success in the use of flexible work schedules. The difficulty in using flexible work schedules is introduced with interdependent tasks. The scheduling of shifts and workers becomes more difficult and restrictive under such conditions. Unless the nature of the task(s) can be redesigned in content to enhance the use of flexible work schedules, the dictates of the task outweigh the issues of scheduling.

Managerial work lends itself to flexible work scheduling because of the reduced interdependence of detailed tasks and the greater responsibility associated with these positions. The manager's role is increasingly one of establishing a productive and healthy emotional environment within which to work, which is not necessarily contingent upon the manager's presence. This does not mean that the manager's presence in the workplace is not important, even critical. What it does mean is that the manager often has more discretion and latitude about working hours than may exist for individuals whose specific tasks are highly interdependent.

Flextime in the Oil Industry

Because of rapid growth and urban traffic congestion in Houston during the 1970s, many of the oil companies established flextime programs. Gulf Oil Corporation and Tenneco, Inc., were among the companies which implemented such programs in downtown Houston and in some of their suburban locations. Gulf Oil offered their program to selected departments while Tenneco, Inc., allowed their personnel to apply for the flextime program. In each case, the program was intended to aid individuals in managing the difficulties associated with getting to and from work in the congested urban location. A second motivation in establishing these programs was to remain competitive with other oil companies in the area which were implementing flexible work programs. In addition to enabling individuals to manage work demands more effectively, these programs enable the individual to manage the demands of a personal and professional life with less distress.

Professional-Personal Balance

Increasing decision latitude and discretion enables an individual to cope better with high job demands, as we have seen in the work of Karasek (1979). A parallel aspect of flexible work schedules is the increased discretion and control that they can give an individual in balancing professional and personal demands. Having the flexibility to focus energy in areas that demand attention enables an individual to distribute energy more effectively and to manage time more efficiently. This improves the integration of individual and organizational needs, both of which must be met if the individual and the organization are to maintain health (Cohen and Gadon, 1978). This notion of flexible work schedules goes somewhat beyond the more systematic approach of eight-hour schedules by allowing individuals time away from work for personal matters.

If such flexibility is to benefit both the individual and the organization, there must be a certain level of maturity and responsibility on the part of the individual. When that is present, flexible work schedules can improve the individual-organizational exchange, increase the discretion the individual has in managing personal stress demands, and dissipate some of the cumulative effects which stress can cause. We will address the issue of "maintaining a balance" in more detail in Chapter 10.

CAREER DEVELOPMENT

As noted in Chapter 1, occupations vary substantially in the amount of stress they cause individuals in the occupation. Occupations also vary in how individuals may pursue their careers within the occupation. Careers are commonly thought of as the sequence of vocational activities an individual engages in over the course of time. Career development is an important aspect of an individual's career and refers to the actions an individual undertakes alone or in collaboration with other people to improve his career in specific ways. From an organizational perspective, inattention to individual career development may result in organizational dysfunctions, such as poor quantity and quality performance, lower levels of commitment, or dysfunctional turnover due to frustrated aspirations. From an individual perspective, poor career choices and decisions may lead to prolonged stress and strain. In this context, it is management's responsibility to take certain career development initiatives as well as to make available opportunities for individuals to undertake certain actions on their own behalf.

Mobil Oil Corporation is among those major corporations which have focused attention on career development. Their use of structured instruments and workshops for self-assessment and career planning is aimed at benefiting both Mobil and the individual. Through this process, Mobil is pushing its managers to plan for their futures with the help of the company. Any such preventive management method must incorporate two key aspects of the occupation-career issue. These are self-assessment and opportunity analysis. The framework at Mobil considers both of these aspects by getting individuals to look at their assets, liabilities, and interests as well as to identify the people with whom they would like to work and the job(s) they would like to consider.

Self-assessment and opportunity analysis may be undertaken by the individual with available published materials, or they may be accomplished with the assistance of a career counselor. The counselor may be a member of the organization or an independent consultant. This is one form of employee counseling, other forms of which will be addressed in Chapter 11.

Self-Assessment

Individuals cannot undertake effective career planning and develop-ment activities without having undertaken a thorough assessment of their own needs, interests, skills, abilities, and knowledge (Kotter, Faux, and McArthur, 1978). The two key self-assessment questions are: (1) What do I want and like to do? (2) What are my present strengths, abilities, and talents?

Individual interests   Individuals differ in their likes and interests. There will be varying degrees of distress associated with engaging in activities which the individual does not like. Some such activities will always be present in any job or occupation. However, these points of disinterest can be minimized through effective self-assessment. Two of the most widely used measures of individual interests are the Strong-Campbell Interest Inventory (Strong and Campbell, 1974) and the Kuder Occupational Interest Survey (Kuder and Diamond, 1979). These inven-tories assess an individual's preferences for various courses of study, activities, people, amusements, and occupations. While these two interest inventories are the most widely used and best researched, Buros (1978) lists additional interest inventories that may be chosen. Regardless of the measurement tool employed, it is essential to the self-assessment process that individuals have a basis for understanding their interests and preferences.

Individual abilities   While interests are an important part of the self-assessment process, it is also essential for individuals to have a realistic and largely objective understanding of their abilities. This aspect of the self-assessment process concerns the special knowledge and intellectual capability that the individual has as well as the unique physical skills and talents. Both areas of ability are important. Each ability area can be developed with the proper drive and interest, but there are upper limits to the development which may occur. This is not to say that through keen interest one cannot overcome what appear to be limitations or lack of ability. However, these must be accurately assessed when examining the individual's ability base.

No one or two standardized tests will provide the diverse information base needed in this area of self-assessment. The Educational Testing Service and the Psychological Corporation provide a diversity of aptitude tests which may be useful in assessing intellectual functioning. Probably the best resource for one to use in selecting an aptitude test is Buros' *Eighth Mental Measurement Yearbook* (1978). Its two volumes include a wide range of mental and aptitude tests along with an assessment of the quality of each, based on validity and reliability studies.

As difficult as it is, it is important for an individual and an organization to undertake an individual ability and talent assessment. Whenever possible, this assessment should be formalized. However, even informal assessments by alert, experienced individuals can be useful and may suffice. From the individual's perspective, it is only after both the interest and the ability assessments have been completed that he or she may effectively turn to the second dimension of the career development process. It is in this second dimension, opportunity analysis, that each organization may play a vital role in structuring opportunities for career development which minimize the dysfunctions of frustrated ambitions and wasted talents.

Opportunity Analysis

Opportunity analysis is concerned with the process of identifying the range of organizational and occupational roles which are available for an individual. As organizations and societies change, the available roles will also change. Each role will require the incumbent to exhibit various behaviors and talents, and it is essential to develop information about these role requirements if one is considering fulfilling one.

A key part of the opportunity analysis from the individual's standpoint is to determine the educational and physical requirements for the occupations or specific jobs under consideration. The requirements of various job levels in one industry and one organization will differ markedly. For example, lower-level managerial positions will require substantially greater technical knowledge, while top-level managerial positions will require much more conceptual skills and knowledge (Bracey, Sanford, and Quick, 1981). In some cases there is some flexibility in requirements; for example, the administrators in a hospital corporation may either possess the M.B.A. degree, the M.P.H. degree, or the M.H.A. degree. In other cases there is virtually no flexibility in a requirement; for example, an Air Force combat pilot must have 20-20 vision and superior mechanical aptitude.

Defining career paths   Organizations have the responsibility to establish career paths, that is, sequences of jobs to be followed by an individual in pursuing his career or opportunities of switching into different functions within the organization. There are various ways to create career paths that will enhance the individual's growth and development. The blockage of such growth and development in and of itself may have detrimental effects upon organizational health. Organizations and professions differ in what may constitute individual growth and development. Some organizations, like private-sector corporations and military services, lend themselves to upward mobility as a characteristic of career development. Others, like professional organizations and universities, lend themselves to the horizontal cultivation of professional skills and talents as the key characteristic of career development.

The profession of nursing has recently been embroiled in much career development turmoil. Many nurses feel frustrated and distressed about the lack of available opportunities for advancement and development. The avenue into hospital administration has not been traditionally open to the nursing directors, although that is changing. Another change that is occurring is the establishment in some hospitals of professional ladders, which allow nurses to pursue professional development as opposed to administrative development.

Creating opportunities   In an effort to minimize the disruption associated with the replacement of key executives, Tenneco, Inc., and Ken Davis Industries, among other corporations, require key executives to designate an heir apparent who is able and prepared to step into the key position. This form of career development and planning has advantages for both the individual and the organization in coping with the stressful aspects of career development and turnover. For the individual, it affords him time to develop the necessary skills and information required in the new position. For the organization, it minimizes the disruption of a change in leadership which can have adverse effects upon performance and productivity.

One of the more structured approaches to careers is carried out by the United States military services, each of which has a force structure to which it must conform by law. This approach inevitably keeps individuals moving through sequences of assignments designed to develop their abilities as well as utilize their talents. It also requires that individuals achieve promotions to the next higher pay and responsibility grade or be terminated by the service. This policy of promotion or termination has the advantage of ensuring the availability of opportunities for younger military members. The possible drawback is the loss of an able, effective performer who lacks the upward drive for promotion and achievement.

The processes of self-assessment and opportunity analysis are integrally related to career development. All are ongoing activities of concern to the organization as well as the individual. Failure to make available opportunities for able individuals may be just as detrimental to organizational health as allowing key positions of responsibility to go unfilled.

In summary, career development is eustressful to the extent to which it requires the individual to learn new skills, acquire new knowledge, and overcome previous limitations to his or her full development. The lack of career development opportunities for an individual will lead to frustration, distress, and other negative outcomes. Therefore, career development opportunities are an integral aspect of preventive management and organizational health.

DESIGN OF PHYSICAL SETTINGS

The first four preventive management methods discussed in this chapter are primarily concerned with the task, role, and interpersonal demands of work. This last primary prevention method is concerned with the physical factors which cause individuals stress in organizations. Despite our established mastery over many aspects of our physical environment, there are still work settings that are especially demanding physically—for example, the various divisions of oceangoing freighters and naval ships. Mastery over such naturally powerful forces as hurricanes and tornadoes has not been established. Nevertheless, the vast majority of white-collar office workers and blue-collar factory workers spend their days in physical settings that are far more controlled than they were 100 years ago.

For a manager or consultant to undertake the design of physical settings as a preventive management intervention or for a researcher to study the role of the physical setting in creating or alleviating organizational stress entails a thorough understanding of the six functions of physical settings (Steele, 1973). To reiterate from Chapter 2, these functions are (1) shelter and security, (2) social contact, (3) symbolic identification, (4) task instrumentality, (5) pleasure, and (6) growth.

All these functions are of importance in stress management and in the design of physical settings, though their relative importance will vary according to department, managerial preference, organizational level and function, as well as other formal and informal organizational considerations. Not everyone using a physical setting will agree on the priority of these various functions, however. For example, various trainees in one organization had some markedly different perceptions regarding the key functions of the training space. Some considered its most important function to be task instrumentality, while others considered it to be growth.

Many aspects of a physical setting fall in the category of what Herzberg would call hygienic factors, and these are typically what people think about when examining their physical environment. Steele suggests that this may be a convenient place to start people thinking, but the examination of the physical setting must eventually turn to viewing the organization as an entire ecological system. In this case, the ecological concerns are with how individuals relate to and interact with their organizational environments. While individuals often attend to the aesthetic and hygienic aspects of their work environments, they less frequently attend to the natural fit between themselves and their surroundings. It is the interdependence of individuals and their work environments which is the key concern of this ecological perspective in the analysis of physical settings.

Designing Physical Settings

The actual design or redesign of a physical setting involves creativity and an understanding of the functions of space as well as some careful forethought and planning. Each physical setting should be approached without preconceptions about its limitation, since such preconceptions will limit one's imagination in redesigning the space. Once one's imagination is fully opened to the redesign opportunities, it may be possible to use the following sequences of activities for effectively designing or redesigning the space.

Ecological analysis of the physical setting   Identifying the functions of any physical setting requires input from the various individuals and groups who use the setting. Questionnaires or interviews can be used for this purpose. Questionnaires are most efficient when there are a large number of individuals whose opinions and perceptions are needed. This step is critical because a misidentification might result in an extremely dysfunctional setting. For example, if there is a need for privacy and restricted contact in a set of counseling offices and if the setting is inadvertently designed to enhance social contact, individuals using the counseling services will be distressed.

The function identification is only part of the overall ecological analysis. It is also necessary to consider how the space and people in it interact. Such an examination will result in a dynamic analysis that complements the analysis of the functions. The dynamic analysis requires that one examine how the setting places demands and stresses upon individuals who are moving within it and through it. This dynamic examination is an equally important aspect of the overall ecological analysis.

Examination of the present setting   Once the purposes of the physical setting have been identified, then the actual space must be carefully examined for several reasons. First, it is necessary to determine which aspects of the setting are fixed and which are not. Very few aspects of a physical setting are actually fixed in a strict sense, though they may be perceived that way. The use of movable partitions and half-walls is a good example of how a fixed aspect of a physical setting may be converted into easily changed aspects of the physical setting.

Second, the setting needs to be examined for natural advantages and/or disadvantages. For example, a university classroom building designed with two large 250-person lecture halls, fifteen 70-person lecture halls, twenty 40-person classrooms, and four 15-person classrooms is well-suited for large undergraduate classes but particularly ill-suited for very many graduate seminars.

Changes in the physical setting   Once the functions of the setting and the space itself have been carefully examined, then the changes to be made should be identified and carried out. This may include bringing in furniture, removing or adding walls, lowering or raising ceilings, raising the floor, or removing unnecessary furniture. Such identified changes should be made only after a consideration of other aspects of the work environment, budgetary constraints, and the effects of these changes upon the individuals in related areas of the organization. Some possible alterations in the physical setting are listed in Table 8.2. The result of the entire redesign effort should be a natural fitting and flowing together of people and their environment in a smooth ecological system.

Impact of the analysis   The final aspect in the design or redesign of a physical setting is to evaluate the effect of any changes that were made. This may be done by examining accident rates and performance and pro-

TABLE 8.2
SOME POSSIBLE ALTERATIONS
IN THE PHYSICAL SETTING

Structural changes
- Points of entry and exit
- Wall placement and height
- Ceiling height and angle
- Openings for vistas and lighting
- Floor angles and elevations
- Furniture, fixtures, and placements

Accoustical changes
- Wall coverings, finishing, and insulation
- Cushions and draperies
- Floor coverings and finishing
- Ceiling coverings and finishing
- Plants and natural additions

Lighting changes
- Natural openings
- Placement of artificial lights
- Intensity of lighting
- Color of interior furnishings
- Plants and natural additions

(a) ORIGINAL FACILITY DESIGN

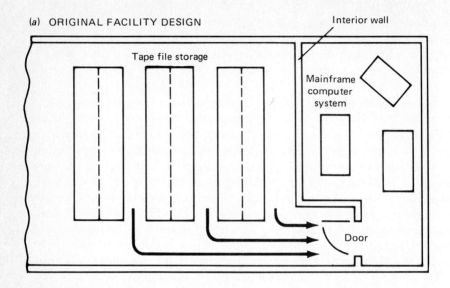

(b) REDESIGNED FACILITY

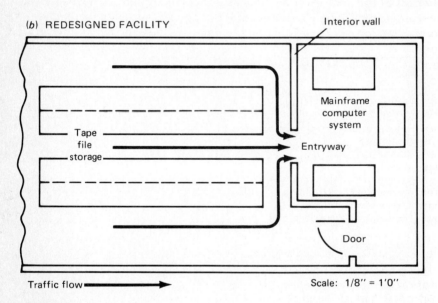

Traffic flow ▬▬▬▬▬▶   Scale: 1/8'' = 1'0''

FIGURE 8.4
Redesigning a physical setting.

ductivity data or by the use of questionnaires and interviews. This analysis of the impact of the changes should be done some months after the changes are made to avoid or minimize the more temporary effects of the change.

A Computer Operations Redesign Effort

The redesign of a physical setting is illustrated in the changes made at a computer facility. The mainframe computer, tape drives, and tape file storage facilities were installed in an area of a building not originally designed for a computer operations branch. This area of the building is shown in Figure 8.4a. The operations personnel experienced some inefficiency in their work flow and task accomplishment because of the location of the door between the tape file storage area and the mainframe computer system.

The branch chief realized that the area might be redesigned more effectively if the tape file storage cabinets and the computer system were more directly connected. He was able to accomplish this by creating a new entry way in the interior wall between the two operations areas. In conjunction with the new entry way, he redesigned the layout of the computer system and tape file cabinets, as shown in Figure 8.4b. This redesign effort created a more efficient and natural flow so that, ecologically, the operations personnel and the setting worked more harmoniously in accomplishing the task for which the setting was intended. The two areas in operations were still somewhat distinct, yet more easily and efficiently connected.

SUMMARY

This chapter presents five organizational-level methods of preventive management aimed at moderating the effects of organizational stressors upon individuals at work. These five methods are task redesign, participative management, flexible work schedules, career development, and the design of physical settings. A brief description of each appears in Table 8.1. The references at the end of the chapter list sources of information for managers interested in learning more about these methods. They are fundamentally concerned with the formal organization and the effects of the formal organization upon the individual. The differences and distinctions between the formal and the informal organizations will be more carefully distinguished at the outset of Chapter 9.

These five prevention methods do not exhaustively list the potential methods for preventing organizational distress within the formal system. They were chosen based upon the documented evidence of their applicability in organizations. Some less extensive and elaborate methods aimed at specific sources of distress may include efforts to change pay and benefit systems, formal company policies and procedures, performance appraisal systems, various aspects of the quality of work life, or equal opportunity programs. There are a wide variety of ways to change and/or modify the formal organization so as to minimize the distressful and maximize the eustressful effects which it has on the individual.

Chapter 9 will address four organizational-level methods of preventive management which are aimed at the informal, interpersonal, and role-related sources of stress in organizations. These aspects of organizational life generate as many demands as does the formal organizational system. Altering these demands requires different techniques than those required to redesign the formal and physical organization.

FURTHER READINGS

Task Redesign

Davis, L., and J. Taylor (eds.): *Design of Jobs*, 2d ed., Goodyear, Santa Monica, Calif., 1979.

Griffin, R. W.: *Task Redesign: An Integrative Approach*, Scott, Foresman and Company, Glenview, Ill., 1982.

Hackman, J. R.: "Work Redesign," in J. R. Hackman and J. L. Suttle (eds.), *Improving Life at Work*, Goodyear, Santa Monica, Calif., 1977, pp. 96–162.

Hackman, J. R., and G. R. Oldham: *Work Redesign*, Addison-Wesley, Reading, Mass., 1980.

Participative Management

Likert, R.: *New Patterns of Management*, McGraw-Hill, New York, 1961.

Marrow, A. J.: *Making Management Human*, McGraw-Hill, New York, 1960.

Flexible Work Schedules

Cohen, A. R., and H. Gadon: *Alternative Schedules: Integrating Individual and Organizational Needs*, Addison-Wesley, Reading, Mass., 1978.

Nollen, S. D.: "What Is Happening to Flexitime, Flexihour, Gliding Time, the Variable Day? and Permanent Part-Time Employment? and the Four-Day Work Week?" *Across the Board*, April 1980, pp. 6–21.

Ronen, S.: *Flexible Working Hours: An Innovation in the Quality of Work Life*, McGraw-Hill, New York, 1981.

Career Development

Bolles, R. N.: *What Color is Your Parachute?* Ten Speed Press, Berkeley, Calif., 1979.

Hall, D. T.: *Careers in Organizations*, Goodyear, Santa Monica, Calif., 1976.

Kotter, J. F., V. A. Faux, and C. McArthur: *Self-Assessment and Career Development*, Prentice-Hall, Englewood Cliffs, N.J., 1978.

Van Maanen, J., and E. J. Schein: "Career Development," in J. R. Hackman and J. L. Suttle (eds.), *Improving Life at Work*, Goodyear, Santa Monica, Calif., 1977, pp. 30–95.

Design of the Physical Setting

Becker, F.: *Work Space: Creating Environments in Organizations*, Praeger, New York, 1981.

Sommer, R.: *Tight Spaces: Hard Architecture and How to Humanize It*, Prentice-Hall, Englewood Cliffs, N.J., 1974.

Steele, F.: *Physical Settings and Organization Development*, Addison-Wesley, Reading, Mass., 1973.

CHAPTER 9

ORGANIZATIONAL METHODS FOR IMPROVING RELATIONSHIPS AT WORK

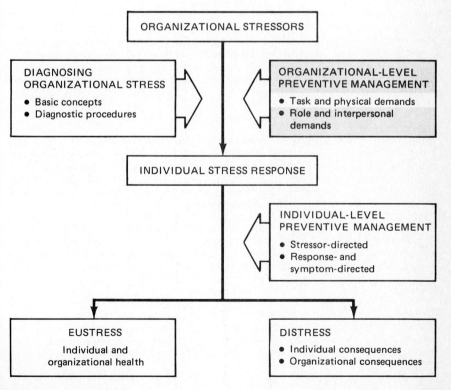

The four primary prevention methods discussed in Chapter 8 focused on reshaping the formal organization to prevent excessive or insufficient work demands. Our focus in this chapter is on methods for preventing distress caused by informal and interpersonal demands placed on individuals in organizations. This may be accomplished through one of several prevention methods directed at role and interpersonal stress factors. The four methods to be covered in this chapter are identified and briefly discussed in Table 9.1. The empirical evidence regarding these methods is modest, suggesting the need for additional research.

The emphasis in Chapter 8 was primarily upon the formal organization. The specific concerns of the formal organization are the tasks that individuals perform and the physical settings in which they work. Any organization is, however, a blend of formal and informal elements. The prevention methods discussed in this chapter deal with the integration

TABLE 9.1
ORGANIZATIONAL-LEVEL METHODS OF PREVENTIVE MANAGEMENT
Role and Interpersonal Demands

Role analysis

This method is aimed at clarifying an individual's work role to reduce distressful confusion and conflict. A role profile is developed based on the expectations of superiors, peers, subordinates, and other key people with whom the individual must work. This *expected role* is then clarified by eliminating conflicts and confusion in the expectations. It is also integrated with the *enacted role*, resulting in reduced role stress for the individual. (French and Bell, 1978)

Goal setting

This method focuses on the primary relationship between an individual and his immediate superior. The aim of this method is to clarify the individual's work role by specifying major areas of responsibility and specifying performance goals in each responsibility area. This should result in increased motivation and reduced role stress. (Quick, 1979b)

Social support

This is a method for ameliorating many of the effects of work stresses upon the individual. The idea is to buffer the impact of stressors upon the individual's psychological and physiological functioning by providing the necessary emotional, informational, appraisal, and instrumental support that the individual needs. (House, 1981)

Team building

This is a method for intervening in the interpersonal processes of an intact work group. The aim of this method is to confront, work through, and resolve interpersonal conflicts that naturally evolve within work groups. The process of resolution is thought to be better than repression for the management of these interpersonal stresses. (French and Bell, 1978)

---

of the informal and the formal organization. Two of these methods, role analysis and goal setting, are primary prevention methods aimed at changing the demands placed upon the individual at work. The other two methods, social support and team building, are a mixture of secondary and tertiary prevention methods. They are intended to assist individuals in managing the various demands of work. The ability to understand individual and organizational functioning is hinged in part on grasping the distinction between the formal and the informal, the overt and the covert, the conscious and the unconscious. This distinction is depicted in Table 9.2.

One of the underlying assumptions of organizational-level preventive management is that the informal, covert, and unconscious elements of organizations and individuals are important to health (French and Bell, 1978; Freud, 1956a). Some organizations and individuals attempt either to ignore the informal or to repress it. While such a strategy may be successful in the short term, it is rarely successful for long periods of time. Organizational and psychiatric literature document numerous cases of organizational and individual health problems arising from lack of integration of the informal and unconscious with the formal and the conscious. For example, if management ignores the feelings and needs of employees, the employees may retaliate by using work slowdowns or other disruptive activities to frustrate management. An individual-level example would be illustrated in the case of a manager who becomes very angry with his boss but represses the feeling at work, only to have a headache or upset stomach later.

The formal and informal aspects of organizational life are important

TABLE 9.2
THE FORMAL AND THE INFORMAL

The organization	The individual
Formal (overt) aspects	**Conscious aspects**
• Goals and objectives	• Thoughts
• Organization and job structure	• Intentions
• Policies and procedures	• Feelings of joy and anger
• Capital and operating budgets	• Voluntary behavior
• Organization technology	• Performance
Informal (covert) aspects	**Unconscious aspects**
• Perceptions	• Repressed feelings
• Attitudes	• Prejudices
• Values	• Involuntary reactions
• Group behavior norms	• Subliminal perceptions
• Feelings	• Psychological processes

when dealing with role and interpersonal demands because there are formal and informal requirements in all working relationships. For example, Payne (1980) has pointed out that we receive social support from both the formal organization, as in the case of rules about work behavior, and the informal organization, as in the case of a supervisor covering a friend's shift for a few hours. Recognizing the formal and informal components of organizations and individuals may lead to alternative and complementary ways of managing the demands of organizational life.

Organizational-level preventive management requires an attention to both the formal and the informal when dealing with the relationships that influence an individual's behavior and stress level at work. In one way or another, each of the prevention methods in this chapter is concerned with the individual's working relationships. The formal aspects of these relationships may cause distress or eustress. The same is true of the informal aspects of these relationships. Which of the two outcomes occurs—distress or eustress—is partially dependent upon the application of one or more of the following preventive measures.

ROLE ANALYSIS

Role analysis is a method of clarifying and defining an individual's work role to reduce distressful confusion and conflict. An individual conducts a role analysis by first asking people at work what they expect of him or her. By identifying the points of confusion and/or inconsistency in these expectations, the individual may then take action to resolve the confusion and eliminate the inconsistencies. The result of role analysis is a clearer, more consistent work role for the individual.

Organizational Roles

Organizational roles may be defined in one of two ways. One way is to define the role in terms of what other people at work expect of the individual, which is the *expected role* and the most common way of defining an organizational role. The other way is to define the role in terms of how the individual in the role behaves, which is the *enacted role*. Thus an individual's actions and behaviors "in role" define the enacted role. The expected role and the enacted role are not necessarily the same. The whole process of assuming an organizational role causes individuals stress at work (Kahn et al., 1964).

Organizational roles are more easily understood in a role set framework. In this framework, the individual is viewed from the position of a focal role. Figure 9.1 depicts this focal role with its various role senders. People inside the organization as well as outside the organization are

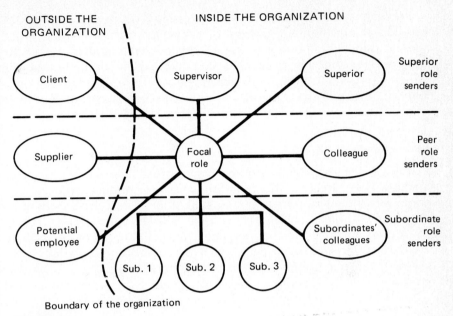

OUTSIDE THE ORGANIZATION

INSIDE THE ORGANIZATION

FIGURE 9.1
An organizational member's role set.

important in the individual's role set, each being a source of behavioral expectations.

Role senders are individuals who expect the focal person to behave in certain ways and meet certain obligations at work. As shown in the figure, there are three general categories of role senders. These are superior, peer, and subordinate role senders. Some are inside the organization and others are outside. Every organizational member will have formal as well as informal relationships with various role senders, and behavioral expectations are generated in all these relationships. Therefore, each role sender will have both formal and informal expectations of the focal person.

Typically, an individual is more concerned with what his supervisor wants and expects of him than with what one of his subordinates wants or expects. However, stress will be generated by ambiguity and conflict in either case. Some roles will typically generate more stress than others. For example, the boundary-spanning roles are typically very stressful (Miles, 1980). This is due to the great variety of expectations communicated to these individuals, the diverse performance feedback which they receive, the evaluation criteria used for these positions, and several other considerations discussed by Miles (1980).

Preventive management of role stress is an active process which requires clarification and integration of the various expectations which role senders communicate to the focal role as well as alteration of the behaviors exhibited by the focal person. Any activity or method of role stress management must focus on these essential processes of clarification and integration. For these two essential processes to go on, both role expectations and behaviors must be observed and analyzed.

The Procedure

Dayal and Thomas (1968) were the first to discuss the actual use of role analysis. There are a number of different ways to conduct a role analysis, some ways being more regimented than others. These are discussed by Dayal and Thomas (1968), French and Bell (1978), and Huse (1980). Regardless of which specific approach is taken, the key elements of a role analysis are the same in each approach. Based on French and Bell (1978), the following paragraphs outline how to conduct a role analysis. The procedure involves identifying key role senders and their behavioral expectations of the focal person, and developing the focal person's role profile.

Role-set identification   The focal person must identify his or her role set, making sure to include all relevant role senders who may have legitimate expectations of the focal person. Classification and categorization of the various role senders is necessary to avoid ignoring any relevant role senders.

Role definition   Once the role set has been identified, it is necessary to define the focal role in terms of its place in the organization. The rationale for the focal role and the contributions of the incumbent to overall organizational functioning and goal attainment are developed by the focal person. This rationale is a broad justification of the role's necessity to the organization. The responsibilities and authorities of the focal person are identified here.

Focal person's expectations   None of us functions entirely independently in any organization. We have certain expectations regarding what other organizational members will do for us in our role performance. In this step, the focal person identifies what is expected of each member of the role set, discussing these expectations with the various role senders.

Role-sender expectations   The next step requires the focal person to identify all the specific expectations which each member of the role set has of him or her. In identifying each role sender's expectations, the focal person should be particularly mindful of expectations which are ambiguous. In addition, the focal person should be aware of points of inconsistency and/or incompatibility between the expectations of one or more role senders.

In using this approach, the focal person should be attendant to any informal expectations which various role senders may place on the role. These will often not be made explicit without the focal person probing for them. However, these informal expectations may play an important role in the dynamics of the relationship between focal person and role sender and should, therefore, be explored. For example, a supervisor who likes to be left alone in the morning until after his first cup of coffee will be very upset with anyone who bothers him before that time. This illustrates one of his informal expectations.

Role profile   The final step in the role analysis technique is the development of a written role profile which delineates the expected role of the focal person. This profile should consist of a set of clear, specific, and internally consistent expectations of the focal person. Any inconsistencies in the profile or expectations which are not clear or explicit should be examined by the focal person in conjunction with the affected role sender(s). These inconsistencies and ambiguities should be eliminated from the profile as much as possible. Those which cannot be eliminated will require the focal person to devise some alternative ways to manage this role stress, such as drawing on social support contacts. Role analysis is a systematic way of profiling an individual's work role so that the confusion and inconsistency in the role may be clearly identified. Stress is reduced for the individual as the inconsistencies and confusion are eliminated from the role profile through discussion and negotiation with the involved role senders. There will always be stress associated with assuming an organizational role, and that is not necessarily bad. What needs to be eliminated through role analysis are the distressful elements of role stress.

Practical Difficulties

Several contemporary forms of organization pose peculiar difficulties for the use of role analysis. These include matrix and project organizations. Both forms of organization have become more prevalent as a result of an increasingly complex and changing business environment. Bennis (1966) suggests that these and other forms of flexible and temporary organizations are better suited to current conditions than the traditional bureaucracy. These organizations will be complex, decentralized, flexible, and informal (Burns and Stalker, 1961). Because of their increasing presence, it is important to examine the difficulties in using role analysis in these organizations.

Matrix organization The matrix form of organization arose in an effort to combat some of the difficulties in managing large groups of employees where coordination and interfacing at the operating level are important. The aircraft industry and the shipbuilding industry are among those who have most heavily used this matrix form of organization.

A matrix organization will typically look like the one depicted in Figure 9.2. The focal role incumbent in this example is responsible in a formal fashion to both Theresa L. and Carol L. As we noted earlier, any person will have several superiors to deal with in a role set. However, it is only in the matrix structure that the person has two managers to report to. This results in a structural arrangement with great potential for role conflict to occur through conflicting expectations from Theresa L. and Carol L.

This situation in the matrix structure leads to a greater need for a method such as the role analysis technique. It may also lead to some real difficulties, such as power struggles between managers, unless the potentially conflictual situation for the focal role incumbent is properly managed (Davis and Lawrence, 1978).

Project organization Many companies now use a project form of organization in an operating division to accomplish a specific task. For example, an international construction firm used this form of organization to complete an engineering contract for the Iranian government (Riddle, 1979). This temporary form of organization faces a predictable and finite life cycle (Kimberly, Miles, and associates, 1980). There is a period of growth, a period of task accomplishment, and a period of decline. Because of the rapidity of the changes that occur within the role relationships in a project organization, it is unlikely that any role profile developed would be useful for an extended period. However, it is clear that a real need for role clarity would be present in this form of organization. Therefore, a less formal role analysis procedure, conducted on a more frequent basis, might be very appropriate in this organizational arrangement.

Organic organization Burns and Stalker (1961) clearly delineate the advantages of the organic organization form in an unstable and/or changing environment. One of the characteristics of this form of organization is the constantly changing role relationships that occur between organizational members. This circumstance creates a substantial amount of role stress for the members of organic organizations. As a result, there

FIGURE 9.2
Matrix organization in a northwestern power company.

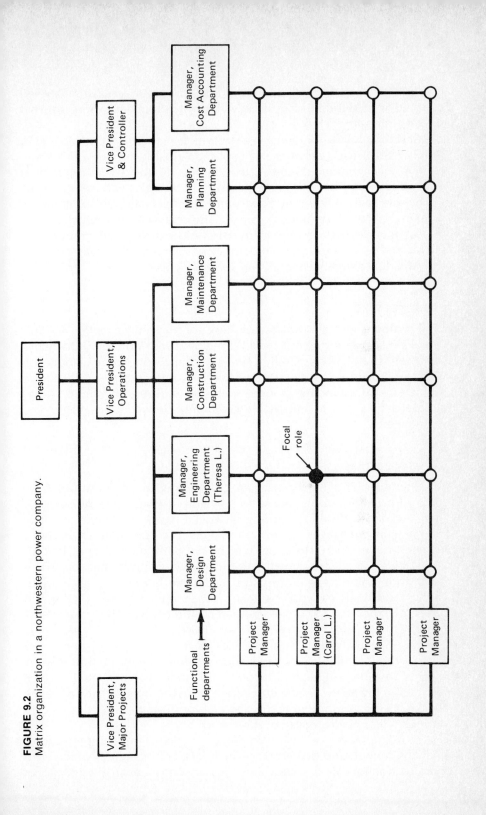

is a greater need for role analysis in this form of organization, a need coupled with difficulties in its execution in situations where role set relationships are in flux.

Therefore, in the organic organization, it may well be necessary for employees to use one of the several individual-level methods of preventive management discussed in Chapters 10 and 11 in conjunction with an organizational-level method such as the role analysis technique.

The role analysis technique deals with the expectations of all members of an organizational member's role set. The next technique which we will discuss focuses on the primary relationship existing between an employee and his or her supervisor. The supervisor is the key role sender in an individual's organizational role set (Kahn, 1964).

GOAL SETTING

Goal setting is a method of establishing specific objectives for an individual's job. These objectives will direct and motivate the individual's behavior and actions. Goal setting is often done in collaboration with the individual's supervisor and, when done correctly, will lead to a clearer understanding of one's job and work environment. It may also lead to a better mutual understanding between a manager and employee.

Goal-Setting Theory

The literature and the practice of goal setting in organizations have focused primarily on its motivational value in stimulating task performance (Locke, 1968). According to Locke, work incentives, such as money, may contribute to motivation when used in conjunction with a goal-setting program. However, it is the difficulty and clarity of an individual's work goals which will determine their motivational value. This basic notion about the importance of difficult but clear goals in motivating individuals at work has been supported by a well-established series of laboratory and field research studies over the past twenty years (Latham and Yukl, 1975; Locke, 1968).

According to Locke (1968), individuals must also accept their work goals if they are to serve a motivational value at work. In one case he reports that the subjects did *not* accept their assigned goals, which resulted in the goals' having little effect upon the subjects' performance (Locke, 1968). In other words, individuals perform better if they accept difficult, clear goals regarding their work.

According to Locke (1968), employee participation, competition for goal attainment, and performance feedback are incentives which elicit individual action. He does not view these incentives as an integral part of the goal-setting process. Using a slightly different interpretation, Steers and Porter (1974), Latham and Yukl (1975), and Quick (1979b) view participation, competition, and feedback as behavioral dimensions of the goal-setting process. It is the behavioral focus in the goal-setting literature that is relevant to goal setting as an organizational-level method of preventive management.

Integrating Role Theory and Goal Setting

Latham and Yukl (1975), Miles (1976b), and Quick (1979b) have extended Locke's theory by integrating it with role theory and examining how goal-setting activities can clarify an individual's organizational role. This is done primarily through the manager-employee relationship. The employee's relationship with the manager is particularly important because the manager is the primary source of role expectations for the employee (Carroll and Tosi, 1973; Gerloff and Quick, 1978; Kahn, 1964). The manager is also the individual's key link to the organization.

Both Locke (1968) and Taylor (1911) would refer to goals as standards of performance. On the other hand, role theorists would view goals as behavioral expectations (Miles, 1976a, 1976b). As such, the manager and employee would establish a limited task-related set of behavioral expectations for the employee's role through goal-setting activities. Quick (1979b) has proposed that this process may be useful for managing role stress. Whereas goal difficulty and clarity are the key concerns in motivating an individual's task performance, it is behavioral dynamics in the manager-employee relationship which are the focus in goal setting as a method for reducing distress. Goal clarity might reasonably be expected to reduce distress caused by role ambiguity and confusion. Furthermore, through the employee's active participation in the goal-setting process and the manager's regular performance review and feedback, it is reasonable to expect an overall reduction in an employee's distress at work.

A model for understanding the motivational and stress-reducing functions of goal-setting programs is presented in Figure 9.3. The upper linkages in the model are based on Locke's task motivation and performance ideas. The lower linkages suggest that the interaction between manager and employee will lead to reduced role stress. Specifically, the more frequent and useful the manager's performance feedback and the more participation exhibited by the employee, the lower the employee's role stress. This stress-reducing function will be most pronounced when the manager and employee achieve consensus with regard to the employee's task goals.

Because the stress-reducing function of goal-setting programs focuses on both task goals and manager-employee behaviors, as seen in Figure

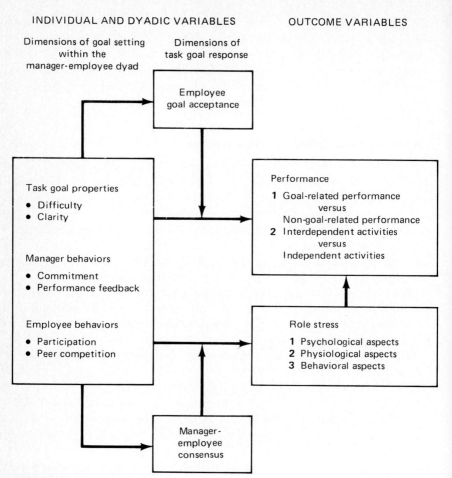

FIGURE 9.3
A suggested framework for goal-setting programs.

9.3, it is essential for the training program used in an organization to focus on both knowledge acquisition and skill development (Streidl, 1976). Acquiring new behavior patterns and modifying old behavior patterns is essential to the use of goal-setting programs as a way of preventively managing stress.

A Training Program Based on Role Play

By using a training program for goal setting which provides the participant an opportunity to role-play the "manager" role and the "employee" role, an individual is able to acquire goal-setting skills in addition to knowledge. Streidl (1976) of Tenneco, Inc., has designed a three-phase training program in goal setting which involves (1) individual employee performance planning, (2) effective performance evaluation by the manager, and (3) developmental coaching and counseling by the manager. This three-phase training program is outlined in Table 9.3. The program may be completed in a three-day period. The manager's roles as evaluator and developmental counselor are handled separately (phases II and III) to emphasize the distinction between these roles and reduce the dysfunctions associated with the two roles (Meyer, Kay, and French, 1965). Each training phase should be completed so that the trainee can digest the materials before the next phase. Therefore, it would be best to complete the three phases over a one-month period.

TABLE 9.3
GOAL-SETTING TRAINING PROGRAM

Phase I: Performance planning (1 day)

    Module 1 1 hour, 30 minutes
        Introduction and historical background

    Module 2 2 hours
        Identification of major responsibility areas
        Practice in preparing specific goals for each responsibility area

    Module 3 3 hours, 30 minutes
        Performance planning sessions role plays

Phase II: Performance evaluation (1 day)

    Module 1 1 hour
        Introduction to evaluation concepts

    Module 2 2 hours, 30 minutes
        Review of traditional evaluation techniques
        Evaluation based on goal setting
        Performance-based MBO

    Module 3 3 hours, 30 minutes
        Performance evaluation session role plays

Phase III: Developmental counseling (1 day)

    Module 1 1 hour
        Introduction of the supervisory counseling role

    Module 2 2 hours, 30 minutes
        Why do developmental needs require identification?
        Practice in identifying developmental needs

    Module 3 3 hours, 30 minutes
        Coaching and counseling session role plays

Source: James C. Quick and David A. Gray, "Dyadic Goal Setting as a Developmental Technique: Training Through Role Planning," *Proceedings of the 1979 Academy of Management, Southwest Division,* p. 151.

Performance planning During this phase, participants define managerial roles and identify major authority and responsibility areas. This helps participants better understand their organizational roles in a general fashion. They then practice developing specific goals for each major responsibility area. For example, one objective in the major responsibility area of "service" might be "to receive less than two complaint letters each quarter." A series of three *role playing exercises,* each lasting about one hour, including feedback and review of performance, are an important part of the learning process. Participants have the opportunity to role-play the managerial and employee roles in a performance planning session, getting both practice and feedback on their behavior and performance.

Performance evaluation Phase II of the training focuses upon evaluating employee performance. This is particularly important because of the stressfulness of this process for both parties (Beehr and Newman, 1978). In this phase of the training it is shown how goal setting may be used as an improved basis for evaluating performance as compared to the more traditional approaches to performance evaluation (McGregor, 1957). Participants are provided sample performance plans for several hypothetical employees (typically three or four) in various jobs together with measures of the employee's actual performance. The participants then practice evaluating the employee's performance levels against planned performance. As in the first phase of the training, each individual has the opportunity to role-play a performance evaluation session. The participants are given a different set of three performance plans and actual performance results. The participants again work in groups of three and role-play three performance evaluation sessions. The focus in these sessions is upon the review of actual performance.

Developmental counseling The final phase of the training focuses upon the developmental coaching and counseling aspects of the managerial role (Athos and Gabarro, 1978). The importance and nature of the counselor role is reinforced in this phase of training. A key aspect of this phase is reviewing sample performance plans and evaluations for the purpose of *diagnosing* employee skills and/or attitude deficiencies and developmental needs. The manager who is a good counselor will be able to efficiently diagnose performance problem areas and actively work with the employee in coming to grips with those problems. Therefore, a good manager also needs to be a good diagnostician. The diagnostic work is done individually and is followed again by three-person role plays.

Effectiveness of Goal-Setting Programs

In evaluating the effectiveness of using goal-setting programs for stress management, significant declines in both role conflict and ambiguity were found during one fourteen-month study in an insurance company (Quick, 1979a). This suggests that the individual's work role can be clarified through the goal-setting process, thus reducing the amount of stress it generates. A later review suggests that this result may be dependent upon the existence of a participatory, interactive process between the individual and his supervisor (Tolchinsky and King, 1980). In a second study conducted over a two-year period in a large western bank, similar reductions in role stress owing to the presence of a goal-setting program were not found (Quick, Kulisch, Jones, O'Connor, and Peters, 1981). This may well have been due in part to the much lower levels of employee participation found in the bank.

The insurance company study also found a significant decline in illness-related absenteeism at five months following the implementation of the goal-setting program. This decline was not maintained eight months after implementation. The reduction in absenteeism is consistent with improved role clarity because individuals feel less confused at work and less prone to avoid work. Also, absenteeism was found to be significantly related to conflicting expectations from supervisors. As these conflicting expectations were reduced, it is not surprising that absenteeism declined. Again, the results in the bank were not consistent with these results. The individuals using the goal-setting program were absent more because of personal illness and absent less on holidays than those not on the goal-setting program. This suggests that the bank's program had the reverse effect upon its employees, in fact *increasing* their stress level. These findings suggest that a participatory approach to the goal-setting process is an essential prerequisite to achieving the intended stress reduction.

SOCIAL SUPPORT

Social support is a means of augmenting the natural physiological and psychological resources that each individual has to manage the demands at work which cause stress. House (1981) suggests that this may be accomplished in one of three ways. First, social support may have a direct effect upon work stress by altering a work demand or modifying one's response to the demand. Second, social support may have a direct effect upon health by improving one's physical or psychological well-being. Third, social support may buffer the adverse effects work stress may have on one's health. Figure 9.4 illustrates these three ways that social support

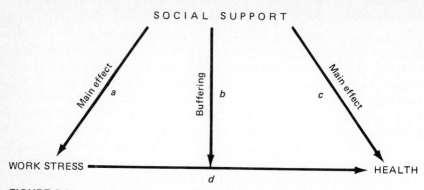

FIGURE 9.4
Potential effects of social support on work stress and health. [Source: *James S. House*, Work Stress and Social Support, *p. 31, copyright © 1981, Addison-Wesley, Reading, Mass. Used with permission.*]

may affect work stress and health. Social support is primarily a secondary prevention method aimed at assisting the individual to deal with work demands.

Many of the experts on social support are either unclear or tautological in their definitions of social support. A reasonable definition of social support, based on the various definitions of the experts, is the assistance one receives through his or her interpersonal relationships. Operationally, social support comes in one or more of four forms: emotional, appraisal, informational, and instrumental support (House, 1981). Emotional support involves providing empathy, emotional caring, and love, such as quietly listening to the lament of an individual who has just lost a job. Appraisal support involves transmitting information to an individual about role performance and behavior. An example would be the performance appraisal interview. Informational support involves providing information needed to manage demands or problems, for example, receiving specifications for a new computer software system from a user. Instrumental support involves behaviors which directly assist another individual in need, such as taking on part of a colleague's work after your own has been completed.

The Human Dialogue and Loneliness

According to Lynch (1977), human relationships and social support are critical to our emotional, psychological, and physiological well-being. Based upon demographic data, as well as clinical studies, he demonstrates the vital role of human relationship in health and well-being. Premature deaths as well as a variety of medical diseases and disorders may be partially attributable to the fact that the individual involved failed to cultivate the relationships and social supports that are essential to health and the avoidance of distress. In one of the classic studies of social support, Parkes (1969) found the death rate among 4,486 widowers in the first six months after the spouse's death to be 40 percent above that expected for married men of the same age.

Avoiding loneliness for Lynch (1977) is more than spending time around other people. Avoiding loneliness means to open up one's innermost self in a relationship with another human being. While there are varying degrees to which each of us bares our soul to another, it is that capacity to do so which is essential to the avoidance of loneliness. Each of us wants and needs—as much as we may want to deny it—close, committed relationships in which we may invest our love, our caring, and our emotional energy. We also need to have other individuals invest their love and emotional energy in us. Commonly these relationships are with family and kinfolk, but we also need to have emotional and psychological investments with some individuals at work (Quick and Quick, 1984).

The distress and pain of alienation at work can have devastating consequences for an individual's health and well-being in addition to the potentially adverse effects upon performance and productivity. Such distress and pain may be overcome through the dialogue of human relationship. This dialogue is not without risks and hazards either, for it is only through the gradual process of revealing our inner self and risking the pain of rejection that we can know in which relationships to really invest ourselves. However, we can only avoid the medical consequences of loneliness by developing such intimate, trusting relationships in which we can invest ourselves and carry on the human dialogue.

The benefits of the human dialogue are illustrated in the case of a successful Dallas business executive. While he uses such activities as running regularly to manage his stress, he also talks about the central role his relationship with his father plays in managing stress. He has always had a close relationship with his father, an 81-year-old retired oilman. As a youngster, he spent much time with his father in the oilfields. He continues to have a close relationship with his father to whom he can reveal the more distressful and troubling aspects of his work life, getting both emotional support and perspective. He regularly and frequently visits his father, simply sitting and talking with him. Such human dialogue is essential to health and to the avoidance of the medical consequences of loneliness (Lynch, 1977).

Social Support at Work

Every individual has a social support network which varies in both size and composition. This network consists of all the various relationships in which the individual is involved. These relationships may be classified into major categories or arenas, as depicted in Figure 9.5. While these relationships in this social support network provide assistance in managing demands and problems, it should also be noted that these relationships will at times be a *source of demands*. This notion of social exchange is at the foundation of all human relationships. So, it is important to keep in mind that even the most supportive of our relationships will place certain demands upon us at times.

As illustrated in the case of the Dallas business executive, familial support systems can be especially important as a source of guidance, renewal, and emotional support (Bhagat, 1983). In the childhood years, the family plays a vital role in an individual's socialization and adjustment to the broader society. In the adult years, the family is an important source of identification and strength. The family's value as a support system depends in part upon its acceptance of an individual's whole personality, including the flaws and inconsistencies in that personality. It also depends upon the recognition and meeting of the individual's more fundamental needs. In addition, families evaluate and regulate the behavior of their members. Therefore, the family is a vital social support system which combats loneliness and alienation and which provides a source of identity and guidance.

As indicated in Figure 9.5, not all social support systems come from personal and family relationships. Effective support systems are also needed within work organizations. There are several reasons for this. First, the demands of work require a response using various resources available to the individual. Appraisal and informational forms of social support enhance our knowledge and skill utilization in meeting these diverse demands. Without the supplemental outside resources to assist us in managing demands at work, the stress response caused by specific demands will be more intense and sustained than would otherwise be the case. Second, the instrumental form of social support provides us with the additional resources and assistance that we need to manage specific demands. Third, when our emotional needs are not met, we become preoccupied with the particular need deprivation that we are experiencing. If we are getting the emotional support we need at work, then such need deprivation will not be a driving force for our behavior.

While social support systems may not alter the nature of a role or of an interpersonal stressor, they can be instrumental in various coping strategies that the individual attempts. For example, a role conflict may develop if two superiors expect different types of work from a subor-

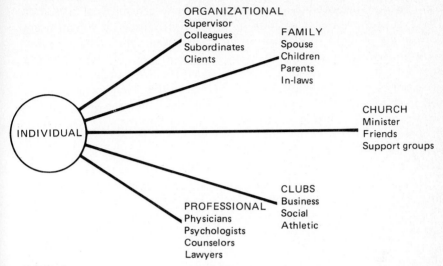

FIGURE 9.5
Social support network.

dinate. Even if the conflict cannot be structurally resolved, it is possible for the individual either to learn how to meet both sets of conflicting expectations with social support from a peer group *or* to feel less upset and troubled by the inability to meet both sets of demands. The sense of mastery and interpersonal competence in a situation will contribute to lower levels of experienced stress. This is attributable to the lower levels of experienced threat and demand posed by the situation.

Building Support Systems

Building effective social support systems at work starts at the top of the organization. Management must be prepared to provide the individuals in an organization with social support, not all of which can be of a formal nature. The formal organization can be designed to provide some social support of various kinds. For example, managerial titles and office settings provide some emotional support by way of esteem and status gratification. Appraisal support may be provided through the performance evaluation and reward allocation processes. Informational support may be provided through policy directives and written procedures. Instrumental support may be provided by way of capital, material, and human resources provided to the manager.

One category within the social support network in Figure 9.5 is professional. Increasingly, organizations are providing various forms of professional support services beyond the standard medical assistance. These support services include alcoholism programs, psychiatric and counseling programs, and support group activities. One such counseling program will be illustrated in Chapter 12, and it should be noted that group therapy, discussed in Chapter 11, is a formalized, professional form of social support. Individual reluctance to utilize such forms of social support reflect traditional and archaic attitudes which are often founded on erroneous assumptions. For example, it is often the strong and more fit individuals who reach out for professional support when it is appropriate (Peck, 1978). Thus, drawing upon one's social support network is a sign of strength as opposed to a sign of weakness.

The support systems of the formal organization will not be completely adequate in and of themselves. There is a need for informal support systems as well. These support systems should be complementary and supplemental to the support systems contained in the formal organization. The support systems of the informal organization may be more effective in shaping behavior and avoiding distress at times. For example, when a teacher in a secondary school admitted a student to class who should not have been in the class, she received feedback (appraisal support) about her behavior in a formal disciplinary note from an assistant principal. The incident left her formally and publicly chastised for her behavior. The teacher's verbally hostile response to the memo distressed the assistant principal. An informal and private conversation between the assistant principal and the teacher might have achieved equal or better performance results with less distress for both parties.

Formal and informal support systems at work may contribute to improved decision making while reducing stress. Maier (1967) has highlighted the assets and liabilities that are associated with group decision-making and problem-solving processes. In a study of decision-making processes in emergency rooms, Quick et al. (1983) found that resident physicians relied increasingly upon social supports for information and emotional support as the decision situation became more complex and stressful. (An exception occurred in the initial stages of a life-threatening crisis situation where one resident made the initial decisions alone.) The effect of the collaborative and consensual decision processes for the residents was to reduce their distress and to improve the quality of the decision-making process.

Effects of Bureaucracy

Burns and Stalker (1961) found that organic bureaucracy, a decentralized form of organization that has few rules or regulations, tends to cause more distress for individuals than mechanistic bureaucracy, which is more formalized and centralized in structure. This appears to be largely attributable to the confusion, ambiguity, and conflict associated with the work-related roles of individuals in organic organizations. In addition, due to the inevitable lack of formalized rules and standardization of procedures in the organic organization, there will be job and role stressors operating which cannot be eliminated. Therefore, the method for preventing excessive distress in such situations must be implemented at the interpersonal level. The need will be greater for both emotional and instrumental support in the organic organization to compensate for the lack of formal appraisal and informational support.

Some social support through the formal organization is possible in such situations, but the informal organization's support systems are critical in a constantly changing environment. Use of the informal organization for this purpose will entail using the informal status system and leadership structure of the organization so as to establish behavioral norms regarding provision of social support. Many American organizations have not viewed provision of social support as an essential or necessary aspect of organizational life, yet it should be viewed as an integral part of coping with the demands and stresses that we do face at work.

In summary, individuals may improve and expand their social support systems through a process of communicating their needs from specific relationships. It is true that one risks not receiving the support asked for, but one surely will not receive it unless it is asked for. In addition to communicating social support needs, individuals must be prepared to give social support to members of their support network when *they* need it. It is through this reciprocal process of giving and receiving social support that support networks grow and flourish.

TEAM BUILDING

Team building is a prevention method aimed at improving performance effectiveness through cooperative, supportive relationships within a work group. It is also concerned with the effectiveness of the work group in accomplishing the tasks set out for it. The outcome of effective team building should be a cohesive, well integrated work group within which individuals give and receive needed support while being highly productive as a group.

Team building is intended for use with naturally occurring work groups of a size not normally greater than fifteen or twenty. The members of the work group must have regular, face-to-face interaction as well as commonality of purpose, task, or objective. Thus, the concern here is with formal work groups of a task-oriented nature. What is an inevitable consequence of such groups is the evolution of emergent sentiments and interactions. These informal dimensions of the group's interpersonal life may interfere with the task objectives and create distress for some members. The informal interactions may also have beneficial effects upon group functioning.

The Team-Building Process

Team building involves three essential steps. First, the group needs to diagnose internal problems, stresses, and/or barriers to the group's effectiveness. Second, the group needs to establish an agenda for working through the issues identified within the diagnostic work. The group should be careful to work on underlying or basic problems, rather than the symptoms of those problems. Third, the group should reassess its performance and interpersonal relations at some time, maybe three months, after the group work is completed.

Diagnostic activities Using one or another of the formal stress diagnostic procedures will be helpful in this phase of the team building. For example, an examination of the "process data" or the data regarding "attitudes and relationships" in Levinson's diagnostic procedure may indicate that stresses of an interpersonal nature are operating in a work group. Or, such symptoms as absenteeism, open conflicts which go unresolved, or excessive tardiness indicate interpersonal distress. The concern in diagnosing the work group's functioning is with the interpersonal and emotional health of the relationships among the work group members as well as with the group's level of productivity. The concern is not with the health of the individual members but with the health of the *relationships* within the group (Laing, 1971).

It is possible, for example, that the work group inadvertently chooses one member to serve as the scapegoat for stresses within the group. This does not necessarily mean that there is anything "wrong" with that member. If preliminary diagnostic activities suggest that the stresses may be of an interpersonal nature, then the group leader or the diagnostician should schedule a block of free time (approximately three hours) for the entire work group to assemble and to examine the interpersonal relationships and performance of the group. The leader (or diagnostician) should take the initiative to establish the purpose of the meeting, the expected outcome, and an atmosphere of open exchange and supportive confrontation. The purpose of the meeting is to identify the sources of interpersonal stress according to the membership.

The outcome of the group diagnosis should be a statement listing the interpersonal stresses which the group members must manage. This listing will most likely be composed of the conflicts existing in the relationships among the members of the group. Until the conflicts are identified, no action to eliminate or minimize them as sources of stress can be taken.

Group work agenda Once the group has developed a diagnostic statement regarding interpersonal stresses within it, the leader must establish a program of activities (i.e., group work) to deal with items on the list. There are a variety of formats for this group work. For example, one way of doing the group work would consist of weekly meetings of one to two hours during which members work on one or two specific conflicts. There are effectively two outcomes which may ensue from this group work. One outcome is to achieve resolution of the conflict. The other outcome is to contain the conflict and minimize its distressful effects.

Conflicts which may be resolved include different approaches to specific aspects of the group's tasks, idiosyncratic behavioral patterns which cause distress for specific individuals, and divergent perspectives on the group's objectives. Conflicts of this nature may be resolved as members of the group explore their unique knowledge and/or perspectives through the process of group dialogue and exchange. The eventual outcome of this process will be increased agreement and consensus and reduced stress tension within the group.

Not all conflicts can achieve resolution, however. Some conflicts in work relationships are based upon differences in personal beliefs or values as well as differences in individual development. It may not be possible to resolve such conflicts to the stage of agreement and consensus. What is possible in such situations is to clearly define the conflict and its basis as well as to identify strategies for minimizing the dysfunctional effects of the conflict.

A natural history of conflict within a work group is depicted in Figure 9.6, incorporating the stages of the evolution of the conflict and the alternative outcomes of the conflict. While informal groups and work groups are not the only place where conflict occurs in the organization, it is within this context that it most often occurs and where it should be resolved.

The various resolution strategies for conflict may be classified as either participant modes or third-party modes. This distinction here is concerned with whether the members of the group can manage and work through their own conflict or whether they require intervention from some outside force, be it a superior or a professional consultant. A failure on the part of the group to resolve its conflicts would lead to the group's destruction.

The aim of the group work is to improve the interpersonal and emotional life within the group to preclude the evolution of symptomatic diseases such as labor strikes, grievances, and high absenteeism rates. In a sense, the work of improving interpersonal relationships within the group is an ongoing activity. However, within the context of this inter-

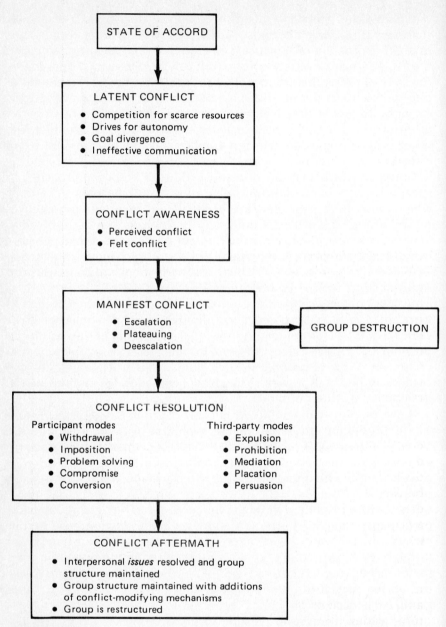

FIGURE 9.6
Natural history of conflict. [*From "Organizational Conflict: Concepts and Models,"
by Louis R. Pondy, in* Administrative Science Quarterly, *vol. 12, 1967, by permission
of* The Administrative Science Quarterly. *Copyright © 1967, Cornell University. All
rights reserved.*]

vention, there is a formal concluding point for the group work. That point must be determined by the leader of the group.

Reassessment   It is important to conduct a follow-up or reassessment of the work group's functioning three to six months after the conclusion of the group work. The improvements that are achieved by the end of the work group may not be sufficiently reinforced within the group to be stable over time. The reassessment activity will determine this. A procedure similar to or the same as that used in the diagnostic activity should be employed for this purpose. This will allow for comparability of results and data.

Cautionary Notes

The process   The team-building activity in the work group is based upon a consensual, participatory approach to confronting and resolving interpersonal stresses. Much of the discussion will relate to the feelings of group members. It is important for the leader to point out that the activity the group will engage in is *not* group therapy. If the group or any of its members feel the need for such therapy, a trained clinician should be engaged to take responsibility for the therapy. This does not mean that there will be no therapeutic benefit from effective group work around interpersonal issues, for there can be. The leader should be always alert to the potential for the group to stray from their objective and drift into material he or she cannot handle.

Organizational norms   Organizations vary markedly in what are acceptable norms and standards of behavior. Groups and individuals which deviate from accepted and established norms will encounter varying degrees of conflict and sanctions aimed at increasing their conforming behavior. For team building to be most effective, an organization must be open to change and communication. Without such receptive norms and a rather participatory philosophy of management, any team-building efforts will encounter resistance and difficulties.

Project teams   Many organizations increasingly use temporary organizational structures, such as project teams or groups, for short-term and/or specialized projects. The life cycle of these organizational structures varies from several months to several years. They are often composed of specialists from various functional areas who must blend their talent. For example, the temporary project team put together by a large American oil company to deal with the Iranians, was composed of engineers, accountants, and design specialists (Riddle, 1979). The potential for interpersonal stress and conflict in this form of organization is particularly great. Depending upon the life cycle of the team, there may not be time for diagnosis, group work, and reassessment. The essential activities are the diagnosis and the group work. While the reassessment is important in an ongoing work group which has an unspecified life cycle, it is not critical for a project team having a near-term termination date.

It is also possible to use this prevention method in the case of project teams by doing some preliminary diagnostic and group work at the outset of the project's formation. Severe interpersonal conflicts are often found in the start-up and growth phases of project teams and entrepreneurial ventures (see Miles, 1979). These may be precluded through the use of early diagnosis and group work.

SUMMARY

This second chapter on organizational-level preventive management has presented four methods of prevention aimed at the role and interpersonal demands of organizational life. *Role analysis* and *goal setting* are methods for clarifying the individual's organizational role. While it may not be possible to prevent such stressors as dual-reporting relationships, it is possible to minimize the ensuing ambiguity and conflict through the use of these prevention techniques. Not only is the emotional distress caused by these circumstances minimized, but the performance level of individuals is enhanced, especially when using goal-setting programs.

These methods will not eliminate all role conflict and ambiguity, nor will they eliminate the interpersonal demands of work life. The use of *social support* and *team building* can be helpful secondary prevention methods used to manage the distressful demands not eliminated by the other organizational-level methods of preventive management. These methods will not necessarily change the demands of the work settings, but can be instrumental in assisting people to use and develop their capacities to manage their demands.

The organizational methods for preventive stress management discussed in these two chapters are ones that management can employ for groups of individuals in order to buffer the impact of the various job, physical, role, and interpersonal stressors. However, these methods will not eliminate all distress. It is important to combine these methods with the individual-level preventive management techniques described in the next two chapters.

FURTHER READINGS

Role Analysis

French, W. L., and C. H. Bell, Jr.: *Organizational Development: Behavioral Science Interventions for Organizational Improvement*, 2d ed., Prentice-Hall, Englewood Cliffs, N.J., 1978.

Huse, E. F.: *Organization Development and Change*, 2d ed., West, St. Paul, Minn., 1980.

Goal Setting

Drucker, P. F.: "Management by Objectives and Self-Control," in *The Practice of Management*, Harper & Row, New York, 1954, pp. 121–136.
Hughes, C. L.: *Goal Setting: Key to Individual and Organizational Effectiveness*, American Management Association, New York, 1965.

Social Support

House, J. S.: *Work Stress and Social Support*, Addison-Wesley, Reading, Mass., 1981.
Lynch, J. J.: *The Broken Heart: The Medical Consequences of Loneliness*, Basic Books, New York, 1977.

Team Building

French, W. L., and C. H. Bell, Jr.: *Organization Development: Behavioral Science Interventions for Organization Improvement*, 2d ed., Prentice-Hall, Englewood Cliffs, N.J., 1978.
Jewell, L. N., and H. J. Reitz: *Group Effectiveness in Organizations*, Scott, Foresman and Company, Glenview, Ill., 1981.

CHAPTER 10

INDIVIDUAL METHODS FOR MANAGING WORK AND PERSONAL DEMANDS

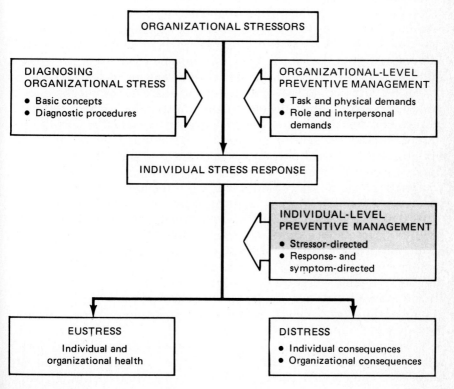

Even with the most successful preventive management activities at the organizational level, individuals will still be faced with stressful demands and they will still experience a certain amount of distress. There are numerous and highly varied techniques for preventing individual distress. Some techniques are aimed at changing one's perception of potential stressors, while others are aimed at altering response patterns, and still others are directed at the treatment of specific stress-induced problems.

Table 10.1 lists the major categories of individual stress management interventions and the individual techniques that will be described in detail in this chapter and in Chapter 11. The summary at the end of Chapter 11 will consider the manner in which an individual might choose specific preventive management techniques and formulate a personal stress management plan.

This chapter discusses primary prevention at the individual level—the use of stressor-directed techniques aimed at preventing or minimizing the occurrence of the stress response in everyday work life. Corporate psychologists, personal development experts, psychiatrists, and a host of popular stress management trainers have suggested a wide range of mental and social devices to assist individuals in preventing personal distress. In contrast to the secondary and tertiary prevention techniques described in Chapter 11, the effectiveness of which has been systematically studied in many cases, the primary prevention techniques have been offered largely on the basis of individual personal experience. The variety of approaches to individual stress management is a direct reflection of the fact that nobody is quite sure what are the best techniques. What works well for one individual might be rejected outright by another person. And the lack of systematic assessment of these techniques makes any sort of objective selection impossible. It is useful, however, to have a notion of the types of techniques which are used and to have a framework in which to consider alternative approaches.

Primary prevention techniques fall into three groups: (1) managing personal perceptions of stress, (2) managing the personal work environment, and (3) lifestyle management. A sampling of individual strategies within each of these categories is given in Table 10.2. Several of the most commonly promoted techniques will be described. Even though many of these methods appear to be common sense, it is striking to discover the number of people who experience significant distress and yet fail to use even the most basic stress control techniques.

One of the most common and most important aids in stress management is social support from coworkers, family, and friends. Although social support is very much a personal matter, it is influenced in the work setting by organizational factors and, therefore, it was considered in detail in Chapter 9. But social support outside the workplace and, in par-

TABLE 10.1
INDIVIDUAL-LEVEL PREVENTIVE MANAGEMENT TECHNIQUES

Primary prevention: Stressor-directed	
Managing personal perceptions of stress • Constructive self-talk • Psychological withdrawal • Recognizing the inevitable • Disputing cognitive distortion • Changing the Type A behavior pattern	**Lifestyle management** • Maintaining a balance • Leisure time use • Sabbaticals
Managing the personal work environment • Planning • Time management • Overload avoidance • Other methods (social support, task variation, leave job)	

Secondary prevention: Response-directed	
Relaxation training • Progressive relaxation • The relaxation response • Meditation • Medical hypnosis and autogenic training • Biofeedback training • Momentary relaxation • Traditional methods	**Emotional outlets** • Talking it out • Writing it out • Acting it out
Physical outlets • Aerobic exercise • Recreational sports • Flexibility and muscular relaxation activities • Muscle strength and endurance building	

Tertiary prevention: Symptom-directed	
Counseling and psychotherapy • Symptom-specific programs • Individual psychotherapy • Behavioral therapy • Group therapy • Career counseling	**Medical care** • Medications • Surgery • Physical therapy

ticular, the family-work interface are critical determinants of both the amount of perceived stress and the ability of an individual to deal effectively with stress.

Even when work demands do not take time away from family activities, work stress frequently spills over into the home as the working spouse brings the day's tensions into family interactions. Conversely, marital and

TABLE 10.2
METHODS OF PRIMARY PREVENTION AT THE INDIVIDUAL LEVEL

Method	Reference
Managing personal response patterns	
• Constructive self-talk	Eliot (1982); Albrecht (1979)
• Psychological withdrawal	Hall and Mansfield (1971, 1976); Nicholson et al. (1976)
• Recognizing the inevitable	Overbeke (1975); Student (1977); Bensahel (1974); Uris (1972); Levi (1967)
• Disputing cognitive distortion	Beech, Burns, and Sheffield (1982); Ellis (1955)
• Changing the Type A behavior pattern	Rosenman and Friedman (1977); Friedman and Rosenman (1974); Suinn, Brock, and Edie (1975); Roskies et al. (1978); Suinn (1978)
Managing the personal work environment	
• Planning	Buck (1972); Oates (1971); Hall (1976); Howard, Rechnitzer, and Cunningham (1975); Howard (1978)
• Time management	Lakein (1973); Albrecht (1979); Schuler (1979)
• Overload avoidance	Oates (1971); Albrecht (1979)
• Social support	House (1980); Student (1977); Caplan and Killilea (1976)
• Task variation	McCann (1972)
• Leave job	McCann (1972); Overbeke (1975)
Lifestyle management	
• Maintaining a balance	Albrecht (1979); McCann (1975); Kiev (1974); Rountree (1979)
• Leisure time use	McCann (1972); Walsh (1975); Uris (1970); Bensahel (1977)
• Sabbaticals	Goldston (1973); Rountree (1979)

other forms of family discord can readily lead to distraction or a quick temper at work. At the same time, the family can serve an important role in countering and attenuating the amount of distress which organizational stressors induce.

Handy (1978) has considered whether the family is a help or a hindrance in confronting stress at work. He concludes that the family can be both a help and a hindrance, depending upon the nature of the marriage, the underlying personal priorities of the individuals, and the demands of the job. Kanter (1977) provides a useful overview of the reciprocal relationship between work and family in the United States and observes that many of the organizational stressors which burden the individual worker also disrupt family relationships which might otherwise serve as an important source of support.

The value of helping individuals to build and maintain strong family relationships is being recognized by some businesses and industries. The Hospital Corporation of America, for example, has recently piloted a series of workshops for hospital administrators and their spouses. The workshops aim at identifying sources of stress and strain for each of the spouses and at delineating ways of managing the distress.

Building family relationships is neither an individual nor an organizational intervention, but an extraorganizational intervention. Although we do not consider family relationships under a separate heading, attention to family support systems and efforts at strengthening these systems should be considered a vital and valid part of any stress management effort.

This chapter is not meant to be a crash course in personal stress management, but an overview for managers and future managers involved in organizational stress management. Additional information about the techniques listed in Table 10.1 can be found in the original references and in the reading materials listed at the end of this chapter.

MANAGING PERSONAL PERCEPTIONS OF STRESS

Fundamental to the definition of "stressor" presented in Chapter 1 is the notion that a condition must be *perceived* as a stressor by an individual if the condition is to be a source of stress. Selecting a $100,000 piece of hospital equipment may be quite stressful to a new administrator whose largest past purchase was the $7,000 family car. But to an administrator of a large chain of hospitals who has occasionally bought equipment costing over $1,000,000 and often contracts for several hundred thousand dollars worth of new equipment, a decision about $100,000 may be made with relative equanimity.

Efforts to alter personal perceptions of stress are directed at changing the way in which individuals respond to potential stressors and the extent to which their internal stress response is activated. Some individuals—those with the Type A behavior pattern, for example—are constantly evoking their stress response and, in doing so, are creating their own stressors. Changing their response patterns involves teaching Type A individuals to view their environment differently. For other individuals, the emphasis is on ways of minimizing the magnitude of response to daily stressors. The essence of this approach is summarized by the 2,000-year-old words of Epictetus: "Men are disturbed not by things but by the views they take of them."

Constructive Self-Talk

During their daily activities most people conduct an intermittent mental monologue or narrative about the events they are experiencing and their reactions to the events. This monologue, or self-talk, can be positive in tone: "Gee that really was a witty remark." Or the content of the self-talk can be negative or self-effacing: "Boy, are you dumb, why not just keep your mouth shut." Self-talk can be unconscious, but usually it is conscious and often a person will find himself saying part of it aloud. Negative self-talk can waste emotional energy by setting up a tension-sustaining mental short-circuit. Constructive self-talk (Eliot, 1982) is a conscious effort to replace negative, self-defeating, self-effacing, often irrational narrative with positive, reinforcing, and more rational self-talk.

Table 10.3 lists examples of several common situations, the typical mental monologues which a person might go through, and constructive self-talk alternatives. The potential benefit of constructive self-talk can be appreciated by imagining oneself in any of the situations listed in Table 10.3 and noting how one would feel after five or ten minutes of the typical monologue.

An important part of constructive self-talk is *rethinking*; that is, recognizing when one has latched onto dead-end or downhill thoughts and consciously beginning to substitute constructive, forward-looking thinking. There are several other related concepts. *Quick recovery*, for example, refers to the ability to rebound in a short period of time from strong emotional experience (Albrecht, 1979). One person might ruminate for several days over a missed promotion or bad grade, while another person will brood about it for a few hours and then bounce back determined to work even harder to earn the promotion or a better grade.

Another concept is that of *thought stopping*. This also involves recognizing dead-end or downhill thoughts, but instead of staying on the same subject and changing the tenor of the thinking, one mentally—or verbally—says "stop," and "changes the subject." The technique of *mental diversion* is also useful in reducing the extent to which one experiences anxiety or distress over daily events. For example, the morning before a test or presentation for which a student has studied thoroughly or for which a manager has prepared completely, the student or manager may allow himself or herself to worry obsessively. This can continue until the test or presentation begins and may prove to be a significant mental drain. Alternatively, having completed preparations the night before, these individuals can choose to occupy their minds with other mental activities of a positive or pleasing nature. Mental diversion requires that one have a few positive topics on hand to substitute.

While the basic notion of constructive self-talk is rather simple and, with practice, can be mastered without special training, most people

TABLE 10.3
TYPICAL MENTAL MONOLOGUES AND
CONSTRUCTIVE SELF-TALK ALTERNATIVES

Situation	Typical mental monologue	Constructive self-talk alternative
Driving to work on a day which you know will be full of appointments and potentially stressful meetings	"Oh brother, what a day this will be!" "It's gonna be hell." "I'll never get it all done." "It'll be exhausting."	"This looks like a busy day." "The day should be very productive." "I'll get a lot accomplished today." "I'll earn a good night's rest today."
Anticipation of a seminar presentation or public address	"What if I blow it?" "Nobody will laugh at that opening joke." "What if they ask about . . . ?" "I hate talking to groups."	"This ought to be a challenge." "I'll take a deep breath and relax." "They'll enjoy it." "Each presentation goes a bit better."
Recovering from a heart attack	"I almost died. I'll die soon." "I'll never be able to work again." "I'll never be able to play sports again."	"I didn't die. I made it through." "The doctor says I'll be able to get back to work soon." "I can keep active and gradually get back to most of my old sports."
Difficulty with a superior at work	"I hate that person." "He makes me feel stupid." "We'll never get along."	"I don't feel comfortable with him." "I let myself get on edge when he's around." "It will take some effort to get along."
Flat tire on a business trip	"Damn this old car." (Pacing around car, looking at flat tire.) "I'll miss all my meetings." "It's hopeless."	"Bad time for a flat." (Beginning to get tools out and start working.) "I'll call and cancel Jenckins at the next phone. I should make the rest of the appointments."

learn it in stress management seminars or in psychotherapy sessions with a clinical psychologist or behaviorally-oriented psychiatrist. It is a concept rooted in self-hypnosis and behavioral therapy. Self-talk is a useful primary prevention technique because it aims not at reversing the stress response, but at redefining a condition or situation in such a way that it is no longer a stressor.

Psychological Withdrawal

In their study of three research and development organizations undergoing considerable stress due to funding cutbacks, Hall and Mansfield (1971) found that the researchers in these organizations showed a remarkable resistance to the stress. Their attitudes about themselves and their work remained positive and productive, but their identification and investment in the organization decreased significantly. The investigators suggest that this decreased investment, or withdrawal, helped the researchers to handle the stress of cutbacks and uncertainty.

Psychological withdrawal, or affective isolation, is, in essence, another way of avoiding distress by redefining a potential stressor as a nonstressor. It would be misleading, though, to think of psychological withdrawal as surrender. Developing emotional detachment does not preclude continued active involvement in the tasks from which you have withdrawn psychologically. In fact, a certain degree of psychological withdrawal may be essential in some jobs. Medical students, for example, learn during their training to develop an attitude of "detached concern" for their patients. The distress generated by working intensely with sick and dying patients would be intolerable without some withdrawal of natural emotional responses.

A variation of psychological withdrawal is *selective ignoring*, a process by which a person looks for the positive aspects of a troublesome situation and anchors his or her attention to these, to the exclusion of the noxious aspects of the situation (Perlin and Schooler, 1978). This process is facilitated by magnifying the importance of the positive aspects and viewing that which is noxious as trivial.

Recognizing the Inevitable

An old prayer petitions that when things are amiss, "Give me the strength to change what I can, the patience to accept what I cannot change, and the wisdom to know the difference." In any organization there will be some things amiss—some conditions or events which are potential stressors—which are unavoidable. Some stress management trainers encourage participants to develop additional perspective on their organizations and to identify situations which are inevitable. If these situations are then accepted as inevitable, the individual may avert some of the stress which might otherwise have been felt.

While this approach may be effective in the short term, it may risk greater distress in the future if the individual begins to accept too many things as inevitable and develops a sense of helplessness or impotency in the organization.

TABLE 10.4
TYPES OF COGNITIVE DISTORTION

---

1 *Overgeneralization.* Here the individual draws some general rule or conclusion as a result of one or a few isolated episodes; this conclusion is then applied across the board to similar or dissimilar circumstances.

2 *Selective abstraction.* This error in thinking involves concentrating on some detail taken out of context while concurrently ignoring some conspicuous features of the event; the experience is conceptualized on the basis of this detail.

3 *Arbitrary inference.* The individual makes a specific inference in the absence of evidence to support the conclusion; indeed, the evidence may even be to the contrary.

4 *Magnification.* This type of distortion can be seen when the individual grossly magnifies and gives excessive prominence to the importance of an event.

5 *Minimization.* Here the individual distorts the significance by grossly playing down the import of the event.

6 *Dichotomous thinking.* All experiences are placed in one of two categories: impeccable or defective, brilliant or crass. Usually the individual classifies himself in the most negative way.

7 *Personalization.* This type of cognitive distortion refers to the individual's proclivity to associate various external events, especially negative ones, to himself when there is no rational basis for making the judgment.

Source: H. R. Beech, L. E. Burns, and B. F. Sheffield, *A Behavioral Approach to the Management of Stress.* Copyright John Wiley & Sons, New York, 1982, p. 73. Reprinted by permission of John Wiley & Sons, Ltd.

Disputing Cognitive Distortion

One of the ways in which an individual can create additional stressors is through a process referred to as "cognitive distortion" in which the individual engages in a self-defeating, high-anxiety, frequently irrational pattern of thinking (Beech, Burns, and Sheffield, 1982). The result is a series of negative beliefs which quickly become self-perpetuating. Table 10.4 lists seven types of cognitive distortion which have been identified and which frequently manifest themselves in the type of negative self-talk described earlier. Unfortunately, these cognitive distortions can manifest themselves as conscious, persistent beliefs.

One systematic approach to modifying cognitive distortion is rational emotive therapy (RET), first presented by Ellis in 1955. The essence of RET is a process of logical questioning aimed at cognitive restructuring by disputing and modifying the irrational beliefs. According to RET, disputing cognitive distortions can be attempted by:

1 Detecting the irrationalities
2 Debating against the irrationalities

3 Discriminating between rational and irrational thinking
4 Defining circumstances to prevent cognitive distortion and to maintain closer contact with reality (Beech et al., 1982, p. 77)

An example of cognitive distortion and the effect of disputing the distortion is provided by the experience of the director of personnel for an east coast shipbuilding firm. The firm had solicited an outside management evaluation which included, among other things, an evaluation of the personnel department. Although the final report contained a relatively even mixture of positive and negative comments, the director of personnel initially saw only the negative ones. He became furious and accused the evaluator of unprofessional, shoddy work. He was both *selectively abstracting* and *magnifying* the negative portions of the report. After a lengthy discussion the director of personnel began to detect his distortion of the report. Eventually he was able to take pride in the positive feedback which the report provided and to learn from the negative feedback.

Changing the Type A Behavior Pattern

In their now classic book, *Type A Behavior and Your Heart,* Friedman and Rosenman (1974) present a lengthy discussion of philosophical guidelines, "reengineering" procedures, and drills aimed at undoing the Type A behavior pattern. The philosophical guidelines upon which the reengineering procedures and drills are based appear with brief elaborations in Table 10.5. Friedman and Rosenman assert that anyone can alter his or her behavior pattern and that this can be done without any deterioration in financial status, social status, or other measures of "success." An honest, in-depth self-appraisal is the first step in the process. This includes exploring some of the philosophical issues related to life goals, means-ends questions, and so on. The next step is contracting with oneself to replace old behavior patterns with new ones, using the reengineering procedures and drills outlined in their book.

Although Friedman and Rosenman's approach is straightforward and logical, there is limited experimental evidence to support its efficacy. Furthermore, there is some debate concerning the appropriateness of this approach to the Type A behavior pattern (Roskies et al., 1978). Friedman and Rosenman hold that insight into their behavior patterns and a major philosophical reorientation is essential for Type A individuals to make an effective change in their behavior pattern.

The opposing view is that the Type A behavior pattern is similar to a chronic illness: it cannot be cured, but it can be treated to decrease the harmful effects of the condition. Some people have linked Type A behavior to an addiction in that immediate gratification (success at work)

TABLE 10.5
PHILOSOPHICAL GUIDELINES FOR CHANGING TYPE A BEHAVIOR PATTERNS

- *You must try to retrieve your total personality.*
  Return to or develop interests in art, music, drama, nature, or spiritual matters outside your normal vocation. Spend time communicating with people on these and other subjects.

- *You must establish life goals.*
  Life goals should include an economic or professional set and a set for private life. They should help prevent sheer hyperactivity from replacing purposeful progress.

- *Make some gestures toward myth, ritual and tradition.*
  Recognize existing and add new rituals and traditions which provide uniquely pleasant experiences, build and maintain social relationships and maintain your humanity.

- *Stop using your right hand to do the work your left hand should be doing.*
  Many daily demands are of a trivial or ephemeral nature. They are the "left-handed" activities, which should require less vigilance and which should be delegated or handled with minimal effort.

- *Let your means justify your ends.*
  Stop trying to excuse daily "errors of living" by looking toward some great end. Each day and each activity should also be valued for its own sake.

- *A successful life is always unfinished.*
  Life is an unfinishedness. Life is structured upon and consists primarily of uncompleted processes, tasks, and events. Only a corpse is completely finished!

Source: Adapted from M. Friedman and R. H. Rosenman, *Type A Behavior and Your Heart*, Fawcett Crest, New York, 1974, pp. 214–233.

is preferred to long-term harm (early heart attacks) and withdrawal symptoms in the form of anxiety with decreased activity are observed (Roskies et al., 1978; Suinn et al., 1975). With the chronic disease or addiction model, treatment is aimed at providing a means to release the tension and hostility inherent in Type A behavior without altering the individual's basic psychodynamics. The goal of change strategies is not to convert Type A individuals into Type B individuals, but to reduce the psychophysiological impact of Type A behavior.

Finally, some authors have questioned whether any form of individual intervention can succeed without changing the cultural, familial, and work environments which appear to generate or at least foster Type A behavior (Howard, et al., 1976; Mettlin, 1976).

To date most clinical studies of attempts to change the Type A behavior pattern have been based on behavioral approaches such as progressive relaxation or biofeedback. Roskies and associates (1978), however, compared brief psychotherapy aimed at providing psychoanalytic insight into the Type A behavior pattern with behavioral therapy based on progressive relaxation and recordkeeping for tension levels and response patterns. Using a sample of 27 professional and executive volunteers, aged 39-59, treated over a period of five months, the investigators found that both interventions were associated with lowered cholesterol levels and systolic blood pressure. Decreases in cholesterol levels were particularly impressive for individuals assigned to behavioral treatment. Participants also reported statistically significant reductions in psychological symptoms and time pressure and greater satisfaction with their lives. Differences in these psychological measures also tended to be greater among those receiving the behavioral treatment.

Using psychotherapy and/or behavioral therapies, other investigators have also found positive physiological and psychological changes can be brought about in Type A individuals (Suinn and Bloom, 1978; Rosenman and Friedman, 1977; Manuso, undated). There is also data which indicates that "beta-blockers," a category of drugs used to treat high blood pressure by inhibiting sympathetic nervous system activity, may reduce the amount of Type A behavior which is observed. Similarly, initiation of a program of regular exercise has been associated with decreases in Type A behavior.

Although these studies provide some data to assess the comparative efficacy of different treatments, they are insufficient to justify recommending a single treatment over others. It should be encouraging, however, that Type A behavior patterns or at least the physiological and psychological consequences of these patterns are amenable to change. The variety of approaches which have favorable effect on Type A behavior suggests that any comprehensive stress management program will have an impact on individuals whose experience of organizational stress is influenced by Type A behavior.

MANAGING THE PERSONAL WORK ENVIRONMENT

At any level in an organization, there are aspects of the daily work routine which are in the individual's control and there are parts of the routine which are totally out of the individual's control. It is sometimes surprising for managers and supervisors to discover that they can control their working life to a greater extent than they had originally thought.

Table 10.2 lists several techniques which are available to managers, supervisors, and employees for reducing work stressors by better management of their personal work environment. Obviously, some techniques are more applicable at certain levels in the organization than at other levels. Similarly, some techniques are more applicable in certain types of organization than in other types. As with the techniques for managing personal response patterns, the techniques for managing the work environment are reported largely on the basis of the experience of management consultants and the other individuals who have described the techniques.

Planning

Possibly because it is such an obvious and commonplace activity, personal planning—planning ahead—is frequently mentioned, but seldom studied by psychologists, organizational behavior specialists, and others in the field. In the work setting, personal planning involves looking into the future, identifying goals and possible job stressors, and developing a strategy to achieve goals, while avoiding the negative impact of anticipated stressors. The process of personal planning parallels that of organizational planning described at the end of Chapter 12.

Personal planning is applicable in several areas. Buck (1972), for example, recommends that job applicants plan ahead to avoid a distressful mismatch of job demands and personal skills and interests. Applicants should learn as much as they can about the job for which they are applying. At the same time, they should make a candid assessment of their own abilities, career goals, and tolerance for stress. Similarly, Oates (1971) emphasizes that planning ahead may help the applicant avoid a job which is too difficult or is not satisfying.

Midlife changes are a frequent source of potentially preventable distress. Planning may assure that a midlife *transition*, rather than a midlife *crisis* occurs. Hall (1976) suggests that individuals should expose themselves to new options, exploring various alternatives, and developing an attitude of flexibility. Thinking realistically about potential midcareer stressors should help the individual to prepare for them.

Howard and associates (1975), in a review of coping mechanisms, suggest that task planning may help an employee to "work smarter, not harder." The planning process thus serves as the mechanism by which some of the other techniques such as time management and overload management are brought into play. But planning should not be confused or equated with time management, which is considered in the next section. Planning involves a more conceptual and comprehensive review of one's goals and activities. It also tends to be more future oriented.

McLean (1979) observes that the personal planning process should occur at two levels. At the concrete level, the process should consider geography, education, career, monetary needs, family needs, and life-time goals. At the more basic level, one should assess current coping strategies and intellectual and emotional resources to determine whether present coping mechanisms are as successful as they might be. If not, then planning is needed to improve stress management activities.

Although there is general agreement on the potential value of personal planning, we are aware of few studies which consider the process of personal planning in any detail. The organizational literature on management by objectives, problem solving and decision making contains some useful ideas. Planning for major work activities is included under the goal-setting programs described in Chapter 9. The guidelines presented in that section should be useful for everyday planning as well. Kirn and Kirn (1978) provide a framework for long-term "lifework planning," which includes suggestions for evaluating one's lifework situation and for systematically establishing future plans.

Time Management

Our language is full of phrases and cliches reflecting the value which we place on time: "time is money," "time . . . is the stuff life is made of," "let's make up for lost time," "time and tide wait for no man," "time is life," "time is running out," and so on. Deadlines, productivity objectives, and project timetables bring the manager and employee face to face with time and, in doing so, create significant distress. *Time management* represents a set of skills and attitudes which can be highly effective in reducing time stress and improving effectiveness. Increased job satisfaction and peace of mind are important consequences of wise time management.

Alan Lakein (1973) a pioneer in time management and one of the leading consultants in the field, has outlined a systematic approach to the effective use of time. Three concepts which are fundamental to his method are (1) the goals statement, (2) the To Do list with priorities, and (3) a schedule.

One major reason for poor time utilization is the lack of a clear sense of purpose. For the individual it is necessary to consider carefully what one wants out of life, to formulate a lifetime goals statement, to review it regularly, and to revise it periodically (Lakein suggests revising the list each birthday). A major stumbling block to effective time utilization in organizations is lack of awareness or agreement about the duties, authority, and responsibilities associated with each individual job. It may be necessary to engage in a formal role analysis, as described in Chapter 9, in order to have a clear enough sense of purpose.

The central concept in time management is that of the written *To Do list*. The list should include all significant time demands and things which need to be accomplished. Some people try to keep their To Do list in their heads. This is less reliable and it makes setting priorities more difficult. The list should be expanded each time new items arise and tasks should be deleted as soon as they are completed. A stack or pocketful of slips of paper with various undone tasks scribbled on them does not constitute a To Do list.

Whenever a list is made, each item should be given a priority. Lakein suggests an ABC priority system, with A corresponding to high-priority items and B and C corresponding to medium- and low-priority items, respectively. The A items can be further classified as A-1, A-2, A-3, and so on. All A items should be completed before going on to B and C items. This is difficult at times, because the B and C items are more numerous and often easier to finish. This reflects a phenomenon referred to as the 80/20 rule: "If all items are arranged in order of value, 80 percent of the value would come from only 20 percent of the items, while the remaining 20 percent of value would come from 80 percent of the items" (Lakein, 1973, p. 71). This means that in a list of ten items, two of them will account for 80 percent of the productivity or value. These two items should be identified, labeled A, and completed as soon as possible.

The purpose of setting priorities is simply to assure that the important items are identified and receive enough time. Most B and C items can wait and often they can be ignored entirely. Completing the A items requires a schedule or time plan. In preparing the plan, one should take advantage of *internal prime time* and *external prime time* by scheduling *quiet time* and *availability time*. Internal prime time is the time during which you concentrate the best, work the most productively; for some people this is before sunrise, while for others it is late afternoon. External prime time represents the best opportunity to deal with other people, including coworkers, business associates, and social contacts. To accomplish the most within limited time, it is useful to set aside portions of one's internal prime time as quiet time. To do this it is necessary to use whatever measures are available to minimize interruptions. Limiting phone calls, educating fellow workers about your time preferences, and closing an otherwise open office door can help to reduce interruptions.

Initially, effective time management may require retraining one's supervisor to avoid interruptions or last-minute requests which inadvertently undo an organized To Do list. It also requires overcoming certain common stumbling blocks. Learning to set limits on meetings and telephone calls, recognizing common "time robbers," controlling paperwork, learning to ignore C items and often B items, and working with superiors and fellow workers to establish clear goals are all important steps in learning to manage time.

Controlling and planning time should not turn a person into a machine, and it should not become a source of distress. To the contrary, putting important items first should assure that the high-value items are completed; this contributes to a greater sense of accomplishment. In addition, an important aspect of time management is putting time aside to relax. Effective use of time also permits one to "slow down" final decisions and reduces some of the pressure inherent in making major decisions at the last minute. Finally, even if better time management were not justified on the basis of increased productivity, it would be justified on the basis of decreased distress.

Overload Avoidance

Time management may reduce some of the stress from a demanding job, but there is a limit to what it can achieve if the demands on an individual are excessive. If preventive efforts at the organizational level have been effective, then overload should be minimized. Nevertheless, there are several avenues open to the individual who is faced with excessive work obligations.

Learning to identify and eliminate busy work is one important step in reducing job demands (Oates, 1971). Learning to delegate wherever and whenever possible is also important.

Equally important is learning how to avoid excessive obligations in the first place. Albrecht (1979) points out that employees are all too often unwilling to negotiate a reasonable deadline or to redefine the scope of a task assigned to them by the boss. Management frequently has only a vague idea of the resources required to complete a specific project and a limited knowledge of the employee's actual workload. If the individual to whom the job is assigned does not negotiate a reasonable timetable at the outset or renegotiate the timetable when it appears unrealistic, then he falls victim to his own obligations.

Many workers as well as managers have a great deal of difficulty saying, "no," or even "yes, but." Even if the request is clearly unreasonable or the timetable unworkable, many people have difficulty saying so. Therefore, an important part of overload avoidance is assertiveness training. A variety of approaches to assertiveness training have been described, but the essence is that of learning to say "no" in a socially acceptable way (Alberti and Emmons, 1974; Bower and Bower, 1976; Jakubowski-Spector, 1973). Assertiveness training has received special attention from women's groups, but it is an equally valuable skill for men.

Thus overload avoidance involves learning to decline, whenever possible, those requests which are unreasonable or overwhelming and renegotiating those obligations which are no longer feasible. Although these sound like easy steps to take, experience has demonstrated that considerable skill may be required to control one's obligations in a demanding or insensitive environment.

Other Methods for Management of the Personal Work Environment

In addition to the techniques already mentioned, there are numerous other methods which have been proposed to help management and employees to gain greater control over their personal working environment and, by doing so, to reduce their stress levels. Table 10.2 lists several of these methods, and brief discussions of other methods can be found elsewhere (Newman and Beehr, 1979; Burke and Weir, 1980).

Building social support among peers and superiors has been mentioned previously as an important buffer against the effects of organizational stressors. It was discussed in Chapter 9 as an organizational intervention since there are a variety of activities which management can undertake to promote social support. However, individuals can also play an important role in building their own support among coworkers, friends, and family.

LIFESTYLE MANAGEMENT

The emphasis throughout this book has been on stress management in the workplace. Yet, there is an undeniably large interaction between work life and home life. The manner in which this interaction is handled will have an important bearing on an individual's overall well-being, influencing both health and work performance. There are two important aspects of the work-life and home-life interaction over which management may have some influence: the ongoing balance between work and home and the use of leisure time. A third area of lifestyle management is that of sabbaticals or career breaks.

Maintaining a Balance

In many organizations individuals are rewarded for "losing themselves" in their work. People who work long hours, put in extra time on weekends, and take work home may advance rapidly and appear to be succeeding marvelously. However, *workaholic* behavior eventually takes its toll. The workaholic behavior pattern is typical of the Type A individual who, as we have already noted, experiences a much higher risk of a heart attack. The workaholic remains chronically in a state of distress. Often the person is unaware of his own signs of distress and may manifest the distress only through increased cigarette or alcohol consumption. This excessive involvement in work is really a form of addiction—an addiction with potentially quite serious consequences.

In contrast to the distress of the workaholic lifestyle is the eustress which is usually achieved by maintaining *balance* between work life and home life. Overinvestment in work activities frequently reflects an effort to gain rewards and a sense of value from work which are not coming from outside activities. Rather than working to make the outside activities more satisfying, the workaholic submerges himself in his job, creating extreme imbalance in his life.

Home life, social life, artistic and cultural activities, and, for many, spiritual and religious life, are all potential sources of satisfaction and significant rewards. Investing oneself in these activities as well as work life provides a more diverse network of social and emotional supports. Individuals with a strong support network are generally better able to weather difficulties in one particular area. Although work stressors may remain the same, the ability to cope with the stressors with the least amount of distress is enhanced by maintaining a balance.

Leisure Time Use

Vacations are accepted as one of the rewards for working, and people will often express the "need" for a vacation. Yet, little attention has been paid to the wise and creative use of leisure time as a stress management tool. One- or two-week block vacations are one use of paid time off. However, three-day weekends and scattered "mental health" days are also useful. One cardiologist who deals extensively with the stress-related aspects of heart disease urges his patients to make frequent use of three-day weekends as stress reducers (Eliot, 1982). We are not aware of any company which has systematically studied the divided use of vacation time for three-day weekends. However, anecdotal evidence suggests that a well-planned three-day weekend can be extremely refreshing, particularly during or following a period of extreme stress. Five three-day weekends may well be more valuable and refreshing than one week of vacation.

Counselors at psychiatric facilities are allowed to periodically take "mental health" days. These are one-day absences which can usually be taken without advance request. They are meant to be used whenever the demands of caring for severely troubled individuals become too great. While unplanned mental health days can be quite disruptive in some businesses and industries, their use should be considered wherever feasible.

Interestingly, the impact of vacations and leisure time on individual health and well-being has received little systematic study. There is some evidence that individuals have a greater tolerance for adversity and a decreased nervous system responsiveness following vacations. There is also some evidence that creative use of leisure time and attention to lifestyle can be as important as diet and exercise in preventing heart attacks (Mayer, 1975). Thus vacation planning should be considered as part of any personal stress management plan. However, it is important to recognize that vacations are not necessarily relaxing. The Type A individual who tries to squeeze as much sight-seeing or golf as possible into a week's vacation may return as stressed and as tired as he was when he left. Vacations may be physically tiring, but they should be planned in a way which makes them mentally relaxing.

Sabbaticals

Sabbaticals, or career breaks, have been a long-standing part of university and religious life aimed at providing a period of rest, reflection, and revitalization. The term is based on the biblical precedent of declaring a one-year "sabbath of solemn rest for the land" every seventh year (Leviticus 25: 1–7). Within the past fifteen years many businesses and industries have recognized the potential benefits of allowing midcareer breaks. A 1972 survey of the "Fortune 500" revealed that nearly one-quarter of the respondents had a form of sabbatical program (Goldston, 1973).

Sabbaticals may be structured through educational programs or social service leaves or they may be unstructured (Rountree, 1979). Educational programs are the most common type of structured sabbatical. University-based programs such as Harvard's Public Health Systems Management Course and the Sloan Programs at MIT are popular examples. Structured sabbaticals are generally funded by the company.

Unstructured or free-lance sabbaticals are often at the expense of the participant. They include such activities as reading and independent research, domestic or foreign travel, or simply rejuvenation through sports and recreation.

An enthusiastic proponent of executive sabbaticals is Eli Goldston who, as president of Eastern Gas and Fuel Associates, took a six-month career break to lecture as a visiting fellow at the London Graduate School of Business Studies. The impact of the sabbatical was apparent to his colleagues, one of whom commented, "You didn't get a recharge, you had a new engine installed" (Goldston, 1973, p. 63).

As with vacation and other leisure-time activities, the impact of sabbaticals has not been systematically studied, but anecdotal experiences suggest that they can play an important role in a comprehensive stress management plan.

SUMMARY

This chapter has described a wide range of primary or stressor-directed methods for individual-level preventive management. Personal response patterns can be influenced by techniques such as constructive self-talk, psychological withdrawal, recognizing the inevitable, disputing cognitive distortion, and changing Type A behavior patterns. The individual can also influence the stressors in his or her work environment through planning, time management, overload avoidance, and related methods. Finally, work demands can be controlled by maintaining a balance between work and other activities and by making effective use of leisure time.

All the methods described in this chapter are concerned with helping the individual to alter the frequency and the intensity of the demands or stressors which he or she faces. Chapter 11 will describe methods intended to dissipate the effects of the stress response, once it has been stimulated, and to treat overt symptoms of distress. Since additional individual techniques are presented in Chapter 11, the discussion of personal stress management plans and the choice of techniques will be presented at the end of that chapter.

FURTHER READINGS

Albrecht, K.: *Stress and the Manager*, Prentice-Hall, Englewood Cliffs, N.J., 1979.

Beech, H. R., L. E. Burns, and B. F. Sheffield: *A Behavioral Approach to the Management of Stress*, John Wiley, New York, 1982.

Cooper, C. L.: *The Stress Check*, Prentice-Hall, Englewood Cliffs, N.J., 1982.

Ellis, A.: "What People Can Do for Themselves to Cope with Stress," in *Stress at Work*, C. L. Cooper and R. Payne (eds.), Wiley, New York, 1978, pp. 209–222.

Friedman, M. D., and R. H. Rosenman: *Type A Behavior and Your Heart*, Fawcett Crest, New York, 1974.

Girdano, D. A., and G. S. Everly, Jr.: *Controlling Stress and Tension: A Holistic Approach*, Prentice-Hall, Englewood Cliffs, N.J., 1979.

Lakein, A.: *How to Get Control of Your Time and Your Life*, Peter H. Wyden, New York, 1973.

Levinson, H.: *Executive Stress*, New American Library, New York, 1975.

CHAPTER 11

INDIVIDUAL METHODS
FOR RELAXATION
AND SYMPTOM RELIEF

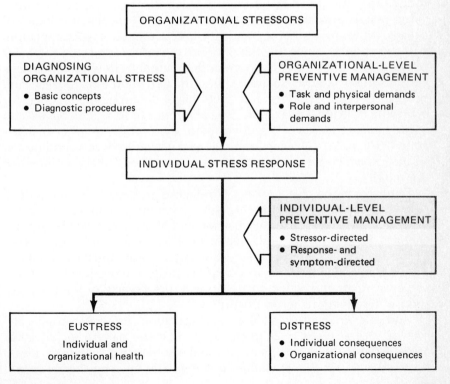

Chapter 10 described a wide range of techniques directed primarily at helping individuals to reduce the demands on their work lives and to minimize their perceptions of these demands as stressors. In this chapter we will consider response-directed (secondary) and symptom-directed (tertiary) prevention techniques—techniques aimed at dissipating the physical and psychological effects of the stress response once it has been evoked and techniques aimed at treating the behavioral, psychological, and medical symptoms of distress. Not only are the techniques in this chapter more widely used for stress management, but, for the most part, they are also the individual-level methods with the best research in support of their effectiveness.

After reviewing the secondary and tertiary individual-level methods of preventive management, this chapter will conclude with a discussion of personal stress management plans and the process by which an individual might formulate such a plan.

RELAXATION TRAINING

Organ (1970, p. 303) describes the long history of systematic efforts to achieve mental and physical relaxation dating at least to the sixth century B.C., when the Indian scripture, the Upanishads, suggested that individuals could reach a state of spiritual unity, "by means of restraint of breath, withdrawal of sense, meditation, concentration, contemplation, and absorption." Since that time, various means for achieving mental or physical relaxation have been described, largely within religious contexts. Chinese Taoism, Japanese Shintoism, Zen Buddhism, Judaism, and various Christian leaders and sects have described techniques for achieving individual relaxation. Similar interest in relaxation has existed in the secular literature. Wordsworth, for example, is described in Spurgeon (1970, p. 61) as having found his own way to achieve a condition of relaxation which he termed, "wise passiveness" or "a happy stillness of the mind."

The recognition that a variety of religious and secular techniques all appear to achieve relaxation through a common physiological mechanism was made by Dr. Herbert Benson and his associates at the Harvard Medical School in the early 1970s (Benson, Beary, and Carol, 1974). Termed the relaxation response, this pattern represents a generalized decrease in sympathetic nervous system activity and possibly an increase in parasympathetic activity. It is virtually the reverse of the stress response described earlier in Chapter 3.

Studies of individuals eliciting the relaxation response through any one of several techniques demonstrate that the pattern includes decreases in metabolic rate, heart rate, and respiratory rate. Initially, blood pressure may remain the same, but regularly eliciting the relaxation response may lower blood pressure. The electroencephalogram (brain wave recording) during the relaxation response shows an increase in the intensity of the slow alpha waves usually associated with feelings of well-being.

In studying the different techniques capable of achieving the relaxation response, Benson and his colleagues (1974) found four elements which seemed to be common to the techniques and which are usually necessary for eliciting the relaxation response:

1 *A quiet environment.* Sound, including background noise, and other distractions may prevent elicitation of the response. Any convenient, quiet place, including an office desk behind a closed door, is suitable and will facilitate relaxation.

2 *A mental device.* Shifting away from logical, externally-oriented thought is aided by a constant mental stimulus. Silently repeating a sound, a word or a phrase (a mantra); fixing one's gaze or one's "mind's eye" on an object; or focusing one's attention on the rhythm of breathing will help keep out distracting thoughts and external stimuli.

3 *A passive attitude.* Worrying about how well one is performing a relaxation technique can be distracting and stressful in itself. A passive attitude helps the individual to simply ignore distracting thoughts or external stimuli and to return to the mental device.

4 *A comfortable position.* The classic cross-legged "lotus position" for certain meditation techniques may be comfortable for Easterners and supple Westerners, but for most relaxation techniques Westerners will probably prefer a comfortable chair. Lying down is avoided because of the tendency to fall asleep.

In addition to these four basic elements, each of the different relaxation methods incorporates its own specific practices, philosophies, and variations. These differences become important when comparing or selecting relaxation techniques. One way in which the techniques vary is the extent to which they can be self-taught. Benson, for example, describes a simple procedure that can be learned from his written descriptions. In contrast, the Transcendental Meditation (TM) program requires that one learn the technique only from a qualified TM instructor. Some experts believe that relaxation techniques can be learned more quickly and more effectively if they are taught by an experienced instructor. Supporting the instructor model is the observation that many people who begin practicing a relaxation method soon lose interest and stop using the method. Having an instructor or peer group may create and sustain the motivation needed to fully incorporate the technique into a person's life. Audiocassette relaxation instruction provides some of the advantages of learning from an experienced teacher, but with less expense. Sources of such instruction are listed at the end of this chapter.

The techniques also differ in the extent to which they emphasize mental or physical relaxation. TM, for example, focuses primarily on mental relaxation, while progressive relaxation is based on systematically relaxing the skeletal muscles. In practice, most techniques that have been studied achieve both mental and physical relaxation, even if one is emphasized over the other.

Finally, the techniques differ in the extent to which they are rooted in religious or spiritual beliefs. Benson's method for achieving the relaxation response and Carrington's clinically standardized meditation are both based upon older meditation practices, but they purposely omit spiritual or mystical teachings which form an important part of advanced TM, Zen and similar methods.

With these comments in mind, we can describe each of the techniques listed in Table 10.1 and summarize some of the research supporting their value as stress management measures. Selection of a specific technique is largely an individual matter, based on level of motivation, personal spiritual beliefs, the need for a mental versus a physical emphasis, the availability of instructors, and price. Selection is also partly a matter of trial and error. If one technique does not seem to work well, an individual should remain open to trying another approach.

Progressive Relaxation

The earliest structured relaxation technique to appear in the medical and psychological literature was progressive relaxation, a technique developed by the physician-physiologist Jacobson in the late 1920s and 1930s for use in the treatment of anxiety. Jacobson (1929) emphasizes physical relaxation and relies on achieving profound relaxation of all major skeletal muscle groups as the means to prevent as well as treat anxiety.

Progressive relaxation, as it is currently taught (Bernstein and Borkovec, 1973), consists of sequential tensing and releasing of each of the sixteen skeletal muscle groups into which Jacobson divides the body. A quiet environment with soft lights and a comfortable seated or reclining position is recommended. The muscles are tensed for five to seven seconds and then relaxed for about thirty seconds. This process begins with the arms, progresses to the face, neck and throat, and then through the chest, abdomen, legs, and finally, the feet. The process provides systematic comparison of the amount of tension in each muscle group and comparison of the tensed and relaxed state for each group. Such comparisons train the subject to become aware of even the slightest degrees of muscle tension, and they are useful in achieving maximal relaxation. The whole process lasts thirty to sixty minutes. With experience, the subject learns to combine muscle groups into first seven and then four groups. It may take thirty hours or more to master the skill.

Dr. Jacobson has continued to refine the technique, incorporating electromyographs (EMGs) to help the subject assess muscle tension and applying the technique to a wide range of conditions (Jacobson, 1978). Although progressive relaxation has not achieved general acceptance as the primary mode of therapy for anxious patients, it is frequently used in conjunction with behavioral therapy, psychotherapy and drugs. In addition, it has served as the basis from which a variety of other relaxation and stress control techniques have been developed.

Research into comparative effectiveness of progressive relaxation has shown it to be helpful for a variety of problems, including insomnia and test anxiety among college students. For individuals in whom stress is manifested primarily by muscle tension, progressive relaxation during workday, evening, or weekend relaxation breaks might prove to be the most effective means of countering their stress response.

The Relaxation Response

On the basis of his study of Transcendental Meditation and other practices which elicit the relaxation response, Benson devised a simple set of instructions designed to bring forth the response (Table 11.1). To practice the technique, the individual sits in a quiet, comfortable place and passively focuses on his breathing and the word "one." Benson suggests that the technique be practiced for ten to twenty minutes once or twice a day. It should not be used immediately following a meal, since the diges-

TABLE 11.1
INSTRUCTIONS TO ELICIT THE RELAXATION RESPONSE

1 Sit quietly in a comfortable position.
2 Close your eyes.
3 Beginning at your feet and progressing up to your face, deeply relax all your muscles. Keep them relaxed.
4 Breathe through your nose. Become aware of your breathing. As you breathe out, say the word "one" silently to yourself. Continue the pattern: breathe in . . . out, "one," in . . . out, "one," and so on. Breathe easily and naturally.
5 Continue for ten to twenty minutes. You may open your eyes to check the time, but do not use an alarm. When you finish, sit quietly for a few minutes, first with your eyes closed and later with your eyes opened. Do not stand up for a few minutes.
6 Do not worry about whether you are successful in achieving a deep level of relaxation. Maintain a passive attitude and permit relaxation to occur at its own pace. When distracting thoughts occur, try to ignore them by not dwelling on them and return to repeating "one." With practice, the response should come with little effort. Practice the technique once or twice daily but not within two hours after any meal, since the digestive processes seem to interfere with eliciting the relaxation response.

Source: H. Benson, *The Relaxation Response*, pp. 162–163. Copyright © 1975 by William Morrow and Company, Inc. Used by permission of the publisher.

tive process may interfere with obtaining a full benefit of the relaxation response.

Instructions for the relaxation response have been published in both the professional and popular literature. No formal training is required to use the technique and no particular aptitude is necessary to experience the relaxation response. People vary greatly, however, in the way in which they experience the relaxation response. A small percentage will "immediately experience ecstatic feelings" (Benson, 1975, p. 164), while some people experience relatively little subjective change.

To date there have been several scientific studies on the effect of the relaxation response on physiological and psychological variables. The largest and most comprehensive was a twelve-week study conducted at the corporate offices of Converse, a division of Eltra Corporation (Peters, 1980; Peters, Benson, and Porter, 1977; Peters, Benson, and Peters, 1977). One hundred thirty-six volunteers were randomly assigned to one of three groups. Group A was instructed in eliciting the relaxation response. Group B was asked not to use any special technique, but to simply sit quietly and relax. Group C, the control group, received no instructions. For the eight-week intervention period, groups A and B took two 15-minute breaks each day, one in the morning and one in the afternoon or evening. The breaks were to be taken from the employee's own time, including coffee breaks, lunchtime, or time before or after work hours. Group C members took their usual breaks, but no relaxation breaks as such.

The effects of regular relaxation breaks were assessed using several physiological and psychological measures. A fifty-one item symptom index indicated the frequency with which participants reported experiencing one of many specific symptoms, including headache, backache, diarrhea, or difficulty sleeping. Group A showed nearly a 25 percent decrease in the symptom index, the largest and only statistically significant change. Group B also reported a decrease in symptoms, but the magnitude of the decrease was much smaller.

The groups were also compared on a performance index, in which the volunteers rated their own daily physical energy, strength of concentration, ability to handle problems, and overall efficiency. A small but significant improvement was noted by group A. Group B also showed improved performance, but this improvement was not statistically significant.

A sociability-satisfaction index was administered biweekly in which participants were asked about relationships at home, with friends, and at work and about satisfaction with work, self-confidence, and satisfaction with oneself. A happiness-unhappiness index was also administered on a biweekly basis. Small improvements in both sociability-satisfaction and happiness-unhappiness were noted in group A and, to a lesser extent, in group B.

Finally, significant decreases in blood pressure were observed in group A. These decreases, the magnitudes of which were comparable to what might be seen with low doses of blood pressure medication, appeared in both sexes, at all ages, and at all levels of baseline blood pressures. Of particular value is the observation that the greater blood pressure decreases tended to occur in individuals with higher initial blood pressures.

Thus, it would appear that in addition to the subjective sense of relaxation which practicing the relaxation response elicits, there are measurable benefits which have practical significance in the workplace.

Meditation

To a certain extent the relaxation response is a distillation of a variety of techniques which induce relaxation. It was Benson's study of transcendental meditation which stimulated the concept of the relaxation response. However, many other forms of meditation, including clinically standardized meditation, Zen, and yoga can achieve similar relaxation effects.

A technique which falls somewhere between Benson's very basic relaxation response and the more intense classical meditation of Eastern origin is clinically standardized meditation (CSM). The technique was developed over a period of several years by Princeton psychologist Patricia Carrington. Dr. Carrington made an extensive study of classical meditation and then synthesized a system of mantra meditation free from a religious or mystic basis and more appropriate for western use. Her book, *Freedom in Meditation* (1977), is one of the most comprehensive, lucid discussions of meditation available.

Carrington emphasizes preparation, attitude, and the mantra. CSM is intended to be taught by a qualified instructor, who will observe its proper use and help to sustain the individual's motivation until it becomes a regular practice for the individual. Apparently some people experience considerable psychological and physical distress during the early stages of learning meditation. Much of this distress stems from a misunderstanding or misuse of the techniques. Therefore, Dr. Carrington places a strong emphasis on the instruction process. To make instruction in CSM more readily available, she has prepared a three-hour taped course which can be purchased for about $50 (see chapter references). To fully anticipate and prevent any misconceptions or problems with the use of the tapes, Dr. Carrington proceeded cautiously and spent nearly two years developing the course.

The effectiveness of CSM in preventive management has been demonstrated in a long-term study of employees of New York Telephone Company who reported very high levels of job stress. Eighteen months after CSM training began, meditators showed a marked decrease in depression, anxiety, hostility, and improvements in several physiological measures. CSM has subsequently been adopted for use in companywide stress-reduction programs (Carrington et al., 1980). The U.S. Mint in Philadelphia also conducted a successful pilot study using CSM, but funding cutbacks prevented complete implementation of the project.

Transcendental Meditation, or TM, is probably the best known of the meditation techniques of eastern origin. Based primarily on Hindu practices, the method was introduced into the western world in the late 1950s by Maharishi Mahesh Yogi. TM training currently costs about $200 for a ten-hour course from an approved instructor.

Meditators are taught to spend two daily twenty-minute periods in a quiet place in a comfortable position while silently repeating their mantra, the sound or word given to the trainee by the instructor. The aim is to develop a passive attitude and a peaceful world view. TM seemed revolutionary when it was introduced into the United States, and its aura of mysticism and secretism added to its appeal for many people.

Promoters of TM have emphasized the beneficial effects of TM in increasing practitioners' ability to cope with stress reactions and in improving physiological measures of stress, such as high blood pressure. To a greater degree than the advocates of other relaxation methods, the advocates of TM have sought to provide systematic documentation of the effects of TM. The movement's International Center for Scientific Research is charged with collecting such information and making it available to business, industry, and management.

Kuna (1975) reviews several studies which demonstrate a beneficial effect of regular meditation on laboratory measures of reaction time, alertness, coordination, perceptual-motor performance, and learning efficiency. In a retrospective study of businessmen who practiced TM, Frew (1974) concluded that regular meditators showed more job satisfaction, more stability in their jobs, better interpersonal relationships with supervisors and coworkers, less anxiety about promotion combined with a record of moving ahead quickly, and improved job performance. Furthermore, the greater the authority and responsibility which the meditator held in the organization, the greater seemed to be the gain in productivity, satisfaction, and work relations.

In considering such studies, it is difficult to determine which effects are due to meditation itself and which effects are due to differences in the individuals who choose to meditate.

In addition to secular forms of meditation such as the relaxation response and clinically standardized meditation and the popularized eastern method of transcendental meditation, there are numerous other meditation techniques of eastern origin including among others, Chakra yoga, Rinzai Zen, Soto Zen, Zazen, Ananda Marga yoga, Mudra yoga, Tantra yoga, Sufism, Kundalini yoga, and Shavasana. Descriptions and comparisons of many of these techniques can be found in Pelletier (1977).

In practice, the choice of a specific form of meditation depends largely on the individual appeal of a particular technique. Most large cities in the United States now have a variety of meditation centers (often found under "meditation" in the Yellow Pages) and the availability of a skilled teacher is probably as good a basis for selecting a technique as any. Suffice it to say that many individuals feel that a spiritually-based eastern meditation technique has proven beneficial in their work and private lives. Many self-instructional works are available for those who are interested in pursuing this form of relaxation (see the listings at the end of the chapter).

Medical Hypnosis and Autogenic Training

Hypnosis is an induced state of altered consciousness characterized by extreme relaxation and a heightened susceptibility to suggestion (Sachs, 1982). A hypnotic trance can be induced by focusing the subject's attention on a mental, visual, or other sensory image and suggesting increasing relaxation and well-being. Although the popular image of hypnosis portrays the subject as falling into a "sleep," the brain wave pattern and the subjective experience of hypnosis are quite different from those of true sleep. Nevertheless, a state of profound muscular relaxation can be suggested and achieved through hypnosis.

Many individuals are capable of learning to induce a hypnotic state in themselves, a process known as *self-hypnosis*. Self-hypnosis can be learned from any one of a number of books on the subject, but it is most easily learned after an individual has experienced a hypnotic trance through induction by a skilled hypnotist, usually a psychiatrist, clinical psychologist, or other trained therapist.

The relaxation achieved through hypnosis is comparable to that realized through other relaxation methods (Benson, Beary, and Carol, 1974). In addition, though, it can be applied to any of a wide variety of common problems, including pain control, smoking cessation, weight control, phobias, and a variety of other stress-related, psychosomatic problems. Hypnosis is of little lasting value when the individual has no firm urge to change. However, when there is a sufficient commitment to change—conscious or unconscious—the technique can be quite useful (Crasilneck and Hall, 1975).

Autogenic training is a method of self-hypnosis developed from experiments with medical hypnosis in the early 1920s by the German psychiatrist, J. H. Schultz. The training emphasizes the development of individual control over physiologic process through organ- and symptom-specific exercises.

TABLE 11.2

SAMPLE FORMULA FOR AUTOGENIC TRAINING

Intentional (behavior change) formulas

Reducing mental tension
- "I meet my troubles calm, collected, and cheerful."
- "Don't think, don't do, don't want anything."
- "Calm, content, comfortable."

Coping with present stress
- "I am free from frustration and fright."
- "Detach! . . . do not mind."
- "Calm, careful, courageous."

Coping with memories of past stress
- "Past pains perish; pleasant peace prevails."
- "The past has passed; the present prevails."

Decision making
- "Correct decisions come quickly (inhalation)."
- "I decide what I want."
- "I decide what seems best."

Reduction of smoking and drug or alcohol abuse
- "Less pills, less poison!"
- "Skip smelly smoking."
- "Alcohol at no time, at no place, on no occasion."

Slimming
- "Break bread briefly."
- "Less bread, less spread."
- "Calm, content, satisfied, and satiated."

Organ-specific formulas

Respiration
- "My breath flows calm and free (exhalation)."
- "Breathe easy (exhalation)."

Eyes
- "Eyes cool (inhalation) and relaxed (exhalation)."
- "Blood circulates in the retina."

Blushing
- "Face is cool and pale (inhalation)—warmth and redness flow to trunk and legs (exhalation)."

Intestines
- "Intestines work warmly, smoothly (exhalation), and strongly (inhalation)."

Hemorrhoids
- "Anus is relaxed and wide (exhalation)—cool water irrigates it (inhalation)."

Itching
- "My . . . is cool (inhalation), relaxed, and soft (exhalation)."

Rheumatic pains
- "Shoulders and elbows stay warm and relaxed (exhalation)."

Source: B. Jencks, *Exercise Manual for J. H. Schultz's Standard Autogenic Training and Special Formulas,* (American Society of Clinical Hypnosis, Des Plaines, Illinois, 1979), pp. 38–39.

Once a subject has mastered the basic techniques of autohypnosis and the six standard autogenic training exercises (a process which Schultz believes should take two to three months in a healthy trainee), then he is ready to use a variety of special formulas. *Intentional formulas* are used to achieve behavioral change by reinforcing mental resolve to omit undesirable behaviors or to perform new behaviors. *Organ-specific formulas* are used to modify specific physiological processes. Examples of these formulas are given in Table 11.2.

Schultz's work is available in English in a rather forbidding six-volume medical text (Luthe, 1969–1973). A more recent and more readable manual for self-instruction has been prepared by Jencks (1979) and is available from the American Society of Clinical Hypnosis. The techniques are best learned, however, from an experienced clinical psychologist or other qualified therapist.

As with biofeedback, the specificity of autogenic formula makes the technique more suitable to the control of individual symptoms or responses to specific stressors.

Biofeedback Training

In Chapter 3 the stress response was defined as a well-organized pattern of autonomic nervous system and endocrine system responses. Figure 3.2 listed many of the physiologic actions of the sympathetic part of the autonomic nervous system. Because physiologic responses such as changes in blood pressure, heart rate, and sweating occur without conscious effort, they were originally thought to be involuntary responses. However, some striking examples of voluntary control of "autonomic" function stimulated medical researchers to explore the extent to which control of visceral functions could be learned. The tool as well as the product of this exploration has been biofeedback.

The term "feedback" was coined around the beginning of this century by the pioneers in radio. Mayr(1970) quotes Norbert Wiener, a mathematician instrumental in feedback research, who described feedback quite simply as, "a method of controlling a system by reinserting into it the results of its past performance." *Bio*feedback is possible whenever a physiological function can be recorded and amplified by electronic instruments and reported back to a person through any of the five senses. The equipment reflects the individual's response much the way a mirror would reflect his appearance. Figure 11.1 illustrates the basic feedback loop in biofeedback. Although any of the five usual senses could be used, feedback is generally auditory (using tones of varying pitch or rhythm) or visual (using blinking lights, colors, graphs).

In clinical biofeedback, the focus is usually on one physiologic measurement—skin temperature, for example. A temperature sensitive

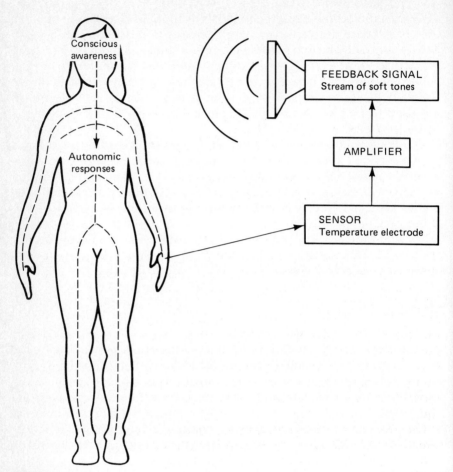

FIGURE 11.1
Example of the feedback loop in biofeedback.

electrode is attached to the skin and an amplifier converts the skin temperature reading to a stream of soft tones. The colder the skin, the faster the tones. The subject is not instructed to make his skin warmer, but to slow the tones. Although medical researchers have demonstrated many of the anatomical and functional nervous system connections which are involved in the feedback loop, the exact way in which an individual "learns" from the feedback remains somewhat of a mystery.

Biofeedback can be applied to any physiological function which can be easily measured. For example, sweating is measured by sensors of galvanic skin response (GSR), muscle tension by electromyography (EMG), brain waves by electroencephalography (EEG), heart rate and heart rhythm by the electrocardiogram (ECG or EKG), blood flow by plethysmography, blood pressure by an electric sphygmomonometer, intestinal movement by amplification of the stethoscope sounds, stomach acid by a pH meter, and so on.

Although any of these measurements can be used, the three most commonly used for relaxation therapy are muscle tension, brain waves, and sweating. To achieve relaxation through control of muscle tension, the EMG sensors are connected to either the forehead (frontalis muscle) or the back of the neck (trapezius muscle). By learning to relax these muscles, many people experience a generalized sense of relaxation. Alternatively, brain waves can be monitored with sensors attached to the scalp and hooked to an EEG machine. One particular type of brain wave, the slow alpha wave, is associated with feelings of relaxation and well-being. The biofeedback EEG machine is programmed to recognize this wave form and to provide visual or auditory information to the subject. Using an "alpha trainer" as some of the specialized EEG devices are called, can result in greater relaxation by teaching the subject how to increase alpha brain waves and reduce other brain waves. Biofeedback has a distinct advantage over other methods in that it provides the individual with precise data about his or her state of relaxation. However, the cost and convenience are significant limiting factors in the use of biofeedback. A skilled instructor is required, as is specialized equipment, ranging in price from $10 to $10,000. The accuracy and reliability of available equipment varies greatly, and quality and price are not always well correlated. A good buy requires an experienced operator of biofeedback equipment.

Girdano and Everly (1979) divide biofeedback equipment into three categories: *home trainers,* which usually cost less than $200 but are "virtually worthless"; *clinical trainers,* which range in price from $250 to $1,000 and are usually dependable, although limited in their capabilities; and *research units,* which can cost over $10,000, are generally accurate, and provide a great deal of versatility.

Successful clinical applications of biofeedback include beneficial effects on such conditions as tension headaches, high blood pressure, potentially serious heartbeat irregularities, and chronic pain (Gentry, 1975; Fuller, 1978; Miller and Dworkin, 1977).

Application of biofeedback in the workplace has been limited, but experience from its use by the Equitable Life Assurance Society's Emotional Health Program suggests that, despite the cost of the necessary equipment, significant net savings can be achieved through the control of work-related stress symptoms. These savings are calculated by comparing the cost of biofeedback training with the savings in employee and physician time from reduced illness-related visits to the medical department (Manuso, 1979; 1981).

Momentary Relaxation

The relaxation techniques described thus far require a place free from interruption and a period of at least ten to twenty minutes. For the typical manager or employee it may be possible to practice a relaxation technique at most once each working day. Yet, the average day is usually filled with a number of small stresses, which can accumulate bit by bit, and with one or two major stressors, such as a report deadline or a public presentation. For such situations, momentary relaxation (Albrecht, 1979; Roskies et al., 1978) or use of the six-second quieting response (Manuso, 1980) can be useful.

Once an individual has mastered a deep relaxation technique such as the relaxation response or progressive relaxation, the skill of momentary relaxation should come almost automatically. Albrecht (1979, pp. 198–199), an experienced organizational development consultant, describes momentary relaxation with the following examples:

> The next time you find yourself about to deal with a challenging, stressful situation, simply pause for a few seconds, turn your attention to your body, and allow your whole body to relax as much as you can, keeping the situation in mind. You can easily learn to do this "quickie" relaxation technique in a few seconds and without the slightest outward sign of what you are doing. Anyone looking at you would notice, at most, that you had become silent and that you seemed to be thinking about something for a few seconds. You need not even close your eyes to do this.
>
> If you happen to have a few moments alone before entering the challenging situation, you can relax yourself somewhat more thoroughly. Sit down, if possible, get comfortable, and close your eyes. Use your built-in muscle memory to bring back the feeling of deep relaxation and hold it for about a full minute. Then open your eyes and, as you go about the task at hand, try to retain the feeling of calmness that came with the relaxation.

Momentary relaxation draws upon an individual's mental and physical "memory" of deep relaxation to rapidly achieve partial relaxation. Taking a few deep, slow breaths will usually help to bring on relaxation. The effectiveness of deep breathing depends not only upon its usual associations with relaxation techniques, but also upon neurological reflexes which result in lowered muscle tone and heart rate following a few deep breaths. In fact, it is theorized that the relaxation which some people derive from smoking a cigarette results in part from the first few deep, slow breaths with which the smoker lights the cigarette and not from the process of smoking.

Traditional Methods

A discussion of relaxation techniques would not be complete without reference to the many "home remedies" which have been used for decades and, in many cases, for centuries. It is unfortunate that many of these accessible and economical traditional methods have received little or no attention by those who study stress, and it is equally unfortunate that they are often neglected in stress management programs. Traditional methods include such activities as hot baths or showers, soft music, a hike in the woods, light reading, and lovemaking. (One of the coauthors of Dr. Benson's original articles on the relaxation responses was well-known to his medical school roommates for his lengthy crepuscular hot baths!)

Data to support the effectiveness of traditional methods is largely anecdotal, but our own clinical experience suggests that these and other traditional methods should be explored and encouraged in any comprehensive stress management program.

PHYSICAL OUTLETS

Although the enthusiasm for exercise as a means of health promotion is relatively recent, the idea itself is rather old. The first printed work recommending exercise as a health-promoting and disease-preventing activity was published in Seville in 1553 by Christobal Mendez (Kilgour, 1960). The first company-supported recreation and fitness program in the United States may have been that started by the National Cash Register Company in 1904 (Duggar and Swengros, 1969).

The popularity of physical exercise as a means of stress management is reflected in the fact that nearly every recent publication on stress management includes a discussion of physical exercise. Corporate fitness programs have proliferated over the last two decades, making the means for regular physical exercise much more widely available to the working population. The growing corporate commitment to such programs is reflected in the growth of The American Association of Fitness Directors in Business and Industry (AAFDBI) from a group of about a dozen individuals in 1974 to an association of some 700 members in late 1978.

Physical exercise includes an extremely wide range of activities, some of which may be quite helpful in stress management and others of which can sometimes be rather unhealthy. Exercise can be grouped into four main categories: (1) aerobic exercise, (2) recreational sports, (3) flexibility and muscular relaxation activities, and (4) muscle strength and endurance building.

Aerobic exercise is any form of repetitive physical activity which produces a sustained heart rate, respirations, and metabolic rate for a period of at least twenty to thirty minutes. Jogging, swimming, aerobic dance, continuous bicycling, vigorous tennis or other racket games, and cross-country skiing are examples of such exercise. Aerobic exercise is the only form of exercise which can predictably achieve cardiorespiratory fitness.

Recreational sports, including bowling, softball, racket games, and such activities as gardening, can sometimes be aerobic in nature, but more commonly they involve intermittent energy expenditure. Such activities can be extremely effective outlets for aggression and frustration. Bowling, racket sports, and woodchopping are among the most cathartic releases.

There are also milder forms of exercise which are aimed at achieving *flexibility and muscular relaxation* through regular, rhythmic routines which are not necessarily intense enough to produce cardiovascular conditioning. Examples include simple calisthenics and "muscle-toning" exercises, modern dance, the recently popular traditional Chinese system of symbolic movements known as Tai Chi Chuan, and other systems of eastern origin such as Hatha yoga and Aikido. Finally, there are the isometric and weight-lifting exercises aimed at *muscle strength and endurance building*. By itself this form of exercise does not usually achieve cardiopulmonary conditioning, but it can be quite effective in venting hostilities, relaxing tense muscles, and building self-image.

The personal and psychological benefits which have been claimed for regular physical exercise are legion. Decreased muscle tension, heightened mental energy, improved feelings of self-worth, greater sense of well-being, improved memory, greater self-awareness, realization of "peak experience," and, in the workplace, decreased absenteeism, improved performance, and lower attrition have all been mentioned. Although the bulk of evidence is anecdotal and consists largely of individual testimonials, the consistency and fervor of these reports is striking. And a few controlled studies have confirmed some of these results.

For example, Lynch and his associates (1973) divided a group of middle-aged men into a half which exercised and a half which did not. After a nineteen-session exercise program consisting primarily of jogging, the exercise group showed significant reduction measures in anxiety, depression, and hostility compared to their preexercise scores and the no-exercise group. In another study, Griest, a psychiatrist from the University of Wisconsin, randomly assigned twenty-eight men and women aged between 18 and 30 with clinically significant depression to either running or individual psychotherapy. Six of the eight patients who were assigned to running and continued it for at least ten weeks recovered from their depression. This result was better than that observed for those assigned to psychotherapy (Griest, Klein, Eischens, and Faris, 1978).

There is even greater support for some of the physiological benefits of aerobic exercise. Regular programs of vigorous conditioning have fairly consistently been found to lower resting heart rate and blood pressure, to improve oxygen utilization, and to create a more favorable cholesterol and triglyceride profile. Clinical studies have demonstrated a salutory effect on such stress-related problems as high blood pressure, back and other muscle aches, chronic lung disease, diabetes, and mobility difficulties in the elderly (Fentem and Bassey, 1979; Yvarvote et al., 1974). Epidemiological studies have confirmed that a sedentary lifestyle increases the likelihood of heart attack in comparison with a lifelong pattern of regular physical activity (Fentem and Bassey, 1979; Froelicher, Battler, and McKirnan, 1980; Pattenbarger and Hyde, 1980). It has not been proved, however, whether initiating a program of regular aerobic exercise later in life will have any effect on cardiovascular disease and heart attack prevention.

The physiological pathways by which exercise achieves its beneficial cardiovascular effects are already partly known, and each year more information is available. The relationship between exercise and the stress response is also becoming more clearly understood. Both stress and exercise stimulate an increase in the catecholamines adrenaline and noradrenaline, the effects of which were described in Chapter 3. But the Institute for Aerobics Research in Dallas, Texas, has found that under resting conditions, aerobically fit individuals have a lower level of catecholamines in their bloodstreams. In addition, the institute has found aerobically fit individuals to have a better interplay between their activating, stress-response sympathetic nervous system and their relaxing, restorative parasympathetic nervous system. This suggests that fit individuals may be less physiologically reactive in stressful situations.

The mechanisms by which exercise achieves its psychological effects are much less clear. Part of the answer may be the improved self-image which comes with a trimmer, well-conditioned body build. Regular exercise also results in more restful sleep. Some researchers have suggested that the primary effect of any form of exercise is diversion—a mental break (Morgan et al., 1980). Most intriguing is the recent evidence that vigorous exercise can lead to a transient quadrupling of the blood levels of *endorphins*, naturally occurring morphine-like hormones associated with pain relief and feelings of well-being (Gambert et al., 1981). Thus, the mood-elevating effect of exercise may in fact be a naturally produced biochemical "high."

Whatever the mechanism, there is general agreement that regular physical exercise is an effective stress reduction technique for many individuals. Management support for exercise programs is reflected in the multimillion dollar health and fitness programs initiated by Kimberly-Clark, Xerox, Exxon, Tenneco, and numerous other corporations. Rather than focusing on only one or two modes of exercise, most programs offer a variety of activities. Fitness programs at many large companies are endowed with a range of sophisticated conditioning equipment and extensive facilities, but managers interested in exercise programs should recognize that a large capital investment is not a prerequisite for an effective program. Classrooms, rooftops, large multipurpose indoor rooms, and parking lots have all been used successfully. More important than facilities, is the availability of a small number of well-trained fitness instructors and the availability of time.

Most individuals are not as physically fit as they lead themselves to believe. In a study of 641 employees in the electronics industry, Kreitner, Wood, and Friedman (1979) looked at the relationship between physical fitness and cardiovascular disease proneness. They drew four conclusions from their study. First, the average employee sees himself or herself as being physically fit and in good health. Second, the average employee is in unsatisfactory shape from the standpoint of objective coronary risk. Third, the average employee engages in no regular, vigorous exercise. Fourth, the average employee is strongly interested in modifying coronary risk factors.

As a final caution, individuals interested in starting a personal or company exercise program should be aware of certain safety guidelines. First, people who have not exercised regularly should begin gradually. Walking or easy bicycling are generally safe and easy ways to start. After working up to being able to walk briskly or bicycle for thirty minutes a day, most people can begin a program of jogging, more vigorous bicycle riding, swimming, or one of a number of other activities. Anyone with diabetes, heart disease, lung disease, or a history of other serious medical illness should undoubtedly see a physician before beginning an exercise program. In addition, many medical organizations and many practicing physicians recommend that those over the age of 35 should check with their physician before starting a program of regular exercise. While this is certainly the cautious approach, it can be quite costly, and it is probably unnecessary for individuals who have been in good health and who use good judgment in choosing their exercise. If a person chooses to see a physician, it should be a physician who is himself in good physical condition and who is attuned to monitoring exercising individuals. The American College of Sports Medicine (1975) provides clear but conservative guidelines for exercise prescription.

A second caution is that there should be an *exercise plan* which includes graded conditioning and sufficient warm-up and cold-down periods. Individuals who suffer adverse consequences of exercise programs have usually attempted to progress too rapidly or have failed to recognize their own limits. Cooper (1970; 1982), Zohman (1979), and the other references cited at the end of this chapter provide useful guidelines for establishing exercise plans.

Finally, exercise is for enjoyment and relaxation. Some individuals, particularly those with the Type A behavior pattern, turn exercise into another form of competition and, as a result, create more tension and distress for themselves.

EMOTIONAL OUTLETS

Physical exercise provides one very good method for ventilating the effects of the stress response. A loud, vigorous game of racketball or tennis can relieve much of the tension from a stressful day at work. But there are also other ways of expressing one's stress-related emotions. Unfortunately, there are often social barriers to emotional outlets. We learn to keep our feelings to ourselves. Men learn not to cry and wish not to appear weak.

Nevertheless, talking with coworkers, friends and other people, writing out one's feelings in one form or another, and acting out the feelings in a controlled way are all viable means to release tension arising from organizational demands.

Talking It Out

Talking with peers or superiors to ventilate one's feelings and to generate some social support is one of the commonest and seemingly effective means of personal stress management. In a survey of supervisors employed in the engineering department of a large corporation, Burke and Belcourt (1974) found that, when asked what they did to cope with work tensions and anxieties, the most frequent response of the supervisors was talking with others (18%).

In a similar study, Howard and associates (1975) asked 300 managers from twelve different companies whether or not they used each of ten coping techniques previously identified by Burke (1971). The most commonly reported stress management techniques were (1) change to a nonworking activity (64%), (2) talk through with others (49%), (3) change strategy of attack (41%), (4) compartmentalize work and nonwork life (40%), and (5) engage in physical exercise (35%). Of interest is the observation that those individuals who reported fewer psychosomatic symptoms made greater use of talk with other individuals. Individuals with fewer symptoms also resorted *less frequently* to changing the strategy of attack on work, talking through with spouse, and changing to a different work activity.

Psychiatrists, psychologists and other counselors have long held that one of the sources of distress among men in the workplace is the denial of emotional expressiveness. Although it has been assumed that women traditionally are more emotionally expressive, some fear that women in the workplace are beginning to develop the same sort of denial. The simple, age-old method of "talking it over" often is quite effective.

Writing It Out

Writing letters and keeping journals or diaries are age-old, socially accepted methods for expressing emotions which do not find adequate expression elsewhere. The use of writing as a means of emotional release at the workplace is most visible in office or interdepartmental memoranda. Corporate executives, secretaries of state, and humble managers have all been embarrassed, demoted, or expelled as a result of angry and intolerably candid memos. At the same time, however, a well-tempered and carefully composed letter or memorandum can be an effective tool for ventilating tension as well as communicating information which may be useful in moderating future demands.

For a written communication to be emotionally cathartic without jeopardizing one's good standing, it may be useful to write the first draft while the frustration or anger is fresh and then save it for a day or two to be revised under calmer circumstances. Often the process of writing the draft is an end in itself; many hostile memos and letters of resignation have landed in the wastebasket, with the writer much relieved and no one the wiser.

Written expressions of emotion, whether kept to oneself or shared with others, should be viewed as a legitimate form of stress control and not, as sometimes happens, a childish self-indulgence. Provided the writing process actually serves to ventilate the feelings, it is useful.

Acting It Out

Finally, there are many ways of releasing tension by acting it out. Crying, shouting, screaming, and even laughing are all legitimate forms of expression. They need not happen in public to be effective. Anger can be talked-out, cried-out, or yelled-out. Other, more creative avenues can also be explored. The manager of a small retail shop, for example, found that beating a pillow with a plastic baseball bat for fifteen or twenty minutes after particularly stressful days during their peak season gave him his appetite back and made his evening at home much more enjoyable.

The two guidelines for acting out emotions are (a) that no one is harmed, including the person who is expressing his or her feelings, and (2) that the action is truly effective in releasing tension. Within these guidelines, pillow fights, punching bags, dart boards and a variety of other creative solutions are all permissible.

COUNSELING AND PSYCHOTHERAPY

Relaxation techniques and physical exercise are principally forms of secondary preventive management; they are aimed at preventing and dissipating the effects of the stress response before symptoms have developed or before some form of mental or physical disability has occurred. Counseling, psychotherapy, and medical therapy are forms of tertiary prevention, aimed at reversing or at least controlling stress-related symptoms and behaviors which could otherwise lead to disability or death.

It is neither possible nor relevant to review in detail the nature and diversity of available counseling and psychotherapeutic measures. Instead, this section will attempt simply to present an overview of the major types of therapeutic interventions and to provide some illustrative examples of their application in the workplace.

We have divided counseling and psychotherapy programs into five categories: symptom-specific programs, individual psychotherapy, behavioral therapy, group therapy, and career counseling.

With the exception of some of the symptom-specific programs such as alcohol counseling, most employee programs aim to provide short-term and supportive therapy. Individuals requiring long-term or intensive therapy are almost invariably referred to outside professionals or community facilities by most companies. Nevertheless, much of the need in preventive stress management is precisely in the areas of short-term and supportive interventions.

Symptom-Specific Programs

Alcoholism, drug abuse, cigarette smoking, and obesity were among the most common stress-related symptoms discussed in Chapter 3. Individual programs directed at each of these behavioral symptoms are basic to comprehensive preventive management.

Many of the earliest ventures of business and industry into the field of counseling were in the area of alcoholism. Eastman Kodak, Dupont, Equitable Life, and Consolidated Edison of New York are among the companies which, decades ago, pioneered the development of employee alcoholism programs. Today the Association of Labor-Management Administrators and Consultants on Alcoholism (ALMACA) have over 1,700 members who manage and staff alcohol abuse programs. And over 4,400 occupational alcoholism programs currently exist in the U.S. The extent of alcoholism and need for corporate involvement is reflected in the comments of Dr. Leon Warshaw (1979, pp. 104–105), an authority on occupational stress and currently corporate medical director of Equitable Environmental Health, Inc.: "In my view, any organization that does not have an alcoholism program, or which has not recently examined an established program to make sure that it is up to date and working well, is needlessly dissipating its human and financial resources and failing its responsibilities as a corporate citizen."

Of the various reasons for incorporating alcoholism programs into the workplace, the two most compelling are that they are capable of achieving high success rates—which many free-standing programs are not—and they are cost-effective. The National Council on Alcoholism cites recovery rates of 33, 40, 50, 70 and 80 percent for occupational programs. "Job jeopardy" or the "performance approach," in which specific penalties, including dismissal, form part of a therapeutic contract with the employee, is an important element in successful programs (Warshaw, 1979).

The loss of productive time and additional expense from alcohol-associated accidents, absenteeism, and interpersonal troubles is considerable and, therefore, it should not be surprising that a review of occupational alcoholism programs concluded that these programs are generally cost-effective when well-managed (Levens, 1979).

Although drug abuse, smoking cessation, and weight control programs have not been as thoroughly studied, they nevertheless have an important role in preventive management programs. The U.S. military, for example, has been particularly concerned with weight control programs. Similar programs aimed at smoking cessation have been slow in developing, but they are now gaining wider support.

Individual Counseling

Whereas fitness and relaxation training usually have been popular and well-supported, personal counseling is often the weakest part of employer-initiated preventive management programs. Counseling has been listed under tertiary prevention, but like other tertiary techniques it also can have an important impact as a primary or secondary prevention measure, depending upon the availability and emphasis of counseling services.

In the context of stress management, most counseling is aimed at reducing or controlling the stress response by providing information and insights about the stressor or about the individual's reasons for perceiving a certain condition as a stressor. But programs vary considerably in their emphasis. Some are concerned primarily with providing psychological first-aid, support for individuals during a time of crisis. Other programs provide short-term individual or family counseling to help resolve a specific problem or to evaluate the need for ongoing therapy. Counseling can be directed at developing specific personal skills, such as greater comfort with common stressful situations like public speaking or meeting new clients. Long-term in-depth psychotherapy to deal with major life issues is generally provided through outside services, although some of the larger companies include comprehensive in-house counseling programs.

Counseling, especially under the heading "psychotherapy," frequently denotes "mental illness" and for this reason is shunned by management and employees alike. Often management wrongly perceives counseling programs as simply providing mental health services for maladjusted, disordered employees. Employees react in a similar way: "I don't need counseling. I'm not crazy." This is unfortunate because work-related stress is ubiquitous, and counseling programs may help prevent the need for more intensive therapy.

Another fear which sometimes inhibits the development of an effective counseling program is that confidentiality will not be maintained. To be accepted and fully utilized by managers and employees, counseling programs must assure absolute confidentiality for those who use the services and for records of such encounters. In a small company, this is sometimes difficult. This issue of confidentiality may in itself be significant enough to necessitate that counseling be handled by outside services.

It is also important to ask who should be doing the counseling. This depends in part, of course, on the type of counseling being undertaken. Psychoanalysis, for example, requires a psychiatrist or psychologist who has had rigorous training in association with a psychoanalytic institute, and it requires three to five sessions a week for five to seven years. Dr. Leonard Moss, a psychiatrist with extensive experience in organizational stress management programs and himself a trained psychoanalyst, suggests that senior management, as well as the organization's medical personnel and outside professional counselors, have an important role to play in individual counseling (Moss, 1981). Senior managers can be especially helpful to young managers and executives through their understanding of peer competition, problems with authority, career development, internal corporate relationships, and related issues.

Some companies do offer formal psychotherapy, of which there are many types: traditional in-depth Freudian psychoanalysis, Carl Rodger's client-centered therapy, Rollo May's existential therapy, Fritz Perls' gestalt therapy, and so on. In the context of stress management, psychotherapy attempts to provide individuals with insights into the psychodynamics of their perceptions and responses to stress and to use these insights to cope more effectively with job stress. Studies of the effectiveness of psychotherapy suggest that it is the ability of the individual therapist, rather than the particular school of therapy, which is the major determinant of outcome. Certainly no one type of psychotherapy has been shown to be preferable for counseling individuals in dealing with organizational stress. It is important, however, that the therapist be familiar with the stressors which are prevalent in a particular company or specific industry.

The cost-effectiveness of individual counseling programs has not been fully determined, but one recent review of twenty-two counseling programs found that significant reductions in the use of general health care services usually followed treatment for stress-related problems (Jones and Vischi, 1979).

Behavioral Therapy

Another form of individual intervention is behavioral therapy. In contrast to most counseling and psychotherapy, behavioral therapy places less emphasis on insight and the understanding of psychodynamics, and relatively greater emphasis on achieving demonstrable changes in behavior. Rather than looking into the past for the origins of behavior, the behaviorist looks at current and ongoing factors which influence and reinforce behavior patterns. The goal is to substitute new, socially effective responses for old, inappropriate or distressing responses. Specific types of behavior therapy include systematic desensitization, modeling, assertive training, token economies, and aversion training.

An important principle of behavior therapy is that of *counter-conditioning*. Counterconditioning is the process of unlearning an old reaction pattern by practicing a more desirable pattern, one which is incompatible with the old pattern. This is commonly done through a procedure known as *systematic desensitization*. The subject is first taught to achieve good relaxation, usually through one of the methods mentioned earlier in this chapter. The subject is then told to imagine a common situation which he finds stressful. The mental image usually undoes some of the relaxation, and the subject must then be reminded of the necessity of maintaining good relaxation. Eventually the therapist works through a hierarchy of events or situations which the subject finds increasingly stressful. Each time the subject begins to respond with tension, he is reminded to substitute relaxation. Thus systematic desensitization involves substituting relaxation for tension in increasingly difficult situations.

Some therapists suggest that individuals prepare their own hierarchy of stressors related to a particular area of difficulty. Table 11.3 presents such a hierarchy for someone who finds public speaking difficult. The individual is asked to use an arbitrary scale (e.g., 1-100) to rank the stressors according to the degree of disturbance or stress which they create. When applied to a specific stressor, such as public speaking, behavioral therapies serve a dual role as both stressor-directed and response-directed interventions.

The technique of making successive approximations to the desired behavior is not just applied in the therapeutic encounter. Consider, for example, a manager with angina pectoris (chest pains from a heart condition) who has severe attacks whenever he speaks to large groups.

TABLE 11.3
SAMPLE HIERARCHY FOR SYSTEMATIC DESENSITIZATION
FOR PUBLIC SPEAKING

Rank	Degree of stress	Event
1	100	Presenting a serious managerial problem to an unsympathetic meeting of the company board—interruptions frequently made
2	95	Presenting as above, but to a more understanding audience
3	90	Presenting as in 1, but to a small, special committee, instead of the full board
4	85	Giving a talk to a large gathering of the Rotary Club at a local hall
5	80	Being interviewed live for a TV news item
6	75	Receiving a telephone call from the managing director to attend a special board meeting as in 2 above
7	70	Briefly introducing a speaker to a large audience at a women's institute
8	65	Driving to the meeting as in 1 above
9	60	Receiving a letter requesting attendance next week at a meeting as in 3 above
10	55	Making a brief, recorded TV appearance
11	50	Giving a speech at a prize-giving ceremony at your old school
12	45	Standing up and heckling a speaker in a crowded hall at a political meeting
13	40	Making a prepared statement to a small workers' delegation about altered conditions of employment
14	35	Receiving a telephone call and invitation from the headmaster with reference to 11 above
15	30	Giving a "pep" talk to the members of your department at work
16	25	Acting as chairman in a light-hearted debate at the workers' social club
17	20	"Officiating" for an hour at the youth club disco patronized by your daughter
18	15	Giving directions to a group of tourists you meet in an art gallery
19	10	Being telephoned by the producer in respect to 10 above
20	5	Telling six of your colleagues in the staff dining room about some news items you have read

Source: Adapted from H. R. Beech, L. E. Burns, and B. F. Sheffield, *A Behavioral Approach to the Management of Stress.* Copyright © John Wiley & Sons, New York, 1982, pp. 69–70. Used by permission of John Wiley & Sons, Ltd.

These episodes might be prevented with larger doses of heart medication, but behavioral therapy may be even more effective. The patient is first taught how to achieve good relaxation. Then, in the therapeutic setting, he imagines himself in front of a small group and, as tension begins to develop, he reestablishes a feeling of calm. Once this can be done in the office, the individual begins by talking in front of a small, informal group. When he is able to remain calm and pain-free in a small group, he begins to speak to even larger groups and, eventually, he can lecture to a large audience and respond to questions and criticisms without pain (Eliot, 1979, pp. 92–93).

A system of *self-reinforcement* is frequently encouraged by behavioral therapists. The individual sets certain behavioral objectives and identifies rewards which are freely available but which he reserves for reinforcing his successes. The manager with angina pectoris, for example, might reward himself for a major presentation with a three-day weekend or lunch at a special restaurant.

Controlled research on systematic desensitization has demonstrated significant positive results. In a two-year follow-up study of fifty-seven college students with severe public speaking anxiety, 85 percent of those treated by systematic desensitization showed lasting improvement, compared with 50 percent improvement among those treated by dynamic psychotherapy and 22 percent improvement among those who received no treatment (Paul, 1967). In another randomized study of thirty-five individuals with three common phobias 72 percent recovered completely through systematic desensitization versus 12 percent recovery in the control subjects (Lazarus, 1961).

Psychoanalysts and other psychodynamic therapists express the fear that treating symptoms without providing the patient with insights into the origin and meaning of the symptom will simply result in the expression of the presumed underlying conflict in some other way. In practice, this has not proven to be a major problem. Experienced behavioral therapists frequently perform a functional analysis of behavior as part of their therapy and do help the patient to gain some insight into the behavior. However, maladaptive behaviors often become self-perpetuating; simply substituting a more rewarding response pattern provides sufficient reinforcement and improvement in an individual's self-image to make insight almost irrelevant at times. Milton Erickson, an unusually inventive psychiatrist who placed his emphasis on achieving therapeutic change, rather than insight, felt that such insight could sometimes be distinctly untherapeutic. Haley (1973, p. 67) states: "His emphasis is upon bringing about change and expanding a person's world, not upon educating [the patient] about his inadequacies."

Behavior therapy has been shown to be effective for changing specific behaviors, but it is understandably less effective for global anxieties, for people with major maladaptive problems, and for individuals with marked personality disturbances.

Group Therapy

Individual counseling offers many potential benefits to employees, but group approaches also have some distinct advantages. Group therapy makes more efficient use of the therapist's time and skills, allowing limited resources to benefit more people. It has the advantage of providing and strengthening social support in the organization, while at the same time using the potent therapeutic influence of peer feedback. Also, peer pressure can serve as a powerful motivating mechanism for participation as well as for constructive personal change and growth.

As with individual therapy, there are many types of group therapy. For practical purposes, occupational stress groups can be divided into *encounter groups* and *self-help groups*. Encounter groups—known variously as sensitivity training groups, marathon groups, or T-groups— lead participants to discover their candid, sometimes quite hidden feelings, to interact on an emotional level, and to explore individual and group relationships. One review of research on the effectiveness of such groups concluded that they should be viewed as recreational activities or, at best, limited therapeutic interventions (Back, 1973). Several authors have commented on the potential psychological hazards of participation in encounter groups, and one review found reported "casualty rates" to range from less than 1 percent to almost 50 percent (Hartley, Roback, and Abramowitz, 1976). Certainly there is no clear evidence supporting the effectiveness of such groups in the preventive management of job stress.

Self-help or support groups are formed with individuals sharing common stressful experiences and may be quite helpful. The common stressors for such a group may be organizational ones, which affect both home and work life, or outside stressors, which are relevant to the workplace because of the global impact which they may be having on the individuals involved. Examples of issues considered by existing groups of managers (and in some cases spouses) are, the problems of living abroad, the problems of managers who are parents without partners, the problems of two-career couples, and the problems of a heavy travel schedule (Moss, 1981).

In some respects group therapy is a formalized version of social support, described in Chapter 9. However, building social support is aimed primarily at preventing stress responses, whereas group therapy is generally entered into once an individual has experienced difficulty with the work situation.

Group therapy is usually on outside time and paid for with the participant's own funds. When groups are provided through the organization, it is responsible for the quality and potential ill-effects of the program. Thus it is important to review the qualifications and experience of the group leader and to assure that, when contracting with an outside professional association, the individual actually assigned to provide the service is qualified.

Career Counseling

Career development is discussed in detail in Chapter 8 as a primary prevention method. In other words, systematic attention to career development should help individuals progress along career paths in which the demands are suited to their skills and interests. If the demands are optimal, then there should be little stress and even less distress. Unfortunately, this is not always the situation.

Sometimes individuals will find themselves in jobs to which they are not suited. The person-job mismatch may result from the individual's personality, temperament, ability or training; from the nature of the work environment and peer group; from having been promoted too rapidly or too slowly; or from a transitional crisis such as that which frequently occurs during midlife. Once any of these circumstances has originated, then career counseling of a remedial nature is warranted. The process is much the same as that described in Chapter 8.

Inevitably, though, some people will find that they simply do not fit in a particular career or organization. Counselors familiar with the company personnel structure and with the outside job market can provide a valuable service to such individuals by directing them to other positions. Although management may resist letting counselors advice employment in other organizations, truly effective career counselors must have this option (Warshaw, 1979).

MEDICAL CARE

Standard medical therapy is the last attempt to prevent discomfort, disability, and death from stress-induced conditions. When organizational interventions have failed to control serious organizational stressors and when individual coping mechanisms have been pushed to their limit, individuals present themselves to physicians with any of a whole range of stress-related conditions described in Chapter 3.

Until recently physicians usually responded to stress-related illness with some ad hoc advice and, in most cases, a drug prescription. More and more frequently, however, family physicians are recommending exercise, relaxation breaks, and other forms of primary and secondary prevention techniques.

Growing public awareness of preventive medicine and health promotion leads people to seek help earlier and has thereby given physicians the opportunity to use more preventive approaches. Nevertheless, much of the care provided by physicians is still aimed at treating major manifestations of stress-related illness with medications, surgery, and sometimes physical therapy. We would prefer to see primary and secondary preventive measures used more frequently and more effectively; nevertheless, it is useful to briefly review the range of benefits which can be derived from standard medical therapies.

Medications

Anxiety or nervousness is probably the most common symptom of distress treated by the family physician and general practitioner. The most widely known and widely prescribed antianxiety drug is diazepam (Valium®). Its popularity with both physicians and patients is a testament to its perceived efficacy. For short-term use to help individuals through periods of crisis or unusually severe stress, diazepam and some of the other antianxiety drugs are quite effective, reasonably safe, and have minimal addictive potential (Rosenbaum, 1982). They are also useful for the short-term treatment of insomnia. Continued use of such agents, however, is fraught with several potentially serious problems. First, although not initially appreciated, diazepam and closely related drugs can be addictive and have a rather complex withdrawal pattern. Second, use of these drugs may be hazardous while performing activities requiring complete mental alertness. If poor work performance is one of the sources of stress, drugs can actually make the problem worse by dulling mental and physical capabilities. Finally, by blunting distressful feelings and by making the individual feel better, antianxiety drugs may eliminate the motivating force for the individual to make effective, permanent life changes.

Although diazepam and closely related drugs are often prescribed as muscle relaxants, they are not particularly effective compared to muscle relaxation training (e.g., progressive relaxation), massage, or the application of moist heat.

Antianxiety drugs can sometimes be used in low doses as an effective alternative to alcohol abuse. Although this is really the substitution of one addiction for another, diazepam probably allows for better work and social performance and is certainly less toxic to the body.

Depression manifested by sleep disturbance, increased alcohol consumption, fatigue, muscle aches, and a variety of other symptoms is another common stress-induced condition. Although antidepressant medications are virtually never a long-term solution, they can be highly effective in elevating a person's mood out of the deepest part of the depression and in making an individual feel more energetic. They provide enough of an improvement in a person's mental outlook to allow the person's own coping mechanisms to begin functioning effectively again. The individual may begin to make constructive life changes as part of a more permanent solution. It is unfortunate that many people shun the use of antidepressant medications, since they are often highly effective as short-term therapy to facilitate the resolution of a serious depression.

Medical therapy for peptic ulcer disease, one of the classic stress-related illnesses, has undergone several advances in the recent past. Optimal healing of ulcers and prevention of ulcer complications requires regular medical care and adherence to medication, diet, and other special advice.

Mild to moderate high blood pressure may respond quite well to these methods. Angina pectoris, heart failure, and some of the other cardiovascular conditions may also benefit from some of these interventions. However, when an individual has any of these potentially quite serious problems, it is important to continue regular medical care and, if relaxation, diet, and exercise are not sufficient, to be willing to begin drug therapy. Similarly, even though diet and exercise are the first-line treatment for adult diabetes, regular office visits and, if necessary, oral medications or insulin injections should not be avoided simply because an individual is being conscientious with diet and exercise regimens.

Surgery

Surgery is obviously not a primary therapy for any of the stress-related illnesses. Nevertheless, individuals suffering the consequences of chronic stress may meet the surgeon in one of several ways. For example, coronary artery bypass surgery has become a popular treatment for arteriosclerosis of the coronary arteries and the resulting chest pains (angina pectoris). Henry Kissinger, Alexander Haig, tennis star Arthur Ashe, actor Rock Hudson, and "Peanuts" cartoonist Charles Schultz are among those who have undergone the procedure.

Bypass surgery is only effective for certain types of heart blockage and, even then, despite the pain and expense of surgery, the procedure adds an average of only about one year of life compared to standard medical therapy. Relief of anginal pains following surgery makes the procedure worthwhile for most people in whom the surgery is indicated, but primary and secondary prevention would have been so much more worthwhile. A related procedure called endarterectomy is available to correct the blood flow in the arteries to the head in individuals having transient ischemic attacks (TIAs) or "little strokes."

Surgery is also available for the treatment of cigarette-induced cancers (of which lung cancer is only one), severe ulcer disease, certain types of arthritic deformities, some alcoholism-induced conditions, and the intractable foot infections to which diabetics are prone. As with heart disease, surgical treatment of these conditions can sometimes be effective. Invariably, however, it is more costly, more painful, and less satisfactory than primary and secondary prevention.

A final caveat regards surgery for abdominal pain. There are many causes for recurrent abdominal pain, one of which is chronic and recurrent stress. Individuals suffering from such pains are constantly looking for a cure, and surgery is sometimes seen as the simple, definitive solution. Unfortunately, unless there is a specific diseased organ, surgery will be fruitless. Individuals suffering from recurrent abdominal pain—particularly women, in whom the potential causes of such pain are more varied—should insist on a careful evaluation and explanation of the likely problem before agreeing upon surgery.

Physical Therapy

In the military and in some large companies, the physical therapist forms an integral part of the medical care team. Often, however, the potential contribution of physical therapists to the treatment of stress-related illness is neglected. Physical therapy is particularly useful for individuals suffering from back trouble, neck trouble, and other forms of muscle tension. Arthritics, whose mobility or functioning is limited, can benefit from evaluation and treatment by a physical therapist. Special exercises, ultrasound treatments, whirlpool treatments for specific muscles and joints, and several other therapeutic modalities are available through the physical therapist.

Home physical therapy in the form of massage or professional massage available through health clubs and many fine hotels provides a direct and extremely effective means of combating backache, neckache, and other stress-related symptoms arising from tense muscles. For most people massage is as effective as or more effective than muscle-relaxant drugs, and it has none of the side-effects of these drugs. Massage by a loved-one also reinforces the role of social support in stress management.

CREATING A PERSONAL STRESS MANAGEMENT PLAN

Whether stress management is handled by the medical department, the personnel or human resources department, separately by the various departments, or left as an individual matter, each employee should be encouraged to develop his or her own stress management plan. The plan need not be elaborate or complex; the process of developing the plan can be as valuable as or more valuable than the final product.

Many early stress management programs took a narrow, almost tunnel-vision approach to stress control: "Exercise your stress away," "Relaxation for low-stress living," and so on. It is apparent from this and the preceding chapter that there is in fact a wide range of methods for individual stress management. These techniques vary widely in their focus, complexity, cost, accessibility, and effectiveness. It is important, therefore, to take a systematic approach to creating a personal stress managment plan. There is no generally agreed upon strategy for formulating such a plan, but we suggest the following five steps: (1) Identify your stressors, (2) Identify your responses, (3) Identify your options, (4) Make your plan, and (5) Modify your plan.

At the present time, making a stress management plan, like diagnosing organizational stress, is as much art as it is science. The process is time-consuming at first, insight-oriented, individualized, and, in the end, one of trial and error. Most people can formulate a basic stress management plan without professional guidance. Information such as that provided at the end of this chapter and Chapter 10 should provide managers and other employees with sufficient background. However, for people who are unsuccessful on their own or who suffer from high levels of stress and resulting distress, professional guidance may be necessary.

Identify Your Stressors

Self-observation is the first step in personal stress management. Stressors can be identified by an individual through an informal process of personal reflection, but as part of a stress management program, stressors can be identified in a more structured way using one of the methods described in Chapter 6. Cooper's Management Audit provides a conceptual framework for identifying stressors, but the Life Events Scale, Stress Diagnostic Survey, and Stressors Checklist are examples of more specific measurement tools (see Chapter 6 for descriptions and specific references).

In using any standardized assessment method, it is important for the individual to bear in mind that it is merely a tool, not an end in itself. The individual should come away from the diagnostic process not with a score or checklist pattern, but with a very specific knowledge of what stressors exist in his or her life and what is the relative impact of these stressors.

Identify Your Responses

The signs of the stress response and resulting distress were listed and described in Chapter 3. Individuals can learn to monitor their own stress responses and to note when, for example, their cigarette consumption is rising. Simply becoming aware of one's own distress is the first step. It is also useful to tune in on one's self-talk patterns.

Responses can manifest themselves as subtle physiological changes such as a rise in heart rate, as behavioral changes such as increased smoking or alcohol consumption, as psychological changes such as depression or sexual dysfunction, or as frank medical symptoms such as headaches or chest pain. It is important for individuals to develop an internal barometer which monitors these responses and tells them when stress responses and distress are increasing.

With some symptoms it is not always easy to decide whether or not they are related to stress. Even the individual's personal physician may have difficulty separating stress from other causes of disease. Therefore, individuals should be cautious in attributing major symptoms, particularly new or persistent symptoms, to stress without having this confirmed with a medical opinion.

Behavioral measures, a daily log of stress-related symptoms, the Maslach Burnout Inventory, the Cornell Medical Index, and other diagnostic procedures described in Chapter 6 are useful devices for structuring the identification of responses.

Identify Your Options

Most people develop certain coping habits of their own. Identifying these habits, deciding which ones seem to work best, and learning to apply these methods when tension begins to develop is an important first step. But, as Table 10.1 indicated, there is a rather broad set of options for individual stress management. An effective stress management plan will depend upon narrowing these options to those that seem to be acceptable, feasible, and appropriate to the individual's particular stressors and stress responses.

Acceptability of a specific method is a prerequisite for including it in a stress management plan. For example, a traditional method such as knitting or a mystic relaxation technique such as Zen meditation may be wholly unacceptable to a Chase Manhattan bank vice president whose life might be greatly improved by a structured relaxation technique such as progressive relaxation. Thus the techniques must be selected and adapted to fit one's lifestyle.

Feasibility also limits the available options. Although most individual-level methods of preventive management require little in the way of equipment, many require trained instructors, psychologists, physicians, or other professionals. If these individuals are unavailable or their cost is prohibitive, then the options are limited to those which involve minimal expense. However, the cost of not dealing effectively with distress can be considerable. It is important, therefore, to weigh the expense of preventive management against the losses to oneself, one's family, and one's occupation from mismanaged stress.

In contrast to those whose choices are restricted by the cost of a particular technique, there are those individuals who value a thing only when they have spent a significant amount of money on it. The Transcendental Meditation program and some types of biofeedback training are appealing to people for precisely this reason.

Finally, the options should be appropriate to the person's particular stressors and stress responses. One of the reasons for looking at stress management techniques as being stressor-directed, response-directed, and symptom-directed was that this classification may help in selecting specific methods. For example, the manager who deals with all aspects of his job except public presentations may benefit from using a stressor-directed technique. One of the illustrations of constructive self-talk given in Table 10.3 was of anticipation of a public address. Earlier in this chapter we demonstrated how systematic desensitization, a behavioral therapy technique, can be used as a stressor-directed technique for this same problem.

Other individuals will be troubled more by specific responses than by specific stressors. Low backache is a common symptom which people may experience in response to a whole variety of demands. Relaxation training, physical exercise, or massage are response-directed and symptom-directed techniques which can be very useful in countering the discomfort of low back pain.

In considering organizational stressors, it is useful for the individual to make an assessment of which stressors appear to be changeable, which appear to be avoidable, and which are inevitable. While efforts are being pursued to invoke organizational-level preventive management to moderate organizational demands, the individual can best use his or her own energy by directing it towards stressors which the individual can influence.

Make Your Plan

After an individual has identified the range of options available, it is important to select those options which seem most feasible and most attractive and to formulate these into a personal stress management plan.

STRESS MANAGEMENT PLAN

Name: _Jon Dickinson_   Date: _11-20-82_

Personal Perceptions of Stress

(1) _Practice constructive self-talk_

(2) _Learn to recognize the inevitable_

(3) _____

Personal Work Environment

(1) _Learn to say No! (nicely)_

(2) _Each day make a do list_

(3) _and daily plan_

Lifestyle Choices

   Leisure time use:

   Other:

(1) _Take an out-of-town 3-day weekend every 2 months_

(2) _Don't forget vacations_

Relaxation Method(s)

(1) _Practice progressive relaxation each evening_

(2) _Use momentary relaxation at work_

(3) _____

Physical Outlets

(1) _Jog 30 minutes every other day_

(2) _Tennis or golf each weekend_

(3) _____

Emotional Outlets

(1) _Take time to talk-out work frustrations with the wife._

(2) _Practice controlled expression of anger at supervisors_

(3) _____

Professional Help

(1) _None now_

(2) _____

FIGURE 11.2
Personal stress management plan. [*Adapted from Joseph W. Kertesz, "Stress Management Plan," unpublished worksheet, Duke-Watts Family Medicine Center, Durham, N.C., 1982.*]

Figure 11.2 provides a model framework for such a plan and an example of one individual's plan.

Although most people deal with daily stress without a written stress management plan, the written plan helps an individual to think more concretely about stress and the manner in which it might handled. The plan also serves as a contract with oneself. It can be used as a reminder of the options the individual has identified. It can also be used periodically for self-review.

Blanks are provided for the full range of individual-level methods of preventive management, but many people will rely on a limited subset of these methods. Thus, in the example in Figure 11.2, the individual has not planned to alter the personal work environment or identified a need for any professional help. Even though all blanks need not be completed, most basic stress management plans should include some options for relaxation training and for physical and emotional outlets.

Modify Your Plan

Personal stress management is not yet and probably never will be a science. It is impossible to know in advance what methods will work best for a particular individual. Therefore, the personal stress management plan should always be viewed as tentative, and the process of developing a plan should be seen as one of trial and error. The "bottom line" is whether or not the individual feels a sense of relief and achieves the feeling we described earlier as "eustress." The basic question is "When you use the techniques you've outlined, how do you feel at the end of the day?"

If a particular activity in the stress management plan does not seem to make an individual feel any better, then the activity ought to be dropped and replaced with some other activity. For example, some executives will find video games to be quite relaxing, while many will find them annoyingly frustrating. Try different techniques, but be ready to replace those that are not working.

It is also important to guard against turning a releasor into a stressor. Even the most basic relaxation method can become a stressor if the person begins worrying about whether or not he or she is "relaxing correctly." Leisure activities such as vacations can become stressful if tight travel deadlines are set and one is overly concerned with achieving a "successful vacation."

Finally, personal stress management is an evolutionary process. As new or more demanding situations arise and as one's work environment changes, different methods may be needed to achieve the healthy, positive, constructive outcome defined earlier as eustress.

SUMMARY

This chapter and the preceding chapter have reviewed a diverse range of preventive management techniques for the individual. Many of these techniques are available to the individual with or without the help of management. Others, such as counseling or medical care, are available only if management provides them or if the individual seeks them outside the organization. Management, therefore, plays a central role in determining what techniques are made available, what activities are encouraged, and what facilities are provided. Some of the activities, such as comprehensive health promotion programs can be extremely costly. The following chapter will examine some of the programs that organizations are currently using to manage stress. It will also present a model for formulating an overall preventive management strategy and some questions to consider in implementing such a program.

FURTHER READINGS

General Works

Beech, H. R., L. E. Burns, and B. F. Sheffield: *A Behavioral Approach to the Management of Stress*, John Wiley & Sons, New York, 1982.

Crasilneck, H. B., and J. A. Hall: *Clinical Hypnosis*, Grune & Stratton, New York, 1975.

Girdano, D. A., and G. S. Everly: *Controlling Stress and Tension: A Holistic Approach*, Prentice-Hall, Englewood Cliffs, N.J., 1979.

Goldberg, R. J.: "Anxiety Reduction by Self-Regulation: Theory, Practice and Evaluation," *Annals of Internal Medicine*, vol. 96, 1982, 482–487.

Pelletier, K. R.: *Mind as Healer, Mind as Slayer*, Dell Publishing Co., New York, 1977.

Relaxation Training

Benson, H.: "Your Innate Asset for Combating Stress," *Harvard Business Review*, July-August 1974, pp. 49–60.

Benson, H.: *The Relaxation Response*, Avon Books, New York, 1975.

Bernstein, D. A., and T. D. Borkovec: *Progressive Relaxation Training: A Manual for the Helping Professions*, Research Press Co., Champaign, Ill., 1973.

Brown, B.: *Stress and the Art of Biofeedback*, Harper & Row, New York, 1977.

Carrington, P.: *Freedom in Meditation*, Anchor Press, Doubleday, Garden City, N.Y., 1977.

Davis, M., E. R. Eshelman, and M. McKay: *The Relaxation and Stress Reduction Workbook*, New Harbinger Publications, San Francisco, 1980.

Jacobson, E.: *You Must Relax*, 5th ed., McGraw-Hill Book Co., New York, 1978.

Lindemann, H.: *Relieve Tension the Autogenic Way*, Wyden, New York, 1973.

Marcus, J. B.: *TM and Business*, McGraw-Hill Book Co., New York, 1977.

Mitchell, L.: *Simple Relaxation*, Atheneum Publishers, New York, 1979.

Physical Exercise

Anderson, J. L., and M. Cohen: *The West Point Fitness and Diet Book*, Avon, New York, 1977.

Cooper, K.: *The Aerobics Program for Total Well-Being*, M. Evans and Company, New York, 1982.

Cooper, M., and K. Cooper: *Aerobics for Women*, Bantam Books, New York, 1978.

Royal Canadian Air Force, *Exercise Plans for Physical Fitness*, Pocket Books, New York, 1962.

Sheeham, G.: *Doctor Sheeham on Running,* World Publications, New York, 1975.
Zohman, L.: *Exercise Your Way to Fitness and Heart Health,* Mazola Corn Exercise
   Booklet, Dept. 20, Box 307, Coventry, CN 06328, 1979.

Counseling and Psychotherapy

Bergin, A. E., and S. L. Garfield: *Handbook of Psychotherapy and Behavior
   Change,* Wiley, New York, 1971.
Freud, S.: *Collected Papers,* vols. I to V, Hogarth Press, London, 1956.
Jones, K. R., and T. R. Vischi: "Impact of Alcohol, Drug Abuse and Mental Health
   Treatment on Medical Care Utilization: A Review of the Research Literature,"
   Medical Care, vol. 17, no. 12, Supplement, 1979.
Wolberg, L. R.: *The Technique of Psychotherapy,* 3d ed., Grune and Stratton,
   New York, 1977.

RESOURCE GROUPS

General

American Health Foundation, 320 East 43rd Street, New York, NY 10017
American Institute of Stress, Tarrytown House, Executive Conference Center,
   East Sunnyside Lane, Tarrytown, NY 10591

Relaxation Training

Biofeedback Society of America, 4301 Owen Street, Wheat Ridge, CO 80030
International Center for Scientific Research, Maharishi International University,
   Fairfield, IA 52556

Physical Exercise

National Jogging Association, 919 18th St., N.W., Suite 830, Washington, DC 20006
American College of Sports Medicine, 1440 Monroe St., 4002 Stadium, Madison,
   WI 53706
American Medical Joggers Association, Box 4704, North Hollywood, CA 91607
American Association of Fitness Directors in Business and Industry, 400 Sixth
   Street, S.W., Suite 3030, Washington, DC 20201
President's Council on Physical Fitness and Sports, 400 Sixth Street, S.W., Room
   3030, Washington, DC 20201

Counseling and Psychotherapy

American Academy of Psychoanalysis, 40 Gramercy Park N., New York, NY 10010
American Academy of Marriage and Family Counselors, 41 Central Park West,
   New York, NY 10023

American Examining Board of Psychoanalysis, 80 Eighth Ave., Room 1210, New York, NY 10011

Referrals, American Psychiatric Association, 1700 18th Street N.W., Washington, DC 20036

American Psychoanalytic Association, One East 57th St., New York, NY 10032

Office of Professional Affairs, American Psychological Association, 1200 17th Street N.W., Washington, DC 20036

National Clearinghouse for Mental Health Information, National Institute of Mental Health, 5600 Fishers Lane, Rockville, MD 20857

National Mental Health Association, 1800 North Kent Street, Arlington, VA 22209

Alcoholism and Drug Abuse Treatment

Al-Anon Family Group Headquarters and Alateen, P.O. Box 182, Madison Square Station, New York, NY 10010

Alcoholics Anonymous, P.O. Box 459, Grand Central Station, New York, NY 10017

Association of Labor-Management Administrators and Consultants on Alcoholism, 1800 North Kent Street (Suite 907), Arlington, VA 22209

Association of Labor and Management Administrators and Consultants on Alcoholism, Suite 350, Park Plateau, 300 Wendell Court, Atlanta, GA 30336

National Clearinghouse for Alcohol Information, Alcohol, Drug Abuse, and Mental Health Administration, P.O. Box 2345, Rockville, MD 20852.

National Clearinghouse for Drug Abuse Information, Alcohol, Drug Abuse and Mental Health Administration, 5600 Fishers Lane, Room 10-A56, Rockville, MD 20857

National Council on Alcoholism, 733 Third Avenue, New York, NY 10017

Provide Addict Card Today/National Association on Drug Abuse, 355 Lexington Ave., New York, NY 10017

Other Resource Groups

American Society of Clinical Hypnosis, 2400 East Devon Avenue, Suite 218, Des Plaines, IL 60018

Association for Advancement of Behavior Therapy, 420 Lexington Ave., New York, NY 10170

Y's Way to a Healthy Back Program, Pacific Region YMCA, 3080 La Selva, San Mateo, CA 94403

AUDIOVISUAL MATERIALS

American Hospital Association. "Stress!" (educational package program with a Leader's Package including audiocassette, slides, Leader's Guide, audience participation materials; introduction available as a 16-mm film or videocassette). USCAN International, Ltd., 205 W. Wacker Drive, Suite 300, Chicago, IL 60606.

Budhzynski, T. H.: "Relaxation Training Program," BMA Audio Cassette Publications, 200 Park Ave. South, New York, NY 10003.

Carrington, P.: "Clinically Standardized Meditation," (CSM) Self-Regulated Course (audiotapes and manual). Pace Educational Systems, Inc., P.O. Box 113, Kendall Park, NJ 08824.

Cotler, S. B., and J. J. Guerra: "Self-Relaxation Training," Research Press Co., Box 3177, Champaign, IL 61820.

Manuso, J.: "Manage Your Stress" (facilitator's guide, film or videotape, audiocassette, exercise books). CRM Multimedia Module, McGraw-Hill Films, 110 Fifteenth Street, Del Mar, CA 92014.

McLean, A. A.: "Dealing with Job Stress" (cassettes and workbooks). Management Decision Systems, P.O. Box 35, Darien, CN 06820.

New Harbinger Publications: "Progressive Relaxation and Breathing," "Autogenics and Meditation," "Self Hypnosis," "Thought Stopping" (tapes). New Harbinger Publications, 2200 Adeline, Suite 305, Oakland CA 94607.

Stroebel, C. G.: "Quieting Response Training," BMA Audio Cassette Publications, 200 Park Ave. South, New York, NY 10003.

CHAPTER 12

IMPLEMENTING PREVENTIVE MANAGEMENT

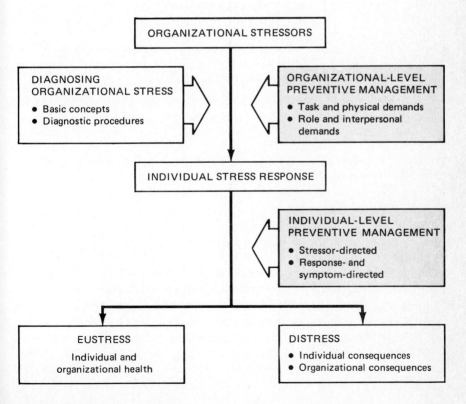

Chapters 8 through 11 have provided detailed discussions of the various organizational- and individual-level techniques which are available to reduce the occurrence and negative impact of organizational stress and to promote the positive aspects of organizational stress. Too often management is aware of stress reduction techniques which could be applied in the organization, but it is unable to establish a feasible mechanism for utilizing these techniques on a continuing basis. Therefore, this chapter will review some of the ways in which preventive management techniques may be implemented. Brief examples and several detailed case studies will be reported to illustrate some of the successful approaches to establishing stress management programs.

The distinction between organizational-level and individual-level programs is as valid for companywide programs as it is for the specific techniques already described; generally, there appears to be little integration between the two levels. Interventions at the organizational level are usually initiated as part of organizational development efforts or in response to specific crises. In contrast, the individual-level techniques are usually originated by the medical or personnel department. We are unaware of any truly integrated companywide stress management efforts. This is unfortunate, since the best use of company resources will probably result from an integration of both the organizational and individual levels of preventive stress management.

PROGRAMS AT THE ORGANIZATIONAL LEVEL

The design and implementation of stress management activities at the organizational level can occur through one of several mechanisms, including consultation, training, organizational development, and task forces. These mechanisms are not mutually exclusive and, in fact, successful preventive management at the organizational level may involve the use of two or more approaches.

Management Development

Management training or management development is a formal internal program to expand the skills of managers. It may involve courses and other structured educational activities within and outside the organization, rotation of job assignments to add breadth to the manager's experiences, and periodic evaluation and constructive feedback. Course work and in-house training related to stress management has been added to many management development programs. As more rising managers learn about job enrichment, task redesign, role analysis, goal setting, and other preventive management techniques, these techniques will receive wider application. In addition, new techniques are likely to be developed and tested as a natural, evolutionary extension of preventive management.

Training in stress management skills is also important at the supervisory level. Effective management depends upon the quality of training received by front-line supervisors and middle management. This training may be provided through in-house programs or by one of a large number of firms who specialize in prepackaged supervisor training programs. In the past, many of these programs have dealt largely or exclusively with the technical aspects of the job: recordkeeping, personnel policies, organization of production activities, and so on. Recently, human relation issues have begun to appear in supervisor and middle-management training. These training programs are thus an ideal setting for teaching supervisors and middle management about organizational stress and the range of interventions which are available for reducing organizational stressors or minimizing their impact. Training and periodically retraining key employees in organizational stress management techniques should provide a source of ongoing self-assessment.

It should also be kept in mind that supervisors and middle management are among the most stressed individuals in the organization. These individuals are the "men in the middle," getting intense pressures from both labor and top-level management. First-line supervisors experience this stress most intensely. This was illustrated very vividly in a large appliance manufacturing company during some diagnostic work. The major complaint that the first-line supervisors had was the lack of knowledge and skills in coping with the demands of their jobs, which they reported to be very distressful. Therefore, it is especially important for new supervisors to gain the knowledge and skills to manage the demands and stresses of their new positions.

Most management training programs are conceptually and cognitively oriented, which is only one component of good preventive training for stress management. It is also essential that the behavioral and skill components of such training be given adequate attention. Individuals who do not know how to establish effective social supports, or how to exercise, or how to relax require experiential practice and feedback regarding the conduct of these activities.

Organizational Development

Just as management development programs are important to the continued expansion of the skills of individual managers, organizational development programs are important to the continued growth and well-being of the organization. Organizational development activities are aimed primarily at group processes such as decision-making patterns, communication channels and styles, conflict management, structure of lines of authority, and so on. The goal of organizational development work is organizational health, in terms of both productivity and adaptability. The diagnosis of organizational stress and the search for effective intervention techniques should be a part of any organizational development program.

The tenants of preventive management and organizational development are very consistent. The implementation of preventive management through an organizational development function is compatible with the general thrust of that function. There are two fundamental, though not major, differences between preventive management and organizational development. First, the primary level of analysis for organizational development is the work group, whereas the primary level of analysis for preventive management is the organization. This makes some difference in the framework for strategies and intervention methods. Second, preventive management has a holistic concern with both the formal and informal organization. The emphasis in much of traditional organization development is on the informal organization, although the formal is not ignored. The balanced perspective of preventive management is important in creating a whole and healthy organization. Inevitably, it will shape the methods of intervention as well as the strategies and preferred points of intervention.

It is possible, though historically it has not been done, to use the organizational development function as the point of integration for the various stress-oriented activities of the organization. Because of the host of ways in which distress may be manifested and the very diverse intervention methods, from medical to psychological to administrative, for responding to distress, it is essential that a coordination function for these services and activities be provided in the organization.

Organizational development activities may manifest themselves in a variety of ways. One manifestation is in the form of specific structural changes in the workplace, an example of which is work scheduling, described in Chapter 8. The experience of Tenneco demonstrates this organizational approach to reducing employee stress.

In the 1970s flextime became popular in many organizations. Ronen (1981) lists over 250 companies using flextime programs. Because of the severe traffic problems for employees in downtown Houston during the late 1970s and the establishment of flextime programs by many competitors, Tenneco, Inc., initiated its own flextime program. A written corporate policy specified the purpose and operation of this program.

The program operates under a corporate policy which establishes a number of alternative eight-hour flexible work schedules around a "core" period of 8 a.m. to 4:45 p.m. The Tenneco employee may apply for a daily schedule which begins between 7 a.m. and 9 a.m. (in thirty-minute increments) and ends between 3:45 p.m. and 5:45 p.m. As long as the department is adequately staffed during the "core" period and the department head approves, the individual is then able to work during his chosen hours. Much of the impetus for this and other programs is aimed at assisting individuals in dealing with the stress of urban commuting and traffic problems.

In conjunction with the flextime program, Tenneco, Inc., has established another corporate program aimed at the problems of urban commuting and energy shortage. This is a program of corporate van pools which operate from the suburbs of Houston to downtown. There are 130 van pools in the company, each of which is composed of individuals working the same flextime schedule. More than one-third of Tenneco's employees in downtown Houston participate voluntarily in these van pools. The van pool and flextime programs are designed to mesh together in relieving the stress of commuting.

Tenneco, Inc., has also designed and built an employee health and fitness center, established to promote employee health and physical fitness. The center, which is in operation from 6 a.m. to 7 p.m. daily, is adjacent to the company's headquarters. Company policies support employee use of the center anytime before, during, or after working hours, as long as supervisors concur and the employee otherwise can complete a full daily work schedule. The center hours and operation are also designed to mesh with the flextime program established by the company.

Overall, Tenneco, Inc., has found their flextime program to be working quite well. Despite a number of operational issues still being resolved, flextime represents a successful organizational-level intervention which reduces individual stress by moderating the unusually difficult demand of traveling to and from work.

Consultation

Frequently changes in job design, organizational roles, physical environment, support systems, career development opportunities, or decision-making patterns will occur as a result of the analysis and recommendations of a consultant charged with improving the work environment and reducing stress or conflict in an organization. Often the work is done by an internal consultant—a corporate vice president, a new personnel manager, the medical director, a staff industrial psychologist, or someone else from management adept in the methods of organizational behavior. The internal consultant may be charged with a one-time evaluation, with periodic stress assessment, or with an ongoing role in monitoring the organization's stress patterns. Preventive management activities can also be initiated as a result of the work of an outside consultant. Psychologists, psychiatrists, and other mental health professionals from universities or private practice are often hired to analyze company stress patterns and to suggest changes. Management consultants from universities and private consulting groups are also becoming active in the area of stress management. Like internal consultants, their preventive management "tools" are essentially those described in Chapters 8 and 9 and variations thereon.

Outside consultants may offer the advantage of greater objectivity and lack of any vested interest in existing management practices and behavior patterns. At the same time, however, without a long-term knowledge of the organization and subtleties of its operation, an outside consultant may be less able to discern which intervention techniques will have the greatest likelihood of success.

Selection of an outside consultant should be done with great care. Management consulting firms may lack expertise in the psychodynamics and complex social psychology of organizational stress, while consultants drawn from mental health fields sometimes lack experience and insight with regard to business and industry. One organization, for example, contracted with the Department of Psychiatry at a local university to study work-related stress among its employees and to evaluate the medical department's stress management program. After over one year of diligent probing and careful analysis by the multidisciplinary team, the chairman of the department presented the team's findings. Although quite interesting, the report unfortunately contained nothing of practical value which had not already been known by the medical director and management (Warshaw, 1979, pp. 83–84).

When carefully selected, however, external consultants can play an invaluable role as resources for managerial decision making about preventive management programs. This was illustrated in the case of a pharmaceutical laboratory which called in two university professors for consultation. The management of the production functions in the lab was convinced that the turnover and absenteeism rates were unacceptable and required action. An examination of the work areas, the physical layout of the plant, a close examination of the employee comments and complaints, as well as the actual absenteeism and turnover rates suggested a healthy organization. It was recommended that no training program be undertaken at that juncture because it would be a waste of money. Thus, an independent external consultation may play a key role in preventive management, especially if the opinion is that no specific action is currently required.

An important caution with regard to the use of outside consultants is that they too may have vested interests. Consultants hired by management and dependent upon this relationship for their livelihood may cater to the interests and desires of management, rather than make suggestions which benefit the whole organization. This potential conflict may be most apparent in the balance which is struck between organizational-level interventions aimed at changing the demands which the organization puts on the individual and interventions aimed at helping the individual to deal more effectively with those demands.

Preventive Management Task Force

Using the task force concept, it is possible to integrate and implement preventive management programs. One of the things that we have noticed in discussions with diverse organizations is both the lack of integration between individual and organizational health and the lack of integration between various specialties concerned with different aspects of health. Fitness programs, counseling services, dietary functions, and alcoholism programs are scattered throughout various parts of an organization. In fact, all of these functions are related and connected to the functional (fitness) as well as dysfunctional (alcoholism) ways in which individuals respond to stress.

A preventive management task force would accomplish two primary purposes. First, this approach would lead to coordination and integration of the variously related programs that bear upon organizational stress management. This integration would result in resource savings through reduced duplication of services and/or equipment. Second, because of the relationships between such diverse activities as fitness programs and psychiatric counseling, the task force would provide for the interdisciplinary blending of medical, physiological, psychological, and administrative specialties. The knowledge exchange as well as skill blending are both essential to the comprehensive response to organizational stress.

PROGRAMS AT THE INDIVIDUAL LEVEL

Chapters 10 and 11 described a wide range of methods for personal stress management. Most of these methods are accessible to the average employee outside the workplace. Depending upon the specific method, it may be available through self-study, the employee's personal physician, local counseling and human service agencies, or organizations such as the Transcendental Meditation program. Increasingly, however, training in personal stress management is available at the workplace through the medical or health department, a separate stress management program, fitness programs or comprehensive health promotion programs. These programs are often viewed as being part of the employee benefit package, although they could easily be justified as "preventive maintenance" costs for the company's human resources.

Medical and Health Departments

Many of the activities which are now considered part of preventive stress management have traditionally fallen to the medical or occupational health departments. These departments may be staffed by various occupational physicians, occupational nurses, family physicians, psychiatrists, psychoanalysts, psychologists, and social workers. Union counselors, industrial·chaplains, and pastoral counselors may work separately or through the medical department to provide additional services. The skills and potential contributions of each of these professional groups are well described in Warshaw's *Managing Stress* (1979).

Routine medical care, relaxation training, exercise prescription, and a host of different types of counseling programs are among the services which may be offered by medical departments. In many companies, the medical or health department offers the best point of entry for introducing new programs aimed at individual stress reduction. Basic medical department services are usually offered without charge, but optional stress management activities sometimes must be funded by charging employees for the service.

Introducing stress management activities through the medical department has its potential difficulties and limitations. As long as the medical staff is on management's payroll, they are "company doctors," the connotation of which is that the needs of management come first. Occupational physicians have become quite sensitive to this criticism, so much so that in 1976 the American Occupational Medical Association adopted a new Code of Ethical Conduct for Physicians Providing Occupational Medical Services. Among other things, the code specifies that physicians should "practice on a scientific basis with objectivity and integrity" and "avoid allowing their medical judgment to be influenced by any conflict of interest." To the extent that medical departments follow this code, there should be no difficulty in introducing stress management activities through the medical or health department.

Another concern is that the medical staff may lack background in organizational and administrative sciences and, therefore, may not fully appreciate the context of organizational stress and available nonmedical interventions. It is in part this concern which has led some firms to initiate stress management programs through employee relations, the personnel department, or newer divisions such as human resources management.

Warshaw, who has practiced and written about occupational health and stress management for over twenty years, points out that there are several different elements which may be involved in clinical stress management programs at the workplace (Table 12.1). The extent to which the company provides on-site treatment versus referral service depends in part upon finances. The following case study (adapted from Reardon, 1976, pp. 50–54) suggests one way in which small companies

TABLE 12.1
ELEMENTS IN A CLINICAL STRESS MANAGEMENT PROGRAM

1. *First aid.* Provision of immediate telephone or personal contact with a health professional for crisis situations
2. *Case finding.* Identification of persons with indications of stress-related difficulties and making arrangements for their evaluation.
3. *Evaluation.* Establishment of an accurate diagnosis and estimation of the severity and rate of progression of the stress-related difficulty
4. *Treatment.* Provision of short-term counseling and supportive therapy in the workplace
5. *Referral.* Making arrangements for the individual to receive treatment which is appropriate to his or her needs and suitable in terms of immediacy, convenience, cost, and acceptability.
6. *Rehabilitation.* Facilitation of continuation on the job during therapy or return to work after a bout of absence or disability
7. *Screening.* Periodic examination and evaluation of individuals in highly stressful positions or with high-risk personal characteristics to detect early indications of impending difficulty
8. *Prevention.* Educating and persuading individuals at high risk for stress-related difficulties to adopt lifestyles and work habits that will enhance their coping abilities and decrease their levels of distress

Source: Adapted from L. J. Warshaw, *Managing Stress*, Addison-Wesley, Reading, Mass., 1979, pp. 33–35.

can provide valuable counseling services with a limited financial investment by the company:

> The Southern Connecticut Gas Company, an employer of fewer than 600 persons in both white- and blue-collar occupations, could not afford to establish an in-house program staffed with psychologists, social workers, or nurses. Like many firms, however, the company was deeply concerned about the increasing number of workers who, because of alcohol or drug abuse or other personal problems, were unable to function properly.
>
> In recent years, as the energy situation worsened, utilities began to take a harder line toward employee performance, but claimed to value experienced, trained employees as human beings as well as assets in whom they had invested years of time and considerable money. So rather than move to discharge poorly performing employees too quickly, it seemed better to try to develop a program that would help solve their problems—a program that would be corrective rather than punitive and would benefit both the employee and the company.
>
> **Help from the outside**   A tight budget eliminated the possibility of offering full-time services of a special staff or setting up an on-site facility. So they investigated the feasibility of using outside agencies to

carry out the program through referrals from the company. Evaluation of the available services indicated that the family service agencies of the United Way offered an ideal vehicle to conduct the program. They had the personnel, resources, facilities, and experience. The agencies are part of the Family Services of America, Inc., the parent organization for more than 300 such agencies throughout the United States and Canada, a network that offers the potential for the same kind of aid to companies with similar problems.

Organizing the program The Southern Connecticut Gas Company began to progress early in 1975 after they reached agreement with Family Services of Greater New Haven and Family Services in Woodfield, the two local family service agencies that operate in the area of the company's headquarters.

The agencies promised the complete confidentiality of the counselor-client relationship. No employees would be required or expected to discuss their personal problems with their on-the-job supervisor or with the employee relations manager.

The next step in designing the program was training the company's 90 supervisors. In a series of comprehensive three-hour sessions, every supervisor received details of the mechanics of the program and learned what to do when on-the-job performance began to deteriorate.

Union participation and support The company's two local unions endorsed the program and were represented at the training sessions. Union officials were quick to recognize the program's advantages: It saved jobs for members; it avoided the traditional adversary relationship between union and management, emphasizing cooperation rather than confrontation; and it removed the pressures of having to defend employees who had become virtually indefensible.

How the plan works When an employee reaches the point where disciplinary action becomes mandatory, his supervisor recommends a voluntary visit to the personnel department. The supervisor is careful to point out that the visit is offered on a private basis and will be conducted in confidence.

If the employee accepts, the personnel department coordinates a meeting between the employee and Family Services where the individual meets—away from the job—with a qualified case worker.

Once the problem is identified, a course of action is set. The service agency may work with the employee directly, conduct ongoing counseling with him and his family, or refer him to another agency or medical care facility.

If the employee remains in the program, the company is notified of his satisfactory attendance. It does not get details of the nature of the problem nor is it told what treatment the employee may be receiving.

This confidentiality is an important point, particularly to corporate managers. Further, an employee often regards his problem as "his business" and not that of the company—even though he is about to lose his job as a result. He would rather protect his psyche than his job—a basic human trait.

Cost vs. benefits   What has it cost the Southern Connecticut Gas Company to establish this program? To start, it cost $4,620 in worker hours to train the 90 supervisors and union officials. The contract with the social service agencies calls for the company to pay $35 for each initial "intake" interview. Additional costs, however, are borne directly by the employee or by his major medical and other health insurance coverage.

In terms of time required to design the program, the effort was well worth making. The first memorandum on the program was submitted to top management in September 1974. The first meetings with the family service counselors were held in January 1975, and by April training sessions for supervisors had begun. By July nine employees had enrolled in counseling programs, and by September several had responded successfully to treatment. Eight are still on the payroll, although each was considered in a "last chance" category.

The cost involved in this counseling effort, the timetable under which the program was established, and the availability of similar family counseling services in most cities make this approach feasible and accessible for most small and medium-sized companies. Its apparent success in saving jobs and possibly preserving families and promoting individual well-being, suggests that such programs can be quite cost-effective.

Many companies offer extensive on-site counseling programs aimed at specific problem areas such as poor coworker relations, alcohol or drug abuse, marital troubles, and personal finances. Among the companies offering such programs are 3M, B. F. Goodrich Company, General Mills, and The Equitable Life Assurance Society of the United States. Some of these programs are provided through the corporate medical department, while others have been initiated by human resources management, personnel, employee relations, or employee benefits.

Stress Management Programs

In recent years there has been a move to establish ongoing personal stress management programs or hold periodic stress management seminars at the workplace. These may be organized through the personnel department, the medical department, or a joint effort among departments. The content of these programs varies from place to place.

Commonly they include training in one or more of the relaxation techniques, discussion of the role of physical exercise, and a description of some of the personal coping techniques and lifestyle management issues discussed in Chapter 10. Often, however, early company stress management programs have restricted themselves to teaching one relaxation technique. Although useful, this limited approach should probably be viewed as only a starting point for a more comprehensive stress management program. Examples of existing programs include:

• Metropolitan Life Insurance Company's Center for Health Help offers a program in worksite stress management to employees and markets the program to other corporations. The program emphasizes reduction of distress through behavior modification techniques such as reducing time urgency pressure, developing interpersonal communication skills, and relaxing voluntary muscle.
• Illinois Bell's Training and Development Department periodically offers a stress management course at the request of employees.
• Equitable Life Insurance Company's Emotional Health Program utilizes biofeedback to help employees learn to ease their tensions. The company informally estimates that each $15 which it spends on a treatment session relieves symptoms that would have cost three times that much in lost productivity.
• New York Telephone Company piloted the use of Clinically Standardized Meditation for stress management and, on the basis of its success, has made CSM training regularly available to employees.
• B. F. Goodrich Tire's Group Learning Center has prepared a training program entitled "Manage Your Stress," a nine-hour program in three sessions designed to teach employees to identify their own stress responses and to assume responsibility for altering their responses.

Several modular stress management programs are now available on audiocassettes with supplementary films and videocassettes. Manuso (1980) has developed one of the most comprehensive sets of audiovisual materials. It is particularly well-suited to individual stress management in the workplace. This and other audiovisual programs are listed at the end of Chapter 11.

Fitness Programs

Of the preventive management techniques described in Chapters 10 and 11, physical fitness training has probably received the greatest financial commitment from business and industry. The extent of this commitment to some programs is impressive:

• Weyerhaeuser Company in 1972 invested $73,000 to construct and equip a colorful gymnasium at the company's headquarters in Tacoma,

Washington. The facility, which includes indoor courts, a well-equipped exercise room, saunas, and a locker room, is open daily to employees and their families.

• Johns-Manville spent $17,000 to equip a small company gym at its Denver headquarters. Like many corporate fitness programs, participants must have a medical examination before beginning and are given specific exercise guidelines.

• Exxon Corporation, when it planned its Manhattan headquarters building which opened in 1972, set aside a 2,900-square-foot area for its physical fitness laboratory. Under the supervision of the medical department, over 300 executives have participated in regular prescribed exercise, achieving significant improvements in several health parameters.

• The Life Insurance Company of Georgia set up a Tower Health Club atop its building in Atlanta. Its executives, over 200 of whom are members, pay a subsidized membership fee which is about one-third of the fee for other tenants in the building. Facilities, which include handball and squash courts, massage and exercise rooms, and a rooftop track, are open twelve hours daily on weekdays.

Although corporate fitness programs seem to attract larger management investments in facilities and staffing than other techniques with stress reduction potential, the fitness program frequently serves as the focal point from which a variety of other programs, including relaxation training, develop. Often the elaborate facilities constructed for fitness programs also serve as meeting places for broader stress management seminars and training programs.

Comprehensive Health Promotion Programs

In an effort to stem the tide of rising employee health care costs and health insurance premiums and to reduce the high cost of premature death and disability among executives, managers, and skilled employees, an increasing number of companies are organizing comprehensive health promotion and disease prevention programs. Thorough health examinations to detect asymptomatic disease and disease risk factors, fitness programs, behavior change efforts aimed primarily at smoking and weight control, and stress management are key components of most programs.

Comprehensive health promotion programs offer a tremendous potential for reducing the individual and organizational costs of stress-related illnesses. Not only do they attack some of the consequences of organizational stress, including smoking, excessive alcohol consumption, and obesity, but these programs also deal with basic stress responses as well as individual risk factors which can multiply the adverse health effects of stress.

One of the earliest, best-known, and most ambitious programs is the Health Management Program initiated by Kimberly-Clark (Dedmon 1979, 1980; Dedmon et al., 1979; also based on pamphlets and progress reports from the Health Management Program listed under resource groups, end of this chapter). The history, progress, and goals of the program are described in the following paragraphs:

Kimberly-Clark's Health Management Program began full operation in 1977 with the stated goal of significantly reducing absenteeism, health care costs, and cardiovascular risk factors within ten years. The home of the program is a $2.5 million health services center at the corporate office in Wisconsin's Fox Valley. It is available to 2,600 salaried and 1,900 hourly employees of the office. The center includes a 7,000-square-foot multiphasic health testing center and a 32,000-square-foot fitness center featuring a 25-meter Olympic pool, a 100-meter suspended track, exercise equipment, a sauna, and a lounge and dining area. A staff of 40, including 17 health professionals, is responsible for the evaluation, counseling, fitness training, and lifestyle modification programs.

Participants enter the program through a series of five steps. First, participants are asked to complete a comprehensive, computerized health history. Next, the employee is given a series of laboratory tests to assess liver, heart, kidney, and lung functions as well as hearing and vision. The third step is a complete physical examination and a treadmill test. A periodic follow-up examination is offered every two to three years, depending on age. Following the initial evaluation, the results are reviewed and recommendations are made for health promotion and, where necessary, further medical care. A health prescription is prepared with the approval of the employee's personal physician. The fifth and final step is admission to the fitness facility. The health prescription includes an exercise program which usually offers swimming, jogging, cycling, or walking.

The center opened with a large promotional effort, including three weeks of presentations to employees. The medical director kept an open telephone hotline in his office to answer questions and receive feedback about the program. Initially, 60 percent of the salaried employees signed up—10 percent more than expected. To date, over 90 percent of the employees have been through the health screening, 50 percent have received exercise orientation, and 25 percent use the facilities regularly.

The screening program has uncovered a significant number of treatable health conditions and has already succeeded in lowering blood pressure and triglyceride levels in the participants. The Employee Assistance Program provides counseling services. About one-half of its clients have alcohol or drug problems, and they report a favorable rehabilitation rate of 65 percent. Over 200 employees and family members have received training in cardiopulmonary resuscitation.

In addition to the screening, exercise, and counseling programs, the center has a full schedule of health education classes on stress management, obesity, nutrition, and alcohol and drug abuse.

The services and facilities are available to employees on a voluntary basis and without charge. The estimated cost is about $435 per person per year. On the basis of current operations, and projected reductions in absenteeism and use of medical services, it is estimated that the overall break-even point will be 8½ years—3 years for the Employee Assistance Program and about 6½ years for the remainder of the program. The entire range of services has been well received by employees. The cooperation and participation of local physicians has also been obtained. The Health Management Program has further enhanced Kimberly-Clark's public reputation and has assisted in corporate recruitment efforts. Current indications suggest that the ten-year goal for reducing absenteeism, health care costs, and cardiovascular risk factors will be realized.

In addition to Kimberly-Clark, a growing number of other major corporations are initiating comprehensive health promotion programs which include a variety of stress management activities. The Xerox Health Management Program, Control Data Corporation's Stay Well Self-Health Management Program, the General Dynamics Health Fitness Center, and Citicorp's Manage Your Health program are all examples of such programs. Although many of the major corporate health promotion programs are based in large new physical fitness facilities, such facilities are not necessary to design and implement a comprehensive health promotion program.

THE IMPLEMENTATION CYCLE FOR
PREVENTIVE MANAGEMENT

Knowing the range of organizational and individual stress management techniques and potential mechanisms for their implementation will accomplish little without a specific implementation strategy. Formulating and implementing a program of preventive stress management involves the same basic steps which are required for the introduction of any change in an organization: (1) organizational stress diagnosis, (2) planning for prevention, (3) organizational and individual action, and (4) outcome evaluation. These steps form the the implementation cycle

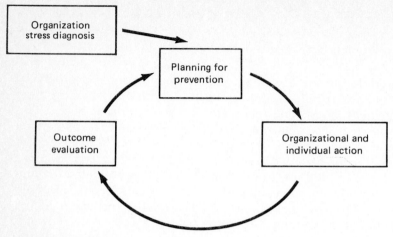

FIGURE 12.1
The implementation cycle for preventive management.

for preventive management (Figure 12.1) which is fundamental to systematic organizational growth and development.

Organizational Stress Diagnosis

The initial diagnostic process should be a comprehensive effort to discover the major sources of stress and unique demands to which the organization and the individuals within it are subjected. The diagnostic effort can draw heavily on the measures described in Chapter 6. As Albrecht (1979) notes, such an assessment involves a *listening orientation*: management should proceed with a sense of curiosity, investigation, and sensitivity to the total organization, its individual components, and the individual employees. A complete assessment would include a survey of conditions and relationships which employees find stressful, a survey of employees to determine the incidence of stress reactions, a general health survey, a review of worker-management or union-management relationships, and a review of absentee rates, productivity, and other objective measures listed in Chapter 6.

As we noted in Chapter 5, selection of the diagnostician is an important consideration. A knowledgeable occupational physician should be involved in the selection and interpretation of health surveys; a trained clinical or industrial psychologist or organizational behavior specialist should be involved in the use of psychological surveys. The most accurate and useful assessment will probably result from the interaction of a multidisciplinary assessment group and interested, enlightened management.

In the process of conducting this diagnosis of organizational stress, there are a variety of key questions which management should consider. These questions should guide the diagnostic process, but they should not limit it. As other questions arise, they should also be pursued to completion.
- What are the unique characteristics of the industry in which the organization operates?
- What are the unique demands placed on employees by the nature of the work and by the technology used by the organization?
- What changes are likely to occur in the industry? How soon?
- What key events may affect suppliers, competitors, and customers?

Planning for Prevention

The objective of planning for prevention is to establish the organization's goals for the preventive management program as well as the means by which these goals will be achieved within available resources. The planning process itself lays the groundwork for implementation; therefore, it is important to involve key decision makers and the individuals who will implement the plans in the planning process. Support building for any organizational change begins with the planning process.

The assessment should have identified the major areas for improvement. Often it will be necessary to address the most "symptomatic" area first, before attempting a broader, long-term program. Drawing on the interventions described in Chapters 8 through 11, the planners should identify the most attractive potential solutions and estimate the cost, expected benefits, time for implementation, and feasibility for each. Two or three of the most promising interventions, aimed at the high-priority problems, should be selected for implementation. These and the most attractive interventions not selected for immediate implementation should be used to create a longer-term three-to-five-year preventive management plan.

As in the organizational stress diagnosis stage, there are several key questions which are important in this stage of implementing preventive management in an organization. These key questions should again stimulate the planning process, not constrain it. As additional questions arise, they should be addressed by the planning group.
- What is the burden of suffering (human and organizational costs) attributable to stress in the organization?
- What has been previously attempted to reduce this burden of suffering? With what results?
- What outside community resources are available to prevent distress?
- What are the priorities of identified problems and possible preventive interventions?

- What resource people (inside and outside the organization) are available?
- What are other companies in the industry doing?

The planning group may also refer to the tables in Chapter 6 as a source for ideas about measures to consider and as a basis for developing strategies for preventive managerial interventions.

When addressing these questions, and when selecting among proposed interventions, the balance between organizational and individual approaches should be kept in mind. When certain levels of stress are unavoidable, then programs aimed at teaching individual employees how to minimize distress are reasonable. However, individual stress management programs should not be used to buffer the consequences of correctable and sometimes inexcusable organizational demands. Implementation of organizational techniques will generally involve different individuals and different resources than techniques aimed at the individual. These differences may influence the perceived feasibility and cost of alternative interventions.

Organizational and Individual Action

Any change is itself a potential stressor. Wherever possible, preventive management actions should be presented in a desirable way: the support and participation of those affected should be solicited, they should be introduced on a voluntary basis (e.g., in the case of counseling or relaxation training), and they should be supported by key individuals in the organization. If the planning process has adequately involved these key individuals, much of the support should exist even before the program is initiated. Unnecessary delays should, of course, be avoided, but at the same time false starts can be costly, frustrating, and harmful to the credibility of preventive management efforts. A program which starts and fails may be worse than no program at all.

The scope of the program should be realistic. Setting ambitious expectations can be a useful motivating force, but if they are too ambitious, the implementation of the program may only increase distress. Once a program has been introduced, consistent follow-through is necessary to assure its continuation. Commitment of time and resources on the part of management should be sufficient to support the program.

Imbalance in American programs   The major emphasis in American industry in the past several years has been upon the more active approaches to coping with stress-induced energy such as the construction of large gymnasiums. While physical fitness is a very important part of effective stress management for individuals, it may be overdone. This occurred in the case of a young dietitian who trained for and ran a marathon while also playing in a soccer league and participating in some other sports. She was overdoing her exercise and became unable to meditate, relax, or pray.

The active approaches to managing stress need to be balanced with the more passive approaches of meditation and relaxation. The origins for these more passive approaches are found in both the Judeo-Christian tradition as well as eastern philosophy. These passive approaches clash with some twentieth-century American values. This clash, for example, appeared to account for the kind of difficulties a southwestern stress management clinic had selling their services to local businesses. They had a program based largely on passive approaches. After two years of operation and much red ink, the operation was terminated. It may take years before the benefits of some approaches will be accepted by and incorporated into American industry.

Organizational politics   Organizational politics have not been written about extensively by academicians nor are they always very well understood by the actors in an organization. Therefore, the political processes of any organization may appear irrational to those attempting to understand them; they have eddies, undercurrents, and crosscurrents which are not easily discernible. Every manager and executive knows how essential these processes are to organizational life and the success of any idea or program. The best ideas and programs will be of little or no value unless they have the support of key organizational participants.

Allen and Madison (1979) have identified several characteristics of political actors in organizations. They have a good understanding of the organization's social norms and blend in well with the organization. They are ambitious but also sensitive to other individuals at work. Using these characteristics, political actors gain power through tactics such as blaming and attacking opponents for problems at work, projecting a very positive self-image, and building support groups in the organization to advance their cause(s).

The implementation of preventive management will succeed only with the support and encouragement of the key political actors and coalitions within the organization. If one is insensitive to these individuals and groups or does not gain their backing, the implementation of the intended program will be very difficult at best and will fail at worst. Because the political processes in an organization do not operate rationally or logically at times, one cannot always rely upon reason as a basis for countering political opposition in the implementation process. More likely, one must rely upon internal political proponents of the ideas and programs.

Outcome Evaluation

Any major planned organizational change needs to be followed up by a systematic evaluation. Initially, informal feedback may be useful for making minor modifications in the program and for responding to significant misperceptions of the program. A more structured evaluation should be conducted three, six, or twelve months after the changes have been put into effect. The evaluation should focus on the various individual and organizational health indicators which have been previously discussed, for health is the ultimate objective of preventive management. The results of this evaluation are used to determine whether the change was worthwhile and, if so, what modifications might be made to make the changes even more effective. As Figure 12.1 indicates, the evaluation feeds back into the planning process.

The evaluation process may utilize many of the same diagnostic instruments which were used in the initial assessment. Comparison of before and after scores provides an excellent method of determining the impact of the intervention. Obviously, *any* single intervention can only be expected to influence a subset of the organizational and individual markers of distress. The results of a formal evaluation can also be useful in modifying the three- or five-year plans for preventive stress management.

COST BENEFIT RATIO OF PREVENTIVE MANAGEMENT

Management has a responsibility for the well-being of its employees, but it also has a responsibility to those who own or support the organization. Therefore, the relative economic costs and benefits of preventive interventions are of considerable importance. Manuso (1982) has provided an excellent review of this issue, upon which much of the following discussion is based.

Alcohol treatment programs are among the oldest of the symptom-directed interventions, and they are the ones about which the most cost-benefit information is available. Pritchett and Finley (1971), for example, found that the annual cost of providing an alcoholism control program for a corporation of 1,700 employees amounted to $11,400. The costs of not providing the program—measured by lateness and absenteeism, poor decisions, terminations, early retirement, and such—were over $100,000 annually. Similarly, Hilker and associates (1972) estimated that the Illinois Bell Telephone–sponsored alcoholic rehabilitation program resulted in annual corporate savings of over $90,000 for extended illnesses alone. Taking into consideration their documented reductions in off-duty and on-the-job accidents, improved job efficiency, and reductions in hospitalization expenses would make the savings even higher.

Evidence from General Motors (Stessin, 1977) also demonstrates substantial benefits from alcoholism treatment programs.

There is some evidence that short-term psychotherapy is associated with financial benefits. Follette and Cummings (1967) found that both outpatient and inpatient medical services decreased significantly for a group of individuals receiving short-term psychotherapy. In another study of people seeking outpatient psychotherapy, Reiss (1967) found that patients increased their earnings by an amount four times that of a control group of individuals in comparable occupations. Finally, Jameson and colleagues (1978) report that average hospital utilization costs were decreased by 50 percent among a Blue Cross population utilizing the program's psychiatric benefits.

Employee counseling programs have received less attention. In a study at Kennecott Copper Company in Salt Lake City, Egdahl and Walsh (1980) found that their employee assistance program was associated with a 50 percent decrease in absenteeism and a 55 percent reduction in hospital medical and surgical costs.

The best cost-benefit data on organizational stress management comes from a study by Manuso (1981) in which biofeedback formed a central part of an in-house corporate stress management training program. Experience with fifteen employees suffering from headaches and fifteen with anxiety suggested a return on investment of over five dollars for every dollar invested. This return is based on comparing pretreatment costs of employing an individual with chronic headache or anxiety with the posttreatment costs. The costs of headaches and anxiety were found to result not from lateness and absenteeism, but from visits to the health center, interference with one's capacity to work, and the effect of these symptoms on one's coworkers, boss, or subordinates.

In concluding his review of the cost-benefit ratios of stress management programs, Manuso (1982) observes that through his contacts in the field, "It is reported that stress management interventions enjoy a return on investment on the order of 200 to 800 percent, depending upon the type of program, the setting, and the variable examined."

Although continued research into the cost-benefit ratios of alternative preventive management strategies is important, it is equally important to recognize that a favorable cost-benefit ratio is not always necessary to stimulate corporate action. For example, large sums of money have been spent on corporate exercise facilities simply because they were felt to be worth having. There is great popular support for fitness programs, but there is virtually no cost-benefit data to justify such expenses. Considerations of quality of life alone may justify effective preventive management programs. A favorable cost-benefit analysis may be sufficient to obtain approval for a new program, but it should not always be necessary.

SUMMARY

Simply knowing the range of possible preventive management techniques described in Chapters 8 and 11 will not necessarily lead to effective prevention of distress. At the organizational level, management training programs for all levels of management, organizational development activities, internal or external consultants, and ad hoc task forces can all be useful in introducing preventive management activities. At the individual level, medical or health departments, stress management programs, fitness programs, and comprehensive health promotion programs can each be vehicles for bringing individual stress management techniques into the organization. Implementing preventive management in an organization requires (1) organizational stress diagnosis, (2) planning for prevention, (3) organizational and individual action, and (4) outcome evaluation. These functions form an iterative model for implementing preventive management which is intended to foster continuing growth and development of the organization and the individuals within it.

Integration of individual and organizational approaches is essential for optimal use of available human and material resources. Individual interventions should not be used to pacify employees in the face of unnecessarily distressful organizational practices. At the same time, individuals should learn how to minimize the distress caused by inevitable and unchangeable stressors.

FURTHER READINGS

Albrecht, K: *Stress and the Manager,* Prentice-Hall, Englewood Cliffs, N.J., 1979.

Brief, A. P., R. S. Schuler, and M. Van Sell: *Managing Job Stress,* Little, Brown and Company, Boston, 1981.

Collins, M. L.: *Employee Fitness,* Ministry of Supply and Services of Canada, Ottawa, Canada, 1977.

Dedmon, R. E.: "Employees as Health Educators: A Reality at Kimberly-Clark," *Occupational Health and Safety,* April 1980, pp. 18–24.

Dedmon, R. E., et al.: "An Industry Health Management Program," *The Physician and Sports Medicine,* vol. 7, no. 11, November 1979.

Fitness in the Workplace: A Handbook on Employee Programs, President's Council on Physical Fitness and Sports, Washington, D.C., undated.

Moss, L.: *Management Stress,* Addison-Wesley, Reading, Mass., 1981.

Warshaw, L. J.: *Managing Stress,* Addison-Wesley, Reading, Mass., 1979.

RESOURCE GROUPS

General

Center for Health Promotion, American Hospital Association, 840 North Lake Shore Drive, Chicago, IL 60611

American Institute of Stress, Tarrytown House, Executive Conference Center, East Sunnyside Lane, Tarrytown, NY 10591

American Occupational Medical Association, 150 N. Wacker Drive, Chicago, IL 60606

American Occupational Health Nurses Association, 79 Madison Avenue, New York, NY 10016

Boston University, Center for Industry and Health Care, 53 Bay State Road, Boston, MA 02215

Human Economy Center, 358 North Pleasant Street, Amherst, MA 01002

National Institute for Occupational Safety and Health, 5600 Fishers Lane, Rockville, MD 20857

Office of Health Information and Promotion, Department of Health, Education and Welfare, 721 B Hubert Humphrey Building, 200 Independence Avenue, S.W., Washington, D.C. 20201

Washington Business Group on Health, 605 Pennsylvania Avenue, S.E., Washington, D.C. 20003

Corporate Programs Cited in Chapter

Employee Assistance Center, B. F. Goodrich Company, 500 South Main Street, Akron, OH 44318

Manage Your Health, Citicorp, 399 Park Avenue, 25th Floor, Zone 10, New York, NY 10043

Medical and Personal Concerns Department, The Equitable Assurance Society of the United States, 1285 Avenue of the Americas, New York, NY 10019

Physical Fitness Laboratory, Exxon Corporation, 1251 Avenue of the Americas, New York, NY 10020

Employee Assistance Program, Health and Safety Department, General Mills, Inc., P.O. Box 1113, Minneapolis, MN 55440

Training and Development Department, Illinois Bell, 212 West Washington Street, 14F, Chicago, IL 60606

Johns-Manville Corporation, Ken-Caryl Ranch, Denver, CO 80217

Health Management Program, Kimberly-Clark Corporation, Neenah, WI 54956

Tower Health Club, Life Insurance Company of Georgia, 600 West Peachtree Street N.W., Atlanta, GA 30365

Center for Health Help, Metropolitan Life Insurance Company, One Madison Avenue, New York, NY 10010

Medical Department, New York Telephone Company, 1095 Avenue of the Americas, New York, NY 10036

Southern Connecticut Gas Company, 880 Broad Street, Bridgeport, CT 06609

Tenneco, Inc., Tenneco Building, P.O. Box 2511, Houston, TX 77001

Weyerhaeuser Exercise Club, Weyerhaeuser Company, Tacoma, WA 98477

Xerox Health Management Program, Xerox Corporation, Building 337, 800 Philips Road, Webster, NY 14580

Human Resources Management, 3M, 3M Center, St. Paul, MN 55144

CHAPTER 13

PREVENTIVE MANAGEMENT: LOOKING AHEAD

The thesis of this book has been that *individual and organizational distress are not inevitable. Stress,* on the other hand, *is inevitable*; it is a naturally occurring experience which may be channeled in constructive or destructive ways. Channeled constructively, the energy which stress induces assists the individual in dealing with the demands of organizational and personal life. It provides the vitality which gives an individual and an organization the luster of good health. Stress is not a disease. But channeled improperly, it can lead to significant distress—to troublesome individual and organizational consequences.

Our purpose has been to present a logically consistent and integrated discussion of organizational stress—its nature, its causes, its consequences, its diagnosis, and, most important, its management. This comprehensive model for preventive management of organizational stress is summarized in Figure 13.1. This chapter will review the main points which have been made and conclude with a description of what steps can be taken by executives, stress researchers, managers, and individual employees.

ORGANIZATIONAL STRESSORS (Chapter 2)

Task demands
  Occupational category
  Managerial jobs
  Career progress
  Routine jobs
  Boundary spanning
  Performance appraisal
  Work overload
  Job insecurity

Physical demands
  Temperature
  Illumination, other rays
  Sound waves, vibrations
  Office design

Role demands
  Role conflict:
    intrasender
    intersender
    person-role
    interrole
    overload
  Role ambiguity

Interpersonal demands
  Status incongruence
  Social density
  Abrasive personalities
  Leadership style
  Group pressures

INDIVIDUAL STRESS RESPONSE (Chapter 3)

Physiology
  Sympathetic nervous system
  Endocrine system

Individual modifiers
  Achilles heel
  Type A behavior
  Personality
  Sex
  Age
  Ethnicity
  Social support
  Peer group
  Diet

DIAGNOSING ORGANIZATIONAL STRESS

Basic concepts (Chapter 5)

Diagnostic procedures (Chapter 6)
  Measures of organizational stressors
  Measures of individual distress
  Measures of stress response modifiers

ORGANIZATIONAL-LEVEL PREVENTIVE MANAGEMENT

Task and physical demands (Chapter 8)
  Task redesign
  Participative management
  Flexible work schedules
  Career development
  Design of physical settings

Role and interpersonal demands (Chapter 9)
  Role analysis
  Goal setting
  Social support
  Team building

INDIVIDUAL-LEVEL PREVENTIVE MANAGEMENT

Stressor-directed (Chapter 10)
  Managing perceptions of stress
  Managing the work environment
  Lifestyle management

Response-directed (Chapter 11)
  Relaxation training
  Physical outlets
  Emotional outlets

Symptom-directed (Chapter 11)
  Counseling and psychotherapy
  Medical care

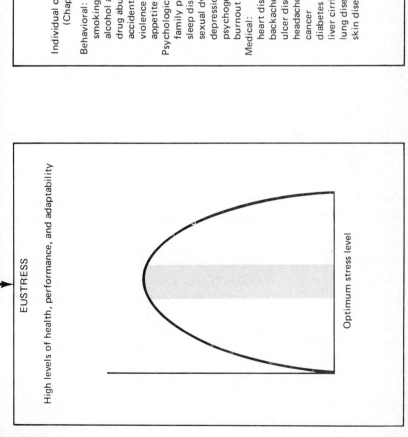

EUSTRESS

High levels of health, performance, and adaptability

Optimum stress level

DISTRESS

Individual consequences
(Chapter 3)

Behavioral:
  smoking
  alcohol abuse
  drug abuse
  accident proneness
  violence
  appetite disorders
Psychological:
  family problems
  sleep disturbances
  sexual dysfunction
  depression
  psychogenic disability
  burnout
Medical:
  heart disease, stroke
  backache and arthritis
  ulcer disease
  headache
  cancer
  diabetes mellitus
  liver cirrhosis
  lung disease
  skin disease

Organizational consequences
(Chapter 4)

Direct costs:
  Participation-membership:
    absenteeism
    tardiness
    strikes, work stoppages
    turnover
  Performance-related:
    quality of production
    quantity of production
    grievances
    accidents
    machine downtime, repair
    material, supply overuse
    inventory shrinkages
  Compensation awards

Indirect costs:
  Loss of vitality
    low morale
    low motivation
    dissatisfaction
  Communication breakdowns
    decline of frequency of contact
    distortions of messages
  Faulty decision making
  Quality of work relations
  Opportunity costs

FIGURE 13.1
The comprehensive preventive management model for organizational stress.

STRESS AND ITS CONSEQUENCES

There are four main concepts relevant to organizational stress. These are *organizational stressors* (demands), *stress*, *distress*, and *eustress*. The naturally occurring experience of stress is caused by any stressor or demand, either of a physical or psychological nature, confronting an individual. Stress is the unconscious, generalized psychophysiological response of the individual to any demand. The amount of stress caused by a demand will depend on the frequency and intensity of the demand as well as the individual's past experiences and perception of the demand. The two alternative outcomes of the stress response are *distress* and *eustress*.

Distress is the destructive, unhealthy outcome, which has detrimental consequences for both individuals and organizations. Eustress is the constructive, healthy outcome, which leads to the productivity, adaptability, and flexibility characterizing healthy individuals and organizations.

Sources of Organizational Stress

Stressors in organizational life provoke the individual's stress response, and there are a wide range of such demands. In Chapter 2 we examined four categories of demands affecting individuals at work: task, role, physical, and interpersonal demands. The most prevalent and important of these demands are the task and role demands.

The task demands that an individual faces at work are all related to the specific activities of the job. Jobs fall into various occupational groupings, some of which are highly stressful while others are minimally stressful. The nature of one's work will, therefore, be a major determinant of the amount of stress encountered on the job. However, because of differences in skills, abilities, knowledge, and other individual characteristics, no two individuals will experience the same amount of stress doing the same tasks.

Role demands are related to other people's expectations of a person at work. When these expectations are confusing or conflicting, an individual encounters role stress. While task demands are all related to formal involvement with the organization, role demands may be informal as well as formal. For example, a hospital administrator may not be required by his corporation to socialize with the medical community, but it may be an essential informal expectation by the various members of that community.

Depending on the setting, the physical and interpersonal demands which individuals face may not be as common as the task or role demands, but when they occur, they cause just as much stress. For some individuals or occupational groups, these demands may be a greater source of organizational stress than task or role demands. For example, naval crewmen aboard ship and Air Force flight personnel face physical demands as a very important, regular part of their work.

Individual Consequences of Stress

Distress is *not an inevitable* consequence of stressful events at work or at home, but it is a common consequence of mismanaged stress. In Chapter 3, we examined the psychological, behavioral, and medical consequences of stress. These various consequences are listed in Figure 13.1. They constitute the many ways in which individuals may suffer from mismanaged stressful experiences. The particular consequences any given individual suffers will depend upon the nature and susceptibility of that individual. While one person may experience a heart attack as a result of distress, another will suffer from alcoholism.

One reason why each individual and organization reacts differently to stress is the operation of modifiers of the stress response such as Type A behavior pattern, age, sex, and the individual's unique physiological and psychological life history. Stress will affect each person at their most vulnerable point(s), or their Achilles heel, either psychologically, behaviorally, or physiologically. However, these adverse consequences of distress may be averted through careful preventive measures to achieve eustressful consequences.

Organizational Consequences of Stress

Individuals are not the only ones who suffer the consequences of distress or reap the benefits of eustress. Organizations as well suffer various direct and indirect costs of distress, as we detailed in Chapter 4. Many of these costs are related to the individual consequences of distress. They are listed in Figure 13.1. The procedures for identifying and valuing these different organizational costs are in the early stages of development. As organizational scientists become more precise and accurate in their methods for measuring organizational functioning, more realistic figures for the costs of distress will become available.

If some of the organizational costs of distress proceed from individual consequences and suffering, then organizational and individual health are also related. Thus, healthy organizations will foster health among the individuals involved with the organization, and healthy individuals will contribute to a more vital organization. Effective prevention of the adverse consequences of distress depends in part upon accurate and timely diagnosis of organizational stress. It is the diagnostic process which enables us to link specific organizational demands with particular individual and organizational consequences of stress.

DIAGNOSING ORGANIZATIONAL STRESS

Organizational stress diagnosis is a process of identifying the sources and consequences of stress through in-depth knowledge of a particular individual or organization. As described in Chapter 5, it is often a complex process which can require the skills of several professional disciplines. Of the disciplines which deal with organizational stress, knowledge and expertise from three disciplines are required for effective diagnosis: organizational science, psychology, and medicine. Each discipline makes a unique contribution to an accurate assessment of individual and organizational stress.

Organizational science is needed for an understanding of the structure and processes of an organization, as well as the administrative principles related to the management of the organization. Without this knowledge, it would be difficult or impossible to know when stress-related organizational problems were occurring. By the same token, it is necessary to have the knowledge of psychology to understand individual psychological functioning. Distress may lead to various disorders and to failure in normal psychological processes. The identification and diagnosis of such problems is difficult without a working knowledge of psychology.

Finally, effective organizational stress diagnosis requires medical expertise. Stress manifests itself in the individual's physiology. When stress is mismanaged and becomes distress, it often manifests itself in physical illness. Therefore, medical expertise is required for reliable and accurate stress diagnostic work.

Depending on the purpose of stress assessment, an interdisciplinary and team-oriented approach to the diagnostic process may be the most effective. The many procedures and methods that the diagnostician(s) might draw upon for the assessment were reviewed in Chapter 6. There are several approaches to diagnosing stress at the organizational level, and there are other approaches to diagnosing stress at the individual level. In either case, some professional judgment is required in interpreting the diagnostic data and findings.

There are scientific elements of organizational stress diagnosis found in the organizational, psychological, and medical procedures used. However, there are important artistic aspects to the diagnostic process as well. These craft elements are captured in the skill and judgment required of the diagnostician in selecting the proper diagnostic procedure(s), applying the procedure(s) with a particular individual or organization, and evaluating or interpreting the data that are generated in the diagnostic process. An erroneous diagnosis may be, at best, wasteful of organizational resources and at worst, dangerous because of serious diseases or problems left unidentified. Because of the risks, hazards, and devastating consequences of distress, an accurate stress diagnosis is essential.

A key reason why organizational stress diagnosis is so important is its fundamental role in responsible preventive action by management. The diagnosis is the basis for selecting methods of preventive management, the aim of which is to prevent distress and enhance eustress. Accurate diagnosis contributes to prevention of the individual and organizational consequences of distress. It is a fundamental and central element to understanding organization stress as well as preventing distress.

PREVENTIVE MANAGEMENT

Preventive management is a philosophy as well as a set of principles concerned with the responsible management of organizations and individuals. As was discussed in Chapter 7, preventive management has two aims. The first aim is to promote individual and organizational health. We defined health along three dimensions: productivity, adaptability, and flexibility. Healthy individuals and organizations are productive, adaptive, and flexible. The second aim is to prevent individual and organizational distress by controlling the stressor (primary prevention), the stress response (secondary prevention), or the symptoms of distress (tertiary prevention).

These aims are achieved by the use of organizational-level and individual-level methods of preventive management. These methods are selected on the basis of the organizational stress diagnosis and an organization-specific implementation strategy. The specific implementation strategy is guided by the following five principles of preventive management:

1 Individual and organizational health are interdependent.
2 Management has a responsibility for individual and organizational health.
3 Individual and organizational distress are not inevitable.
4 Each individual and organization reacts uniquely to stress.
5 Organizations are dynamic, ever-changing entities.

These guiding principles may be used as the basis for designing and implementing preventive management programs.

Organizational-Level Preventive Management

Preventive management deals first with the organizational level. The methods of organizational-level preventive management discussed in Chapters 8 and 9 are listed in Figure 13.1. Most of these methods are stressor-directed. They aim at changing the design of the organization so as to alter the demands it places upon individuals. The intent of organizational-level preventive management is not to eliminate or even minimize the demands to which individuals are subject at work. Instead, the intent is to eliminate unnecessarily distressful aspects of organizational life. As noted in the fifth principle of preventive management, organizations are ever-changing. Organizational-level preventive management will help them change in adaptive healthy ways.

Much distress may be averted through responsible management action at the organizational level by employing task redesign, participative management, career development activities, physical-setting design, role analysis, team building, and social support efforts within the organization. Because of the nature of stress and differences in individuals and organizations, altering organizational demands alone will not prevent all distress. Once management has done what it can at the organizational level, then it is necessary to rely upon individual-level preventive management.

Individual-Level Preventive Management

Organizational life is demanding and at times difficult. It is unreasonable to expect that it will be otherwise. Once this fact has been accepted, it is possible to effectively deal with the demanding and difficult aspects of organizational life. While employees should not be expected to cope with unnecessary demands, they should be assisted in learning to manage the legitimate and necessary requirements of organizational life.

The methods of individual-level preventive management are intended to help individuals manage these requirements. We examined these methods in detail in Chapters 10 and 11. They are listed again in Figure 13.1. These methods act preventively in one of three ways. Stressor-directed methods help individuals to change or adjust the demands to which they are subject. Managing one's personal work environment is an example of such preventive action. Secondary prevention through response-directed techniques aims at the psychological and physical responses to stress. Physical exercise and relaxation training are the principal response-directed techniques. Tertiary or symptom-directed methods are aimed at the behavioral, psychological, and medical consequences of distress. Psychotherapy and routine medical care are examples of symptom-directed activities.

Individual-level preventive management should be used in conjunction with organizational-level preventive management since the two approaches are complementary in their effects. These two levels of preventive action may be implemented using the preventive management cycle presented at the end of Chapter 12 (see Figure 12.1).

LOOKING AHEAD

Acknowledging the sources of organizational stress, recognizing the consequences, understanding the diagnostic process for organizational stress, and knowing the available preventive management methods are all important. But distress will not be avoided and eustress will not be fostered until someone takes action. The type of action may vary, depending upon where one is in an organization. Nevertheless, realization of the potential value of preventive stress management means that executives, stress researchers, managers, and individual employees must act.

What Can Executives Do?

Board chairpersons, company presidents, chief executive officers, directors of foundations, university chancellors, vice presidents, city managers, agency directors, military commanders, hospital administrators, and department chairpersons occupy the central positions from which they can see the impact of stress and—*if they choose to*—adopt the philosophy and strategies of preventive management. Executives can begin by accepting stress as an inevitable, even necessary, part of organizational life, while at the same time rejecting the concept that distress is a "necessary evil" of working life. The role of the top executive should be to establish an environment which promotes *eustress*—the stimulating, healthy, productive outcome of stress—and minimizes *distress*.

Once executives understand the basic nature of organizational stress and once they accept the proposition that management has a responsibility for individual and organizational well-being, the next step is to assess the prevalence, intensity, and impact of stress in the organization. A good diagnostician is fundamentally a keen observer who knows his subject well. Executives, therefore, may be in the best position to diagnose stress in their own organizations. They may wish, however, to complete the diagnostic process by using some of the objective diagnostic techniques described in Chapters 5 and 6. Executives may also want to take advantage of the third-party perspective offered by outside consultants or the expertise offered by psychologists, physicians, organizational behaviorists, or other professionals within the organization.

Whatever the specific diagnostic process selected, the important executive action is that of initiating the diagnosis of organizational stress. Once the sources and consequences of stress are known, it is then possible to design and implement a preventive management program which is appropriate to the organization and the stressors it faces. Some executives may wish to play a central role in planning stress management activities, while others will prefer to appoint an appropriate subordinate. The person responsible for the program must have sufficient skill, experience, and authority to implement whatever plans are laid out.

For preventive management activities to succeed, they must have visible, credible support from top management. Once action has been taken, executives can increase the likelihood of success by participating in the stress management activities and setting an example themselves. Executives should undertake an assessment of their own personal stress and outline a personal stress management plan for themselves.

Executives must bear in mind principle 5 of preventive management, which holds that organizations are dynamic, ever-changing entities. Even after an initial diagnosis and plan have been made, management should remain sensitive to the demands which the organization is placing on individuals and the levels of distress which are being generated. Preventive management plans should always be open to appropriate amendments.

Attempting to reduce distress in the organization does not require an executive to cease being demanding of employees. It is important that the manager be sufficiently demanding of employees to create the kind of healthy stress portrayed in the eustress block of Figure 13.1. At the same time, the manager who is overly demanding will not achieve the best performance from his employees. Therefore, it is necessary to be demanding, while providing the informational, emotional, and instrumental resources and support whereby the individual may meet the demands levied on him or her.

In considering alternative stress management methods, executives must strike a balance between individual-level and organizational-level preventive management by using methods from both levels of prevention as appropriate to achieve the most desirable benefits. Stress management programs are always at risk of becoming tools by which management attempts to mollify employees in the face of unconscionably distressful organizational practices. Responsible executives should guard against this tendency and seek equity in stress management activities.

Finally, executives can make an invaluable contribution to the future directions of organizational stress through collaborative efforts with researchers. The best research on organizational stress and preventive management must come from the workplace. Through the support and encouragement of management, advances in both understanding and practice are made possible. As an evolving process, management must grow both through new knowledge and new practice. Managers can encourage and sustain growth through active interest in pursuing what preventive methods will work as well as those that will not work.

What Can Stress Researchers Do?

Although we have provided extensive descriptions of organizational stress, stress diagnosis, and preventive management, many of the ideas have not yet been fully tested or clearly proven. In addition, there are many aspects of organizational stress about which little or nothing is known. Progress in these areas will depend upon research which confirms or modifies current notions about stress and research which adds new insights into preventive management.

In the past few years investigators have focused on the sources and consequences of organizational stress. While there may be fruitful research yet to be done along this line, there is a greater need for studies of various preventive and coping methods. There has been a paucity of research aimed at evaluating the effectiveness of most prevention strategies, especially organizational strategies. Toward this end, there are several specific research needs that currently exist.

First, there is a need for more systematic examination of the intrapersonal and interpersonal demands which cause stress for individuals. There have been numerous studies detailing the task, role, and physical demands of organizational life. The intrapersonal and interpersonal demands have not been as clearly defined nor as extensively studied. The identification and definition of these stressors is an important prerequisite to studies of how coping mechanisms may reduce their adverse effects.

Second, there is a strong need for further information about the process of organizational stress diagnosis. The techniques described in Chapters 5 and 6 represent a potpourri of concepts and objectives in stress assessment. Although the available measures provide some interesting and, in many cases, objective data about the prevalence, intensity, and impact of stress, the results are not always linked to or used as a basis for preventive action. Further refinement and testing of diagnostic techniques would provide executives and practitioners of organizational development with invaluable tools for formulating effective preventive management plans.

Third, there is a need to design field experiments and field studies aimed at evaluating the effectiveness of the various organizational-level prevention techniques for reducing individual and organizational distress. These investigations need to consider the many sources of stress as well as consequences of distress. In addition to testing the efficacy of previously described techniques, it would be useful for organizational researchers and executives to generate ideas for other organizational-level methods of preventive management.

Fourth, there is a need for research designed to evaluate the effects of the primary individual-level methods of preventive management discussed in Chapter 10. While there have been investigations of the role of aerobic exercise and relaxation in stress management, there are virtually no studies which have examined the impact of the stressor-directed methods upon the consequences of distress.

Fifth, there is a related need to develop better measures of and research regarding social support. Given the initial findings about the important role of social support in long-term health and well-being (Lynch, 1977), there is a need for investigations of the effects of social support on both episodic and chronic stress. What forms of social support are most relevant to chronic stress management? to episodic stress management?

For additional research agenda items for the 1980s, a comprehensive discussion appears in Payne, Jick, and Burke (1982). The aim of research in the area of organizational stress is to improve the practice of management through scientific inquiry. In an applied discipline, such as management, the primary benefits of the research process should be found in improved practice. For this reason, the bulk of the research should be conducted in field settings, in organizations, and in related settings where management is practiced. Basic research in the area of organizational stress is also appropriate if the findings have external validity, as well as implications for parallel field research and management practice. Because of this applied orientation, there is an important role for executives and managers in the study of organizational stress and the advancement of preventive management.

What Can Managers Do?

Depending on the level at which stress is being confronted, middle-level managers may have many of the same opportunities and responsibilities for stress management that top executives have. Many managers will be in the position to diagnose organizational stress and to initiate preventive management programs. Some managers will find the responsibility for intervening in stressful events or circumstances stressful in itself. It is important, therefore, for managers to have the opportunity and the approval to seek necessary advice from superiors or other professionals within the organization.

Managers and supervisors are closer to the majority of individual employees than are top executives. From their vantage point, middle-level managers are more likely than top management to observe the early signs of individual and organizational distress. They can thus serve as an "early warning system" for increasing levels of distress.

Finally, managers, like executives, have a responsibility to monitor their own stress responses and their own manifestations of distress. They can set an example for other employees by taking advantage of stress management programs made available by the organization. They can also enhance their own ability to handle organizational stressors by developing a personal stress management plan.

What Can Individual Employees Do?

It is one of the saddest and most baffling paradoxes that individuals work long, hard, stressful hours to provide for their families and then, as a result of the stress, engage in habits which significantly reduce life expectancy, thereby prematurely depriving their loved ones of their companionship. It is hardly a benefit to a family if a person earns a generous salary, responds to the demands of the job by smoking two packs of cigarettes a day, and dies from a cigarette-induced heart attack at age 55.

Individual employees, like executives, must begin by rejecting the idea that distress is just part of the job. Organizational stressors—the demands of work—will always be present. They are important in stimulating productivity and efficiency. But they need not be overwhelming or disabling. Individual employees have a right to expect that organizational demands will not be unnecessarily stressful. But they also have a responsibility to themselves, their families, and the organization to learn how to manage the demands which are present.

Principle 2 of preventive management asserted that *management has a responsibility for individual and organizational health*. This principle should not be taken to mean that the individual does not have a responsibility also. In fact, although management has a responsibility, the individual still maintains *ultimate responsibility* for his or her own well-being. For individuals experiencing significant work-related distress, this responsibility includes participating in stress management programs provided by the employer as well as seeking outside help when necessary.

Individual employees can begin by recognizing stress management as an important element in maintaining good health. Curbing smoking, controlling excessive use of alcohol and other drugs, engaging in regular exercise, and choosing a reasonable diet are also part of maintaining good health. Stress at work may have an impact on home life and, likewise, stress at home can affect work. At the same time, preventive techniques learned in one environment can often be used in the other environment. Thus, individual employees, like executives and managers, would benefit from performing an assessment of their own levels of stress and distress and then, with the assistance of an experienced professional if necessary, developing a personal stress management plan.

A Reasonable Balance

It is unreasonable to expect individuals to manage unnecessary and unreasonably harsh organizational demands. Some organizations wrongly expect individuals to adjust to inhumane working environments. However, individuals should expect organizational life to be demanding, and they must learn to manage reasonable demands effectively. Therefore, the preventive management of organizational stress involves changing demands and practices within organizations as well as teaching individual methods for managing these stressors and their own responses to them.

Integration of individual and organizational approaches to preventive management is essential for optimal use of available human and material resources. Individuals should learn how to minimize the distress caused by inevitable and unchangeable stressors. At the same time, individual interventions should not be used to pacify employees in the face of unnecessarily distressful organizational practices. Organizational and individual health will be promoted by a balanced program of preventive management.

BIBLIOGRAPHY

Prepared by Suzanne Warner and Michele Bock

Abercrombie, M. L. J.: "Architecture: Psychological Aspects," in S. Krauss (ed.), *Encyclopaedic Handbook of Medical Psychology*, Butterworths, London, 1976.

Abramson, J. H.: "The Cornell Medical Index as an Epidemiological Tool," *American Journal of Public Health*, vol. 56, no. 2, 1966, pp. 287–298.

Adams, J. D.: "Improving Stress Management: An Action-Research-Based OD Intervention," in W. W. Burke (ed.), *The Cutting Edge*, University Associates, San Diego, Calif., 1978.

Adams, John D.: *Understanding and Managing Stress: A Workbook in Changing Life Styles*, University Associates, San Diego, Calif., 1980.

Adams, L., and E. Lenz: *Effectiveness Training for Women*, Wyden, New York, 1979.

Affemann, R.: "Mental Causes of Social Stress Factors, Spiritual Causes of Susceptibility to Stress and Educational Approaches to Stress Relief," *Offentliche Gesunditeitswesen*, vol. 41, no. 3, 1979, pp. 117–123.

Alberti, R. E., and M. Emmons: *Your Perfect Right*, rev. ed., Impact Press, San Luis Obispo, Calif., 1974.

Albrecht, Karl: *Stress and the Manager*, Prentice-Hall, Englewood Cliffs, N.J., 1979.

Alderfer, Clayton P.: "Change Processes in Organizations," in Marvin D. Dunnette (ed.), *Handbook of Industrial and Organizational Psychology*, Rand McNally, Chicago, 1976, pp. 1591–1638.

Alderfer, Clayton P.: *Existence, Relatedness, and Growth: Human Needs in Organizational Settings*, The Free Press, New York, 1972.

Allen, R. W., and D. L. Madison: "Organizational Politics: Tactics and Characteristics of Its Actors," *California Management Review,* vol. 22, no. 1, Fall 1979, pp. 77–82.

American College of Sports Medicine: *Guidelines for Graded Exercise Testing and Exercise Prescription,* Lea and Febiger, Philadelphia, 1975.

American Heart Association: *The Cost of Doing Business,* American Heart Association, 1980.

Anderson, C. R.: "Locus of Control, Coping Behaviors, and Performance in a Stress Setting: A Longitudinal Study," *Journal of Applied Psychology,* vol. 62, 1977, pp. 446–451.

Anderson, Harry: "Executives Under Stress," *Newsweek,* August 24, 1981, p. 53.

Anderson, Col. James L., and Martin Cohen: *The West Point Fitness and Diet Book,* Avon, New York, 1977.

Anderson, Robert A.: *Stress Power,* Human Sciences, New York, 1978.

Anthony, William A.: *The Principles of Psychiatric Rehabilitation,* Human Resource Development Press, Amherst, Mass., 1979.

Argyris, Chris: "The Impact of Budgets on People," The School of Business and Public Administration, Cornell University, Ithaca, N.Y., 1952.

Athos, A. G., and J. J. Gabarro: *Interpersonal Behavior,* Prentice-Hall, Englewood Cliffs, N.J., 1978.

Back, K. W.: "Encounter Groups and Society," *Journal of Applied Behavioral Science,* vol. 9, 1973, pp. 7–20.

Baker, D. G.: "Influence of a Chronic Environmental Stress on the Incidence of Methycholanthrene-Induced Tumors," *Cancer Research,* vol. 37, no. 11, 1977, pp. 3939–3944.

Bandura, A.: *Principles of Behavior Modification,* Holt, Rinehart & Winston, New York, 1969.

Barber, T. X., et al. (eds.): *Biofeedback and Self-Control,* Aldine Publishing Company, Chicago, 1976.

Bar-Khama, Lt. Col. Amos, Yehuda Shoenfeld, M.D., and Eric Shuman: *The Israeli Fitness Strategy: A Complete Program of Diet and Exercise Based on the Training System of the Israeli Defense Forces,* William Morrow and Company, New York, 1980.

Barnes, L. B., and S. A. Hershon: "Transferring Power in the Family Business," *Harvard Business Review,* vol. 54, July–August 1976, pp. 105–114.

Barnett, R. C., and G. K. Baruch: *The Competent Woman: Perspectives on Development,* Irvington, New York, 1978.

Basil, Douglas C., and Curtis W. Cook: *The Management of Change,* McGraw-Hill, London, 1974.

Beary, John F., et al.: "A Simple Psychophysiologic Technique Which Elicits the Hypometabolic Changes of the Relaxation Response," *Psychosomatic Medicine,* vol. 15, no. 2, 1974, pp. 115–120.

Beatty, R. W.: "Blacks as Supervisors: A Study of Training, Job Performance, and Employers' Expectations," *Academy of Management Journal,* vol. 16, no. 2, 1973, pp. 196–206.

Becher, F.: *Work Space: Creating Environments in Organizations,* Praeger, New York, 1981.

Beech, H. R., L. E. Burns, and B. F. Sheffield: *A Behavioral Approach to the Management of Stress*, John Wiley, New York, 1982.

Beehr, Terry A., and John E. Newman: "Job Stress, Employee Health, and Organizational Effectiveness: A Facet Analysis, Model, and Literature Review," *Personnel Psychology*, vol. 31, 1978, pp. 665–696.

Beer, Michael: *Organization Change and Development: A Systems View*, Goodyear, Santa Monica, Calif., 1980.

Bennett, A. E., and K. Ritchie: "General Health Questionnaires," in A. E. Bennett and K. Ritchie, *Questionnaires in Medicine: A Guide to Their Design and Use*, Oxford University Press, New York, 1975, pp. 68–83.

Bennis, William: "The Coming Death of Bureaucracy," *Think*, 1966.

Bennis, W. G., and H. A. Shepard: "A Theory of Group Development," *Human Relations*, vol. 9, 1956, pp. 415–457.

Bensahel, J. G.: "How to Stay Sane During a Corporate Crisis," *International Management*, vol. 29, 1974, pp. 17–18.

Bensahel, J. G.: "Taking Heat Out of a Tense Situation," *International Management*, vol. 32, 1977, pp. 31–32.

Benson, Herbert: *The Relaxation Response*, Avon Books, New York, 1975.

Benson, Herbert: "Your Innate Asset For Combating Stress," *Harvard Business Review*, July–August 1974, pp. 49–60.

Benson, H., J. F. Beary, and M. P. Carol: "The Relaxation Response," *Psychiatry*, vol. 37, 1974, pp. 37–46.

Benson, Herbert, and Robert Allen: "How Much Stress Is Too Much?" *Harvard Business Review*, September–October 1980, pp. 86–92.

Benson, H., B. A. Rosner, B. R. Marzetta, and H. P. Klemchuk: "Decreased Blood-Pressure in Borderline Hypertensive Subjects Who Practiced Meditation," *Journal of Chronic Disease*, vol. 26, 1974, pp. 163–169.

Benson, H., B. A. Rosner, B. R. Marzetta, and H. P. Klemchuk: "Decreased Blood-Pressure in Pharmacologically Treated Hypertensive Patients Who Regularly Elicited the Relaxation Response," *The Lancet*, February 23, 1974, pp. 289–291.

Bergin, A. E., and S. L. Garfield: *Handbook of Psychotherapy and Behavior Change*, Wiley, New York, 1971.

Bernstein, D. A., and T. D. Borkovec: *Progressive Relaxation Training: A Manual for the Helping Professions*, Research Press Co., Champaign, Ill., 1973.

Bettelheim, B.: "Individual and Mass Behavior in Extreme Situations," in E. E. Maccoby, et al., *Readings in Social Psychology*, 3d ed., Holt, Rinehart, & Winston, New York, 1958, pp. 300–310.

Bhagat, R. S.: "Effects of Stressful Life Events upon Individual Performance Effectiveness and Work Adjustment Processes within Organizational Settings: A Research Model," *Academy of Management Review*, vol. 8, no. 4, October 1983, pp. 660–671.

Bhagat, R. S., and M. B. Chassie: "Determinants of Organizational Commitment in Working Women: Some Implications for Organizational Integration," *Journal of Occupational Behavior*, vol. 2, 1981, pp. 17–30.

The Bible, Revised Standard Version.

Biddle, B. J., and E. J. Thomas: *Role Theory: Concepts and Research*, Wiley, New York, 1966.

Billings, Andrew G., and Rudolf H. Moos: "Work Stress and the Stress-Suffering Roles of Work and Family Resources," *Journal of Occupational Behaviour,* vol. 3, 1982, pp. 215–232.

Blanchard, E. G., and L. H. Epstein: *A Biofeedback Primer,* Addison-Wesley, Reading, Mass., 1978.

Blau, Peter M.: *Exchange and Power in Social Life,* John Wiley & Sons, New York, 1964.

Bluedorn, Allen C.: "Managing Turnover Strategically," *Business Horizons,* vol. 25, no. 2, March–April 1982, pp. 6–12.

Bolles, R. N.: *What Color Is Your Parachute?* Ten Speed Press, Berkeley, Calif., 1979.

Bower, S. A., and G. H. Bower: *Asserting Your Self,* Addison-Wesley, Reading, Mass., 1976.

Bowman, G. W., N. B. Worthy, and S. A. Greyser: "Problems in Review: Are Women Executives People?" *Harvard Business Review,* vol. 43, 1965, pp. 52–57.

Bracey, Hyler, Aubrey Sanford, and J. C. Quick: *Basic Management,* rev. ed., Business Publications, Dallas, 1981.

Brandt, M., and M. I. Siegel: "The Effects of Stress on Cortical Bone Thickness of Rodents," *American Journal of Physical Anthropology,* vol. 49, no. 1, 1978, pp. 31–34.

Brenner, B., and M. L. Selzer: "Risk of Causing a Fatal Accident Associated with Alcoholism, Psychopathology, and Stress: Further Analysis of Previous Data," *Behavioral Science,* vol. 14, 1969, pp. 490–495.

Bridges, P. K.: "Recent Physiological Studies of Stress and Anxiety in Man," *Biological Psychiatry,* vol. 8, no. 1, 1974, pp. 95–111.

Brief, Arthur P., Randall S. Schuler, and Mary Van Sell: *Managing Job Stress,* Little, Brown and Company, Boston, 1981.

Brodman, K., A. J. Erdman, Jr., I. Lorge, and H. G. Wolff: "The Cornell Medical Index," *Journal of the American Medical Association,* vol. 140, no. 6, 1949, pp. 530–534.

Brodman, K., et al.: "The Cornell Medical Index—Health Questionnaire: II. As a Diagnostic Instrument," *Journal of the American Medical Association,* vol. 145, no. 3, 1951, pp. 152–157.

Brousseau, Kenneth R., and Mark A. Mallinger: "Internal-External Locus of Control, Perceived Occupational Stress, and Cardiovascular Health," *Journal of Occupational Behaviour,* vol. 2, 1981, pp. 65–71.

Brown, Barbara: "The Implications for Concepts of Healing: Biofeedback," *Journal of Holistic Health,* 1977, pp. 29–32.

Brown, Barbara: *Stress and the Art of Biofeedback,* Harper & Row, New York, 1977.

Buck, V. E.: *Working Under Pressure,* Crane, Russak, New York, 1972.

Buell, James C., and Robert S. Eliot: "The Role of Emotional Stress in the Development of Heart Disease," *Journal of the American Medical Association,* vol. 242, no. 4, 1979, pp. 365–368.

Burack, E. H., F. J. Staszak, and G. C. Pati: "An Organizational Analysis of Manpower Issues in Employing the Disadvantaged," *Academy of Management Journal,* vol. 15, no. 3, 1972, pp. 255–271.

Burke, R. J.: "Are You Fed Up With Work?" *Personnel Administration*, vol. 34, 1971, pp. 27–31.

Burke, R. J., and M. L. Belcourt: "Managerial Role Stress and Coping Responses," *Journal of Business Administration*, vol. 5, 1974, pp. 55–68.

Burke, R. J., and Tamara Weir: "Coping with the Stress of Managerial Occupations," in C. L. Cooper and R. Payne, *Current Concerns in Occupational Stress*, John Wiley & Sons, New York, 1980, pp. 299–335.

Burke, R. J., T. Weir, and R. E. DuWors, Jr.: "Type A Behavior of Administrators and Wives' Reports of Marital Satisfaction and Well-Being," *Journal of Applied Psychology*, vol. 64, 1979, pp. 57–65.

Burns, L. E.: "Relaxation in the Management of Stress," in J. Marshall and C. L. Cooper (eds.), *Coping with Stress*, Gower, London, 1981.

Burns, Tom, and G. M. Stalker: *The Management of Innovation*, Tavistock, London, 1961.

Buros, Oscar: *Eighth Mental Measurements Yearbook*, 2 vols., Gryphon Press, Highland Park, N.J., 1978.

Campbell, D. T., and J. C. Stanley: *Experimental and Quasi-Experimental Designs for Research*, Rand McNally, Chicago, 1973.

Cannon, W. B.: *The Wisdom of the Body*, W. W. Norton, New York, 1932.

Caplan, Gerald, and Marie Killilea (eds.): *Support Systems and Mutual Help: Multidisciplinary Explorations*, Grune & Stratton, New York, 1976.

Caplan, R.: "Organizational Stress and Individual Strain: A Social-Psychological Study of Risk Factors," Ph.D. Dissertation, University of Michigan, 1971.

Caplan, Robert D., et al.: *Job Demands and Worker Health: Main Effects and Occupational Differences*, Research Report Series, Institute for Social Research, The University of Michigan, 1980.

Carrington, P.: *Freedom in Meditation*, Anchor Press/Doubleday, New York, 1978.

Carrington, P., G. H. Collings, H. Benson, H. Robinson, L. W. Wood, P. M. Lehrer, R. L. Woodfolk, and J. W. Cole: "The Use of Meditation-Relaxation Techniques for the Management of Stress in a Working Population," *Journal of Occupational Medicine*, vol. 22, no. 4, 1980, pp. 221–231.

Carroll, S. J., and J. L. Tosi: "Goal Characteristics and Personality Factors in a Management-by-Objectives Program," *Administrative Science Quarterly*, vol. 15, 1970, pp. 295–305.

Carroll, S. J., and J. L. Tosi: *Management by Objectives: Applications and Research*, Macmillan, New York, 1973.

Chan, K. B.: "Individual Differences in Reactions to Stress and Their Personality and Situational Determinants," *Social Science and Medicine*, vol. 11, 1977, pp. 89–103.

Chesney, M. A., and R. Rosenman: "Type A Behavior in the Work Setting," in C. L. Cooper and R. Payne (eds.), *Current Concerns in Occupational Stress*, John Wiley & Sons, New York, 1980, pp. 187–212.

Cobb, S.: "Social Support as a Moderator of Life Stress," *Psychosomatic Medicine*, vol. 38, no. 5, 1976, pp. 300–314.

Coburn, David: "Work and General Psychological and Physical Well-Being," *International Journal of Health Services*, vol. 8, no. 3, 1978, pp. 415–435.

Coffey, R. E., A. G. Athos, and P. A. Raynolds: *Behavior in Organizations: A Multidimensional View*, Prentice-Hall, Englewood Cliffs, N.J., 1975.

Cohen, A. R., and H. Gadon: *Alternative Work Schedules: Integrating Individual and Organizational Needs*, Addison-Wesley, Reading, Mass., 1978.

Cohen, J.: "Stress and Wound-Healing," *Acta Anatomica*, vol. 103, no. 2, 1979, pp. 134–141.

Cohn, Richard M.: "The Effect of Employment Status Change on Self-Attitudes," *Social Psychology*, vol. 41, no. 2, 1978, pp. 81–93.

Coleman, James C.: "Life Stress and Maladaptive Behavior," *The American Journal of Occupational Therapy*, vol. 27, no. 4, May–June 1973, pp. 169–180.

Colligan, Michael J., and William Stockton: "The Mystery of Assembly-Line Hysteria," *Psychology Today*, vol. 12, no. 1, 1978.

Colligan, Michael J., Michael J. Smith, and Joseph J. Hurrell: "Occupational Incidence Rates of Mental Health Disorders," *Journal of Human Stress*, vol. 3, no. 3, 1977, pp. 34–39.

Collins, M. L.: *Employee Fitness*, Minister of Supply and Services Canada, Ottawa, Canada, 1977.

Conway, T. L., R. R. Vickers, Jr., H. W. Ward, and R. H. Rahe: "Occupational Stress and Variation in Cigarette, Coffee, and Alcohol Consumption," *Journal of Health and Social Behavior*, vol. 22, no. 2, June 1981, pp. 155–165.

Cooper, C. L.: *The Stress Check*, Prentice-Hall, Englewood Cliffs, N.J., 1982.

Cooper, C. L., and J. Crump: "Prevention and Coping with Occupational Stress," *Journal of Occupational Medicine*, vol. 20, no. 6, 1978, pp. 420–426.

Cooper, C. L., and M. J. Davidson: "The High Cost of Stress on Woman Managers," *Organizational Dynamics*, Spring 1982, pp. 44–53.

Cooper, C. L., and Judi Marshall, "An Audit of Managerial (Di) Stress," *Journal of Enterprise Management*, vol. 1, 1978, pp. 185–196.

Cooper, C. L., and Judi Marshall: *Understanding Executive Stress*, PBI, New York, 1977.

Cooper, C. L., and Andrew Melhuish: "Occupational Stress and Managers," *Journal of Occupational Medicine*, vol. 22, no. 9, September 1980, pp. 588–592.

Cooper, C. L., and R. Payne (eds.): *Current Concerns in Occupational Stress*, John Wiley & Sons, New York, 1980.

Cooper, C. L., and R. Payne (eds.): *Stress at Work*, John Wiley & Sons, New York, 1978.

Cooper, Kenneth: *The Aerobics Program for Total Well-Being*, M. Evans & Co., New York, 1982.

Cooper, Kenneth: *The Aerobics Way*, M. Evans and Co., Inc., New York, 1977.

Cooper, Kenneth: *The New Aerobics*, Bantam Books, New York, 1970.

Cooper, Mildred, and Kenneth Cooper: *Aerobics for Women*, Bantam Books, New York, 1978.

Coronary-Prone Behavior Review Panel: "Coronary-Prone Behavior and Coronary Heart Disease: A Critical Review," *Circulation*, vol. 63, 1981, pp. 1199–1215.

Cosper, R.: "Drinking as Conformity: A Critique of Sociological Literature on Occupational Differences in Drinking," *Journal of Studies on Alcohol*, vol. 40, no. 9, 1979, pp. 868–891.

Cox, Tom: "Repetitive Work," in Cary L. Cooper and Roy Payne (eds.), *Current Concerns in Occupational Stress*, John Wiley & Sons, New York, 1980, pp. 23–41.

Cox, Tom: *Stress*, University Park Press, Baltimore, 1978.

Cox, Verne C., Paul B. Paulus, Garvin McCain, and Marylie Karlovac: "The Relationship between Crowding and Health," in A. Baum and J. Singer (eds.), *Advances in Environmental Psychology*, vol. 4, Lawrence Earlbaum, Hillsdale, N.J., 1982.

Crasilneck, Harold B., and James A. Hall: *Clinical Hypnosis*, Grune & Stratton, New York, 1975.

Cummings, T. G., and C. L. Cooper: "A Cybernetic Framework for Studying Occupational Stress," *Human Relations*, vol. 32, no. 5, 1979, pp. 395–418.

Dalton, D. R., D. M. Krackhardt, and L. W. Porter: "Functional Turnover: An Empirical Assessment," *Journal of Applied Psychology*, vol. 66, no. 6, 1981, pp. 716–721.

Dalton, D. R., W. D. Tudor, and D. M. Krackhardt: "Turnover Overstated: The Functional Taxonomy," *Academy of Management Review*, vol. 7, no. 1, 1982, pp. 117–123.

Davis, Louis, and James Taylor (eds.): *Design of Jobs*, Goodyear, Santa Monica, Calif., 1979.

Davis, M., E. R. Eshelman, and M. McKay: *The Relaxation and Stress Reduction Workbook*, New Harbinger Publications, San Francisco, 1980.

Davis, S., and P. Lawrence: "Problems of Matrix Organizations," *Harvard Business Review*, May–June 1978, pp. 131–142.

Dayal, I., and J. M. Thomas: "Operation KPE: Developing a New Organization," *Journal of Applied Behavioral Science*, vol. 4, no. 4, 1968, pp. 473–506.

Dedmon, R. E.: "Employees as Health Educators: A Reality at Kimberly-Clark," *Occupational Health and Safety*, April 1980, pp. 18–24.

Dedmon, R. E.: "Kimberly-Clark's Health Management Program—Results and Prospects," Kimberly-Clark Corporation, Neenah, Wis., 1979. (mimeographed)

Dedmon, R. E., et al.: "An Industry Health Management Program," *The Physician and Sports Medicine*, vol. 7, no. 11, November 1979, pp. 56–67.

Dembroski, Theodore M., et al. (eds.): *Coronary-Prone Behavior*, Springer-Verlag, New York, 1978.

Depue, Roger L.: "Turning Inward: The Police Officer Counselor," *FBI Law Enforcement Bulletin*, vol. 48, no. 2, 1979, pp. 8–12.

Derogatis, Leonard R.: "Description and Bibliography for the SCL-90-R," Johns Hopkins University School of Medicine, Baltimore, 1981. (mimeographed)

Derogatis, L. R., R. S. Lipman, L. Covi, and K. Rickels: "Factorial Invariance of Symptom Dimensions in Anxious and Depressive Neuroses," *Archives of General Psychiatry*, vol. 27, November 1972, pp. 659–665.

Dimsdale, J. E., and J. Moss: "Plasma Catecholamines in Stress and Exercise," *Journal of the American Medical Association*, vol. 243, no. 4, January 25, 1980, pp. 340–342.

Duggar, B. C., and G. V. Swengios: "The Design of Physical Activity Programs for Industry," *Journal of Medicine*, vol. 11, 1968, pp. 322–329.

Dobrzanski, T., and R. Rychta: "Cattell 16 Personality Factors and Biochemical

Responses to Occupational Noise Exposure," *Polskie Archiwum Weterynaryjne*, vol. 58, no. 5, 1977, pp. 427–435.

Dohrenwend, B. S., and B. P. Dohrenwend (eds.): *Stressful Life Events: Their Nature and Effects*, Wiley, New York, 1974.

Drucker, Peter F.: *The Practice of Management*, Harper and Row, New York, 1954.

Dunham, Randall B., and Frank J. Smith: *Organizational Surveys: An Internal Assessment of Organizational Health*, Scott, Foresman and Company, Glenview, Ill., 1979.

El-Batavi-Mostafa: "Work Related Diseases," *World Health Magazine*, June 1978, pp. 10–13.

Eliot, R. S.: *Stress and the Major Cardiovascular Disorders*, Futura Publishing Co., Mt. Kisco, N.Y., 1979.

Eliot, R. S.: "Stress Reduction: Techniques That Can Help You and Your Patients," *Consultant*, February 1982, pp. 91–112.

Ellis, A.: *How to Live with a Neurotic*, Crown, New York, 1955.

Ellis, A.: "What People Can Do for Themselves to Cope with Stress," in C. L. Cooper and R. Payne (eds.), *Stress at Work*, Wiley, New York, pp. 209–222.

Engdahl, R., and D. Walsh: *Mental Wellness Programs for Employees*, Springer-Verlag, New York, 1980.

Engel, G. L.: "Psychologic Stress, Vasodepressor (Vasovagal) Syncope and Sudden Death," *Annals of Internal Medicine*, vol. 89, 1978, pp. 403–412.

Evans, Gary W.: "Behavioral and Physiological Consequences of Crowding in Humans," *Journal of Applied Social Psychology*, vol. 9, no. 1, 1979, pp. 27–46.

Eysenck, H. J., and G. D. Wilson: *A Textbook of Human Psychology*, MTP Press, Lancaster, 1976.

Feinstein, A. R.: *Clinical Biostatistics*, C. V. Mosby, Saint Louis, 1977.

Feinstein, A. R.: *Clinical Judgment*, Williams & Wilkins, Baltimore, 1967.

Fentem, P. H., and E. J. Bassey: "The Case for Exercise," *Sports Council Research Working Papers*, no. 8, The Sports Council, London, 1979.

Ferguson, M., and J. Gowan: "TM: Some Preliminary Findings," *Journal of Humanistic Psychology*, vol. 16, no. 3, Summer 1976, pp. 51–60.

Fiedler, Fred E., et al.: "Organizational Stress and the Use and Misuse of Managerial Intelligence and Experience," *Journal of Applied Psychology*, vol. 64, no. 6, 1979, pp. 635–647.

Fineman, Stephen: "A Psychosocial Model of Stress and Its Application to Managerial Unemployment," *Human Relations*, vol. 32, no. 4, 1979, pp. 323–345.

Folkman, S., and R. J. Lazarus: "An Analysis of Coping in a Middle-Aged Community Sample," *Journal of Health and Social Behavior*, vol. 21, no. 3, September 1980, pp. 219–239.

Folkman, S., C. Schaefer, and R. S. Lazarus: "Cognitive Processes as Mediators of Stress and Coping," in V. Hamilton and D. M. Warburton (eds.), *Human Stress and Cognition*, Wiley, New York, 1979, pp. 265–298.

Follette, W., and N. Cummings: "Psychiatric Services and Medical Utilization in a Prepaid Health Plan Setting: Kaiser Foundation Hospital, San Francisco," *Medical Care*, vol. 5, 1967, pp. 25–35.

Ford, D. L., Jr. (ed.): *Readings in Minority-Group Relations*, University Associates, La Jolla, Calif., 1976.

Forrest, W. R.: "Stress and Self-Destructive Behaviors of Dentists," *Dental Clinics of North America*, vol. 22, no. 3, 1978, pp. 361–371.

French, J. R. P., Jr., R. D. Caplan, and R. V. Harrison: *Mechanisms of Job Stress and Strain*, Wiley, New York, 1982.

French, J. R. P., Jr., and R. D. Caplan: "Organizational Stress and Individual Strain," in A. J. Marrow (ed.), *The Failure of Success*, AMA Committee, New York, 1972, pp. 30–66.

French, J. R. P., Jr., and R. L. Kahn: "A Programmatic Approach to Studying the Industrial Environment and Mental Health," *Journal of Social Issues*, vol. 18, 1962, pp. 1–47.

French, Wendell L., and Cecil H. Bell, Jr.: *Organization Development: Behavioral Science Interventions for Organization Improvement*, 2d ed., Prentice-Hall, Englewood Cliffs, N.J., 1978.

Freud, Sigmund: *Civilization and Its Discontents*, W. W. Norton and Co., New York, 1961.

Freud, Sigmund: *Collected Papers: Volumes I–V*, Hogarth Press and The Institute of Psycho-Analysis, London, 1956a.

Freud, Sigmund: *The Interpretation of Dreams*, Basic Books, New York, 1956b.

Frew, D. R.: "Transcendental Meditation and Productivity, *Academy of Management Journal*, vol. 17, 1974, pp. 362–368.

Friedman, M. D., and R. H. Rosenman: *Type A Behavior and Your Heart*, Knopf, New York, 1974.

Friedman, M., R. H. Rosenman, and V. Carroll: "Changes in Serum Cholesterol and Blood Clotting Time in Men Subjected to Cyclic Variations of Occupational Stress," *Circulation*, vol. 17, 1958, pp. 852–861.

Froelicher, V., A. Battler, and M. D. McKirnan: "Physical Activity and Coronary Heart Disease," *Cardiology*, vol. 65, 1980, pp. 153–190.

Fromm, E.: *The Anatomy of Human Destructiveness*, Holt, Rinehart, and Winston, New York, 1973.

Fuller, G. D.: "Current Status of Biofeedback in Clinical Practice," *American Psychologist*, vol. 33, 1978, pp. 39–48.

Gallup, G. H.: *The Gallup Poll: Public Opinion 1972–1977*, vol. 2, Scholarly Resources, Wilmington, Del., 1978.

Gambert, S. R., et al.: "Exercise and the Endogenous Opioids," *New England Journal of Medicine*, vol. 305, no. 26, 1981, pp. 1590–1591.

Gentry, W. D.: "Behavioral Treatment of Somatic Disorders," *University Programs Modular Studies*, 1975, pp. 1–16.

Gentry, W. D., et al.: "Habitual Anger-Coping Styles: I. Effect on Mean Blood Pressure and Risk for Essential Hypertension," *Psychosomatic Medicine*, vol. 4, no. 2, May 1982, pp. 195–202.

Gerloff, E., and J. C. Quick: "A Study of Hierarchical Communication and Consensus within the Context of a Goal-Setting Program," *Academy of Management Proceedings*, 1978, pp. 324–328.

Girdano, Daniel A., and George S. Everly, Jr.: *Controlling Stress and Tension: A Holistic Approach*, Prentice-Hall, Englewood Cliffs, N.J., 1979.

Goldberg, D. P., K. Rickels, R. Downing, and P. Hesbacher: "A Comparison of Two Psychiatric Screening Tests," *British Journal of Psychiatry*, vol. 129, July 1976, pp. 61–67.

Goldberg, R. J.: "Anxiety Reduction by Self-Regulation: Theory, Practice, and Evaluation," *Annals of Internal Medicine*, vol. 96, 1982, pp. 483–487.

Goldston, E.: "Executive Sabbaticals: About to Take Off?" *Harvard Business Review*, September–October 1973, pp. 57–68.

Grant, I., et al.: "Recent Life Events and Diabetes in Adults," *Psychosomatic Medicine*, vol. 36, 1974, p. 121.

Greenberger, Robert S.: "How 'Burnout' Affects Corporate Managers and Their Performance," *Wall Street Journal*, vol. 67, no. 79, April 23, 1981, pp. 1, 18.

Griest, H. H., M. H. Klein, R. R. Eischens, and J. W. Faris: "Antidepressant Running," *Behavioral Medicine*, vol. 5, no. 6, 1978, pp. 19–24.

Griffin, R. W.: *Task Design: An Integrative Approach*, Scott, Foresman and Company, Glenview, Ill., 1982.

Gunderson, E. K. Eric: "Organizational and Environmental Influences on Health and Performance," in B. T. King, S. Streufert, and F. E. Fiedler (eds.), *Managerial Control and Organizational Democracy*, Halsted Press, New York, 1978, pp. 43–60.

Hackman, J. Richard: "Work Design," in J. Richard Hackman and J. Lloyd Suttle (eds.), *Improving Life At Work*, Goodyear, Santa Monica, Calif., 1977, pp. 96–162.

Hackman, J. Richard, and Greg R. Oldham: *The Job Diagnostic Survey: An Instrument for the Diagnosis of Jobs and the Evaluation of Job Redesign Projects*, Department of Administrative Sciences, Yale University, New Haven, 1974.

Hackman, J. R., and G. R. Oldham: "Motivation through the Design of Work: Test of a Theory," *Organizational Behavior and Human Performance*, vol. 16, 1976, pp. 250–279.

Hackman, J. R., and G. R. Oldham: *Work Redesign*, Addison-Wesley, Reading, Mass., 1980.

Haley, J.: *Uncommon Therapy: The Psychiatric Techniques of Milton H. Erikson, M.D.*, W. W. Norton & Co., New York, 1973.

Hall, Douglas T.: *Careers in Organizations*, Goodyear, Santa Monica, Calif., 1976.

Hall, Douglas T., and Francine S. Hall: "Stress and the Two-Career Couple," in C. L. Cooper and R. Payne (eds.), *Current Concerns in Occupational Stress*, Wiley, New York, 1980, pp. 243–266.

Hall, Douglas T., and Roger Mansfield: "Organizational and Individual Response to External Stress," *Administrative Science Quarterly*, vol. 16, 1971, pp. 533–547.

Hall, Douglas T., and Samuel Rabinowitz: "Changing Correlates of Job Involvement in Three Career Stages," *Journal of Vocational Behavior*, vol. 18, 1981, pp. 138–144.

Handy, C.: "The Family: Help or Hindrance," in C. L.Cooper and R. Payne (eds.), *Stress at Work*, John Wiley & Sons, New York, 1978, pp. 107–123.

Harrison, R. Van: "Person—Environment Fit and Job Stress," in C. L. Cooper and Roy Payne (eds.), *Stress at Work*, John Wiley & Sons, New York, 1978, pp. 175–205.

Hartley, D., H. B. Roback, and S. I. Abramowitz: "Deterioration Effects in Encounter Groups," *American Psychologist*, vol. 31, 1976, pp. 247–255.

Haynes, Graham: "The Problem of Stress," *Nursing Times*, vol. 74, no. 18, 1978, pp. 753–754.

Haynes, S., et al.: "The Relationship of Psychosocial Factors to Coronary Heart Disease in the Framingham Study: II. Prevalence of Coronary Heart Disease," *American Journal of Epidemiology*, vol. 107, 1978, pp. 384–402.

Hawkins, N. G., R. Davis, and T. H. Holmes: "Evidence of Psychosomatic Factors in the Development of Pulmonary Tuberculosis," *American Review of Tubercular Pulmonary Disease*, vol. 75, no. 5, 1957, pp. 768–780.

Herold, D. M., and E. G. Conlon: "Alcohol Consumption as a Coping Response to Job Induced Stress," *Academy of Management Proceedings*, 1982, pp. 292–296.

Herzberg, Frederick, B. Mausner, and B. Snyderman: *The Motivation to Work*, John Wiley and Sons, New York, 1959.

Hess, W. R.: *The Functional Organization of the Dienchephalon*, Grune and Stratton, New York, 1957.

Hilgard, E. R., R. L. Atkinson, and R. C. Atkinson: *Introduction to Psychology*, 7th ed., Harcourt, Brace, Jovanovich, London, 1979.

Hilker, R. R. J., F. E. Asma, and R. L. Eggert: "A Company-Sponsored Alcoholic Rehabilitation Program," *Journal of Occupational Medicine*, vol. 14, no. 10, 1972, pp. 769–772.

Hillier, S.: "Stresses, Strains and Smoking," *Nursing Mirror*, February 12, 1981, pp. 26–30.

Hinkle, L. E., and S. Wolf: "The Effects of Stressful Life Situations on the Concentration of Blood Glucose in Diabetic and Nondiabetic Humans," *Diabetes*, vol. 1, 1952, p. 383.

Hirschfeld, A. H., and R. C. Behan: "The Accident Process: I. Etiological Considerations of Industrial Injuries," *Journal of the American Medical Association*, vol. 186, 1963, pp. 193–199.

Hirschfeld, A. H., and R. C. Behan: "The Accident Process: III. Disability: Acceptable and Unacceptable," *The Journal of the American Medical Association*, vol. 197, no. 2, 1966, pp. 125–129.

Holmes, D. S., and B. K. Houston: "Effectiveness of Situation Redefinition and Affective Isolation in Coping with Stress," *Journal of Personality and Social Psychology*, vol. 29, 1974, pp. 212–218.

Holmes, T. H., N. G. Hawkins, C. E. Bowerman, E. R. Clark, Jr., and J. R. Joffee: "Psychosocial and Psychophysiological Studies of Tuberculosis," *Psychosomatic Medicine*, vol. 19, 1957, pp. 134–143.

Holmes, Thomas H., and Minoru Masuda: "Life Change and Illness Susceptibility," in B. S. Dohrenwend and B. P. Dohrenwend, *Stressful Life Events: Their Nature and Effects*, Wiley, New York, pp. 45–72.

Holmes, T. H., and R. H. Rahe: "The Social Readjustment Rating Scale," *Journal of Psychosomatic Research*, vol. 11, 1967, pp. 213–218.

House, J. S.: "The Relationship of Intrinsic and Extrinsic Work Motivation to Occupational Stress and Coronary Heart Disease Risk," Ph.D. Dissertation, University of Michigan, 1972.

House, J. S.: *Work Stress and Social Support*, Addison-Wesley, Reading, Mass., 1981.

House, J. S., and J. A. Wells: "Occupational Stress, Social Support, and Health," in A. McLean, G. Black, and M. Colligan (eds.), *Reducing Occupational Stress: Proceedings of a Conference*, DHEW (NIOSH) Publication 78-140, 1978, pp. 8–19.

House, R. J., and J. R. Rizzo: "Role Conflict and Ambiguity as Critical Variables in a Model of Organizational Behavior," *Organizational Behavior and Human Performance*, vol. 7, 1972, pp. 467–505.

Howard, J. H.: "Managing Stress and Job Tension," *The Labour Gazette*, vol. 78, 1978, pp. 61–64.

Howard, J. H., P. A. Rechnitzer, and D. A. Cunningham: "Coping with Job Tension—Effective and Ineffective Means," *Public Personnel Management*, vol. 4, 1975, pp. 317–326.

Howard, J. H., D. A. Cunningham, and P. A. Rechnitzer: "Health Patterns Associated with Type A Behavior: A Managerial Population," *Journal of Human Stress*, vol. 2, no. 1, 1976, pp. 24–31.

Howard, J. H., D. A. Cunningham, and P. A. Rechnitzer: "Work Patterns Associated with Type A Behavior: A Managerial Population," *Human Relations*, vol. 30, 1977, pp. 825–836.

Hughes, C. L.: *Goal Setting: Key to Individual and Organizational Effectiveness*, American Management Association, New York, 1965.

Huse, Edgar F.: *Organizational Development and Change*, West, St. Paul, Minn., 1980.

Ivancevich, John M., and Michael T. Matteson: *Stress and Work*, Scott, Foresman and Company, Glenview, Ill., 1980.

Jacobson, B.: *The Ladykillers: Why Smoking Is a Feminist Issue*, Pluto Press, New York, 1981.

Jacobson, E. J.: *Progressive Relaxation*, University of Chicago Press, Chicago, 1929.

Jacobson, E. J.: *You Must Relax*, McGraw-Hill Book Co., New York, 1978.

Jakubowski-Spector, P.: "Facilitating the Growth of Women Through Assertiveness Training," *The Counseling Psychologist*, vol. 4, 1973, pp. 75–86.

Jameson, J., L. Shuman, and W. Young: "The Effects of Outpatient Psychiatric Utilization on the Costs of Providing Third-Party Coverage," *Medical Care*, vol. 16, 1978, pp. 383–399.

Jencks, B.: *Exercise Manual for J. H. Schultz's Standard Autogenic Training and Special Formulas*, American Society of Clinical Hypnosis, Des Plaines, Ill., 1979.

Jenkins, C. D., R. H. Rosenman, and M. Friedman: "Components of the Coronary-Prone Behavior Pattern: Their Relation to Silent Myocardial Infarction and Blood Lipids," *Journal of Chronic Diseases*, vol. 19, 1966, pp. 599–609.

Jenkins, C. D., R. H. Rosenman, and M. Friedman: "Development of an Objective Psychological Test for Determination of the Coronary-Prone Behavior Pattern in Employed Man," *Journal of Chronic Diseases*, vol. 20, 1967, pp. 371–379.

Jenkins, C. D., S. J. Zyzanski, and R. H. Rosenman: *Jenkins Activity Survey (Form C)*, The Psychological Corporation, New York, 1979.

Jenkins, C. D., S. J. Zyzanski, and R. H. Rosenman: "Progress Toward Validation of a Computer-Scored Test for the Type A Coronary-Prone Behavior Pattern," *Psychosomatic Medicine*, vol. 33, no. 3, May–June 1971, pp. 193–202.

Jewell, L. N., and H. J. Reitz: *Group Effectiveness in Organizations*, Scott, Foresman and Company, Glenview, Ill., 1981.

Jick, Todd D.: "As the Ax Falls: Budget Cuts and the Experience of Stress in Organizations," in Rabi Bhagat and Terry Beehr (eds.), *Stress and Cognition in Organizations: An Integrated Perspective*, John Wiley, New York, 1984.

Jones, E. W., Jr.: "What It's Like to Be a Black Manager," *Harvard Business Review*, July–August 1973, pp. 108–116.

Jones, K. R., and T. R. Vischi: "Impact of Alcohol, Drug Abuse, and Mental Health Treatment on Medical Care Utilization: A Review of the Research Literature," *Medical Care*, vol. 17, no. 12, Supplement, 1979.

Kahn, R. L.: "Role Conflict and Ambiguity in Organizations," *The Personnel Administrator*, vol. 9, 1964, pp. 8–13.

Kahn, R. L., et al.: *Organizational Stress: Studies in Role Conflict and Ambiguity*, John Wiley & Sons, New York, 1964.

Kahn, R. L., and R. P. Quinn: "Strategies for Management of Role Stress," in A. McLean (ed.), *Occupational Mental Health*, Rand McNally, New York, 1970.

Kales, A., and J. D. Kales: "Sleep Disorders: Recent Findings in the Diagnosis and Treatment of Disturbed Sleep," *New England Journal of Medicine*, vol. 290, 1974, pp. 487–499.

Kanner, A. D., J. C. Coyne, C. Schaefer, and R. S. Lazarus: "Comparison of Two Modes of Stress Measurement: Daily Hassles and Uplifts Versus Major Life Events," *Journal of Behavioral Medicine*, vol. 4, no. 1, 1981, pp. 1–39.

Kanter, R. M.: *Work and Family in the United States: A Critical Review and Agenda for Research and Policy*, Russell Sage Foundation, New York, 1977.

Karasek, Robert A., Jr.: "Job Demands, Job Decision Latitude, and Mental Strain: Implications for Job Redesign," *Administrative Science Quarterly*, vol. 24, June 1979, pp. 285–308.

Kasl, S. V., and S. Cobb: "Blood Pressure Changes in Men Undergoing Job Loss: A Preliminary Report," *Psychosomatic Medicine*, vol. 32, 1970, pp. 19–38.

Katz, C. A.: "Reducing Interpersonal Stress In Dental Practice," *Dental Clinics of North America*, vol. 22, no. 3, 1978, pp. 347–359.

Kessler, Ronald C., and Paul D. Cleary: "Social Class and Psychological Distress," *American Sociological Review*, vol. 45, 1980, pp. 463–478.

Kiev, A.: *A Strategy for Handling Executive Stress*, Nelson-Hall, Chicago, 1974.

Kiev, A., and V. Kohn: *Executive Stress*, An AMA Survey Report, American Management Association, New York, 1979.

Kilgour, F. G. (ed.): *Christobal Mendez Book of Bodily Exercise*, Elisabeth Licht, New Haven, 1960.

Kimberly, John R., Robert H. Miles, and Associates: *The Organizational Life Cycle*, Jossey-Bass, San Francisco, 1980.

Kinzer, N. S.: *Stress and the American Woman*, Anchor Press/Doubleday, New York, 1979.

Kirn, A. G., and M. O. Kirn: *Life Work Planning*, 4th ed., McGraw-Hill, New York, 1978.

Korff, Ernst: "Leisure—Free Time: The Way to Creative Organization of Free Time Activities," *Praktische Psychologie*, vol. 29, no. 5, 1975, pp. 152–157.

Kostrubala, T.: *The Joy of Running*, J. B. Lippincott, Philadelphia, 1976.

Kotter, J. P., V. A. Faux, and C. C. McArthur: *Self-Assessment and Career Development*, Prentice-Hall, Englewood Cliffs, N.J., 1978.

Krackhardt, D. M., et al.: "Supervisory Behavior and Employee Turnover," *Academy of Management Journal*, vol. 24, 1981, pp. 249–259.

Kraus, Hans: *Clinical Treatment of Back and Neck Pain*, McGraw-Hill, New York, 1970.

Kraus, Hans, A. Melleby, and R. R. Graston: "Back Pain Correction and Prevention," *New York State Journal of Medicine*, vol. 77, 1977, pp. 1335–1338.

Kraus, Hans, M.D., and Wilhelm Raab, M.D.: *Hypokenetic Disease*, Charles C Thomas, Springfield, Ill., 1961.

Kreisberg, L.: *The Sociology of Social Conflict*, Prentice-Hall, Englewood Cliffs, N.J., 1973.

Kreitner, R., S. D. Wood, and G. M. Friedman: "Just How Fit Are Your Employees?" *Business Horizons*, August 1979, pp. 39–45.

Kuna, D. J.: "Meditation and Work," *Vocational Guidance Quarterly*, vol. 23, no. 4, June 1975, pp. 342–346.

Laing, R. D.: *The Politics of the Family and Other Essays*, Pantheon Books, New York, 1971.

Laing, R. D., and A. Esterson: *Sanity, Madness, and the Family: Vol. 1, Families of Schizophrenics*, Tavistock, London, 1964.

Lakein, Alan: *How to Get Control of Your Time and Your Life*, Peter H. Wyden, New York, 1973.

Latham, G. P., and G. A. Yukl: "A Review of Research on the Application of Goal Setting in Organizations," *Academy of Management Journal*, vol. 18, 1975, pp. 824–845.

Lazarus, A. A.: "Group Therapy of Phobic Disorders by Systematic Desensitization," *Journal of Abnormal Social Psychology*, vol. 63, 1961, pp. 504–510.

Lazarus, R.: *Psychological Stress and the Coping Process*, McGraw-Hill, New York, 1967.

Lazarus, Richard S.: "Little Hassles Can be Hazardous to Health," *Psychology Today*, July 1981, pp. 58–62.

Lehmann, P.: "Job Stress: Hidden Hazard," *Job Safety and Health*, vol. 2, 1974, pp. 4–10.

LeShan, L.: "An Emotional Life-History Pattern Associated with Neoplastic Disease," *Annals of New York Academy of Science*, vol. 125, no. 3, 1966, pp. 780–793.

Levens, Ernest: "The Cost-Benefit and Cost-Effectiveness of Occupational Alcoholism Programs," *Professional Safety*, vol. 21, no. 11, 1979, pp. 36–41.

Levi, Lennart: *Occupational Stress: Sources, Management, and Prevention*, Addison-Wesley, Reading, Mass., 1979.

Levi, Lennart: *Preventing Work Stress*, Addison-Wesley, Reading, Mass., 1981.

Levi, Lennart: "Social Structures and Processes as Producers of Stress and Illness," *Scheizer Archiv Fur Neurologie, Neurochirurgie und Psychiatri*, vol. 121, no. 1, 1977, pp. 21–31.

Levi, Lennart: *Society, Stress, and Disease: The Psychosocial Environment and Psychosomatic Diseases*, Oxford University Press, London, 1971.

Levi, Lennart: *Stress: Sources, Management, and Prevention*, Liveright, New York, 1967.

Levinson, D. J., et al.: *The Seasons of a Man's Life*, Knopf, New York, 1978.

Levinson, Harry: "The Abrasive Personality," *Harvard Business Review*, vol. 56, May–June 1978, pp. 86–94.

Levinson, Harry: "Conflicts That Plague Family Businesses," *Harvard Business Review*, vol. 44, 1971, pp. 90–98.

Levinson, Harry: *Executive Stress*, New American Library, New York, 1975.

Levinson, Harry: "A Psychoanalytic View of Occupational Stress," *Occupational Mental Health*, vol. 3, no. 2, 1978, pp. 2–13.

Levinson, Harry: "When Executives Burn Out," *Harvard Business Review*, vol. 59, May–June 1981, pp. 73–81.

Levinson, Harry, Janice Molinari, and Andrew G. Spohn: *Organizational Diagnosis*, Harvard University Press, Cambridge, Mass., 1972.

Levitt, Harold: "Applied Organizational Change in Industry: Structural, Technological, and Humanistic Approaches," in J. G. March (ed.), *Handbook of Organizations*, Rand McNally, Chicago, 1965, pp. 1144–1170.

Lewin, Kurt: "Group Decision and Social Change," in J. Newcomb and E. Hartely (eds.), *Readings in Social Psychology*, Holt, Rinehart and Winston, New York, 1974, pp. 197–211.

Lewin, Kurt, Ronald Lippitt, and Ralph K. White: "Patterns of Aggressive Behavior in Experimentally Created 'Social Climates,'" *Journal of Social Psychology*, vol. 10, 1939, pp. 271–299.

Likert, Rensis: *New Patterns of Management*, McGraw-Hill, New York, 1961.

Lindemann, Hannes: *Relieve Tension the Autogenic Way*, Wyden, New York, 1973.

Lindenthal, J. J., J. K. Myers, and M. P. Pepper: "Smoking, Psychological Status, and Stress," *Social Science Medicine*, vol. 6, 1972, pp. 583–591.

Lindsey, K.: "Sexual Harassment on the Job and How to Stop It," *Ms*, November 1977, pp. 48–51 and 76–78.

Locke, E. A.: "Toward a Theory of Task Motivation and Incentives," *Organizational Behavior and Human Performance*, vol. 3, 1968, pp. 157–189.

Lublin, Joann S.: "On-the-Job Stress Leads Many Workers To File—and Win—Compensation Awards," *Wall Street Journal*, September 17, 1980, p. 33.

Luthe, W. (ed.): *Autogenic Therapy, Volumes I to IV*, Grune and Stratton, New York, 1969.

Lynch, James J.: *The Broken Heart: The Medical Consequences of Loneliness*, Basic Books, New York, 1977.

Lynch, S., C. H. Folkins, and J. H. Wilmore: "Relationships between Three Mood Variables and Physical Exercise," unpublished data, February 1973.

Lyons, T.: "Role Clarity, Need for Clarity, Satisfaction, Tension, and Withdrawal," *Organizational Behavior and Human Performance*, vol. 6, 1971, pp. 99–110.

MacCrimmon, K. R., and R. N. Taylor: "Decision Making and Problem Solving," in Marvin D. Dunnette (ed.), *Handbook of Industrial and Organizational Psychology*, Rand McNally, Chicago, 1976, pp. 1397–1453.

MacKinnon, C. A.: *Sexual Harassment of Working Woman*, Yale University Press, New Haven, 1979.

Macy, Barry A., and Philip H. Mirvis: "A Methodology for Assessment of Quality of Work Life and Organizational Effectiveness in Behavioral-Economic Terms," *Administrative Science Quarterly*, vol. 21, June 1976, pp. 212–226.

Macy, Barry A., and Philip H. Mirvis: "Organizational Change Efforts: Methodologies for Assessing Organizational Effectiveness and Program Costs Versus Benefits," *Evaluation Review*, vol. 6, no. 3, June 1982, pp. 301–372.

Maier, N. R. F.: "Assets and Liabilities in Group Problem Solving: The Need for an Integrative Function," *Psychological Review*, vol. 74, 1967, pp. 239–249.

Manuso, J. S. J.: "Biofeedback Helps in Dealing with Stress," *Equinews*, vol. 8, no. 12, July 2, 1979, p. 1.

Manuso, J. S. J.: "Manage Your Stress," CRM Multimedia Module, McGraw-Hill Films, Del Mar, Calif., 1980. (Facilitator's guide, film or videotape, audiocassette, exercise books)

Manuso, J. S. J.: *Preventive Health Care in the Work Setting: The Relative Efficacy of Two Intervention Strategies in Ameliorating Type A Coronary Prone Behavior Patterns*, The Equitable Life Assurance of the United States, New York, undated.

Manuso, J. S. J.: "Stress Management and Behavioral Medicine: A Corporate Model," in M. O'Donnell and T. Ainsworth (eds.), *Health Promotion in the Work Place*, John Wiley & Sons, New York, 1982.

Manuso, J. S. J.: *Stress Management Training in a Large Corporation*, unpublished book, 1979.

March, J. G., and H. Simon: *Organizations*, Wiley, New York, 1958.

Marcus, J. B.: *TM and Business*, McGraw-Hill, New York, 1977.

Margolis, B. L., W. H. Kroes, and R. R. Quinn: "Job Stress: An Unlisted Occupational Hazard," *Journal of Occupational Medicine*, vol. 16, 1974, pp. 659–661.

Marrow, A. J.: *Making Management Human*, McGraw-Hill, New York, 1960.

Maslach, Christina, and Susan E. Jackson: *Maslach Burnout Inventory: Research Edition*, Consulting Psychologists Press, Palo Alto, Calif., 1981b.

Maslach, Christina, and Susan E. Jackson: "The Measurement of Experiential Burnout," *Journal of Occupational Behavior*, vol. 2, 1981a, pp. 99–113.

Maslow, Abraham H.: "A Theory of Human Motivation," *Psychological Review*, vol. 50, 1943, pp. 370–396.

Masuda, Minoru, Kenneth P. Perko, and Robert G. Johnston: "Physiological Activity and Illness History," *Journal of Psychosomatic Research*, vol. 16, no. 2, April 1972, pp. 129–136.

Matteson, M. T., and J. M. Ivancevich: "Organizational Stressors and Heart Disease: A Research Model," *The Academy of Management Review*, vol. 4, 1979, pp. 347–358.

Mayer, N.: "Leisure—or a Coronary?" *Psychology Today*, vol. 8, 1975, pp. 36–37.

Mayr, O.: "The Origins of Feedback Control," *Scientific American*, vol. 223, no. 4, October 1970, p. 111.

Mazzaferri, Ernest (ed.): *Endocrinology: A Review of Clinical Endocrinology*, 2d ed., Medical Examination Publishing, New Hyde Park, N.Y., 1980.

McCann, J.: "The Uptight Executive," *Dun's Review*, vol. 99, 1972, pp. 79–80.

McClelland, D. C.: *The Achieving Society*, Van Nostrand Reinhold Company, Princeton, N.J., 1961.

McGrath, Joseph E.: "Stress and Behavior in Organizations," in Marvin D. Dunnette (ed.), *Handbook of Industrial and Organizational Psychology*, Rand McNally, Chicago, 1976, pp. 1351–1395.

McGregor, Douglas: "An Uneasy Look at Performance Appraisal," *Harvard Business Review*, May–June 1957, pp. 89–94.

McLean, Alan A.: *Dealing With Job Stress*, Management Decision Systems, Darien, Conn., 1976. (cassettes and workbook)

McLean, Alan A.: *Work Stress*, Addison-Wesley, Reading, Mass., 1979.

Melton, C. E., et al.: "Stress in Air Traffic Personnel: Low-Density Towers and

Flight Service Stations," *Aviation Space and Environmental Medicine*, vol. 49, no. 5, 1978, pp. 724–728.

Mendelson, W., J. Gillis, and R. Wyatt: *Human Sleep and Its Disorders*, Plenum, New York, 1977.

Mettlin, C.: "Occupational Careers and the Prevention of Coronary-Prone Behavior," *Social Science and Medicine*, vol. 10, July–August 1976, pp. 367–372.

Meyer, H. H., E. Kay, and J. R. P. French: "Split Roles in Performance Appraisal," *Harvard Business Review*, vol. 43, 1965, pp. 123–129.

Michaels, R. R., M. J. Huber, and D. S. McCann: "Evaluation of Transcendental Meditation as a Method of Reducing Stress," *Science*, vol. 192, 1976, pp. 1242–1244.

Miles, Robert H.: "A Comparison of the Relative Impacts of Role Perceptions of Ambiguity and Conflict by Roles," *Academy of Management Journal*, vol. 19, 1976a, pp. 25–35.

Miles, Robert H.: *The Jim Heavner Story (A), (B)*, Harvard Case Clearing House, Harvard Business School, Boston, 1979.

Miles, Robert H.: "Organizational Boundary Roles," in Cary L. Cooper and Roy Payne (eds.), *Current Concerns in Occupational Stress*, John Wiley & Sons, New York, 1980, pp. 61–96.

Miles, Robert H.: "Role Requirements as Sources of Organizational Stress," *Journal of Applied Psychology*, vol 61, 1976b, pp. 172–179.

Miller, N. E., and B. R. Dworkin: "Effects of Learning on Visceral Functions—Biofeedback," *New England Journal of Medicine*, vol. 296, June 1977, pp. 1274–1278.

Mintzberg, Henry: *The Nature of Managerial Work*, Prentice-Hall, Englewood Cliffs, N.J., 1973.

Mirvis, Philip H., and Edward E. Lawler, III: "Measuring the Financial Impact of Employee Attitudes," *Journal of Applied Psychology*, vol. 62, no. 1, 1977, pp. 1–8.

Mirvis, Philip H., and Barry A. Macy: "Evaluating Program Costs and Benefits," in S. E. Seashore, E. E. Lawler, P. H. Mirvis, and C. Cammann, *Observing and Measuring Organizational Change: A Guide to Field Practice*, Wiley Interscience, New York, 1982.

Mirvis, Philip, and Barry A. Macy: *Guide to Behavioral Costing*, Institute for Social Research, University of Michigan, Ann Arbor, 1974.

Mitchell, Alexander, "Problems and Pressures of Rural Life," *Mental Health*, Winter 1969, pp. 2–4.

Mitchell, L.: *Simple Relaxation*, Atheneum, New York, 1979.

Mobley, William H. *Employee Turnover: Causes, Consequences, and Control*, Addison-Wesley, Reading, Mass., 1982.

Modlin, Herbert C.: "Does Job Stress Alone Cause Health Problems," *Occupational Health and Safety*, vol. 47, no. 5, 1978, pp. 38–39.

Monat, Alan, and Richard S. Lazarus (eds.), *Stress and Coping*, Columbia University Press, New York, 1977.

Moorhead, G.: "Organizational Conditions as Sources of Stress," Paper presented at the Southwestern Meeting of the Academy of Management, Dallas, 1982.

Morgan, W. P., D. H. Horstman, A. Cymerman, and J. Stokes: "Exercise as a Relaxation Technique," *Hospital Physician*, August 1980, pp. A22–A31.

Morris, J. N.: *The Uses of Epidemiology*, 2d ed., E&S Livingston, Edinburgh, 1964.

Morris, J. N.: "The Uses of Epidemiology," *British Medical Journal*, vol. 2, 1955, pp. 395–401.

Morse, D. R., and M. L. Furst: *Stress for Success: A Holistic Approach to Stress and Its Management*, Van Nostrand Reinhold, New York, 1979.

Moss, Leonard, M.D.: *Management Stress*, Addison-Wesley, Reading, Mass., 1981.

Mott, Paul E.: *The Characteristics of Effective Organizations*, Harper & Row, New York, 1972.

Mueller, E. F.: *Psychological and Physiological Correlates of Work Overload Among University Professors*, unpublished doctoral dissertation, University of Michigan, Ann Arbor, 1965.

Mulford, Harold A.: "Stages in the Alcoholic Process: Toward a Cumulative, Nonsequential Index," *Journal of Studies on Alcohol*, vol. 38, no. 3, 1977, pp. 563–583.

Myers, David Charles: "A Correlational Causal Analysis of the Relationships between Role Stress and Work Attitudes and Behavior," *Dissertation Abstracts International*, vol. 39, no. 5, 1978.

Nason, Robert W.: "The Dilemma of Black Mobility in Management," in D. L. Ford, Jr. (ed.), *Readings in Minority-Group Relations*, University Associates, La Jolla, Calif., 1976, pp. 297–314.

Newbury, C. R.: "Tension and Relaxation in the Individual," *International Dental Journal*, vol. 29, no. 2, 1979, pp. 173–182.

Newman, G.: *Understanding Violence*, J. B. Lippincott, New York, 1979.

Newman, John E., and Terry A. Beehr: "Personal and Organizational Strategies for Handling Job Stress: A Review of Research and Opinion," *Personnel Psychology*, vol. 32, 1979, pp. 1–41.

Newton, D. A.: *Think Like a Man. Act Like a Lady. Work Like a Dog*, Doubleday, Garden City, N.Y., 1979.

Nicholson, N., C. A. Brown, and J. K. Chadwick-Jones: "Absence from Work and Job Satisfaction," *Journal of Applied Psychology*, vol. 61, 1976, pp. 728–737.

Noble, E. P. (ed.): *Third Special Report to the U.S. Congress on Alcohol and Health from the Secretary of Health, Education, and Welfare*, National Institute on Alcohol Abuse and Alcoholism, Rockville, Md., 1978.

Nollen, S. D.: "What Is Happening to Flexitime, Flexihour, Gliding Time, the Variable Day? and Permanent Part-Time Employment? and the Four-Day Work Week?" *Across the Board*, April 1980, pp. 6–21.

Nunnally, J. C.: *Psychometric Theory*, McGraw-Hill, New York, 1967.

Nunneley, S. A.: "Psychological Responses of Women to Thermal Stress: A Review," *Medicine and Science in Sports*, vol. 10, no. 4, Winter 1978, pp. 250–255.

Oates, W.: *Confessions of a Workaholic*, World, New York, 1971.

Oh, S. H., et al.: "Biological Function of Metallothionein versus Its Induction in Rats by Various Stresses," *American Journal of Physiology*, vol. 234, no. 3, 1978, pp. 282–285.

Ohlbaum, M. K.: "The Visual Stresses of the Aerospace Environment," *Journal of the American Optometric Association*, vol. 47, no. 9, 1976, pp. 1176–1186.

Ojesjo, L.: "The Relationship to Alcoholism of Occupation, Class, and Employment," *Journal of Occupational Medicine*, vol. 22, no. 10, October 1980, pp. 657–666.

Olbrisch, Mary Ellen: "Evaluation of a Stress Management Program for High Utilizers of a Prepaid University Health Service," *Medical Care*, vol. 19, no. 2, 1981, pp. 153–159.

Organ, T. W.: *The Hindu Quest for the Perfection of Man*, Ohio University Press, Athens, Ohio, 1970.

Orpen, C.: "The Effects of Job Enrichment on Employee Satisfaction, Motivation, Involvement, and Performance: A Field Experiment," *Human Relations*, vol. 32, 1979, pp. 189–217.

Ouchi, William: *Theory Z*, Addison-Wesley, Reading, Mass., 1981.

Overbeke, J. E.: "Pressures Build on Today's Manager," *Industrial Week*, vol. 187, 1975, pp. 21–24.

Paffenbarger, R. S., and R. T. Hyde: "Exercise as Protection against Heart Attack," *New England Journal of Medicine*, 1980, pp. 1026–1027.

Paoline, A. M., et al.: "Sexual Variations in Thermoregulation During Heat Stress," *Aviation Space and Environmental Medicine*, vol. 49, no. 5, 1978, pp. 715–719.

Parikh, D. J., M. B. Ghodasara, and N. L. Raumanathan: "A Special Thermal Stress Problem in Ceramic Industry," *European Journal of Applied Physiology*, vol. 40, no. 1, 1978, pp. 63–72.

Parkes, C. M., et al.: "Broken Heart: A Statistical Study of Increased Mortality among Widowers," *British Medical Journal*, vol. 1, 1969, pp. 740–742.

Paul, G. L.: "Insight versus Desensitization in Psychotherapy Two Years after Termination," *Journal of Consulting Psychology*, vol. 31, 1967, pp. 333–348.

Paykel, Eugene S.: "Life Stress, Depression, and Attempted Suicide," *Journal of Human Stress*, September 1976, pp. 3–12.

Payne, Roy: "Epistemology and the Study of Stress at Work," in C. L. Cooper and R. Payne (eds.), *Stress at Work*, Wiley, New York, 1978, pp. 259–283.

Payne, Roy: "Organizational Stress and Social Support," in C. L. Cooper and R. Payne (eds.), *Current Concerns in Occupational Stress*, Wiley, New York, 1980, pp. 269–298.

Payne, Roy, T. D. Jick, and R. J. Burke: "Whither Stress Research: An Agenda for the 1980's," *Journal of Occupational Behaviour*, vol. 3, no. 1, January 1982, pp. 131–145.

Pearlin, L. I., and C. Schooler: "The Structure of Coping," *Journal of Health and Social Behavior*, vol. 19, 1978, pp. 2–21.

Peck, M. Scott: *The Road Less Traveled: A New Psychology of Love, Traditional Values and Spiritual Growth*, Simon and Schuster, New York, 1978.

Pelletier, K. R.: *Mind as Healer, Mind as Slayer*, Dell Publishing Co., 1977.

Peters, R. K.: *Daily Relaxation Response Breaks*, National Institute for Occupational Safety and Health, Division of Biomedical and Behavioral Science, Cincinnati, Ohio, 1980.

Peters, R. K., and H. Benson: "Time Out From Tension," *Harvard Business Review*, vol. 56, January–February 1978, pp. 120–124.

Peters, R. K., H. Benson, and D. Porter: "Daily Relaxation Response Breaks in a Working Population: I. Effects on Self-Reported Measures of Health, Performance, and Well-Being," *American Journal of Public Health*, vol. 67, no. 10, 1977, pp. 946–952.

Peters, R. K., H. Benson, and J. M. Peters: "Daily Relaxation Response Breaks in a Working Population: II. Effects on Blood Pressure," *American Journal of Public Health*, vol. 67, no. 10, 1977, pp. 954–959.

Plant, M. A.: *Drinking Careers*, Tavistock, London, 1979b.

Plant, M. A.: "Occupations, Drinking Patterns and Alcohol-Related Problems: Conclusions from a Follow-Up Study," *British Journal of Addiction*, vol. 74, no. 3, September 1979a, pp. 267–273.

Pondy, L. R.: "Organizational Conflict: Concepts and Models," *Administrative Science Quarterly*, vol. 12, no. 2, 1967, pp. 297–320.

Porter, Lyman W., Edward E. Lawler, III, and J. Richard Hackman: *Behavior in Organizations*, McGraw-Hill, New York, 1975.

President's Council on Physical Fitness and Sports: *Fitness in the Workplace: A Handbook on Employee Programs*, Washington, D.C., undated.

Pritchett, S., and L. Finley: "Problem Drinking and the Risk Management Function," *Risk Management*, vol. 18, 1971, pp. 16–23.

Quick, J. C.: "Dyadic Goal Setting and Role Stress: A Field Study," *Academy of Management Journal*, vol. 22, no. 2, 1979a, pp. 241–252.

Quick, J. C.: "Dyadic Goal Setting within Organizations: Role Making and Motivational Considerations," *Academy of Management Review*, vol. 4, no. 2, 1979b, pp. 369–380.

Quick, J. C., and David A. Gray: "Dyadic Goal Setting as a Developmental Technique: Training through Role Planning," *Proceedings of the 1979 Southwest Division, Academy of Management*, pp. 147–151.

Quick, J. C., and R. W. Griffin: "Situational Determinants of Goal-Setting Behaviors and Evaluation: Task Variability," paper presented at the Southwestern Academy of Management Meeting, San Antonio, Texas, 1980.

Quick, J. C., A. Kulisch, N. D. Jones, E. J. O'Connor, and L. Peters: *The Goals and Objectives Program: 1981 Evaluation Report*, Technical Report #1, Department of Management, University of Texas at Arlington, May 1981.

Quick, J. C., and J. D. Quick: "Preventing Distress through Better Working Relationships," *Management Review*, vol. 30, no. 4, 1984, in press.

Quick, J. C., and J. D. Quick: "Reducing Stress through Preventive Management," *Human Resource Management*, vol. 18, no. 3, 1979, pp. 15–22.

Quick, J. C., C. Shannon, and J. D. Quick, "Managing Stress in the Air Force: An Ounce of Prevention!" *Air University Review*, vol. 34, no. 4, 1983, pp. 76–83.

Quick, J. D., G. Moorhead, J. C. Quick, E. A. Gerloff, K. L. Mattox, and C. Mullins: "Decision-Making among Emergency Room Residents: Preliminary Observations and a Decision Model," *Journal of Medical Education*, vol. 58, February 1983, pp. 117–125.

Quick, J. D., and J. C. Quick: "Organizational Stress and Preventive Management," *Chronic Diseases and Therapeutics Research*, vol. 3, no. 13, 1979, pp. 185–205.

Quinn, R. P., and L. J. Shepard: *The 1972–1973 Quality of Employment Survey*, Survey Research Center, Ann Arbor, Mich., 1974.

Rabinowitz, S.: "Towards a Developmental Model of Job Involvement," *International Review of Applied Psychology*, vol. 30, 1981, pp. 31–50.

Rahe, R. H.: "The Pathway between Subjects' Recent Life Changes and Their Near-Future Illness Reports: Representative Results and Methodological Issues," in Barbara S. Dohrenwend and Bruce P. Dohrenwend (eds.), *Stressful Life Events: Their Nature and Effects*, Wiley, New York, 1974, pp. 73–86.

Rahe, R. H.: "Subjects' Recent Life Changes and Their Near-Future Illness Reports," *Annals of Clinical Research*, vol. 4, 1972, pp. 250–265.

Rahe, R. H. "Subjects' Recent Life Changes and Their Near-Future Illness Susceptibility," *Advances in Psychosomatic Medicine*, vol. 8, 1972, pp. 2–19.

Rahe, R. H., et al.: "Illness Prediction Studies: Use of Psychosocial and Occupational Characteristics as Predictors," *Archives of Environmental Health*, vol. 25, September 1972, pp. 192–197.

Rahe, R. H., R. T. Rubin, and E. K. E. Gunderson: "Measures of Subjects' Motivation and Affect Correlated with Their Serum Uric Acid, Cholesterol, and Cortisol," *Archives of General Psychiatry*, vol. 26, April 1972, p. 357.

Ramsey, J. D.: "Abbreviated Guidelines for Heat Stress Exposure," *American Industrial Hygiene Association Journal*, vol. 39, no. 6, June 1978, pp. 491–495.

Raskin, M., et al.: "Muscle Biofeedback and Transcendental Meditation," *Archives of General Psychiatry*, vol. 37, 1980, pp. 93–97.

Reardon, R. W.: "Help for the Troubled Worker in a Small Company," *Personnel*, vol. 53, January–February 1976, pp. 50–54.

Reischl, V., et al.: "Radiotelemetry-Based Study of Occupational Heat Stress in a Steel Factory," *Biotelemetry*, vol. 4, no. 3, 1977, pp. 115, 130.

Reiss, B.: "Changes in Patient Income Concomitant with Psychotherapy," *International Mental Health Research Newsletter*, vol. 9, 1967, pp. 1–4.

Riddle, Steven C.: *A Life Cycle Analysis of a Temporary Project Organization*, unpublished masters thesis, The University of Texas at Arlington, 1979.

Ritzer, G.: *Working: Conflict and Change*, Prentice-Hall, Englewood Cliffs, N.J., 1977.

Rizzo, J. R., R. J. House, and S. J. Litzman: "Role Conflict and Ambiguity in Complex Organizations," *Administrative Science Quarterly*, vol. 15, 1970, pp. 150–163.

Rodahl, K., and Z. Vokac: "Work Stress in Long-Line Bank Fishing," *Scandinavian Journal of Work Environment and Health*, vol. 3, no. 3, 1977, pp. 154–159.

Roethlisberger, F., and J. J. Dickson: *Management and the Worker*, Harvard University Press, Cambridge, Mass., 1939.

Roman, P. H., and H. M. Trice: "Psychiatric Impairment among 'Middle Americans': Surveys of Work Organizations," *Social Psychiatry*, vol. 7, 1972, pp. 157–166.

Rome, Howard P.: "Emotional Problems Leading to Cardiovascular Accidents," *Psychiatric Annals*, vol. 5, no. 7, 1975, pp. 6–14.

Ronen, Simcha: *Flexible Working Hours: An Innovation in the Quality of Work Life*, McGraw-Hill, New York, 1981.

Rosenbaum, J. F.: "The Drug Treatment of Anxiety," *New England Journal of Medicine*, vol. 306, no. 7, 1982, pp. 401–404.

Rosenman, R. H., and M. Friedman: "Modifying Type A Behavior Patterns," *Journal of Psychosomatic Research*, vol. 21, 1977, pp. 323–331.

Rosenman, R. H., M. Friedman, and R. Strauss: "CHD in the Western Collaborative Group Study," *Journal of the American Medical Association*, vol. 195, 1966, pp. 86–92.

Rosenman, R. H., M. Friedman, et al.: "A Predictive Study of Coronary Heart Disease," *Journal of the American Medical Association*, vol. 189, 1964, pp. 103–110.

Roskies, Ethel, et al.: "Changing the Coronary-Prone (Type A) Behavior Pattern," *Journal of Behavioral Medicine*, vol. 1, 1978, pp. 201–216.

Rotter, Julian B.: "Generalized Expectancies for Internal versus External Control of Reinforcement," in Julian B. Rotter, June C. Chance, and E. Jerry Phares, *Applications of a Social Learning Theory of Personality*, Holt, Rinehart and Winston, New York, 1972, pp. 260–294.

Rotter, Julian B.: "Generalized Expectancies for Internal versus External Control of Reinforcement," *Psychological Monographs*, vol. 80, no. 1, 1966.

Rotter, J. B., J. E. Chance, and E. J. Phares: *Applications of Social Learning Theory of Personality*, Holt, Rinehart and Winston, New York, 1972.

Rountree, G. D.: "Renew Your Career—Take a Sabbatical," *Hospital & Health Services Administration*, Fall 1979, pp. 67–80.

Royal Canadian Air Force: *Exercising Plans for Physical Fitness*, Pocket Books, New York, 1962.

Russek, H.: "Stress, Tobacco, and Coronary Heart Disease in North American Professional Groups," *Journal of the American Medical Association*, vol. 192, 1965, pp. 189–194.

Russek, H. I., and B. L. Zohman: "Relative Significance of Heredity, Diet, and Occupational Stress in Coronary Heart Disease of Young Adults," *American Journal of Medical Science*, vol. 235, 1958, pp. 266–275.

Sachs, B. C.: "Hypnosis in Psychiatry and Psychosomatic Medicine," *Psychosomatics*, vol. 23, 1982, pp. 523–525.

Sales, S. M.: "Organizational Role as a Risk Factor in Coronary Disease," *Administrative Science Quarterly*, vol. 14, 1969, pp. 325–336.

Schaertel, Terry: "Meditating Housestaff," *Hospital Physician*, vol. 12, no. 7, 1976, pp. 28–31.

Schein, V. E.: "Relationship between Sex Roles, Stereotypes, and Requisite Management Characteristics among Female Managers," *Journal of Applied Psychology*, vol. 60, 1975, pp. 340–344.

Schneider, Helmut: "Frustration: A Disruptive Factor in Cooperation and Performance," *Personnel*, vol. 53, no. 1, 1976, pp. 12–13.

Schuler, R. S.: "Time Management: A Stress Management Technique," *Personnel Journal*, vol. 58, 1979, pp. 851–854.

Seashore, Stanley S.: *Group Cohesiveness in the Industrial Work Group*, University of Michigan, Institute for Social Research, Ann Arbor, 1954.

Seashore, S. E., E. E. Lawler, P. H. Mirvis, and C. Cammann: *Observing and Measuring Organizational Change: A Guide to Field Practice*, Wiley Interscience, New York, 1982.

Sekigudi, C., et al.: "Evaluation Method of Mental Workload under Flight Conditions," *Aviation Space and Environmental Medicine*, vol. 49, no. 7, 1978, pp. 920–925.

Selkurt, E. E. (ed.): *Basic Physiology for the Health Sciences*, Little, Brown & Company, Boston, 1975.

Selye, Hans: "Evolution of the Stress Concept," *American Scientist*, vol. 61, no. 6, 1973, pp. 692–699.

Selye, Hans: "Forty Years of Stress Research: Principal Remaining Problems and Misconceptions," *Canadian Medical Association Journal,* vol. 115, 1976c, pp. 53–56.

Selye, Hans: "On the Real Benefits of Eustress," *Psychology Today,* March 1978, pp. 60–70.

Selye, Hans: *Stress in Health and Disease,* Butterworths, Boston, 1976b.

Selye, Hans: *The Stress of Life,* 2d ed., McGraw-Hill, New York, 1976a.

Selye, Hans: *Stress without Distress,* J. B. Lippincott, Philadelphia, 1974.

Selzer, M. L., and A. Vinokur: "Life Events, Subjective Stress, and Traffic Accidents," *American Journal of Psychiatry,* vol. 131, no. 8, 1974, pp. 903–906.

Sewil, C.: "Those Patients with Wall Street Sickness," *Medical Economics,* November 10, 1969, pp. 102–104.

Shapiro, A. P.: "An Experimental Study of Comparative Responses of Blood Pressure to Different Noxious Stimuli," *Journal of Chronic Disorders,* vol. 13, 1961, p. 293.

Sheehan, George: *Doctor Sheehan on Running,* Anderson World, Mountain View, Calif., 1975.

Shostak, Arthur B.: *Blue-Collar Occupational Stress,* Addison-Wesley, Reading, Mass., 1980.

Silver, B. J., and E. B. Blanchard: "Biofeedback and Relaxation Training in the Treatment of Psychophysiological Disorders: Or Are the Machines Really Necessary?" *Journal of Behavioral Medicine,* vol. 1, 1978, pp. 217–239.

Sime, W. E.: "Comparison of Exercise and Meditation in Reducing Physiological Response to Stress," *Medicine and Science in Sports,* vol. 9, 1977, p. 55.

Smith, M. J., M. J. Colligan, and J. J. Hurrell, Jr.: "A Review of NIOSH Psychological Stress Research—1977," The UCLA Conference on Job Stress, November 1977.

Smith, P. C., L. M. Kendall, and C. L. Hulin: *The Measurement of Satisfaction in Work and Retirement,* Rand-McNally, Chicago, 1969.

Sommer, R.: *Tight Spaces: Hard Architecture and How to Humanize It,* Prentice-Hall, Englewood Cliffs, N. J., 1974.

Sorensen, James E., and Thomas L. Sorensen: "The Conflict of Professionals in Bureaucratic Organizations," *Administrative Science Quarterly,* vol. 19, March 1974, pp. 98–106.

Spielberger, C. D., R. L. Gorsuch, and R. E. Lushene: *STAI Manual for the State-Trait Anxiety Inventory,* Consulting Psychologists Press, Inc., Palo Alto, Calif., 1970.

Spurgeon, C. F. E.: *Mysticism in English Literature,* Kennikat Press, Port Washington, N.Y., 1970.

Steele, Fred I.: *Physical Settings and Organizational Development,* Addison-Wesley, Reading, Mass., 1973.

Steers, R. M.: *Organizational Effectiveness: A Behavioral View,* Goodyear, Santa Monica, Calif., 1977.

Steers, R. M.: "Problems in the Measurement of Organizational Effectiveness," *Administrative Science Quarterly,* vol. 20, 1975, pp. 546–548.

Steers, R. M., and L. N. Porter: "The Role of Task-Goal Attributes in Employee Performance," *Psychological Bulletin,* vol. 81, 1974, pp. 434–452.

Steers, R. M., and Susan R. Rhodes: "Major Influences on Employee Attendance: A Process Model," *Journal of Applied Psychology*, vol. 63, no. 4, 1978, pp. 391–407.

Steiner, Jerome: "What Price Success?" *Harvard Business Review*, vol. 50, March–April 1972, 69–74.

Sterling, T. D.: "Does Smoking Kill Workers or Working Kill Smokers?"'*International Journal of Health Services*, vol. 8, 1978, pp. 437–452.

Sterling, T. D., and J. J. Weinkam: "Smoking Characteristics by Type of Employment," *Journal of Occupational Medicine*, vol. 18, no. 11, November 1976, pp. 743–760.

Stessin, L.: "When an Employer Insists," *New York Times Business and Financial Section*, April 3, 1977.

Stewart, N.: *The Effective Woman Manager*, Wiley, New York, 1978.

Streidl, J. W.: *Manager's Guide to Effective Performance Evaluation, Coaching and Counseling*, Tenneco, Houston, Texas, 1976.

Strong, David, and David Campbell: *Manual for the Strong Vocational Inventory Blank—Strong Campbell Interest Inventory*, 2d ed., Stanford University Press, Stanford, Calif., 1977.

Student, K. R.: "Changing Values and Management Stress," *Personnel*, vol. 54, 1977, pp. 48–55.

Stumpf, Stephen A., and Samuel Rabinowitz: "Career Stage as a Moderator of Performance Relationships with Facets of Job Satisfaction and Role Perceptions," *Journal of Vocational Behavior*, vol. 18, 1981, pp. 202–218.

Suinn, R. M., and L. J. Bloom: "Anxiety Management Training for Pattern A Behavior," *Journal of Behavioral Medicine*, vol. 1, 1978, pp. 25–35.

Suinn, R. M., L. Brock, and C. A. Edie: "Letters to the Editor: Behavior Therapy for Type A Patients," *American Journal of Cardiology*, vol. 36, 1975, p. 269.

Sullivan, Harry Stack: *The Interpersonal Theory of Psychiatry*, W. W. Norton and Co., New York, 1953.

Szilagyi, Andrew D., and Winford E. Holland: "Changes in Social Density: Relationships with Functional Interaction and Perceptions of Job Characteristics, Role Stress, and Work Satisfaction," *Journal of Applied Psychology*, vol. 65, no. 1, 1980, pp. 28–33.

Taché, Jean: "Stress as a Cause of Disease," in Jean Taché, Hans Selye, and Stacey B. Day (eds.), *Cancer, Stress, and Death*, Plenum Medical Book Company, New York, 1979, pp. 1–9.

Tannenbaum, Robert, and Fred Massarik: "Participation by Subordinates in the Managerial Decision-Making Process," *The Canadian Journal of Economics and Political Science*, vol. 16, no. 3, August 1950, pp. 408–418.

Taylor, J. W.: *The Principles of Scientific Management*, Harper and Brothers, New York, 1911.

"Tension in the Public Schools: Teachers under Stress," *Behavioral Medicine*, vol. 6, no. 3, 1979, pp. 28–31.

Terborg, James R.: "Women in Management: A Research Review," *Journal of Applied Psychology*, vol. 61, no. 6, 1977, pp. 647–664.

Thacher, F. J., P. Esmiol, H. R. Ives, and B. Mandelkour: "Can Onsite Counselling Programs Aid Workers, Reduce Health Costs?" *Occupational Health & Safety*, vol. 46, December 1977, pp. 48–50.

Theorell, J., E. Lind, and B. Floderus: "The Relationships of Disturbing Life Changes and Emotions to the Early Development of Myocardial Infarctions and Other Serious Illnesses," *Revue D' epidemiologie et de Sante Publique*, vol. 24, no. 1, 1976, pp. 41–59.

Thompson, James D.: *Organizations in Action*, McGraw-Hill, New York, 1967.

Timio, M., et al.: "Urinary Excretion of Adrenaline, Noradrenaline and Ilhydroxy-corticoids under Job Stress," *Giornale Italiano Di Cardiologia*, vol. 17, no. 11, 1977, pp. 1080–1087.

Tolchinsky, P. D., and D. C. King: "Do Goals Mediate the Effects of Incentives on Performance?" *Academy of Management Review*, vol. 5, 1980, pp. 455–467.

"Tower of Stress: The Plight of Air Traffic Controllers," *Behavioral Medicine*, vol. 6, no. 4, 1979, pp. 38–41.

Tracy, Lane, and Thomas W. Johnson: "What Do the Role Conflict and Role Ambiguity Scales Measure?" *Journal of Applied Psychology*, vol. 66, no. 4, 1981, pp. 464–469.

Triandis, H. D., J. M. Feldman, D. E. Weldon, and W. M. Harvey: "Designing Pre-employment Training for the Hard to Employ: A Cross-Cultural Psychological Approach," *Journal of Applied Psychology*, vol. 59, no. 6, 1974, pp. 687–693.

Trice, Harrison, and Paul Roman: "Perspectives on Job-Based Programs for Alcohol and Drug Problems," *Journal of Drug Issues*, vol. 11, 1981, pp. 167–169.

Tuckman, Bruce W.: "Developmental Sequence in Small Groups," *Psychological Bulletin*, vol. 63, June 1965, pp. 384–399.

Uris, A.: "How Managers Ease Job Pressures," *International Management*, vol. 27, 1972, pp. 45–46.

Van Dosterom, A.: "Psychosocial Problems of the Working Man," *Metamedical*, vol. 54, no. 7, 1975, pp. 218–220.

Van Maanen, John (ed.): "Qualitative Methodology," special issue of *Administrative Science Quarterly*, vol. 24, no. 4, December 1979.

Van Maanen, J., and E. J. Schein: "Career Development," in J. R. Hackman and J. L. Suttle (eds.), *Improving Life at Work*, Goodyear, Santa Monica, Calif., 1977, pp. 30–95.

Van Sell, Mary, A. P. Brief, and R. S. Schuler: "Role Conflict and Role Ambiguity: Integration of the Literature and Directions for Future Research," *Human Relations*, vol. 34, no. 1, 1981, pp. 43–71.

Von, Grun, and Leopald P. Von: "Stress," *Law and Order*, vol. 26, no. 2, 1978, pp. 54–55.

Walker, C. R., and R. H. Guest: *The Man on the Assembly Line*, Harvard University Press, Cambridge, Mass., 1952.

Walsh, R. J.: "You Can Deal with Stress," *Supervisory Management*, vol. 20, 1975, pp. 16–21.

Warshaw, Leon J.: *Managing Stress*, Addison-Wesley, Reading, Mass., 1979.

Weber, A., et al.: "Relationship between Objective and Subjective Assessment of Experimentally Induced Fatigue," *Ergonomics*, vol. 18, no. 2, 1975, pp. 151–156.

Weider, A., H. Wolff, K. Brodman, B. Mittlemann, and D. Wedsler: *Cornell Index Manual*, Cornell Medical School, New York, 1949.

Weiss, D. J., et al.: *Manual for the Minnesota Satisfaction Questionnaire*, XXII, University of Minnesota Industrial Relations Center, Work Adjustment Project, Minnesota Studies in Vocational Rehabilitation, 1967.

Weiss, S. M. (ed.): "Coronary Prone Behavior and Coronary Heart Disease: A Critical Review," *Circulation*, vol. 63, 1981, pp. 1199–1215.

Wesley, E.: "Preservative Behavior in a Concept-Formation Task as a Function of Manifest Anxiety and Rigidity," *Journal of Abnormal and Social Psychology*, vol. 48, no. 1, 1953, pp. 129–134.

"What Stress Can Do for You," *Fortune*, January 1972.

Whitlock, F. A., J. R. Stoll, and R. J. Rekhdahl: "Crisis, Life Events and Accidents," *Australian and New Zealand Journal of Psychiatry*, vol. 11, 1977, p. 127.

Wilensky, Harold L.: "The Professionalization of Everyone?" *American Journal of Sociology*, September 1964, pp. 137–158.

Wolberg, L. R.: *The Technique of Psychotherapy*, 3d ed., Grune and Stratton, New York, 1977.

Wolf, Stewart, and Harold G. Wolff: *Gastric Function: An Experimental Study of a Man and His Stomach*, Oxford University Press, New York, 1943.

Wolff, H. G.: *Stress and Disease*, Charles C Thomas, Springfield, Ill., 1953.

Wright, G., S. Iam, and E. Knecht: "Resistance to Heat Stress in the Spontaneously Hypertensive Rat," *Canadian Journal of Physiology and Pharmacology*, vol. 55, no. 5, 1977, pp. 975–982.

Yarvote, P. M., T. J. McDonheh, M. J. Goldman, and J. Zuckerman: "Organization and Evaluation of a Fitness Program in Industry," *Journal of Occupational Medicine*, vol. 16, no. 9, September 1974, pp. 589–598.

Yates, A. J.: *Biofeedback and the Modification of Behavior*, Plenum, New York, 1980.

Yerkes, Robert M., and John D. Dodson: "The Relation of Strength of Stimulus to Rapidity of Habit-Formation," *Journal of Comparative Neurology and Psychology*, vol. 18, 1908, pp. 459–482.

Zaleznik, A. M., F. R. Kets de Vries, and J. Howard: "Stress Reactions in Organizations: Symptoms, Causes, and Consequences," *Behavioral Science*, vol. 22, 1977, pp. 151–162.

Zohman, Lenore: *Exercise Your Way to Fitness and Heart Health*, Mazola Corn Exercise Booklet, Coventry, Conn., 1979.

INDEX